Decolonization in Britain and France

DECOLONIZATION
IN BRITAIN AND FRANCE

The Domestic Consequences
of International Relations

MILES KAHLER

Princeton University Press — Princeton, New Jersey

Published by Princeton University Press, 41 William Street,
Princeton, New Jersey 08540
In the United Kingdom: Princeton University Press,
Guildford, Surrey

ISBN: cloth 0-691-07672-3   paper 0-691-02224-0

This book has been composed in Linotron Sabon type

Clothbound editions of Princeton University Press books are printed
on acid-free paper, and binding materials are chosen for strength
and durability. Paperbacks, although satisfactory for personal
collections, are not usually suitable for library rebinding

Printed in the United States of America by Princeton University
Press, Princeton, New Jersey

FOR MY PARENTS

If, then, the acquisition of territory did so much harm to the Romans at a time when their conduct was conspicuous for prudence and virtue, what effect will it have upon states whose conduct is very far removed from this?

Niccolò Machiavelli, *The Discourses*, II, xix.

CONTENTS

LIST OF TABLES

THE FIRST glimmerings of this study came during the Vietnam War, when, as a student, I attempted to comprehend the choice of an imperial role and the opposition that it inspired, at home and abroad. By the time that I began the first version of this study, my interest had been transformed into a concern with societies that lose their empires and are forced to adjust their self-images and their domestic politics. In the course of that investigation, I become increasingly dissatisfied with the existing, rigid division between the fields of international relations and domestic political development. The substantive problem of domestic adaptation to international change and the theoretical dissatisfaction lie at the base of this book.

Many of those who inspired this research and my approach to these events are cited in the text, but several individuals deserve special mention. My two dissertation advisers, Samuel H. Beer and Stanley Hoffmann, provided a standard for the intelligent use of history and theory that I could only aspire to match, as well as offering suggestions, support, and prodding of the most helpful kind. Philip Williams, who remains the most reliable source available on the intricacies of Fourth Republic politics in France, offered his assistance to a novice setting out into that labyrinth. Peter Gourevitch was central to the beginning and the end of this study: he supervised the seminar paper that eventually became this book and much later read the entire manuscript, offering valuable advice for revision. D. Bruce Marshall and Tony Smith, two scholars whose grasp of European decolonization is unique among American academics, also read and commented on the entire manuscript. Robert G. Gilpin not only offered useful comments on this work, but also pushed me along, when, as a harried assistant professor at Princeton, it was all too easy to set the work aside. Finally, James R. Kurth, in his course on imperialism at Harvard University, set me on the path that has culminated in a book on the end of (one form of) imperialism. None of these teachers and friends bears any responsibility for that which follows.

In the course of research for this book, my work has been supported by the National Science Foundation, by a Krupp Foundation Graduate Fellowship, by the Council for European Studies, and by the William Hallam Tuck '12 Memorial Fund at Princeton University. The Center for European Studies at Harvard University provided a hospitable location for my dissertation research. The Woodrow Wilson School of Public and International Affairs at Princeton University offered much more than the usual assistance in completing the final manuscript. I would like to thank the editors of *World Politics* for permission to use in Chapter IV material originally published in that journal.

Although the documentary sources for a complete study of decolonization remain in many cases inaccessible, many libraries were generous in offering far more than I might have expected. In particular, I wish to thank the library of the Royal Commonwealth Society, Rhodes House Library, the Section Outre-Mer of the Archives Nationales, and, that invaluable source for the study of French politics, the Services de Documentation of the Fondation National des Sciences Politiques. M. Roger Fauroux very kindly permitted me access to selected archives of the Compagnie Saint-Gobain-Pont-à-Mousson.

Sanford Thatcher at the Princeton University Press has offered the combination of patience and meticulous concern that one hopes for in an editor. Carol Ryner and Judith Tilton undertook the monumental task of entering the manuscript onto the computer and then revising it.

Finally, the manuscript could not have been completed without friends to hear the complaints and to provide the distractions that made it bearable. Three in particular should share in the thanks: Robyn Katcoff Roberts, Carol Sternhell, and James Trussell.

Decolonization in Britain and France

CHAPTER I

Introduction. Decolonization: Domestic Consequences of International Relations, Domestic Sources of Foreign Policy

IN FRANCE discussions of decolonization frequently evoke the word *drame*. Few would deny the tragic and apparently inexorable quality of the events that accompanied the end of the colonial empires, stretching from the partitions of India and Palestine to the final episodes enacted today in southern Africa. The birth of dozens of new states came at a high cost to their future citizens in displacement and death; their heritage has been, in many cases, lingering conflict. For the European states, decolonization seemed the last precipitous act in their decline from world preeminence, leaving doubts about their place in the international order. But *drame* connotes more: an event on such a scale that judgments, particularly moral judgments, are difficult; an occurrence unique in its impact on the history of our century and the societies in question. Decolonization, like the world wars, has been viewed as a great watershed, which it undoubtedly was. Unfortunately, declarations of its unique quality have served to suspend efforts by social scientists and historians to situate decolonization within the context of either international or comparative political analysis.

Perhaps the simplest way to frame these events would be to consider European colonial policies as a special case of foreign policy, even though the ties between colonial power and empire were of a different order than those between two "foreign" states. In comparing the two cases, one would ask why the French elite seemed to resist change so tenaciously; why their British counterparts conceded more gracefully. In this view, Britain and France were challenged by colonial nationalists, yet remained "in control."

A second glance, however, brings into the field of vision aspects of decolonization that a conventional analysis of this kind cannot explain. Under the pressure of external events, political parties split. Settlers and soldiers raised the banner of resistance. Investors and traders dependent on the empire shifted their position from hostility to acquiescence in political change. Britain and France did not seem to be "in control"; elites had to examine carefully the domestic consequences of alternative courses of action. Any explanation of the contrasting French and British courses in decolonization must, then, take a further step: recognizing that the domestic sources of external policy (colonial policy in this case) may be affected in their turn by changes in the international environment or in other societies. The overarching argument presented here is that Britain and France were not entirely "in control" of the process, that they were not simply actors in their relations with the colonial empires, but were also *acted upon* by the empires, or, put another way, that the empires themselves, directly and indirectly, entered into the shaping of colonial policy during these years.

Two superficially similar episodes during the 1950s vividly illustrate the necessity of taking this second step and examining the ways in which changes on the periphery could undermine or strengthen the position of those at the center. In January 1953, at the height of the emergency in Kenya, the murder of a European family by African insurgents (the Mau Mau) led to a threatening demonstration by white settlers at Government House in Nairobi. Although it is difficult to imagine now, the threat by Kenyan settlers to "take matters into their own hands" or to ally with the South African Nationalists was a persistent worry for those in London. In this instance, however, events took a course rarely seen in the French case. The governor, Evelyn Baring, refused to receive the unruly mob; when they attempted to storm the building, he sent their own leaders out to placate them. Following the dispersal of the protesters, his only remark to one of those leaders, Michael Blundell, was "Well done."[1] The British military—hardly allies of the settlers—were not involved in the attempted storming of Government House or in the dispersal of the crowd. The incident caused hardly a ripple in the politics of Britain.

Five years later, in May 1958, a similar crowd of European settlers, this time in Algeria, moved against the Government-General in the center of Algiers. The governor himself, Robert Lacoste, who was a strong supporter of the cause of French Algeria, had left his post. Led by students, the mob seized the building and began to pillage its official files; a cry went up for a Committee of Public Safety to be formed, in defiance of the Paris government. The army command, headed by General Salan, threw in their lot with the settlers, increasing the danger for the metropolitan regime. Confronted with this challenge, the parliamentarians in Paris replied in kind, by investing the government of Pierre Pflimlin, whose alleged intention to negotiate a solution to the Algerian conflict had spurred the revolt in Algiers. In the face of military threats and efforts by the Gaullists to bring their leader back to power, however, the regime's will to resist crumbled. What had begun as a riot in a colonial capital had been transformed into a change of political regime.[2]

The events of May 1958 were only the most significant exemplars of the manner in which decolonization was able to shape politics in Paris to a greater degree than Paris was able to shape and contain the course of decolonization on the periphery. Two years earlier, a Socialist premier elected on a peace platform had visited Algiers, been greeted by a similar display of settler hostility, and returned to Paris to escalate the war that France was conducting in Algeria. In similar

[1] Accounts of this episode can be found in Charles Douglas-Home, *Evelyn Baring: The Last Proconsul* (London: Collins, 1978) and Michael Blundell, *So Rough a Wind* (London: Weidenfeld and Nicolson, 1964), pp. 123-128.

[2] These events are described in greater detail in Chapter III. The best review of the large literature on the events of May 1958 is Philip Williams, "The Fourth Republic—Murder or Suicide?" in *Wars, Plots, and Scandals in Postwar France* (Cambridge: Cambridge University Press, 1970), chap. 7.

fashion, the ability of the British representatives in Kenya to assert their authority and to insulate British politics from events in Africa was also characteristic of a national pattern of policy, in which the metropolis was far less influenced by events in the colonial empire. Despite assiduous efforts by settlers and others to undermine governments intent on decolonization, Britain managed to decolonize while minimizing its domestic political costs. Noting the effects of external events on metropolitan politics and society, however, raises a further question, the importance of such a viewpoint for explaining outcomes in the two national cases. Does it illuminate essential aspects of decolonization that other approaches omit?

An answer to this question cannot be provided before presentation of the argument in the chapters that follow. Numerous competing explanations have been advanced for the difficulties encountered by France during decolonization and the apparent "success" of Britain. Some of these explanations, discussed in the final chapter, can be incorporated into an approach based on the domestic consequences of external change; others cannot. The explanation offered here, however, should not be taken as a total one: it emphasizes the metropolis and its links with the empire; it does not attempt to explain the contrasting colonial nationalisms which provided most of the pressure for change during these years.[3] Nor will each instance of decolonization be considered: in an effort to ensure comparability between the British and French cases, only postwar decolonization will be considered, excluding the decolonization of Ireland and India. The settler colonies—most troublesome politically—offer the most complete and parallel instances of the international-domestic links at the center of the argument. The causal sequence under consideration is one of two steps: first explaining the differing effects that change in a particular set of external relations—those with the colonial empires—could produce within the metropolitan societies, and second, using those effects as partial explanations of

[3] This is a task ably undertaken by Tony Smith in *The Pattern of Imperialism* (Cambridge: Cambridge University Press, 1981), pp. 110-132.

the contrasting courses followed by France and Britain in divesting themselves of colonial rule.

Four means by which the empires implanted themselves have been chosen for closer examination: *political parties* and ideology; *economic actors*, particularly interest groups and individual firms; the *populations* of the empires, European and non-European; and the *state*, including colonial administrators and the military.

In the terms developed later in this chapter, political parties and the ideologies that they incorporated exemplify an *indirect* external influence. The metropolitan societies themselves had constructed an indirect link or anchorage for the empires in individual beliefs and political organizations; these ties proved the most resilient. Because of these links, political parties of the Right suffered contrasting fates—successful survival for the British Conservatives and the Gaullists, failure and eventual disintegration for the French *modérés* and the Poujadists.

The political competition that reinforced or weakened these indirect ties was organized on a spectrum of accommodation or resistance characteristic of societies under external pressure. Differences in the structure and content of nationalist and imperialist ideologies influenced outcomes in each national case, but these ideologies were more than lenses for interpreting changes on the colonial periphery; they were also significant organizationally to political groups on the Right. Relying upon nationalist incentives to maintain the support and participation of their members, representing a disproportionate share of colonial economic and political interests, these parties were the most vulnerable to disruption by the political disputes accompanying decolonization. In confronting the *internal* disengagement from empire that was required, the British Conservative Party possessed numerous advantages in the structure of political competition in Britain, the pattern of power within the party, and its long-established monopoly over the loyalties of a substantial portion of the British electorate. In France, a succession of right-wing parties were willing to employ resistance to decolonization as a means of attracting a nationalist constituency and hesitant to endorse moderate or liberal colonial policies for fear of their competitors in the next election. The causes and the consequences of contrasting conservative responses to decolonization are investigated in Chapter II.

Although the parties of the Right in Britain and France governed and influenced those who governed throughout the years of decolonization the parties of the Left, discussed in Chapter III, were not without effect on the course of decolonization. Their organizational sensitivity to the changes underway in the empires was also determined by ideological attachment, in this instance a commitment to "socialist foreign policy." The contrasting outcomes for British Labour—unified by that ideological core and pressing for speedy decolonization—and the French Socialists—who escalated the Algerian War under Guy Mollet in the face of dissidence and eventual rupture—substantially affected the course of national policy toward the pressure for change abroad. As in the case of the conservative parties, a particular link to the exterior in the form of party ideology had profound effects on the future of the organization.

In contrast to political parties, rendered sensitive to external change by their ideological stakes, *economic actors*, examined in Chapter IV, could influence metropolitan politics by both direct and indirect means. In a curious reversal of the pattern of penetration examined by students of developing economies, firms attempted to enter the metropolitan political arena in order to influence the pace of change on the periphery, singly and as represented by business organizations. Their resistance to or acquiescence in change—determined by their political exposures—also led them to attempt to influence the course of events indirectly, by shaping political debates in London or Paris on the economic value of empire. Influence of both sorts was finally limited by the overriding economic estimates and strategies of the metropolitan political elites, including their perceptions of the costs of a precipitous disengagement, all weighed against a calculation of political benefits and liabilities shaped by the ideological considerations described in Chapters II and III.

The *populations* that inhabited the empires could also influence metropolitan politics directly. Quickly situating themselves at the resistance pole of the nationalist spectrum, the settlers, representatives of fragment societies described below, were central actors in the imperial grip on French and British societies. Disparity of access to metropolitan society set them apart from their Arab or African adversaries and ensured that the pace of disengagement was slowed.

One sector of the colonial populations was particularly important in its political impact: the representatives of the state itself. Decolonization, like other forms of external pressure, could place disintegrative pressures on the bureaucracy that conveyed metropolitan authority to the colonial empires. Analysis of the social groups that are particularly sensitive to nationalist appeals and external threat correctly predicts the trials of France at the hands of rebellion within the state, by the military and administrators of empire. The men who ruled not only thwarted implementation of metropolitan policy on many occasions; they also openly attempted to influence the formulation of that policy in Paris, a pattern of meddling that culminated with the downfall of the Fourth Republic in May 1958. Britain's empire had relied upon indirect means of control; the principal role of the British Army was not colonial and the shift to the nuclear era had thus come more easily. The contrast between the two national cases is perhaps greatest in the impact that decolonization had upon the state itself. This final contrast is described in Chapter V.

DECOLONIZATION AND THE STUDY OF INTERNATIONAL RELATIONS

The domestic consequences of international politics, as typified in the course of decolonization, provide illumination and explanation of the contrast between British and French politics. Domestic consequences in their turn have implications for external policy and for the ways in which international relations are studied, setting a second task for this study. The approach taken here has two sorts of applications for international relations. First, in contrast to most studies of external policy-making, an examination of decolonization suggests that the determinants of foreign policy must be viewed as themselves influenced by the international environment or external actors. One cannot assume that feedback from a society's environment is mediated *exclusively* by state elites, particularly in relatively open societies such as the two under consideration. The effects of a particular choice in external relations may in turn undermine the bases of political power or economic success of those very elites. Like the politicians of the French Fourth Republic, those responsible for foreign policy must constantly look over their shoulders at the domestic effects of their actions and the international events with which they must contend. Those domestic consequences can paralyze the shaping of an external response or force leaders into courses of action difficult to explain by means of a state-centered reading of the national interest.

Attention to the domestic consequences of external change also has a second, broader set of implications for the analysis of international relations: by directing attention to questions of *structure*, it lends support to a different paradigm for research and explanation. Instead of emphasizing decision-makers and their stream of actions, attention is directed to obstacles in the path of any change in external orientation, to the anchors that particular patterns of external relations create within societies.

Structure is an awkward term to employ for a less than clearly defined outlook. Within the social sciences, structure has been claimed by many schools with opposing ideological points of view, from Marxists of different hues to sociologists as different as Parsons and Skocpol to anthropologists such as Claude Lévi-Strauss.[4] The variety of "structuralists" suggests that the term may be nearly empty of meaning, but close examination produces at least a "weak" definition of the struc-

---

[4] Not to mention its wide and more precise use outside the social sciences. For an interesting introduction to the uses of the word structure, see Jean Piaget, *Structuralism* (London: Routledge & Kegan Paul, 1971).

tural approach (as compared to the "strong" definitions advanced by Piaget or, in international relations theory, by Kenneth Waltz).[5] Such a "weak" definition points to two prerequisites of a structural perspective: an emphasis on the relatively fixed or unchanging character of a particular set of relations (contrasting with conjuncture) and an implicit or explicit distancing from voluntaristic or subjective modes of explanation. Both of these characteristics suggest the contrast in international relations theory between structural theories (whether Waltz's systemic variant or Marxist dependency theorists) and conventional foreign policy analysis. The first directs us to what Fernand Braudel calls the "mechanisms that withstand the march of time," "the slow-moving" as opposed to the fast.[6] To ponder such resistance to change as an element requiring explanation corrects a long-standing bias within the social sciences and international relations that was noted by Barrington Moore, Jr.—the pernicious effects of assumptions of cultural inertia:

There is a widespread assumption in modern social science that social continuity requires no explanation. Supposedly it is not problematical. Change is what requires explanation. This assumption blinds the investigator to certain crucial aspects of social reality. . . . The assumption of inertia, that cultural and social continuity do not require explanation, obliterates the fact that both have to be recreated anew in each generation, often with great pain and suffering.[7]

Examining persisting features or sets of relations raises its own problems of division and classification: one observer's structure is another's conjuncture. Constraints that seem fixed for one set of actors may be transformed by others.[8] And just

---

[5] Piaget, *Structuralism*, chap. 1, and Kenneth Waltz, *Theory of International Politics* (Reading, Mass.: Addison-Wesley, 1979), chap. 5.

[6] Fernand Braudel, *The Mediterranean and the Mediterranean World in the Age of Philip II*, Vol. 1 (London: Collins, 1972), p. 353.

[7] Barrington Moore, *Social Origins of Dictatorship and Democracy* (Boston: Beacon Press, 1966), pp. 485-486.

[8] For a treatment of this question in the context of Marxist theory, Bob Jessop, *The Capitalist State* (Oxford: Martin Robertson, 1982), pp. 252-253.

as a structural perspective emphasizes the relatively fixed relations of a given situation, it may stumble into the opposite difficulty: an inability to explain change. Certainly, much of dependency theory, which seems to point to the most pessimistic reading of alternatives for developing societies, often falls into this trap. Or, if change is assumed in many structural accounts, it is assumed that change must occur gradually, imperceptibly, in an evolutionary fashion.

The second element in a structural perspective—an attack on voluntaristic modes of explanation—also has shortcomings, despite its appeal in such accounts as Waltz's theory of international politics or Skocpol's structural theory of revolutions. While traditional views of international relations would overstress the importance of the aims of metropolitan elites and their colonial nationalist opponents—producing a "Whig" view of decolonization that is overly deterministic—a purely structural explanation posited on the collapse of the bases of empire without reference to the aims of actors is difficult.[9] Perhaps the best means of emphasizing the importance of structure in this sense is to recognize the nonintentionality in the account that follows. Actors (party leaders, businessmen, the military) with different goals served, in the face of rising external pressure, to strengthen or erode the structural ties that bound metropolis and periphery. In certain cases, they *did* know that they were moving in that direction (though the pace and the final outcome were almost always unknown). In other cases, they were unaware of and did not intend the consequences of their action. (Perhaps the most celebrated example is the 1958 rebellion in Algiers, intended to cement

---

Jessop makes the distinction one of possible alteration "by a given agent (or set of agents) during a given time period. . . ."

[9] A structural view of decolonization would parallel closely Skocpol's model of revolutionary change: ". . . No successful social revolution has ever been 'made' by a mass-mobilizing, avowedly revolutionary movement." In similar fashion, one could argue that the overthrow of colonial relations was hardly the result of nationalist movements acting alone, though pressure from nationalists contributed to the collapse of colonial structures. *States and Social Revolutions* (Cambridge: Cambridge University Press, 1979), p. 17.

Algeria to France, but in fact bringing to power the man who would finally grant Algeria its independence.)

The structural perspective that is developed here is not alien to international relations. Dependency theory has already been mentioned (Galtung's "structural" theory of imperialism draws much of its inspiration from that literature); political integration theory, as developed in the early 1960s, and Waltz's recent contribution to systemic theory are all structural in the senses described here. Existing theory, however, retains the shortcomings described above. In dependency theory, the links between societies are taken to be economic; the static quality of the analysis gives little sense of the potential for transformation within existing structures. In political integration theory, the domestic side of the linkage between international and national is ignored.[10]

Taking the structural perspective as a lens through which to examine decolonization, then, may not only illuminate that process of international and internal change, but also contribute to refining the structural paradigm. For it is the *transformation* of structures that is at issue here, structures that once appeared impervious to change. That transformation occurred, not in the imperceptible fashion expected by many of the participants, but suddenly and violently. By examining the domestic anchors of the colonial empires and their agents in the metropolitan societies, the dynamic by which the imperial structures were undermined will be clearer—not a dynamic in which far-seeing statesmen willingly granted independence to subject peoples, but one in which politicians subject to conflicting pressures, capitalists making uncertain calculations, bureaucrats and soldiers protecting their interests all produced an outcome that only now we see as inevitable.

One prerequisite for a structural view of international re-

---

[10] A good example of political integration analysis that is a precursor of linkage studies is Bruce Russett, *Community and Contention: Britain and America in the Twentieth Century*, (Cambridge: MIT Press, 1963). Russett admits that the analysis of transactions omits "a whole class of variables which may be described as internal factors; that is they are not measurable as international transactions" (p. 209).

lations is the elaboration of the "missing link" between international relations and domestic politics. The first task of this study—explaining the contrasting courses of French and British decolonization—also demands the tentative placement of this episode in a wider class of events which, like decolonization, have been regarded as external and hence impossible to analyze or incorporate theoretically. Although the array of external or international influences on domestic politics has received growing attention in recent years from social scientists and historians, a common vocabulary must be developed and some tentative generalizations made about international-domestic causality.[11] That step, toward a pre-theory of the domestic consequences of international relations, is begun in this chapter and constitutes the third task in this examination of decolonialization.

AN INITIAL FRAMEWORK

Apart from the literature of imperialism and dependency, societies have for the most part been studied in isolation from their common environment and from each other. As Machiavelli's acute comments on the subject attest, some students of politics have long recognized the shortcomings of this exclusion of the external. Certainly, classical theory in international politics asserted the "primacy of foreign policy," but that phase was more a guide to statesmen than an analysis of the effects that external pressures had on states involved in international competition. Classical social theory, on the other hand, was born of the nineteenth century, an era of prolonged peace when the European states held unchallenged primacy in the international system. The shock of the international would not be felt with full force until our own century.

---

[11] Peter Gourevitch in political science and Theda Skocpol in sociology are among the social scientists who have recently examined these questions; their work is discussed later in this chapter. Mention should be made of Eric R. Wolf, an anthropologist, whose *Europe and the People without History* (Berkeley: University of California Press, 1982) appeared after this study was completed.

In contemporary political science, "linkage politics" has become the rubric under which domestic and international arenas are related to one another. Unfortunately, linkage has seldom been specified, and, with few exceptions, such studies have emphasized the domestic sources of foreign policy, a time-honored tradition in the study of international relations, rather than the domestic *consequences* of international politics.[12]

THE INADEQUACY OF CONCEPTS: THE STATE AND NATIONALISM

The weaknesses of existing theory are demonstrated in the treatment of two concepts central to any theory of the domestic impact of international politics: the state and nationalism. Viewing societies from the outside increases the importance of the state and of political phenomena: while the state as an *internal* allocator of values often seems to dissolve into a pluralistic morass of competing economic and social groups, its distinctive features are enhanced when viewed in its external mediating role. Despite the increasing attention devoted to the state in contemporary social science, however, its external aspect is still relatively neglected. Contemporary debate surrounding Marxist theories of the state is principally concerned with the degree of autonomy that the state can achieve vis-à-vis dominant classes *internally*. Only the theorists of dependency, discussed below, have emphasized the *external* mediating role of the state.[13] Theda Skocpol, a rare

---

[12] Karl Deutsch, "External Influences on the International Behavior of States," in *Approaches to Comparative and International Politics*, ed. R. Barry Farrell (Evanston, Ill.: Northwestern University Press, 1966), pp. 5-26; James N. Rosenau, ed., *Linkage Politics* (New York: Free Press, 1969); James N. Rosenau, "Toward the Study of National-International Linkages," in *The Scientific Study of Foreign Policy* (New York: Free Press, 1971), pp. 307-338; in a volume edited by Jonathan Wilkenfeld, only one chapter treats domestic events as the dependent variable: *Conflict Behavior and Linkage Politics* (New York: David McKay Co., Inc., 1973).

[13] Despite the recent flowering of Marxist theories of the state, an external dimension has seldom been included. For efforts to take these theories into

exception to this pattern, has revealed in her study of social revolutions the connection between the autonomy of the state and its situation in an international context.[14] One could argue that a final and irreducible justification for *political* science lies precisely in this external role of the state.

The second concept, *nationalism*, is implicit in the boundaries that a modern state sets and in the response of the society or its affected segments to an external impact. Defined to exclude the external, however, nationalism has not been well-served by the emphases of contemporary social science. Perhaps the most influential single work in this regard has been Karl Deutsch's *Nationalism and Social Communication*. Its circumscription of nationalism has been widely accepted: nationalism as the development of nations from endogenous sources; nationalist movements as secessionist movements within existing states; the bases of nation-building in a process of integration rather than in differentiation from the outside. Deutsch draws many of his illustrations from East European experience, examples for which his assimilation-mobilization model seem particularly apt. What Deutsch's approach neglects is the question of nationalism *after* the nation-state, why certain movements, policies, and attitudes in relatively homogeneous national societies are termed "nationalist." This flaw in his approach to nationalism as social communication results from an excessively internal point of view: the role of the external in a process of national self-definition is neglected, particularly after the nation-state has been formed and relative integration achieved.[15]

---

account in the domestic sources of foreign policy, see Stephen D. Krasner, *Defending the National Interest* (Princeton: Princeton University Press, 1978) and Pat McGowan and Stephen G. Walker, "Radical and Conventional Models of U.S. Foreign Economic Policy-Making," *World Politics* 33 (April, 1981).

[14] Theda Skocpol, *States and Social Revolutions* pp. 24-33.

[15] A study that is typical of the internal explanations of nationalism advanced by contemporary social science, and particularly sociology, is Anthony D. Smith, *Theories of Nationalism* (New York: Harper & Row, 1971). Conventional social science is not alone in its lack of attention to nationalism. Tom Nairn has described the theory of nationalism as "Marxism's great historical failure." "The Modern Janus," *New Left Review* 94 (November-December, 1975), pp. 3-29.

Contemporary social science has surrounded societies with a theoretical insulation from the intrusions of the external; such insulation cannot simply be stripped away. To admit every international influence would destroy the possibility for theory or even typology. Instead, in reviewing the disparate islands of scholarship that contribute to an understanding of the domestic consequences of international, three sets of organizing concepts will be used, ones that throw into relief the external dimension to domestic political development.

a) *The nature of external changes or intrusions.* A distinction can be made between those that are dealt with by the existing state and remain outside the boundaries of a society (*indirect*) and those that slip around the elites that guard the ramparts (often with the collusion of those elites) and enter into the political life of the society (*direct*). In the first class of events, since the boundaries of a society remain intact, mediation by the state or other domestic actors occurs. *Interpretation of the environment* is the critical determinant of the internal political and social effects of this type of external impact: the perception of the environment as one of high or low threat, assessment of the costs of political and economic autonomy, the uniformity of such perceptions across society, the response of resistance or adaptation that is elicited, the internal changes that follow from that response. *Direct* international impacts are characterized by the *penetration* of the society's boundaries by the external, whether by another state or some other organization, such as a multinational corporation. To the questions of response and interpretation is added a second set of questions: whether the external presence can be incorporated in the internal political arrangements of the society and how that presence might change those arrangements.

b) *Sensitivity.* A concept that has been used in the study of interdependence, sensitivity can be expanded to assess the relative attention and the likely response of societies or groups within societies to international change. Explaining relative sensitivity is a principal task in explaining responses to indirect international impacts. In many cases, sensitivity—of societies or parts of societies—may be induced by previous international shocks. For example, the Gaullist concern for France's international position, described in Chapter II, was born of the experience of invasion and war. A different sort of intrusion, immigration, explains the lingering attentiveness of certain sectors of the American population to events in other societies.

c) *Resistance/collaboration*. Conventional views of nationalism are not helpful in analyzing the domestic consequences of international politics. What is needed is a distinction similar to that drawn by Hoffmann between national consciousness and nationalism.[16] More precisely, three strands are typical of the nationalist syndrome of attitudes or policies: a high independent value placed upon national autonomy, an intense concern with national status vis-à-vis other national communities, and a tendency to expand the community of fellow nationals or "kith and kin" beyond the boundaries recognized by those who are not nationalists. These three criteria of nationalism may be labeled the "patriotic," the "comparative," and the "irredentist," although the latter may refer to maintaining attachments to colonial nationals, as in French North Africa, as well as to the strengthening of ties with those under alien rule. In terms of a spectrum of responses on the part of the state or society, the nationalist is one who chooses to *resist* the external in the interests of maintaining national autonomy, status, or a wider conception of nation; the collaborator or adaptor places a lower value upon autonomy for its own sake, has far less concern for status vis-à-vis other nations, and possesses a narrower conception of the national community. These definitions do not center upon concern for national security, although they may have a great deal to do with the strategy chosen to ensure security.

Responses may include elements of both resistance and adaptation: de Gaulle, the classic exemplar of resistance to the "tyranny of the external," in Hoffmann's phrase, also adapted and conceded in certain circumstances. One may collaborate

---

[16] Stanley Hoffmann, *Decline or Renewal?* (New York: Viking Press, 1974), pp. 367-368.

initially, as many of the Western-trained nationalists did, only to turn to resistance at a later time. Nevertheless, the ideal-types of resistance and collaboration are useful in categorizing the responses of individuals and societies to external intrusions, both political and economic. Also, although it is difficult to separate a term, such as collaboration, from negative evaluations in a nationalist world, here the word will be used in a neutral way.

Using this cluster of concepts, the existing, widely scattered fragments of theory and research on the domestic consequences of international relations can be organized, beginning with the impact of the international state system and then considering the effects of the international economy. In each case, it is *political* consequences that will be of principal concern, although political change may follow the imprint left on economic and social development by the international system.

THE INTERNATIONAL STATE SYSTEM: INDIRECT AND DIRECT IMPACT AT THE LEVEL OF THE POLITICAL SYSTEM

Most of the attention directed to effects on a society of the international state system has been directed to explaining changes at the level of *political regime*. The consequences of implantation within a structure of competitive and divergent states can be divided into two sorts. The first is the most difficult to evaluate, that of a demonstration or diffusion effect.[17] Revolutions abroad, for example, encourage similar movements at home: witness the proliferation of the student revolts during 1968. Revolutions and other political events can also provide models for later imitators, sometimes with considerable effect upon the political forms chosen in a period of upheaval. Most modern political regimes, revolutionary as well as military or authoritarian, have appeared in clusters, such as those that sprang up in Latin America after the mid-

[17] Rosenau labels this an "emulative" linkage process, in Rosenau, "Toward the Study of National-International Linkages," p. 320.

1960s.[18] But clustering and influence cannot be equated with cause, and separating the international influence from domestic determinants is difficult. Even the demonstration effect itself may have been associated with other international pressures. The adoption of new military technology or political organization, for example, can be induced by the exigencies of competition within the state system.

The reality of that state competition and the risk of war within the international system is the second and most significant means by which the international state system, by indirect means and direct penetration, can shape the political structures of societies. Normal foreign policy involves the indirect impact of an environment usually perceived as low in threat. Interpretation and response is restricted to a small part of the population, typically members of the state bureaucracy, although the cast of characters involved may change from issue to issue. In the case of normal foreign policy, effects upon the society are limited, and a response that spreads beyond the makers of policy within the state are rare. Even in this restricted sphere, however, questions arise concerning the *evaluation* of the level of threat and the *cost* of dealing with perceived threats. In evaluating the military budget or the introduction of conscription, a determination of who benefits and who pays for a particular foreign policy can become an open political issue.[19]

In the day-to-day routine of normal foreign policy, any wider social and political effects of international competition are limited; as the resources demanded by that competition increase and the level or nature of the threat becomes a greater source of contention, the political impact of such international

[18] Gabriel A. Almond, Scott C. Flanagan, and Robert J. Mundt, eds., *Crisis, Choice, and Change: Historical Studies of Political Development* (Boston: Little, Brown and Co.,1973), p. 629; the impact of the demonstration effect on revolutions is discussed by Skocpol, *States and Social Revolutions*, pp. 265-269.

[19] Charles W. Maynes, Jr., "Who Pays for Foreign Policy?" *Foreign Policy*, no. 15 (Summer 1974), 152-168; also *Foreign Policy*, no. 18 (Spring 1975), 80-122.

pressures may become more profound. The effect of external conflict on internal social cohesion and political institutions has been a persistent concern of those engaged in politics. The views of the revolutionary Left, for example, have fluctuated between an equation of war with the overthrow of existing regimes and a belief that war is the final social cement. Karl Marx, in surveying the course of the Crimean War, repeatedly expressed hopes that the war would bring a resumption in progress toward a proletarian revolution, brutally interrupted in France during the June Days of 1848.[20] The Crimean conflict belied such hopes, but the Paris Commune, which followed French defeats in the war with Prussia, revived them once again. The *union sacrée*, proclaimed throughout Europe in August 1914, seemed to confirm the consolidating effects of warfare, but the pendulum swung back again in the interwar years: the 1930s, in particular, were dominated by the memory of revolutionary discontent in 1917-1918, a memory that explains certain aspects of appeasement and the calculations of the men of Vichy in 1940.[21]

Social theorists, notably Georg Simmel and Lewis Coser, have attempted to specify the conditions under which external conflict leads to internal solidarity or to social disintegration. Coser concludes that the degree of group consensus prior to the outbreak of conflict and the uniformity of threat perception across groups within a society are the most important elements in determining the effects of international conflict.[22] To uniformity and intensity of the threat perception should be added the *costs* of meeting the threat. Perceptions of the required response and of the threat itself could change if the resources demanded to meet the threat grew precipitously or

[20] Karl Marx, *The Eastern Question* (London: Swan Sonnenschein & Co., Ltd., 1897), p. 535.

[21] Charles A. Micaud, *The French Right and Nazi Germany, 1933-1939: A Study in Public Opinion* (Durham, N.C.: Duke University Press, 1943), pp. 99, 228; Robert O. Paxton, *Vichy France: Old Guard and New Order* (New York: Knopf, 1972), pp. 14-15.

[22] Lewis Coser, *The Functions of Social Conflict* (New York: Free Press of Glencoe, 1956), pp. 93-94.

were imposed inequitably. Even in the case of enormous resource demands, however, effective social unity can be preserved, given the prerequisite of uniform perceptions of an intense threat.[23]

Political integration in the face of external threat:
State formation, total war, and fragment societies
The history of early modern Europe confirms that military competition and war can contribute to the formation of states and the expansion of their internal power. As Perry Anderson has noted, "the virtual permanence of international armed conflict [was] one of the hallmarks of the whole climate of Absolutism." Anderson describes a billiard-ball process in which threatened invasion from Denmark led to an explosion of state power in Sweden, which in turn served as "the hammer of the East," forcing the consolidation of modern state structures and military organizations in Eastern Europe.[24] One of the states so affected was Prussia, whose position at the center of the European state system profoundly affected the course of its political development and the political role of its military. The most prominent counter-example, of course, was England, spared the persistent military threats experienced by the Continental powers. Its weak state and its relatively small military apparatus reflected those historical conditions.[25]

Western imperialism had a similar effect upon political or-

[23] Arthur Stein argues that domestic cohesion will decline in all wars because of the effects of mobilization, although a total war, in which an intense, uniformly perceived threat is present, will display a smaller increase in disunity. Arthur Stein, *The Nation at War* (Baltimore: The Johns Hopkins University Press, 1978), pp. 53, 87-88.

[24] Perry Anderson, *Lineages of the Absolutist State* (London: New Left Books, 1974), pp. 33, 198-212.

[25] On Prussia, Anderson, *Lineages*, pp. 240-246; for a later period (response to the Napoleonic Wars), Skocpol, *States and Social Revolutions*, pp. 104-109. A more general statement of this argument is given by Otto Hintze, "Military Organization and the Organization of the State," in *The Historical Essays of Otto Hintze*, ed. Felix Gilbert (New York: Oxford University Press, 1975), pp. 178-215. Also Peter A. Gourevitch, "The Second Image Reversed: The International Sources of Domestic Politics," *International Organization* 32 (Autumn 1978), 881-912.

ganization in certain stateless societies in Africa and Asia. In what is now Libya, the Sanusi, a Muslim religious order, permitted quarreling Bedouin tribes to deal with the outside; what gave stability to the relationship between order and tribes was "common hostility to outside interference, an ingredient supplied in measured quantities by the Turks and copiously by the Italians."[26] When the light demands of the Turks—taxation and a modicum of order—were replaced by the total demands of the Italians, the Sanusi ceased to mediate and turned to leading an armed resistance. Intense pressure from the Italian invaders in this case secularized a religious order and created a political structure and a nation where one had not existed before.[27]

Just as military competition and war has spurred the formation of modern political organization, so each round of advance in military technology and capability forced new extensions of state power and changes in political structure. For much of European history, France set the pace. The wars of Louis XIV imposed reforms of taxation and administration on his rivals. The ability of France's new revolutionary state to mobilize resources and manpower hitherto undreamed of imposed an even more difficult political dilemma on the elites of the *ancien régime*: "The threat of the French armies posed for regimes of the old order the grave choice of risking destruction either from without or within."[28]

In contemporary nation-states, the onset of intense threat and the need to mobilize resources to meet that threat can have the same effects in more measured form: at least temporarily, political divisions are submerged; an increase in the power of the state and the scope of government action takes place. In two industrial societies attached to political liberalism and laissez-faire economics—Britain and the United States—the world wars illustrated the effects that intense ex-

[26] E. E. Evans-Pritchard, *The Sanusi of Cyrenaica* (Oxford: Clarendon Press, 1949), p. 70.

[27] Ibid., p. 166.

[28] Paul Y. Hammond, "The Political Order and the Burden of External Relations," *World Politics* 19 (April, 1967), 443-464.

ternal threat and mobilization demands could have on domestic politics. In both countries, World War I brought an increase in government involvement in the economy; scientific research took place under state aegis for the first time; curbs upon dissent and an increase in regimentation could be observed. In Britain the form of the executive changed: the War Cabinet, established by Lloyd George in December 1916, was not only smaller in size but also divorced from customary legislative oversight, a virtual "committee of public safety," as A.J.P. Taylor calls it.

The world wars also produced a leveling of disposable income through heavier taxation; in Britain, the tax burden contributed to the destruction of the landed aristocracy as an independent economic and social force in British society.[29] Other "rewards for participation" offered to the working class also had egalitarian implications, strengthening the trade union movement and the Labour Party in Britain. Political participation also widened: temporarily, women played a far more important economic role in the industrial sector, and they were included in an expanded electorate after the war.[30] In Britain and the United States, many of these changes, particularly state intervention in the economy, were reversed after the wartime emergency had passed. In other European countries the wartime demand for a reduction in economic conflict and the introduction of new forms of bargaining pushed toward a more permanent corporatist organization of society.[31]

[29] Arthur Marwick, *The Deluge* (Harmondsworth: Penguin, 1967), especially chap. 9; by the same author, *Britain in the Century of Total War* (London: Penguin, 1970), chaps. 3 and 6; Alan S. Milward, *The Economic Effects of the Two World Wars on Britain* (London: Macmillan, 1970); Alan S. Milward, *War, Economy, and Society, 1939-1945* (London: Allen Lane, 1977), pp. 341-343.

[30] Marwick, *Britain in the Century of Total War*, pp. 108-110; the concept of "rewards for participation" is that of Richard Titmuss. The participation of American women in the industrial economy as the result of war, however, was "limited and brief." David Kennedy, *Over Here: The First World War and American Society* (New York: Oxford University Press, 1980), p. 285.

[31] Stein gives evidence on economic concentration and political centralization in the United States in *The Nation at War*, pp. 54-71. The appearance

The darker side of the social cohesion induced by total war is growth in intolerance for dissent and the appearance of scapegoating, particularly in the case of minorities that can in some way be connected with the external foe.[32] Although the specific effects of total war may vary from society to society, the general outcome might be described as a Hobbesian one (as in state consolidation): an increase in the power of the state internally; an increasingly "despotic" political order, as fewer restraints are imposed on the sovereign; and a leveling effect in economic and social terms.

Another example of the effects that a uniformly threatening environment may have on a society can be drawn from the legacy of the colonial empires themselves: fragment societies—Ulster, South Africa, Rhodesia, Algeria (before 1962)—threatened from the outside and sitting atop hostile and ethnically distinct majorities. Politics within such societies can come to resemble the politics of wartime: the external threat, uniformly perceived, serves as a constant backdrop to the political process.

White South African society illustrates the ways in which the political development of a threatened group can be determined by the inescapable fact of a surrounding hostile population. Relations between the English and Afrikaner fragments of white society have become secondary; "the primary phenomenon is that both have been established amidst more numerous peoples of non-European origins."[33] The same melding of Europeans took place in Algeria, where Italians, Maltese, and others rioted for *Algérie française*. Not only are ethnic lines within the transplanted European society blurred, but open class divisions may nearly disappear. Efforts to found a socialist party among South African working-class whites

---

of corporatist forms of organization is labeled by Kennedy the "most durable and important economic transformation to come out of the war [World War I]." On the European transformation, Charles Maier, *Recasting Bourgeois Europe* (Princeton: Princeton University Press, 1975), pp. 3-87.

[32] Coser, *The Functions of Social Conflict*, p. 103.

[33] Leonard M. Thompson, "The South African Dilemma," in *The Founding of New Societies* (New York: Harcourt, Brace & World, Inc., 1964), p. 179.

ultimately failed; in Ulster the most fervent diehards in the Unionist party have drawn their support from the working class; in North Africa, Julien noted that those who by their social station would have been Socialist or Communist in France, were in the Maghreb utter reactionaries.[34] The dominant ideology in such societies is often a peculiar mixture of populist and anti-democratic elements, satisfying the need to maintain the solidarity of the threatened group, while repudiating the arguments advanced for majority rule.

As perceived hostility from the outside increases, parallels with societies in wartime increase: dissent from the majority line is not tolerated and the use of arbitrary police or vigilante power increases; the political process becomes more centralized and interest groups are increasingly excluded from the making of policy. Such was the course of the Verwoerd regime in South Africa during the early 1960s, as international pressure for the dismantling of apartheid rose.[35] The internal political logic that accompanies a growing external threat may destroy any possibility for accommodation with the outside, an outcome characteristic of societies engaged in total war as well. The process of self-closure so vividly described by Deutsch may leave no option for a polity but final destruction, since any concession appears to be an unacceptable defeat.[36]

Israel provides a case that lies between fragment societies such as Ulster or South Africa and the state engaged in total warfare. Through partition Israel has avoided most of the infringements of domestic liberties associated with conditions of threat from below as well as from the outside. Nevertheless, the persistence and intensity of an external threat has produced a situation in which the government is, for domestic political reasons, locked into a position that seems unlikely

---

[34] C. A. Julien, *L'Afrique du Nord en marche: Nationalismes musulmans et souveraineté française* (Paris: Plon, 1952), p. 59.

[35] Newell M. Stultz, "The Politics of Security: South Africa under Verwoerd, 1961-66," *Journal of Modern African Studies* 7 (April, 1969), 7-12, 14.

[36] Karl Deutsch, *Nationalism and Social Communication* (Cambridge: MIT Press, 1953), pp. 181-186.

to lead to peace. While limited concessions might be attempted, a policy undertaken by Vorster in South Africa, substantial change threatens the removal of the government by a faction whose interpretation of the external situation is both more intransigent and more congruent with the perceptions of the population. Democracy in such instances, as in total war, may not serve peace-making or accommodation.

Political fragmentation under external pressure: Regime change and limited wars

Increasing external threat does not always lead to political integration and the corollary political effects described. Without a uniformly perceived and intense external threat, the pressures of international military competition may not produce social unity and increased state power but political fragmentation and even dissolution. In one study of political crises across a wide range of historical cases, "war or the threat of war" was described as "the most important political system destabilizer" among the environmental changes examined.[37] Of modern peasant revolutions, only one—the Mexican revolution—was not substantially affected by foreign intervention or an ongoing international conflict.[38] Theda Skocpol has elaborated the means by which international pressures led to a splintering of state power in the old regimes of France, Russia, and China. In France and China the financial consequences of international pressure led the old regime to attempt reforms that were resisted by the dominant landed classes in those societies, opening a political crisis that led to social revolution.[39] The importance of elite fragmentation in the cases that Skocpol describes is confirmed by the most prominent case of "failed absolutism" in Europe: Poland, where a powerful but divided landed aristocracy and gentry resisted

---

[37] Almond, Flanagan, and Mundt, eds., *Crisis, Choice and Change*, p. 629.
[38] Eric R. Wolf, *Peasant Wars of the Twentieth Century* (New York: Harper & Row, 1969), p. 47.
[39] Skocpol, *States and Social Revolutions*, pp. 60-64, 73-81, 109-111.

efforts at centralization and mobilization by a weak monarchy.[40]

In other cases, external threat or intervention may provide a stimulus for regime change carried out by elements of the state as part of an effort at resistance (a revolution from above) or spur the dynamic of revolutionary change from below set in motion by the process of state disintegration. In her account of revolutions from above in Meiji Japan and Kemalist Turkey, Ellen Kay Trimberger notes that the men who led these radical responses to external threats were servants of the state without being members of an aristocracy or ruling class; they did not possess substantial economic interests in the existing social order as either landlords or entrepreneurs. Although the threat that triggered these revolutions from above could be great, a limited foreign intervention was optimal for their success: enough to ensure at least the tacit support of the population, but not so great as to require their mobilization, rendered superfluous by the use of part of the state machinery and the military by the revolutionaries.[41]

The constellation necessary for a revolution from above on the Japanese or Turkish model seemed to be emerging in Egypt before the British intervention in 1882; the later Nasserist revolution and the Peruvian military takeover of 1968 are other examples of the same model. A more distant parallel might be drawn with the Gaullist resistance during World War II. The London-based Free French resembled the earlier cases in their vague notions of traditional nationalism and renovation, ideas that became more radical as the war progressed. The Gaullists were equally dubious of mass movements of popular resistance, preferring to rely upon the armed forces. Their resistance was the resistance of those who sought a revolution, or at least a renovation from above, a phrase

---

[40] Anderson, *Lineages*, pp. 279-298.

[41] Ellen Kay Trimberger, "A Theory of Elite Revolutions," *Studies in Comparative International Development* 7 (Fall 1972), p. 194; also, by the same author, *Revolution from Above: Military Bureaucrats and Development in Japan, Turkey, Egypt, and Peru* (New Brunswick, N.J.: Transaction Books, 1978).

that encapsulates the program of General de Gaulle. The aim of such a renovation was the same as that of the samurai and the Turkish officers: an ability to resist threats to national sovereignty and preservation of national autonomy.

A "revolution from above," although spurred by external threat, does not seek popular mobilization to meet it: its aim is to "control and depoliticize" the population. Revolutions from below, however, have been characterized by the use of threatened or actual foreign intervention to spur popular participation and to construct new state structures to replace those overthrown. In the French Revolution, threat of intervention by the European powers gave radicals an instrument in carrying out a revolution within the revolution.[42] Chalmers Johnson has emphasized the importance of invasion and occupation in producing the massive disruption important to the success of the Chinese and Yugoslav revolutions: "the war totally destroyed the traditional rural social order and sensitized the Chinese peasantry to a new spectrum of possible associations, identities, and purposes."[43] In both the Chinese and Yugoslav cases, the peasantry often had only two choices: fleeing or losing their lives. The scale of disruption was staggering: while in eighteen Allied countries during World War II the average loss of life was 1 in 143, in Yugoslavia, 1 in 9 died; 3,441,000 were interned in concentration camps, 23 percent of the population.[44] Outside intervention not only provided a program and a disoriented clientele for revolutionary counter-elites, it continued to shape the processes of state construction that took place after the old regime had disintegrated.[45]

Even when the disintegrative effects of military threat and war are not so catastrophic as to produce a change of regime, normally stable societies can experience political division and

[42] Kyung-Won Kim, *Revolution and International System* (New York: New York University Press, 1970), chap. 3.
[43] Chalmers Johnson, *Peasant Nationalism and Communist Power* (Stanford: Stanford University Press, 1962), p. 5.
[44] Ibid., pp. 121-122.
[45] Skocpol, *States and Social Revolutions*, p. 286.

paralysis. In cases of limited war among the great powers and their allies (such as the Crimean War and the Korean conflict) or asymmetric conflict (exemplified by colonial wars, such as those fought in South Africa, Algeria, or Indochina), the level of external threat is not perceived to be intense by a substantial portion of the population and political class. In contrast to a total war, interpretation of the external threat becomes a matter of political contention. A social truce and reduction of political conflict may be conjured into existence briefly by attempting to connect the patently distant or inferior foe with an overriding external fear, such as "international communism." The truce soon breaks down, however, and the strains imposed by mobilization, whether economic (in the form of taxes and inflation) or social (in the form of conscription) are not borne with patriotic quietude. The political elite fragments, and despite efforts at secrecy and executive decision-making, parliamentary institutions are not silenced for the duration of the conflict. The Crimean War in Britain resembles many later limited conflicts in following this pattern. The press, reporting large-scale mismanagement by the military in the Crimea, spurred the Radicals in Parliament to launch an attack on the aristocratic order and its ability to govern. Rather than the "social pause" that had been hoped for, aristocratic institutions came under increasing attack and the class-consciousness of the middle class was heightened.[46]

Limited wars produce political disunity, whether the collapse of the Fourth Republic, the crumbling of Britain's Labour cabinet under Korean War rearmament, or the onset of McCarthyism in the United States during the same conflict. A second contrast with total war is the government's effort to disguise the economic and social costs of the conflict, rather than demanding equality of sacrifice. As a result, the leveling effect characteristic of total wars is seldom a byproduct of such conflicts. Quantitative studies by Michael Stohl and Arthur Stein compare the effects of war on American society in

[46] Olive Anderson, *A Liberal State at War: English Politics and Economics during the Crimean War* (New York: St. Martin's Press, 1967), pp. 97, 101.

this century and demonstrate the different effects of total wars (particularly World War II), in which uniform and intense threat is perceived across society, and more limited conflicts, such as Vietnam and the Spanish-American War. Stohl's evidence supports the arguments made here: economic violence, such as that occurring during strikes, increased after the beginning of the Spanish-American War, but decreased with the onset of World War I. A reverse effect appeared for racial and ethnic violence: levels did not change with the outbreak of war with Spain, but did increase after entry into the First World War, presumably as scapegoat groups were attacked. Political violence also increased during the First World War, as the government took stronger measures to suppress dissent against the military effort.[47] Stein suggests that limited wars (Korea and Vietnam in particular) produced a smaller decline in measures of inequality in American society; concentration of government power, a result of higher levels of mobilization, was an effect less noticed in the two limited conflicts. Despite a decline in social cohesion in *all* the wars studied, that decline was slightest, given the level of mobilization demanded, in World War II.[48]

The problem of peace-making is as pressing in limited wars, but the political obstacles are different from those in which mobilization levels and threat perception are greater. Efforts at peace are stalled through a dynamic that differs from that of total war: not the logic of increasing intransigence within domestic politics, but the fact that the war becomes a domestic issue early on. A process of competitive mobilization ensues, led by the government and its dissident challengers; the result

[47] Michael Stohl, "Linkages between War and Domestic Political Violence in the United States, 1890-1923," in *Quasi-Experimental Approaches*, ed. James A. Caporaso and Leslie L. Roos, Jr. (Evanston, Ill.: Northwestern University Press, 1973), pp. 156-179. The extension of Stohl's cases to include Korea and World War II suggests a spectrum with World War II at one end, the two limited wars (Spain and Korea) at the other, and World War I lying somewhere in between. Stohl, *War and Domestic Political Violence* (Beverly Hills: Sage, 1976), pp. 111-122.

[48] Stein, *Nation at War*, pp. 38-53.

is often a long-lasting deadlock.[49] If the conflict is one involving a great power and a much weaker adversary, the outcome is often determined by the very asymmetry that seems to give the more powerful party a decisive advantage. For the stronger power, the war is not total, its costs are disguised, and political conflict is rampant. For the weaker power, because of the disparity in military means, the war must be a total war in its political and psychological effects. Thus, paradoxically, the small triumph; the apparently weak are ultimately victorious.[50]

International competition and threat, then, can have quite different consequences, depending upon internal perceptions of the threat and the preexisting level of consensus, particularly among the political elite. If a firm elite consensus exists and the external threat is perceived as intense across society, the probability of an increase in political cohesion and centralization is high. Complicating such outcomes, however, is the question of costs and the effect of the political system. Costs will tend to increase with the intensity of the threat, offsetting the bias toward political solidarity, particularly if the costs are not distributed in an equitable fashion. The political system can affect both elite consensus, by offering the ability to mobilize support for an opposing reading of the threat, and threat perception itself, since certain political systems award elites greater control of information. Beyond these conclusions, much remains unanswered, particularly defining that tip-point within each society at which an external threat, even one requiring a substantial sacrifice, leads either to the suppression of internal cleavage or to political disarray. At least part of the answer to the differing responses of societies must be sought at a different level, by looking within to the responses of particular groups that may regard autonomy or accommodation as preferred solutions.

[49] Robert Rothstein, "Domestic Politics and Peacemaking: Reconciling Incompatible Imperatives," *Annals* 392 (November, 1970), 62-75.

[50] Asymmetric conflicts are examined in Andrew Mack, "Why Big Nations Lose Small Wars: The Politics of Asymmetric Conflict," *World Politics* 28 (January, 1975), 175-200; for this point, p. 183.

THE IMPACT OF THE INTERNATIONAL STATE
SYSTEM: DIVISIONS WITHIN SOCIETIES

To this point, the domestic consequences of international politics have been assessed at the level of the political system or regime. Some of these empirical studies look beneath the carapace of the state, however, at distinctions among groups, organizations, or classes in response to international impact. One simple distinction, mentioned above, is the relative *sensitivity* of groups to occurrences outside the boundaries of their society. In such cases, the boundaries of the state do not circumscribe the boundaries of sentiment, particularly those established by ethnic ties. In the United States, such ties have survived years of assimilation and provide a basis for political action by groups attuned to the interests of other nations.[51]

Another reason for increased international sensitivity is the resistance/collaboration spectrum of nationalist sensitivity. Differing responses by groups to international pressure is one source of the political consequences just described: in responding to the demands of international political competition or war, particularly when additional resources are demanded, the question of how much autonomy at what price inevitably arises. Even under extreme circumstances groups will differ in their answers to that question. Such circumstances, those of a *direct* external intrusion, the penetration of a society's boundaries, produces the most profound polarization along the lines of collaboration and resistance. In attempting to explain the fissures that appear in such instances, the history of colonial resistance and nationalist movements is illustrative, as well as the experience of European collaboration and resistance during World War II.

Two groups stand at the resistance end of the spectrum, forming the leadership core of a nationalist response. Even in those societies lacking a modern state or the integrating presence of nationalism, groups that define the way of life of a

[51] The activities of ethnic lobbies as they relate to Congress are described by Thomas M. Franck and Edward Weisband, *Foreign Policy by Congress* (New York: Oxford University Press, 1979), pp. 186-194.

people have often assumed a prominent role in leading resistance to outside domination. The role of the Muslim order of the Sanusi in Libyan resistance to the Turks and Italians was described above. The great revolts of 1896-1897 in Ndebeleland and Mashonaland (now Zimbabwe) are also typical of this pattern: an influx of European settlers, massive in scope and unprecedented in kind, the destruction or flight of the old leaders, the emergence of a new, religiously based but innovative leadership to confront the threat.[52] In Egypt and Algeria reform movements of the Muslim ulemas played a similar role in nationalist movements.[53] One is also reminded of the curés in the Vendée, who played a substantial part in that instance of local resistance to bourgeois collaborators with the French Revolution.[54]

Nationalist movements have also been led by intellectuals of a new type, those who accept a Western world-view and Western methods of political organization. No longer religious figures defending an order to which they were bound, these resisters assume not only a position of mediation but also a position in part "outside" their society, much like the European intruder.[55] Frantz Fanon and Albert Memmi have considered the progress of intellectuals in Africa and Asia from fascination with Western life and yearning for assimilation to

[52] T. O. Ranger, "Connexions between 'Primary Resistance' Movements and Modern Mass Nationalism in East and Central Africa: Parts I and II," *Journal of African History* 9 (1968), 437-453; 631-641; T. O. Ranger, *Revolt in Southern Rhodesia, 1896-97* (Evanston, Ill.: Northwestern University Press, 1967). Cf. Eric Stokes, "Traditional Resistance Movements and Afro-Asian Nationalism: The Context of the 1857 Mutiny Rebellion in India," *Past and Present*, no. 48 (August, 1970), 100-118.

[53] Robert Owen, "Egypt and Europe: From French Expedition to British Occupation," in *Studies in the Theory of Imperialism*, ed. Roger Owen and Bob Sutcliffe (London: Longman, 1972), p. 206; Wolf, *Peasant Wars*, p. 230.

[54] Charles Tilly, *The Vendée* (Cambridge: Harvard University Press, 1964), p. 60.

[55] Rupert Emerson, *From Empire to Nation* (Cambridge: Harvard University Press, 1960), presents one of the best expositions of the shift to a new nationalist leadership.

a rediscovery of their own cultures and a conversion to resistance. For Memmi, the end of assimilationist hopes occurs
when the intellectual realizes that such hopes will never be
fulfilled; for Fanon, the severance of intellectuals from their
urban base and their migration to the countryside is essential
to the nationalist transformation.[56]

The ambiguous role of the modern intellectual in both mediating with the external and defining a way of life is further
demonstrated by the prominent part played by intellectuals
in ideological collaboration during World War II. The serious
acceptance by some of the fascist model of the future could
be compared to the wholehearted acceptance of the French
way of life by the *évolués* of the colonial empire.[57] Intellectuals
on the resistance side in France seemed to occupy a functional
niche in a secular society equivalent to that of the religious
leaders described above: those who define a way of life or a
culture. Instructors in *lycées* and schoolteachers, such as Georges
Bidault and Guy Mollet, played a prominent role in the French
Resistance. In part this participation resulted from the long-
standing association of the *instituteur* and left-wing politics,
but their participation might also be attributed to their role
in instilling a republican and nationalist ideology in the young.
One could note that two other intellectuals prominent in the
Resistance, Jacques Soustelle and André Malraux, were students of non-European cultures, which may have accentuated
their awareness of a distinctly French way of life.

The definition of a *direct* external intrusion posits a suspension of the state's ability or willingness to exclude such
intrusions. Nevertheless, in most areas of the world in which
the Europeans attempted to exert influence, they confronted
states, albeit decaying ones. As Trimberger's model of revolutions from above suggests, movements of resistance were

[56] Albert Memmi, *The Colonizer and the Colonized* (Boston: Beacon Press,
1963), pp. 119-141; Frantz Fanon, *The Wretched of the Earth* (New York:
Grove Press, Inc., 1968), pp. 125-128.

[57] The distinctions among collaborationists in the case of France are drawn
from Stanley Hoffmann, *Decline or Renewal?*, pp. 26-31.

often led or assisted by elements of the state, particularly in the ancient bureaucratic empires of the Middle East and Asia. The degree of resistance and its success depended upon a number of circumstances. If the state apparatus were already accustomed to restriction of its sovereignty—as in certain parts of the Ottoman Empire—and the Europeans imposed no additional constraints, resistance was unlikely. Both Skocpol and Trimberger emphasize the importance of relative autonomy of the state apparatus from the dominant social and economic elites, essential not only for the revolutionary renovation from above, but also to circumvent a dynamic of collaboration that could otherwise result. If the state bureaucracy (and its allies) saw in the Western intruder a means of maintaining its position against local opposition or a threat from below, the will to resist was further sapped. In the revolt of Abd el-Kader in Algeria (1832-1847) the French were aided by officials of the Turkish government, and later used a "native aristocracy, who were co-opted as administrators of the rural population on behalf of the state."[58] The Ch'ing dynasty in China, of Manchu origin and thus itself alien, could hardly mobilize Chinese nationalist resistance to the West without sacrificing its own hold on power. In contrast to the Vendée or the Bedouin of Cyrenaica, resistance would have widened the rift between ruler and ruled.

The stability of colonial rule and the failure of resistance despite a massive and threatening external impact, underlines the frequent success of strategies of *collaboration*. Even the harshest military occupations have seldom been able to dispense with collaborators, and Ronald Robinson has noted their importance in sustaining the colonial empires, whether they relied upon indirect or direct means of control:

Whether the official agents of imperialism were working from outside or inside Afro-Asian societies therefore, they still had to work through indigenous collaborators and political processes. Their own power was limited. It was enough to manipulate, but not to abolish them. The substance of ruling authority had to a great extent to be extracted

[58] Wolf, *Peasant Wars*, pp. 218, 221.

from their subjects. Essentially, therefore, colonial rule represented a reconstruction of collaboration.[59]

Although the locus of collaboration, like that of nationalist resistance, could shift from society to society, and the motives for collaboration were diverse, some generalizations about likely collaborating groups can be made.[60]

Machiavelli described the most dependable collaborator: the colonist. Robinson attributes the dependability of colonist-collaborators to the dominance of the export-import sector in the colonial economy; political collaboration thus has its base in economic collaboration, an argument dissected more carefully below. A more significant determinant of the loyalty of colonist-collaborators, however, was the dynamic of fragment societies in hostile surroundings described above: the threat posed by the indigenous population and the means granted by the metropolis for meeting that threat. Among colonial powers, Britain tended to devolve considerable responsibility for the maintenance of order upon its colonists. In Australia, North America, and other British territories, the threat posed by the non-European population was minor; claims for greater autonomy resulted. Paris, on the other hand, kept the means of coercion firmly in its grip, even if its local representatives were influenced by *colon* opinion. As described in Chapter V, the possibility for independent resistance to changes in the colonial status quo was an important determinant of the outcome in decolonizing the British and French settler colonies.

If dependent colonists are ideal collaborators, other groups are also likely candidates. Two in particular have frequently served an external master well: those who felt a sense of deprivation under the old regime, whether on religious, ethnic, or socioeconomic grounds; and, paradoxically, those most

[59] Ronald Robinson, "Non-European Foundations of European Imperialism: Sketch for a Theory of Collaboration," in *Studies in the Theory of Imperialism*, ed. Owen and Sutcliffe, p. 133.

[60] Jorge Dominguez classified collaboration according to motivation in five categories: patriotic, prospective, antagonistic, defensive, and survival, in "Responses to Occupations by the United States: Caliban's Dilemma," *Pacific Historical Review* 48 (November, 1979), 593-597.

favored in material terms, the social and economic elite of a society. Deprived minorities were frequently manipulated by the colonial powers in their policies of divide and rule; the unsuccessful French attempt to divide Arab and Berber in North Africa was characteristic. The Germans pursued a similar policy in constructing their New Order in Europe: Croatian *Ustace* were unloosed upon the Serbs; a puppet state was established in Slovakia; Flemish separatism was encouraged in Belgium.

The social and economic elites of a society may opt for collaboration simply because they have the most to lose in an unsuccessful attempt at resistance. Before British intervention in 1882, the Egyptian national movement incorporated landowners who feared higher taxes as the result of demands by foreign creditors, but they defected as the threat of foreign intervention became more real and as the leaders of the national movement became more successful in obtaining widespread popular support.[61] The threat from below that figured in their defection is a second reason for acquiescing in foreign intervention or occupation, particularly when the only strategy of successful resistance is one of mobilization and reform. Ties of class could outweigh those of nationalism, even among the European democracies facing Germany in the 1930s. Harold Nicolson, a shrewd observer of British Conservatives, noted in his diary:

> We have lost our will-power, since our will-power is divided. People of the governing classes think only of their own fortunes, which means hatred of the Reds. This creates a perfectly artificial bond between ourselves and Hitler. Our class interests, on both sides, cut across our national interests.[62]

Vichy France demonstrates both types of calculation in the choice for collaboration: previous exclusion from power and fear of revolution. The Vichy order was constructed in large

---

[61] Owen in Owen and Sutcliffe, *Studies in the Theory of Imperialism*, pp. 206-207.

[62] Harold Nicolson, *Diaries and Letters: 1930-1939* (New York: Atheneum, 1968), p. 346.

part by those segments of French society "which the Third
Republic had kept on the sidelines or whose assigned role in
it had not been as big as they desired." Vichy was, in short,
"a great revenge of minorities."[63] An additional motivation
was social order and anti-communism, instrumental in the
initial refusal to use chaos as the "ultimate weapon" against
the German invader, and a common thread binding together
the often disparate elements in the new regime.[64] Distrust of
social revolution also explains the reluctance shown by civil
servants and the military in joining the Resistance, even after
November 1942.[65]

A final dimension in the pattern of resistance and collaboration is the balance for either response within agrarian and
urban sectors. A recurrent theme in the writings of Rousseau,
taken up again by Fanon, is the superiority of traditional
agrarian society in protecting the indigenous way of life against
foreign intruders and native collaborators. Contrary to Fanon's claims, however, it could be argued that the modernized
sector of the economy and society usually bears the greatest
brunt of the foreign impact; thus, modern Chinese nationalism
emerged in the treaty ports of the south, particularly Canton,
where students and workers were more easily mobilized against
a visible foreign presence. Weighing against such motivations
for resistance were the high stakes that could be lost in a failed
resistance and the relative ease of control (in contrast to the
countryside) that could be exercised by an occupying or in-
tervening power. Modernity also seems related to the development of a Hobbesian point of view: any sovereign should
be obeyed who performs the all-important task of protecting
his subjects against violent death.[66] In the typology of Herbert
Kelman, instrumental or utilitarian bases of national com-

[63] Hoffmann, *Decline or Renewal?*, p. 5.

[64] Paxton, *Vichy France*, p. 286.

[65] Paxton, *Parades and Politics at Vichy* (Princeton: Princeton University
Press, 1966), p. 401.

[66] Hobbes counsels obedience even to an infidel sovereign under almost all
circumstances (*Leviathan*, ed. Michael Oakeshott [New York: Collier Books,
1962], p. 436).

mitment increase with modernity, while sentimental or affective bases decline, possibly undermining the will to resist a relatively benign alien ruler.[67] At least one comparative study of resistance and collaboration in response to American intervention has supported the Fanon-Rousseau model of resistance and collaboration.[68]

A direct and massive international impact throws into relief the likely poles of a nationalist coalition of resistance and a collaborationist alignment of adaptation. At the core of resistance are likely to be those who define a society's self-image—intellectuals, students, religious figures, parts of the state apparatus, and those parts of a population threatened most directly, whether members of the Communist Party in Hitler's Europe or the peasants of China, who faced uprooting and death at the hands of the Japanese. Likely collaborators can also be singled out: those deprived under the old regime, who are likely to regard an external presence as protective; those with high social and economic stakes, who stand to lose in unsuccessful resistance or in mobilizing less-favored groups; and those with ethnic ties to the outsider—particularly colonists. Where the cleavage between resistance and collaboration will appear in a given society depends, again, on the answer to the question how much resistance, at what cost. The answers given to that question will depend not only on the social roles and domestic positions of groups, but also upon the nature of the external intrusion.

This typology of resistance and collaboration makes clear the poor fit between *externally induced* cleavages and other, preexisting divisions in a society. That observation reinforces an earlier argument that categories of class, religion, and other familiar features of the domestic political landscape are in-

[67] Herbert Kelman, "Patterns of Involvement in the National System," in *International Politics and Foreign Policy*, ed. James N. Rosenau, rev. ed. (New York: Free Press, 1969), pp. 276-288.

[68] Dominguez, "Responses to Occupations," pp. 602-603. Dominguez is generalizing from case studies contained in this number of *Pacific Historical Review*, discussing resistance to American occupation in the Philippines, Cuba, and China.

adequate when dealing with the internal consequences of international politics. On the other hand, externally induced fissures may *not* be the most prominent for all of those involved in movements of collaboration or resistance: in Japan and Turkey, in China and Yugoslavia, in the European resistance movements, there were some who were more intent upon social revolution than expelling foreign influence, more interested in destroying their domestic enemies than the alien, a task made easier by the association of those enemies with the foreign intruder. The persistence of externally created divisions after the external impact has receded also seems related to their overlap with other divisions and to the appearance of new external threats that serve to activate a nationalist response along different lines. The unity of resistance movements in Europe, for example, was broken as temporarily submerged social and religious cleavages reemerged and the new power of the Soviet Union heightened distrust of its internal allies.

DOMESTIC POLITICAL CONSEQUENCES OF THE INTERNATIONAL ECONOMY: CONSTRAINT, COLLABORATION, PENETRATION

Although Immanuel Wallerstein has argued that the shape of the international state system from its beginnings was highly dependent upon the evolution of the world economy, it will be assumed here that the two, while clearly influencing one another, cannot be related in a consistent hierarchy of cause and effect.[69] An investigation of the domestic political consequences of international economic relations can employ some of the same concepts used in examining the effects of international military and diplomatic competition: indirect versus direct influences, the nationalist spectrum of response (resist-

[69] Jean Baechler has pointed to the reverse relationships, that "the expansion of capitalism owes its origins and its raison d'être to political anarchy," in *The Origins of Capitalism* (Oxford: Basil Blackwell, 1975), pp. 76-77. On this point, see Skocpol, *States and Social Revolutions*, p. 22.

ance versus adaptation/collaboration), relative sensitivity to international change. Despite these similarities, analyzing the impact of the international economy brings its own complications. First, whatever the level of penetration by outside economic factors, whatever its quiescence in the face of imports or foreign investment, the state does not disappear; it remains a critical mediator between the international economic environment and the domestic economy and society. Second, any assessment of the balance between nationalist striving for autonomy and adaptation to international economic constraints is complicated by the combination of material and ideological strands in the response of many groups. A "pure" nationalist response, in terms of the attitudes and policies described above, is rare.

The effects of the international economy on domestic politics will be considered first in their *indirect* form, as a *constraint* on state action and as creator of *collaborators* within the domestic economy, and then in *direct* form, as external economic organizations, particularly the multinational corporation, penetrate the boundaries of societies.

Constraints on domestic politics: Interdependence and international economic position

Although theorists of international economic interdependence have employed the concept of sensitivity, most studies of interdependence devote little attention to the domestic political consequences of the growth of interdependence. The case studies of Keohane and Nye, which emphasize regime change and stability as a dependent variable, are more concerned with the development of transgovernmental channels (a variant of normal foreign policy) and with the role of international organizations than with the role of nongovernmental groups whose different responses to the demands of economic interdependence might produce political conflict.[70]

---

[70] Robert O. Keohane and Joseph S. Nye, *Power and Interdependence: World Politics in Transition* (Boston: Little, Brown, and Co., 1977), pp. 33-37.

Typically, the interdependence approach emphasizes economic interdependence, in all its manifestations, as a *constraint* upon state action: the efforts of a state to achieve autonomy, particularly in setting economic policy, are thwarted by the conditions of economic openness.[71]

Several characteristics of the interdependence model divert attention from domestic political effects. Despite an assumption of "multiple channels of influence" linking societies, those channels only seem to produce additional constraints upon a state that is viewed as relatively unified. At least among industrial economies, relations are regarded as relatively symmetric, even though some countries are more hemmed in than others, hence a nationalist reaction is not triggered. An additional reason for the lack of a nationalist reaction is a belief that the costs of expanding state autonomy under conditions of interdependence are so great that few governments or societies would be willing to bear them. The result is a portrait of national responses to economic interdependence that emphasizes homogeneity across societies and one that minimizes differential international impacts.[72] The state remains relatively unified, looking *out*; and interdependence remains a *condition* of the environment, which may occasionally produce political conflict but does not enter more deeply into the political life of a society.

Domestic political consequences have also been traced to the *position of a state in the international economy*. Although the object of his study is the world-system, and not its constituents, Wallerstein has attempted to link international economic position to strong and weak states in early modern Europe. "Core economies" are awarded more highly developed state structures, while the economies of the emerging economic periphery have weak states. Unfortunately for Wal-

[71] For example, Edward Morse, *Foreign Policy and Interdependence in Gaullist France* (Princeton: Princeton University Press, 1973).

[72] The homogenizing character of interdependence analysis has been criticized by Peter Katzenstein in "International Relations and Domestic Structures: Foreign Economic Policies of Advanced Industrial States," *International Organization* 30 (Winter 1976), 1-45.

lerstein's argument, even in this small number of cases the fit is poor: not only did some of the core economies, such as the Netherlands, fail to develop strong absolutist states, many of the strongest states (Prussia or Sweden, for example) were parts of the economic periphery or semi-periphery.[73]

A different model linking international economic position to political structure has been derived from the work of Alexander Gerschenkron. Economies are situated not by their position in the international division of labor (as in the cases of Wallerstein or the *dependencia* theorists), but by their *temporal* position in successive waves of industrialization. The principal cases employed by Gerschenkron are the familiar ones of Germany and Russia: apart from the Veblenesque argument of "advantages of backwardness," Gerschenkron points to institutional differences in these "late industrializers": a larger role awarded to central, directive institutions in the economy (banks or the state), the development of large-scale industry, particularly in capital goods; a pervasive public ideology justifying such institutional development.[74] The specifically *political* consequences of these institutional biases are not made explicit in Gerschenkron's work, but others, such as James Kurth, have used his analysis and later applications to Latin America by Albert Hirschman to suggest a possible connection between late industrialization and political authoritarianism, echoing the *dependencia* arguments described below. Like Wallerstein's model, however, such efforts at international economic determinism show a poor fit with the cases at hand, unless they are supplemented with domestic linkages. Gerschenkron's own explanation assumes an internal source of the "will" or "spirit" to industrialize, presumably nationalist striving for autonomy and rejection of foreign

---

[73] These criticisms are developed by Theda Skocpol in "Wallerstein's World Capitalist System: A Theoretical and Historical Critique," *American Journal of Sociology* 82 (March, 1977), 1083-1088; and in Peter Gourevitch, "The International System and Regime Formation," *Comparative Politics* 10 (April, 1978), 419-438.

[74] Alexander Gerschenkron, *Economic Backwardness in Historical Perspective* (Cambridge: Harvard University Press, 1962), pp. 5-30, 44.

patterns and involvement. As Kurth admits, "the explanatory connections are rather imprecise, and in any event authoritarian governments already existed in Germany and Austria and had for many years when these two countries undertook industrialization."[75] The counter-examples are also compelling: Sweden, so damaging to Wallerstein's core-periphery model, is also a clear exception to any theory connecting late industrialization and authoritarianism.

Dependency: Indirect influence as collaboration or adaptation

The principal weakness of theories deriving political outcomes from international economic circumstances, however parsimonious they may be, is the absence of a causal sequence that connects the international with the domestic. Others have tried to sketch the steps more carefully. Peter Gourevitch, for example, has traced the use of a policy instrument (the tariff) in response to an international economic disturbance (the decline in cereal prices in the late nineteenth century) to the strengthening and rigidifying of political regimes in Western Europe and the United States.[76] Simon Schama has linked the perceived relative economic decline of the Dutch economy in the eighteenth century to the economic discontent and political dissidence that marked the beginnings of revolution in the eighteenth century.[77]

The most ambitious attempt to link international economic demands to internal political order, however, is that contem-

---

[75] James R. Kurth, "Industrial Change and Political Change: A European Perspective," in *The New Authoritarianism in Latin America*, ed. David Collier (Princeton: Princeton University Press, 1979), p. 323.

[76] Peter A. Gourevitch, "International Trade, Domestic Coalitions, and Liberty: Comparative Responses to the Crisis of 1873-1896," *Journal of Interdisciplinary History* 8 (August, 1977), 281-313. Gourevitch models his argument on that of Alexander Gerschenkron in *Bread and Democracy in Germany* (Berkeley: University of California Press, 1943), especially pp. 42-50.

[77] Simon Schama, *Patriots and Liberators: Revolution in the Netherlands, 1780-1813* (New York: Knopf, 1977), p. 33; a reaction against the thriving and "cosmopolitan" center of Amsterdam also appeared (p. 35).

porary descendant of the theory of imperialism, dependency theory (taken to include theories of neo-colonialism). In contrast to the models examined up to this point, the international economy can remain *outside* (indirectly affect) the dependent economy, or it can *penetrate* (directly affect) that economy and society, but in either case, the international economy is no longer simply a *constraint* to which a unified state and society respond. Instead, the international economy has "collaborators" within the dependent economies that transmit its signals and ensure the adaptation of internal political and economic forms to the demands of the international market.

It is this presence of *internal* political and economic collaborators that separates *dependency* from economic *dependence*.[78] Even in Hirschman's classic account of drastic trade asymmetry, the response of the dependent state is portrayed as a relatively unified response to an external constraint; it is the interdependence model, highly skewed.[79] In a relationship of dependency, however, the relationship is accompanied by the implantation of those "representing" the international economy within the dependent economy; economic aggregates are accompanied by political and social corollaries.

Peter Katzenstein's analysis of the small European states further illustrates the difference between the two approaches. By most economic measures, the small European economies lie somewhere between the major industrial states and the developing countries. Despite their level of economic dependence, however, they are able to extract a considerable measure of autonomy from the international economy. Their greater degree of freedom results from a political contrast with the developing countries: political structures "tightly knit in cen-

[78] For a somewhat different argument about the contrast between dependence and dependency, James A. Caporaso, "Dependence, Dependency, and Power in the Global System: A Structural and Behavioral Analysis," and Raymond D. Duvall, "Dependence and Dependencia Theory: Notes Toward Precision of Concept and Argument," both in *International Organization* 32 (Winter 1978), 13-43 and 51-78.

[79] Albert Hirschman, *National Power and the Structure of Foreign Trade* (Berkeley: University of California Press, 1945).

tralizing political power and minimizing the difference between public and private realm," as well as an avoidance of penetration on a large scale by foreign multinationals.[80] Katzenstein's relatively optimistic view is based not only on these differences of fact, but also those of interpretation. It is assumed that the costs of alternative strategies for the small economies would be insurmountable, that a considerable measure of adaptation is necessary for survival. Dependency theorists, on the other hand, posit the possibility of a relatively closed, national capitalist or socialist model of development as an alternative.[81] If one strips away the assumption of consensual political strategies in the small European states, one could develop a model much closer to those used by dependency theorists to describe developing countries. In analyzing the causes for Britain's economic decline, for example, some have portrayed its outward-directed financial sector and the costs of its chosen economic strategy in terms very reminiscent of those used for Latin American societies.[82]

In their assessment of the impact of the international economy on African, Latin American, and Asian societies, the dependency theorists do not share the optimism of those who believe that increased autonomy can be extracted from the pressures and infiltration of the economic environment. The economic consequences that have been attributed to dependency—underdevelopment, technological backwardness, regional and social inequalities of wealth and income—cannot be assessed here.[83] It is the *political* consequences of depend-

[80] Peter J. Katzenstein, "The Small European States in the International Economy" (Paper presented at the Annual Meeting of the American Political Science Association, Washington, D.C., September, 1979), pp. 25, 13-14.

[81] For example, Fernando Henrique Cardoso and Enzo Faletto, *Dependency and Development in Latin America* (Berkeley: University of California Press, 1979), p. xxiv.

[82] For example, Frank Longstreth, "The City, Industry and the State," in *State and Economy in Contemporary Capitalism*, ed. Colin Crouch, (New York: St. Martin's Press, 1979), pp. 157-190.

[83] For one attempt at empirical investigation of these hypotheses, Robert R. Kaufman, Harry I. Chernotsky, and Daniel S. Geller, "A Preliminary Test of the Theory of Dependency," *Comparative Politics* (April, 1975), 303-330.

ency that are our principal concern: how does the international economy, according to this model, not only constrain, but shape political outcomes?

Earlier versions of dependency theory, in which the "conditioning" of the domestic economy was portrayed in its starkest form, argued a simple causal connection: the demands of the international economy upon the open, dependent economy were reflected in the rise and fall of collaborating elites. Certain groups benefited from their ties to the international market; others were crushed by it. Those groups that prospered saw the success of political institutions and ideologies that reflected their interests, as well as the interests of the international economy and its dominant powers. Wallerstein uses this form of argument in his study of early modern Europe. In his model, the pull of an emerging international market for grain produces an Eastern variant of absolutism, an explanation that is rejected by others who award greater importance to the international state system or preexisting agrarian structures.[84] Others have traced more carefully the political progress of sectors that expand in response to the international market. The growing power of coffee interests in Brazil has been linked to demands for regional autonomy and decentralization that eventually led to the establishment of a republican regime.[85] The same export crops produced a resurgence in political liberalism and laissez-faire economics among Colombian political parties during the late nineteenth century.[86]

Such simple cause-and-effect relationships cannot be expected to predict political outcomes in most cases, however. Economic role in relation to the international economy may not translate directly into political attitudes and action. Even the much-maligned comprador of nineteenth-century China,

---

[84] Anderson's alternative argument is presented above; also Skocpol, "Wallerstein's World Capitalist System," pp. 1081-1083.

[85] Donald Coes, "Brazil," in *Tropical Development, 1889-1913,* ed. W. Arthur Lewis (London: George Allen & Unwin, Ltd., 1970), pp. 120-121.

[86] Charles W. Bergquist, *Coffee and Conflict in Colombia, 1886-1910* (Durham, N.C.: Duke University Press, 1978), pp. 8, 49-51.

the prototype of the economic collaborator, was a far more ambiguous figure than is often assumed. As the Chinese most directly involved in the modernized and Western-dominated sector of the Chinese economy, the comprador was often the most sensitive to foreign imperialism; many participated in China's reform and revolutionary movements.[87] The harsh economic determinism of a crude dependency model assumes that threatened economic interests will be unable to forge alliances and utilize the state to protect themselves from the vagaries of the international market, in the manner of the Prussian Junkers. While the intrusion of the international market may add an increment of political instability, final political outcomes are usually far more indeterminate.[88]

The simplified dependency view—collaborating elites that identify completely with their position in the international division of labor, the absence of any element of economic resistance or any means, through state action, to organize that resistance—is of limited use in explaining political consequences, particularly in the post-colonial period. A second and far more complex argument is developed by Guillermo O'Donnell to explain the turn toward bureaucratic-authoritarian regimes in Latin America in the 1960s and 1970s.[89] O'Donnell relies more heavily on domestic determinants in

[87] Yen-P'ing Hao, The Comprador in Nineteenth-Century China: Bridge between East and West (Cambridge: Harvard University Press, 1970), p. 194.

[88] Overly deterministic versions of dependency theory are criticized by Tony Smith, "The Underdevelopment of Development Literature: The Case of Dependency Theory," World Politics 31 (January, 1979), 247-288. For a very subtle and detailed account of the political changes induced locally by international economic shifts, see A. G. Hopkins, An Economic History of West Africa (London: Longmans, 1973), chap. 4.

[89] Statements of the O'Donnell argument are given by him in Modernization and Bureaucratic-Authoritarianism: Studies in South American Politics (Berkeley: Institute of International Studies, University of California, 1973); "Corporatism and the Question of the State," in Authoritarianism and Corporatism in Latin America, ed. James M. Malloy (Pittsburgh: University of Pittsburgh Press, 1977), pp. 44-87; "Reflections on the Patterns of Change in the Bureaucratic-Authoritarian State," Latin American Research Review 12 (Winter 1978), 3-38. See as well the excellent summary by David Collier, "Overview of the Bureaucratic-Authoritarian Model," in The New Authoritarianism in Latin America, ed. Collier, pp. 19-32.

his model; with the onset of an economic crisis that results from the close of one phase of import-substituting industrialization, the elites in these societies

... commonly attempt to shift to more austere 'orthodox' development policies that de-emphasize distribution to the popular sector. They see a long-term solution in the "vertical integration" or deepening of industrialization through domestic manufacture of intermediate and capital goods. However, the levels of technology, managerial expertise, and capital needed in this phase require large, more efficient, highly capitalized enterprises—often the affiliates of multinational corporations. The concern with attracting this type of foreign investment encourages the adoption of orthodox economic policies in order to deal with the economic crisis and to create conditions of long-term economic stability that meet the often exacting requirements imposed by multinational corporations and international lending agencies.[90]

The O'Donnell thesis has been criticized for its economic assumptions (the "exhaustion" of possibilities for import substitution) and for the poor fit between the economic developments described and change of political regime.[91] The interest of his model in terms of the domestic consequences of international economic conditions lies in the connection that O'Donnell draws between international economic demands and internal political solutions. The *interpretation* of those demands by domestic elites led them to orthodox economic policies and political repression in an effort to find the way out of an economic impasse. O'Donnell's theory of "preemptive penetration" by external economic actors points to the next stage in the impact of the international economy on societies: from constraint to collaboration to penetration, in the form of the multinational corporation.

Direct effects of the international economy: The multinational corporation

Thus far, international economic influence has been examined in the form of *trade*, a transaction that need not bring a large

---

[90] Collier, "Overview," pp. 26-27.
[91] For example, the articles by Serra, Hirschman, and Kaufman in *The New Authoritarianism*, ed. Collier.

foreign organizational presence into a society. Foreign direct investment, in the form of the multinational corporation, raises additional political questions. Such corporate outposts can provide domestic elites with political and economic resources to bolster their position. Corporations can also be political actors in their own right, rather than simply remaining passive elements in the life of society. Most important, they can give rise, because of their undisguised economic role, to a nationalist reaction, spurring on those who seek greater economic and political autonomy as well as a degree of closure to international influences. States and groups within them have reacted to this new economic actor in ways that demonstrate fear for their national autonomy rather than simple economic interest. In industrialized European societies, nationalist reaction has centered upon threatened control by American firms of sectors of the economy viewed as essential to military research and development, and thus to national defense and status. The quest for freedom of action in the world was prominent in French sensitivity regarding these sectors:

What is at issue for France and Europe is their political position vis-à-vis the great powers and their capacity for long-term national independence. . . . Today an independent aerospace and electronics industry, along with the supporting sciences, has become crucial for a nation to enjoy diplomatic and military freedom of action.[92]

In developing nations, more permeable and infinitely weaker economically than the European states, the political consequences of a multinational presence may be more profound. As organizations with substantial resources, the multinationals can meddle in local politics; the most blatant recent examples are those of ITT in Chile and United Fruit in Guatemala.[93] In his study of multinationals in Peru, Goodsell suggests that the corporations find direct approaches to officials to be the most beneficial and prudent means of political influence;.

---

[92] Robert Gilpin, *France in the Age of the Scientific State* (Princeton: Princeton University Press, 1968), p. 76.

[93] Joseph S. Nye, Jr., "Multinational Corporations in World Politics," *Foreign Affairs* 53 (October, 1974), 155-157.

such means may also cause the most damage and distortion in the domestic political process, however.[94] Foreign corporations may also be feared as a Trojan horse seeking to involve its home country in political or even military intervention on its behalf or enlisting international monetary and financial institutions in its cause if dispossessed. The controversy surrounding policy toward the Allende government in Chile in part concerns this question; in the case of Peru, however, Goodsell found no significant evidence of persistent collaboration between American companies and the State Department.[95]

A more important political effect, and one more difficult to estimate, is the effect that a large foreign economic sector can have in shaping domestic political alliances and the political system itself. In his study of neo-colonialism in Kenya, Colin Leys traces the consolidation of the power of the foreign sector and its allies during the independence and post-independence periods, a process effected by the "relatively efficient transfer of political power to a regime based on the support of social classes linked very closely to the foreign interests which were formerly represented by the colonial state."[96] Richard Sklar argues that the multinational corporations in Zambia share power with a "managerial bourgeoisie" that they in large measure created.[97] The most detailed empirical study of an alliance between multinationals and local allies has been made by Peter Evans. Unlike the more traditional dependency accounts, Evans's description of dependent industrialization em-

[94] Charles T. Goodsell, *American Corporations and Peruvian Politics* (Cambridge: Harvard University Press, 1974), chap. 4.

[95] Ibid., p. 139. A good review of the existing findings on the political involvement of multinational corporations in the developing countries is H. Jeffrey Leonard, "Multinational Corporations and Politics in the Developing Countries," *World Politics* 32 (April, 1980), 454-483.

[96] Colin Leys, *Underdevelopment in Kenya: The Political Economy of Neo-Colonialism, 1964-1971* (Berkeley: University of California Press, 1974), p. 27.

[97] Richard L. Sklar, *Corporate Power in an African State: The Political Impact of Multinational Mining Companies in Zambia* (Berkeley: University of California Press, 1975), p. 209.

phasizes the importance of a relatively *strong* state on the periphery; a mediator exists between foreign capital and the local economy. The result, in Evans's description of the Brazilian case, is

. . . a complex alliance between elite local capital, international capital, and state capital, which I have called here "the triple alliance." The result is not a monolith. Each of the partners comes at industrialization with different strengths, and their interests vary accordingly. . . . Over and above the differences, however, is the consensus that all members of the alliance will benefit from the accumulation of industrial capital within Brazil.[98]

Other accounts of the political effects of foreign direct investment call into question such an inevitable connection between penetration by multinational corporations and the creation of collaborating elites. In the case of Peru, Goodsell could find no support for the alliance between foreign capital and domestic oligarchy posited by the dependency theorists.[99] Moran discovered that the portrait of such an unholy alliance corresponds only partially with the course of Chilean political conflict after World War II. In the years immediately after the war and again during *Nuevo Trato* period of the mid-1950s, the ideal-type does fit fairly closely: in the first instance, the Chilean Right received political benefits for policies favorable to the foreign copper corporations; in the second, their support of a softer regime for the foreign investor assisted their own drive for less state intervention in the economy.[100] At other times, however, particularly during the early 1950s and the 1960s, the Center and the Right provided harsh criticism of the copper corporations and made the most strident demands for more stringent controls and finally, nationalization. Moran found "scant evidence" for a split between the tra-

[98] Peter Evans, *Dependent Development: The Alliance of Multinational, State, and Local Capital in Brazil* (Princeton: Princeton University Press, 1979), pp. 11-12.

[99] Goodsell, *American Corporations*, p. 29.

[100] Theodore H. Moran, *Multinational Corporations and the Politics of Dependence* (Princeton: Princeton University Press, 1974), p. 192.

ditional oligarchy, with its heavy holdings in land, and any new "national bourgeoisie" over the treatment of the foreign copper companies.[101]

Even in those cases where a fairly stable alliance can be said to exist, questions remain. Is the penetration of foreign capital closely associated with authoritarian political regimes in conditions of dependent industrialization? Is the alliance between multinationals, state, and local capital a stable one in the long run? The answer to the first question seems to be no: even if one accepts the existence of collaborating economic elites, their choice of authoritarianism is only partly affected by the presence of foreign capital. Kaufman disputes O'Donnell's model of a "preemptive authoritarianism" designed to attract foreign capital. All of the existing bureacratic-authoritarian regimes eagerly sought multinational investment, but only two (Argentina and Brazil) met with notable success.[102] Other connections between authoritarianism and dependent industrialization, such as the need for a lid on wages (required for an export-oriented strategy) or redistribution of income toward the middle class (to foster consumer goods industries) have also been questioned. Cardoso rejects any close association: "the same fundamental alliance which constitutes a dependent industrial capitalist state may organize itself institutionally within a context of authoritarianism, restricted democracy, or totalitarianism."[103] Multinational corporations can survive and even prosper within a range of political regimes; following Gourevitch's argument regarding tariffs, they may, however, provide valuable support for an existing political configura-

[101] Ibid., p. 188.

[102] Robert R. Kaufman, "Industrial Change and Authoritarian Rule in Latin America: A Concrete Review of the Bureaucratic-Authoritarian Model," in *The New Authoritarianism*, ed. Collier, p. 186. Kaufman concludes that the "formation and short-term survival of B-A regimes did not depend on the initiative or support of foreign direct investors—the MNCs" (p. 248).

[103] Cardoso and Faletto, *Dependency and Development*, p. 210; also Fernando Henrique Cardoso, "On the Characterization of Authoritarian Regimes in Latin America," in *The New Authoritarianism*, ed. Collier, pp. 33-57.

tion or help to make more rigid alignments that had previously remained fluid.[104]

Evidence is also scarce that collaborating economic elites or the state will remain allies of the foreign investor: multinational corporations frequently evoke a nationalist response. Returning to the models of resistance under external political threat, one would expect the state, and particularly the military, to provide one anchor for nationalist response to a foreign economic presence. Even those who have espoused the model of a relatively stable alliance to further dependent industrialization foresee tensions between the state apparatus and the multinational corporations. O'Donnell has predicted tensions between the nationalist goals of the military elite, dominant within the state, and their economic allies, that part of the national economic elite most "transnationalized" and closely tied to foreign corporations.[105] Evans also sees the potential for disruption in a possible coalition between self-interested local business and nationalistic and disenchanted portions of the military:

The local private sector has ideological legitimacy, at least among the bourgeoisie as a whole. They also have a potentially powerful set of allies in the form of those members of the military who define "nationalism" in terms of local autonomy more than in terms of local accumulation. Should excluded local capital become sufficiently disenchanted as to attempt seriously to upset the triple alliance, and should they be able to persuade equally disenchanted "nationalists" to join them, the combination of cultural legitimacy and access to the means of violence could be quite hazardous to the survival of the triple alliance.[106]

In one prominent example of state action against foreign capital in Latin America, it was the Peruvian military regime after 1968 that "devised one of the Third World's most complex

[104] A similar argument is made by James Kurth, in *The New Authoritarianism*, ed. Collier, p. 361.

[105] Guillermo O'Donnell, "Tensions in the Bureaucratic-Authoritarian States and the Question of Democracy," in *The New Authoritarianism*, ed. Collier, pp. 302-303.

[106] Evans, *Dependent Development*, p. 289.

and ambitious programs of state policies for the control of foreign capital."[107]

Chile's course in nationalizing foreign copper-mining interests directs attention to other groups that may support a stance of economic nationalism, apart from the state and those whose interests are in direct competition with foreign firms. Intellectuals shaped conceptions of the national economic interest through the development of the dependency theory, however vague many of its theses were. The Marxist Left, representing anti-American and anti-capitalist ideology, as well as the workers employed by the foreign firms, also offered programs for increasing control over the operations of the mines. Chilean industrialists, skeptical of the contribution made by the copper multinationals to the development of the country, urged fuller use of the mineral resources of Chile to expand its industrial base.[108]

In general, efforts to make a close causal connection between the exigencies of the international economic environment and a particular political regime, such as bureaucratic-authoritarianism, have not been successful. Greater specification within such models of the economic determination of political outcomes is required. The nationalist dialectic that appears with the growth of foreign economic penetration is evident from a number of developing nations, but the social and political context for its formation has seldom been studied. In similar fashion, the local allies of the multinationals are more often posited than investigated, and the tensions inherent in their mediating position between world market and domestic economy are not given enough attention. The construction and breakdown in patterns of collaboration is often a slow and painful process, not the automatic imprinting of the demands of the world economy upon a weaker national one.

[107] Alfred Stepan, *The State and Society:* (Princeton: Princeton University Press, 1978), p. 231.
[108] Moran, *Multinational Corporations,* p. 172.

DECOLONIZATION: DOMESTIC CONSEQUENCES OF INTERNATIONAL POLITICS

The evidence of this chapter suggests that scholars have of late been learning the lessons of this century: that the political development of most societies has been deeply marked by the effects of war, imperialism, and other features of their environment, and that generalizations and models can be constructed across national cases about these international sources of domestic politics. The external need no longer be regarded as a succession of unique occurrences, similar to natural catastrophes, that impinge upon the placid everyday life of societies.

Despite the advance that such research represents, however, three shortcomings are evident. First, despite the usefulness of the concepts introduced earlier—resistance and collaboration, direct and indirect impacts, sensitivity, boundaries— it is clear that our existing vocabulary is not designed for examining the life of societies from the outside in. A second weakness is the emphasis, for understandable reasons, on smaller states and societies, which are much more likely to be shaped and influenced by external influences. Third, that which is explained in most cases is political change or political outcomes at the national level; important results no doubt, but often obscuring the domestic linkages that lay beneath the larger event.

The perspective of external influences on domestic politics (and ultimately on foreign policy) not only illuminates decolonization, decolonization also provides the means for meeting some of these shortcomings in the analysis of international-domestic linkages. The usefulness of the concepts developed can be tested on a complex historical episode: the impact of the colonial empires upon the metropolitan societies was both direct and indirect; it involved both political and economic actors; it elicited a nationalist response from parts of the British and French societies. Decolonization also meets the second criticism of existing studies on external determinants of domestic politics: as large, developed, and powerful countries,

Britain and France can serve as critical cases for any theory that posits the importance of external influences on societies. Finally, the investigation which follows will center on organizations *below* the level of the state, attempting to delve beneath the questions of regime change or aggregate economic effects and to make specific causal relations clearer. One such set of organizations—political parties—provided an important indirect means by which change in colonial relations could influence metropolitan politics. The trials of political parties, Right (Chapter II) and Left (Chapter III) are considered next.

Decolonizing Nationalism: Conservatives and Empire in Britain and France

EVEN a casual observer of political parties in Europe would notice the often dramatic effects of international events on their unity and morale in the twentieth century. Parties Left and Right were split by the struggle over appeasement and rearmament in the 1930s. After 1945 issues such as German rearmament divided parties of the Left and Center in Britain and France; Khrushchev's secret speech signaling de-Staliniation, followed by Soviet intervention in Hungary, jolted West European Communist parties deeply attached to the Russian model of socialism.

Decolonization was yet another external change that added to the dilemmas of the parties. Political parties served as indirect conduits of influence, interpreting changes in the colonial empires and simultaneously increasing the sensitivity of metropolitan politics to those changes. The parties played a direct role as well. Actors from the colonial empires were offered access to the political life of Britain and France in these organizations: settlers, and sometimes Africans and Arabs expressed their views in these metropolitan forums; disgruntled military men and colonial civil servants found a link by which they could circumvent government control; businessmen discovered representatives who would voice their anxieties. In this chapter and the next, it is the first, indirect role of the political parties that will be examined, considering in turn the parties of the Right and those of the non-Communist Left. The conservative and nationalist parties dealt with in this chapter—the Gaullists and *modérés* in France and the Conservative Party in Britain—had the strongest links to the empires, whether defined as ideology or interest. These parties are also key in explaining outcomes, since they governed alone or in coalition during the years of decolonization.

The divergent paths followed by these parties resulted from their particular attachments to the existing pattern of colonial relations. The argument regarding the indirect impact of decolonization on them can be briefly stated: right-wing political formations, through the incorporation of nationalist and colonialist ideology in their organizations, made themselves sensitive to, and were affected by, changes in the international environment and in the empires. When loss of the empires threatened, parties with such internal ideological stakes in the survival of the colonial relationship (apart from the colonial interests that they represented) saw their ability to maintain themselves and to obtain electoral success placed in jeopardy. Two strategies were possible if the leadership shared this perception. The organizational dilemma could be exported: if concessions to colonial nationalism would cause losses internally, the temptation would be to force the costs of arresting change onto the colonial populations and ultimately the nation as a whole. In this case, efforts to achieve internal organizational success could mean external catastrophe. Alternatively, the party leadership, particularly if it held power, could choose to reshape the ideological appeals and incentives offered by the party, to quell dissent, to "decolonize" the party with as little disruption or loss of membership and votes as possible.

Of the three principal cases described in this chapter, the *modérés* (the French Conservatives) represent an unsuccessful case of decolonization, the Conservatives of Britain a successful instance, and the Gaullists a mixed case, although ultimately successful under the Fifth Republic. Success is defined as limiting internal disruption while disengaging from the imperial attachment. What must be explained are the organizational and historical origins of the sensitivity that these political parties displayed to a particular portion of the international setting, the causes for successful or unsuccessful outcomes in each case, and the implications of those outcomes for the course of decolonization.

IDEOLOGY AND PARTY

The argument begins by taking ideology seriously: its incorporation by the parties was a principal means by which the empires were brought into metropolitan political life, a sturdy tie that bound together Britain and France and their colonies. The hold of the empires through ideology must be examined on two levels: that of the belief systems of individuals, particularly those capable of influencing policy, and that of the organizations and institutions that inculcate, pattern, and perpetuate a particular set of beliefs, in this case, a particular national self-image and view of the national interest. Embedded in organizations, ideologies become more impervious to change. To alter policy one must alter an entire organization or parts of it, not merely change the attitudes of a few decision-makers.

To ignore this second dimension of ideology is to risk two misconceptions. The first views ideology as the collective consciousness of a society or a part of society (usually a class). An ideology's development is thus entirely dependent upon the internal social development of that society or group; the ideology may also be viewed as a simple reflection of the interests of that group. Little attention is paid in this view to the possibility for political mediation or organizational autonomy. The second misconception, a familiar feature of the analysis of foreign policy, suggests that the only manifestation of ideology important for explanations of external policy is the belief systems of *individuals*, particularly the most powerful. This approach tends to sever ideology from society altogether. The individual belief systems of leaders and their behavior are tied to political organizations in two ways at least: through the role that political organizations may have in determining their own political beliefs and attitudes and through the concessions that must be made to the party and its core ideology in the shaping of policy.

Taking ideology seriously in the context of political parties is questioned by some on the grounds that ideological constraint and attention to external affairs is low among the electorate. To this objection, one may reply by noting the ideological *stratification* within political parties: uneven attention to external affairs is matched by uneven distribution of power within political organizations such as parties. A party leader can draw small comfort from a docile electorate, if he must face an unruly party conference or a rebellious parliamentary faction. The findings of Butler and Stokes regarding the British electorate may be contrasted with those of Kornberg and Frasure, which demonstrate significant aggregate differences between groups of Labour and Conservative M.P.'s on three issues. It is striking that two of the issues relate to Britain's position as a world power and that one post-colonial issue—a military presence east of Suez—correctly groups all Labour and Conservative frontbenchers.[1] Even at the level of the electorate, evidence concerning specific and often highly complex external issues may not be indicative of the importance of broader orientations. Also, external events, such as the Cold War, may temporarily produce high salience on a set of issues.

In general, beliefs and attitudes regarding external questions are likely to exhibit in even more exaggerated form the stratification found on questions of domestic import.[2] Also, the awareness of external issues and the sharing of beliefs about them are likely to be related to the level of participation in party affairs, particularly if such questions are a prominent part of a party's ideology and electoral appeal.[3] The gap be-

[1] Allan Kornberg and Robert C. Frasure, "Policy Differences in British Parliamentary Parties," *APSR* 65 (September, 1971), 699. Butler and Stokes offer a description of voter attitudes toward Rhodesian UDI that does not surprise: an electorate aware, on the whole, of party positions regarding treatment of the Smith regime, but one that was willing to follow the government's lead and not entirely firm in its own opinions. David Butler and Donald Stokes, *Political Change in Britain*, College ed. (New York: St. Martin's Press, 1971), p. 194.

[2] Philip E. Converse, "The Nature of Belief Systems in Mass Publics," in *Ideology and Discontent*, ed. David Apter (New York: Free Press, 1964), pp. 247-248.

[3] The relationship of ideology (measured on a "right"-"left" scale) to par-

tween party ideology and the actual beliefs of many party electors does suggest, however, that certain parts of the party ideology or program are "free riders" in terms of the preferences of the party electorate. The shaping and connecting of issues is performed by the party; voters, as Butler and Stokes suggest, may agree or disagree with portions of the "package," but vote for it all the same. The presence of "free-riding" issues also points to their possible source: parties are not only stratified, in terms of an awareness of ideology and program, they also contain "issue pockets," to borrow Converse's term: individuals and groups who are particularly sensitive to certain parts of the party ideology, those who will seek to attach their special concerns to the broader party ideology and appeal. In the parties considered in this chapter such "issue pockets" represented the foci of resistance to decolonization, although their opposition to change found resonance throughout the party organization. In one case, the Poujadists, colonialist ideology may have been almost entirely a "free-riding" electoral issue.

Emphasizing the organizational aspect of ideology requires a theory to account for the ways in which organizations such as political parties make use of ideologies. Such a theory must thread its way between two polar images of the organizations: on the one hand, parties as *sects*, a coalition of those committed to a particular set of principles and a program; on the other hand, parties as *factions*, seeking simply after power or the spoils of power.[4] The evidence gathered from surveys suggests that the image of the party as an intensely ideological movement is not accurate, at least for mass parties in industrial societies. Nevertheless, the debates and schisms that have occurred in parties on ideological questions, often distantly related to the coalition of economic or class interests represented by the party, suggest that the purely power-seeking image has drawbacks as well. The second image seems particularly ill-

---

ticipation is described in Butler and Stokes, *Political Change in Britain*, p. 198.

[4] These images are described in Giovanni Sartori, *Parties and Party Systems: Volume I* (Cambridge: Cambridge University Press, 1976), pp. 76-77.

suited for dealing with ideologies such as nationalism or imperialism, which attracted political constituencies far exceeding any set of interests served by those ideologies.

To circumvent this polarity, the uses of ideology in the pursuit of power must be made clear. Here a theory of political organizations based upon incentives, developed by James Q. Wilson and applied to political parties by William Schneider and Peter Lange, will be employed. Albert Hirschman's concepts of exit, voice, and loyalty will be used to adapt the theory further so that it includes the influence of the political milieu upon the behavior of parties in Britain and France.[5] Wilson has summarized the central axiom of his theory of political organizations:

. . . the behavior of persons occupying organizational roles (leader, spokesman, executive, representative) is principally, though not uniquely, determined by the requirements of organizational maintenance and enhancement and . . . this maintenance, in turn, chiefly involves supplying tangible and intangible incentives to individuals in order that they will become, or remain, members and will perform certain tasks.[6]

The coin of Wilson's organizational realm is incentives, which

[5] The theory described is drawn from the following: James Q. Wilson, *Political Organizations* (New York: Basic Books, Inc., 1973), especially chaps. 1-6; William Schneider, "The Origins of Participation: Nation, Class, Issues, and Party" (Ph.D. diss., Harvard University, 1971), chap. 5; Peter Lange, "Change in the Italian Communist Party: Strategy and Organization in the Postwar Period" (Ph.D. diss. Massachusetts Institute of Technology, 1974), chap. 1; Albert O. Hirschman, *Exit, Voice, and Loyalty: Responses to Decline in Firms, Organizations, and States* (Cambridge: Harvard University Press, 1970), especially chaps. 6 and 7; Albert O. Hirschman, " 'Exit, Voice, and Loyalty': Further Reflections and a Survey of Recent Contributions," *Social Science Information* 13 (1974), 7-26; Brian Barry, "Review Article: 'Exit, Voice, and Loyalty,' " *British Journal of Political Science* 4 (January, 1974), 79-107; A. H. Birch, "Economic Models in Political Science: The Case of 'Exit, Voice, and Loyalty,' " *British Journal of Political Science* 5 (January, 1975) 69-82; Michael Laver, " 'Exit, Voice, and Loyalty' Revisited: The Strategic Production and Consumption of Public and Private Goods," *British Journal of Political Science* 6 (October, 1976), 463-482.

[6] Wilson, *Political Organizations*, p. 13.

"may be tangible or intangible and include any valued benefit, service or opportunity in exchange for which an individual is willing to contribute time, effort, or resources to an organization."[7] Apart from material incentives, which were not significant for the parties under consideration, the principal means used by parties to gain participation are *purposive* incentives, "suprapersonal goals which are constituted as ends for which an organization is maintained and which are open to compromise in order to increase the likelihood of at least partial success in the attempt to achieve them"; and *identity* incentives, "the privilege to identify and be identified with a total value system as expressed by an organizational entity such as a political party. [Identity] incentives are founded on two components, the *ideological* and the *sociability*."[8] Unlike smaller voluntary organizations, political parties can shape the incentives demanded by their followers to a degree; they can create demand, to use an analogy from the theory of the firm. After an incentive structure has been established within the organization, however, change in that structure may be difficult.[9] The provision of incentives may also create organizational dependence upon the environment: in the case of nationalist attachment to the colonial empires, the international environment. The particular mix of incentives used by a political party may also vary from stratum to stratum within the party: the party militants may require identity incentives, while the parliamentarians demand both purposive and identity incentives.

The framework of exit, voice, and loyalty developed by Albert Hirschman enables the nature of the party system to be added as an important determinant of the incentives used by a party. The incentive theory developed to this point does not deal with the problem of *too much* participation of the wrong sort: failure in Wilson's scheme is inadequate participation, or, in Hirschman's terms, *exit*. Dissatisfied members or electors simply slip away if the party's evolution displeases

[7] Ibid., p. 31.
[8] Lange, "Change in the Italian Communist Party," p. 57.
[9] Ibid., p. 65.

them, much like dissatisfied consumers. The disgruntled need not quietly disappear, however, and the experience of political parties in most democratic systems is testimony that before fading away, followers can express their displeasure with the leadership in a variety of ways. They can, in short, utilize *voice*. Many leaders, facing a parliamentary party that threatens rebellion or a party conference passing hostile resolution after hostile resolution, hope for less participation, even fewer participants. Failure for the party leaders thus acquires two meanings: in the case of exit, the unsuccessful leaders have few followers or inactive ones; in the case of voice, the leaders face rebellion or replacement.[10]

Hirschman's concept of *loyalty* has been labeled an outcome, rather than an explanatory variable, an "imputed internalized tax on competing products or organizations" that can only be recognized after the fact.[11] Thinking of loyalty as an added barrier to exit, a party's leadership is likely to attempt an increase in loyalty through the use of identity incentives. The leadership of a party would be expected to employ a strategy relying upon such incentives when exit seemed the greatest threat. And that threat would be greatest in a multiparty system, in which the party faced a number of close competitors for a constituency that was not "locked in" for socioeconomic or other reasons. The French parties on the Right faced just such a fluid political environment during the French Fourth Republic. Their use of ideological incentives was reinforced by their character as *new* parties; in Wilson's terms, such organizations, with few resources and little autonomy, are intensely competitive, attempting to establish a distinctive identity using ideological incentives. Thus, ideological incentives are likely to dominate at the beginning of a

---

[10] The choice of followers is not simply between Exit and Voice, but "two interdependent decisions . . . Voice-Silence and Exit-Stay. They are interdependent since our decision as to whether or not to Exit will be influenced by the likelihood and cost of a successful raising of Voice" (Laver, " 'Exit, Voice, and Loyalty' Revisited," p. 472).

[11] Ibid., p. 481; Barry, "Review Article," p. 96.

party's life when it is attempting to attract and hold new members.

In other party systems the use of ideological incentives may be reduced. If a party is permitted a regular share of power, the supply of purposive incentives is increased. If the party followers are not likely to find easy exit—whether in a two-party system or one with wide "gaps" between the parties—the ideologically committed are unlikely to exit. Their power in party affairs from that source is reduced, but their exercise of voice may become even more vehement as the party leadership bids for the uncommitted voters. In such a situation, one in which voice is the principal threat to the party leadership, the structure of power within the party and *beliefs about* the structure of power are important determinants of the incidence and seriousness of voice.[12]

A system with few parties also increases the importance of the *potential attainment of power* in the strategy of parties: if a party is likely in the foreseeable future to gain a major role in determining government policy, the incentive structure of the party may take that fact into account. As the Gaullist case suggests, the supply of purposive incentives grows immeasurably; specific aims can be fulfilled. With the institution of the Fifth Republic, the importance of attaining a share of governing power grew. In contrast to the Fourth Republic, parties were not forced to pursue a defensive strategy, protecting their clientele and never aspiring to more than a fraction of a governing coalition. The old strategy, with its reliance upon identity incentives, became outdated with the change of regime: as the Gaullists discovered, parties could now pursue a hegemonic strategy, similar to that of their British counterparts. In short, parties could aspire to being parties of government.

In power, the supply of purposive incentives permits the

---

[12] On the party system, Hirschman, *Exit, Voice, and Loyalty*, p. 84. As Barry notes, in certain situations, silence may be more rational than voice, even in the absence of exit: Barry, "Review Article," p. 92. For an analysis of *when* voice is likely to be exercised, and its relationship to exit, Laver, " 'Exit, Voice, and Loyalty' Revisited," pp. 476-477.

party leadership to quell any exercise of voice by the ideologically disenchanted by using the swollen ranks of those willing to compromise to ensure the success of specific goals, those more attracted to the abundance of purposive incentives. When power has been lost, however, particularly if there seems to be little opportunity to regain it, the influx of those attracted by purposive incentives becomes an outflow. In such cases, the ideologically attracted may wreak their revenge upon the unsuccessful leadership. If the hoped-for revival in the party's electoral fortunes does not occur, and the power structure of the party does not limit fractioning, the spiral of decline may be reinforced and ultimately result in the destruction of the party.

A final aspect of political parties resembles closely the notion of loyalty: institutionalization, which encourages individuals to "identify their self-interest in some substantive way with the preservation of an institution," in this case, a political party.[13] As Schneider notes, the more institutionalized the party, the less its leadership will have to rely on the manipulation of incentives to obtain participation from members and supporters. Thus, institutionalization can be a barrier to exit and also to the exercise of voice.

A summary of the uses of exit and voice and the likely strategies of party leaders who confront them is contained in Table I. A number of qualifications should be added to this scheme. The number of parties may or may not be significant: the barriers to exit in some multiparty systems is often greater than in two-party arrangements. The chasm between the Communists and the French Socialists, produced by the Cold War, is a good example. Institutionalization is not absolute security against the exit of a party's clientele; such parties as the Whigs in the United States and the Liberals in Britain have discovered the tenuous quality of longstanding historical attachments. Finally, the party system is not completely given: just as a party may shape the incentive demands of its clientele to a degree, so the party (like an oligopolistic firm) can through

[13] Schneider, "The Origins of Participation," p. 307.

Table I. Determinants of Party Strategy

Party system	Principal problem of leadership	Possible strategies
Two-party system or a system with fairly wide "gaps" between the parties; substantial part of the followers "locked in" for socioeconomic or other reasons; parties are institutionalized	Voice	a) Skew political system to reduce the power of parties: increase the power of the political leadership (presidential system, doctrine of collective responsibility, etc.)
		b) Skew party organization (or beliefs about the distribution of power in the party) in favor of the leadership: hierarchical organization, weak democratic ethos internally
Multiparty system or system in which there is competition for the same constituency; parties are newly formed	Exit	a) Increase identity (ideological) incentives
		b) Rely upon personal loyalties (e.g., de Gaulle)
		c) Choose issues to set one apart from rivals
		d) Shift to purposive incentives, if a share of power is obtained

its strategy encourage a party system with more or fewer participants. Of course, as the cases below will illustrate, the party may also miscalculate its ability to shape its environment, overestimating its hold upon adherents and voters.

Given the historical legacy, which will be described in the next section, political parties of the Right confronted a dilemma after 1945. Dependent upon nationalist ideology, which was central to the incentive structure of their parties, they faced a crisis of nationalism—endangered by European supranationalism, the rise of the superpowers, and the threat to the colonial empires. Although these parties were, to a greater or lesser degree, committed in organizational terms to the maintenance of the empires, the political situation in the empires seemed to require greater and greater repression to continue the colonial relationship. The strategic choice was plain: adaptation or resistance, decolonize the parties or export the organizational dilemma in the form of repressive policies to arrest change. The latter alternative could appear attractive: to revert to the economic analogy, the consumers of repressive policies were not members of the parties, or voters, or even residents in the metropolitan societies. They had, literally, no voice.

The emphasis upon organizational and ideological dimensions of the impact of decolonization should not be interpreted as a stark alternative to explanations based upon economic and other interests, the direct means by which the empires influenced metropolitan politics. Coincident with the debate over party ideology and strategy was a debate over the external interests of capitalism in these two countries, one that intersected at times with the first. This second debate will be described in Chapter IV. Both debates, however, had begun in the nineteenth century: in seeking an explanation of the attachment of nationalist ideology to conservative political parties, one must look to the success or failure of a given strategy in the past.

THE HOLD OF EMPIRE: NATIONALISM, IMPERIALISM, AND CONSERVATIVE STRATEGY

Given the use of ideology by political parties, why nationalist ideology? In a theory of political parties that stresses the uses of ideology in organization and electoral strategy the *content* of ideology does not become unimportant. The attachment of nationalism to conservative political formations, while characteristic of contemporary Western societies, was not an historical given. Until the mid-nineteenth century, nationalism was regarded as a revolutionary force, not a stabilizing one. Only gradually did nationalism become part of the conservative political arsenal in response to the two challenges that threatened elites after 1800: the challenge of *de-*

mocracy, posed by the French Revolution, and, following from the first, the challenge of *class*, as a well-organized working-class movement threatened the claims of property. Conservatism as an organized political movement represented the response in the political sphere to these challenges in both organizational and ideological terms.

Efforts to avoid the concession of a democratic framework included "fancy franchises," gerrymandering of constituencies, and the persistent overrepresentation of rural areas. After the concession of such a framework, however, the chief aim of conservative politics became the *organization of political conflict along lines other than class*. Facing an unenviable minority position, elites in Britain and on the Continent possessed three political alternatives. *Subclass loyalties* (familial, local, clientelistic) could be relied upon to ensure deferential political behavior, reinforced if necessary by economic coercion. Such strategies, even when pursued successfully, had distinct limits, set by the advance of urbanization. *Religion* provided a second potential cleavage; it remains one of the best predictors of political adherence in France and other European countries. Religion could, however, divide members of a potential conservative coalition in defense of property; secularization undermined confessional parties in the way that urbanization reduced subclass loyalties. Only the third strategy, *nationalism*, was fairly resistant to erosion by internal social change; it is, nevertheless, subject to the vagaries of the international environment. While conservatives would employ anti-communism and superior management of the economy ("you never had it so good") as additional strategies for electoral success after 1945, nationalism continued to be a viable alternative in Britain and France.[14]

The historical role of nationalism and imperialism in Britain and France had differed, however: not only did the structure of imperialist ideology differ in the two cases, its organiza-

[14] Ralph Miliband has remarked upon the value of nationalism as the cement in a coalition across classes: *The State in Capitalist Society* (London: Quartet Books, Ltd., 1973), p. 186.

tional uses diverged as well. As early as the time of Disraeli, a bifurcation was evident in British imperialist ideology: an "empire of prestige," centered on India and particularly dear to the Tories; and an "empire of interest," grouping the core of British imperial economic interests in the settler Dominions and appealing to a far wider slice of the political spectrum. By the late nineteenth century, the strategy of the British Conservative Party had forged a close ideological link between nationalism and imperialism and incorporated both in its organizational appeal. The emerging Conservative coalition was a Peelite alliance in defense of property that included the landed classes, who continued to absorb the respectable upper stratum of the middle class; the new suburban middle- and lower-middle class, and a portion of the working class. The imperialist ideology was a means of disguising and diminishing the disparities of class within the party, as well as reducing the declining, but still evident, tensions between industrial and agrarian interests. In short:

If preservation of the Union [with Ireland] was essentially a negative cause, the great positive means of bridging the gaps not only between Old Tories and New Tories was imperialism. Here was a doctrine which subsumed within itself in coherent relationship foreign policy, military and naval policy, social reconstruction, economic and commercial policy, Ireland.[15]

The empire in Britain, then, implanted itself deeply in the organizational strategy of a political party representing a powerful social coalition. Empire and nationalism served as a critical source of ideological incentives for the party; its identity as the national party served to cement a cross-class coalition in support of the "natural" governors of Britain. The Conservatives enjoyed a measure of organizational unity after 1886, developed under the pressure of urbanization, that was not to be equaled by the Right in France until after 1945. This party of the Right—representing English nationalism, the Empire, Anglicanism, the upper and middle classes, and those

[15] Richard Shannon, *The Crisis of Imperialism, 1865-1915* (St. Alban's: Paladin, 1976), pp. 228-229.

members of the working class who deferred to the elite's ability to govern or aspired to its social status—faced, across the overlapping cleavages of class, religion, and region, the Liberal and then the Labour coalition—Nonconformist, opposed to the position and privileges of the traditional governing class, anti-imperialist, representing the Irish, Scottish, and Welsh individuality against English hegemony.

The fact that the Right organized itself around nationalist and imperialist ideology in Britain suggests that, despite the claims of consensus on colonial policy, the implantation of the Empire in British political life was clearly circumscribed. The Empire was a *Conservative* creation: the Conservatives would bear most of the consequences of its loss in the political sphere. Conservative ideology and strategy would require adaptation in the face of external changes. The internal conflicts that beset the party after 1900 suggest the importance of its externally-directed ideology in organizational terms: the tariff reform controversy that racked the party repeatedly during the early twentieth century, threatening two prime ministers, Balfour and Baldwin; the Ulster crisis of 1914, culmination of several years in which the Conservative attachment to constitutional and parliamentary processes had been called into question; the struggle over the Government of India Act, which pushed Churchill into opposition; the conflict over appeasement in the late 1930s; and finally, the lengthy crisis of decolonization.

The penetration of the French polity by its overseas empire was shaped by two features that contrasted with Britain's experience: the fragmented character and organizational weakness of the French Right and the ambivalent relationship of the Right with nationalist and imperialist ideology. While the challenge of democracy had come early in France, the threat of a unified, national working-class party came late, if at all. If a nationalist strategy was thus rendered unnecessary for much of the nineteenth century, the ambiguous attitude of the Right toward nationalism made it impossible. Until the 1880s attitudes toward nationalism were determined principally by hostility toward the Revolution and, to a lesser degree, the Napoleonic Empire. Nationalism found its home on the Left, among republicans and radicals dissatisfied with the established order in Europe. During the 1880s and 1890s, however, a transfer of nationalism from the left to the right of the policital spectrum took place, similar to that which had occurred in Britain a few decades earlier. As Rémond describes, nationalism,

> a phenomenon absolutely unpredictable in the political context of the nineteenth century . . . transferred from Left to Right a whole combination of ideas, sentiments, and values heretofore considered the birthright of Radicalism. It is generally recognized that this crucial mutation occurred in the period 1887-1899. Boulangism drew up nationalism's birth certificate and the Dreyfus Affair its baptismal record.[16]

The coalition born of this ideological transfer in the late nineteenth century continued to constitute the Right in France into the twentieth century. Although the social composition of this coalition increasingly resembled the British model, organizational unification continued to elude French conservatives. In its organizational strategy the Right continued to rely heavily upon subclass loyalties and religion, especially in the rural areas. Extraparliamentary forms of activity also continued to exercise an attraction, as illustrated by the nationalist leagues of the 1930s and the support granted to the authoritarian solution of Vichy.

Despite growing similarities to the British pattern in social coalition and an ideological attachment to nationalism, that nationalism itself remained bifurcated into the twentieth century. Imperialist ideology and the expansion of the French empire after 1880 were *not* products of the French Right. Rather, imperialism in France was the creation of Republican politicians near the center of the political spectrum, the inheritors of Gambetta: Ferry, Freycinet, Delcassé, and the leader of the *parti colonial*, Eugène Étienne. Even the growing acceptance of the colonial *oeuvre* in the years of nationalist

---

[16] René Rémond, *The Right Wing in France: From 1815 to de Gaulle*, 2nd American ed. (Philadelphia: University of Pennsylvania Press, 1969), p. 208.

rivalry before World War I and its incorporation into nationalist ideology did not have an *organizational* corollary. The implantation of the empire in the metropolitan political process remained primarily the task of interest groups, even though these groups often appealed to nationalist or status concerns. By the interwar years, acceptance had broadened into an ideological consensus that was scarcely challenged, apart from Communist attacks: right-wing skepticism had virtually disappeared, and even the Socialists came to accept the colonies as a *fait accompli*.[17]

By 1940 the indirect means by which the empires were implanted in the societies of Britain and France—ideology and political organization—were dissimilar. In Britain the attachment to the colonial empire formed the centerpiece of nationalist ideology and contributed to the political appeal and the incentive structure of the Conservative Party; in France, such an organizational embodiment of the imperial attachment did not exist. In the Third Republic's political system of fragmented right-wing and center parties the colonial cause was most effectively forwarded by a cohesive and determined pressure group, working largely out of the public eye. As a result, while the indirect ideological implantation of the empire in the French body politic was broad, excluding only the PCF on the Left, it remained shallow. In Britain, the imperial cause was deeply implanted on one side of the political spectrum: despite claims of a national consensus, the attachment of the Left to the empire was of a different order of magnitude.

The attachment in the French case was further weakened by the bifurcation of nationalist ideology between a European and a colonial variant. The two orientations seemed to provide alternatives that could not be combined: the attraction of the empire declined in the 1920s when France's hegemonic position in Europe seemed assured; it rose in the 1930s as that position crumbled. This seesaw would also be the pattern after 1945, despite efforts to construct that monster of indecision,

---

[17] Raoul Girardet, *L'Idée coloniale en France, 1871-1962* (Paris: La Table Ronde, 1972), p. 133.

"Eurafrique." After Disraeli's synthesis, no nationalist alternative to Empire existed for the British Conservatives. Despite the three intersecting circles drawn by Churchill, the disappearance of empire would leave the British Right with an ideological void, which Europe was ill-suited to fill.

A final contrast may be drawn concerning the indirect impact of the empires and the international environment upon these two societies. Disraeli and the Conservative Party attached the maintenance of the empire to the organizational success of a political *party* and the defense of the traditional governing class. The international environment was used to pay off domestic supporters, but the party also absorbed external shocks. Those shocks increased in intensity during the 1930s; after the war, the final destruction of Britain's world position would provide the greatest test of all for the Conservatives. The empire in France was not constructed to bolster the position of a particular governing class or a political party; instead, it served to bolster a *regime*, the Third Republic, which represented a predominantly bourgeois coalition of classes. The colonial empire was constructed by Republican politicians of the center; its political support remained centrist until 1940, although a certain bipolarization does appear with the rejection of colonialism by the PCF and criticism by the Socialists. As a result, in France, it is the *regime* that suffers external shocks and appeals for support on the basis of its external performance: Charles X, ordering the expedition to Algiers in 1830 to stave off revolution; Louis Napoleon, addicted to foreign adventure as a means to gain domestic support, finally broken by Bismarck. At no point is the contrast between Britain and France on this point more apparent than in 1940: external disaster causes a *party revolt* in Britain, resulting in the overthrow of the Chamberlain cabinet; in France, it is the Third Republic that is sacrificed, the regime that dies.

The French Fourth Republic would also find itself beleaguered by enemies using external failings as weapons. The regime would continue to be implicated in external success or failure. It would collide with a Right organizing nationally to confront the unprecedented strength of the Communist and Socialist parties, making for the first time a firm commitment to the maintenance of the colonial empire as part of a nationalist political appeal. The French Right discovered the empire just as the full force of colonial nationalism began to be felt.

The Gaullists, because of their wartime competition with Vichy and their explicitly nationalist ideology, pursued this course of action most tenaciously. Ultimately, Gaullism was successfully decolonized, but only after it had played a prominent role in the destruction of the Fourth Republic. The strategic choices of the Gaullists and their effects upon French politics and external policy will be examined next.

GAULLISM: DECOLONIZING FRENCH NATIONALISM

Gaullism, perhaps the most complex of the party cases under consideration, epitomizes the means by which the external, past and present, enters the life of societies. A movement born of invasion and war, Gaullism carried lessons learned from the shock of defeat and resistance into French society after 1945. Gaullism did not employ nationalism in its political strategy; it *was* nationalism. The movement ensured that French society, made sensitive to its environment by external shocks, would remain sensitive. This embodiment of intransigent nationalism would also bear the brunt of the most difficult episode in French decolonization, Algeria, and survive.

The attachment of the Gaullist elite to the colonial empire was born of experience in World War II. What de Gaulle and the Free French sought after 1940 was legitimacy, in the eyes of their potential followers and other nations; legitimacy could only be purchased with territory. Their contest with Vichy engrained in the Gaullist conception of politics an enduring tie between the maintenance of the empire and the legitimacy of the regime. In Gaullist constitutional doctrine the preeminent role of the state was its *external* role in defending national independence; they agreed with the men of Vichy that one of the principal guarantors of the autonomy and status of France internationally was the colonial empire. In addition, the war invested the empire and particularly North Africa with a specific strategic role: in the event of another invasion, the Mediterranean could become "the Marne."[18] If these elements in Gaullist ideology pointed toward nationalist rigidity, an opening for reform also existed. In Gaullist mythology, the greatest achievement in colonial policy was the reforms enacted at the Brazzaville Conference, portrayed after the war as a radically new course that was later abandoned by weak republican governments. In fact, the legacy of Brazzaville and of Félix Eboué—the figure who symbolized both the Conference and Gaullist hopes for the empire—hardly implied a revolutionary break. Despite a very limited degree of decentralization and the advocacy of more positions in the civil service for Africans, "everything pointed toward the more complete integration of an economically and socially more developed Africa into the French national system, for the benefit of France on the international scene."[19]

In North Africa, limited reforms and promises of reform were combined with repression when nationalists demanded more significant measures. A further demonstration of the weakness of Gaullist liberalism in colonial policy was given by French efforts to reestablish control against the Vietminh in Indochina. While de Gaulle's statements of late 1944 seemed to indicate a willingness to compromise, the declaration of 24 March 1945 pointed to French aims that would enclose the states of Indochina in "a tight web of French control."[20] Nevertheless, as a new movement, critical of the preceding

[18] Charles de Gaulle, *Discours et messages: Pendant la guerre* (Paris: Plon, 1970), p. 366. The competition between Vichy and the Free French is described in Robert Paxton, *Vichy France: Old Guard and New Order* (New York: Knopf, 1972).

[19] William Harvey Wainwright, "De Gaulle and Indochina, 1940-1945" (Ph.D. diss., Fletcher School of Law and Diplomacy, Tufts University, 1971), p. 809. For accounts of the Brazzaville Conference, D. Bruce Marshall, *The French Colonial Myth and Constitution-making in the Fourth Republic* (New Haven: Yale University Press, 1973), pp. 104-111, and Brian Weinstein, *Eboué* (New York: Oxford University Press, 1972), pp. 297-304.

[20] Wainwright, "De Gaulle and Indochina," p. 852.

parliamentary regime, Gaullism could not accept the old *pacte colonial* unchanged; this search for a new pattern of colonial relations would provide one of the routes of disengagement from empire finally adopted by de Gaulle and the party loyalists.

The Rassemblement du Peuple Français: Constraints on ideological change

Founded in April 1947 as the first organizational manifestation of Gaullism, the Rassemblement du Peuple Français (RPF) displayed no willingness to concede greater autonomy for the colonial empire, however. Its program continued the wartime commitment to maintaining effective French control. The central statement of colonial policy was de Gaulle's speech at Bordeaux (15 May 1947) in which he restated the limitations placed upon any concessions of home rule to the colonies: the spheres of external relations, defense, economic policy, and public order would remain in the hands of France. The Gaullist emphasis remained that of the Union Française as a bloc; possibilities for autonomy were limited, and independence was unthinkable.[21]

The international milieu provides a partial explanation for this immobility; apart from Indochina, the full force of colonial nationalism was not to be felt until the 1950s; the salience of colonial issues in French political life remained low in the immediate postwar years. Conservatives in both Britain and France were able to bask in illusions that they had cultivated during the war. The importance of this explanation is magnified for the RPF because the organizational constraints upon ideological change seem relatively weak. In contrast to the fragmented localism of traditional formations on the Right in France, the RPF sought to establish a centralized, national party that relied upon militants rather than notables, one that achieved a degree of participation more characteristic of left-wing parties than conservative groups. Such a cadre of party

[21] Charles de Gaulle, *Discours et messages: Dans l'attente* (Paris: Plon, 1970), p. 78-85.

adherents, drawn in many instances from veterans of the Free French forces and the Resistance, would be motivated by nationalist incentives, but the principal identity incentives offered would be those surrounding de Gaulle himself and the image of the movement as the chief bulwark against communism. With these alternative sources of incentives, nationalist attachment to the colonial empire did not play as important a role in the RPF as it would in the later life of the movement.[22]

If the availability of the identity incentives described and the personal loyalty inspired by de Gaulle ·diminished any threat of exit, a threat further reduced by the weakness of right-wing competition, the possibility of voice within the movement was made unlikely by its hierarchical and centralized character. Effective control from the center was even greater than in the British Conservative Party; the ideological role awarded de Gaulle was more a monopoly than that granted the British Conservatives' leader.[23]

Yet despite the low threat of exit or voice and the power for ideological adaptation that this implied for de Gaulle and the RPF leadership, the *electoral strategy* of the Gaullists reinforced their intransigence regarding the evolution of the colonial empire. De Gaulle never accepted the detested name of "party" for any of the Gaullist movements: like the Communist Party on the Left, the RPF had hegemonial aspirations, not to represent a *part* of the French electorate, but to represent *all* Frenchmen, except the "separatists" (Communists). Unlike most of the traditional parties, the Gaullists did not seek to carve out a constituency within the political system, they sought to *change* that system. To accomplish their aims, the Gaullists pursued a strategy of polarization, splitting the

[22] The evidence for this point is drawn from the proceedings of *Assises nationales* of the RPF and from the movement's publications, particularly *Le Rassemblement*.

[23] Philip M. Williams, *Crisis and Compromise: Politics in the Fourth Republic* (New York: Doubleday-Anchor, 1966), pp. 148-149. Christian Purtschet, *Le Rassemblement du peuple français, 1947-1953* (Paris: Editions Cujas, 1965), p. 72.

electorate along lines favorable to their movement. De Gaulle outlined the strategy to the departmental delegates of the RPF: "Everyone is sleeping. There are two currents: communism and ours. All will crystallize on us or on the Communists. We must organize. . . ."[24]

The political strategy of the RPF emphasized anti-communism: just as the threat of the Popular Front had stimulated the organization of the Right in the 1930s, so the onset of the Cold War benefited the RPF. The vote shares of the Communist Party and the Rassemblement tended to rise and fall together. While colonial issues did not play a prominent role in the efforts of the RPF, efforts at polarization based upon anti-communism did spill over into the colonial program of the RPF in several ways.

Most directly, the anti-communist emphasis of the RPF served to reinforce its opposition to decolonization and conciliation in the first colonial war of the Fourth Republic: Indochina, a struggle that was quickly assimilated into the larger confrontation of the Cold War. The Indochina War enabled the RPF to differentiate itself clearly from the Communists; it was the ideal issue for polarizing the electorate, although its salience remained remarkably low until the final years of the conflict. Regarding the French efforts to retain Indochina in the Union Française, the Gaullist movement, from de Gaulle to the RPF electorate, displayed considerable uniformity. For de Gaulle, the French war effort became an emblem of France's continued status as a great power. He repeatedly evoked images of the importance of Indochina that were strikingly similar to later proponents of the "domino theory."[25] As late as August, 1953, André Astoux recalls de Gaulle's advocacy of "winning the war" by "making in one year the effort made in five."[26] While de Gaulle envisaged peace in Indochina as part of a larger settlement with the Communist bloc in November, 1953, and

[24] André Astoux, L'Oubli (Paris: J. C. Lattès, 1974), p. 143.
[25] De Gaulle's comments on the war may be found in his press conferences, Discours et messages: Dans l'attente, pp. 346, 371-372, 472.
[26] Astoux, L'Oubli, p. 340.

advocated seeking such a peace in April, 1954, he was adamant that Indochina remain in the Union Française, and he criticized the participation of Fouchet and Koenig in the cabinet of Mendès-France, committed to ending the war in Indochina.[27] The Rassemblement faithfully reflected de Gaulle's intransigence, linking the struggle in Asia with the internal struggle against the Communists. Repeatedly, the Assises nationales of the movement called for no negotiation with the Viet Minh, who were portrayed as agents of Moscow and collaborators with the Japanese.[28]

The attempt to construct a conservative coalition to oppose the Communists also led the RPF to seek support among the French of North Africa, where wartime support for the Free French had been less than wholehearted. The successful, although temporary alliance between the Gaullists and the North African settlers led to a harsh condemnation of the mild reforms proposed in the Algerian Statute of 1947. The deeper implantation that the Gaullists enjoyed among the settlers of Tunisia would influence their attitude during the crisis in that protectorate in 1951-1952, the first major colonial crisis that could not be fitted into the Cold War pattern. The conflict revolved around the claims of the Tunisians, led by the nationalist Neo-Destour, to further reforms that would increase the internal autonomy of the protectorate. While the French governments (there were three between autumn and spring) moved from repression to liberalism and back again, the Gaullists never wavered from their hostility to change, sometimes more adamant than the attitude taken by the Tunisian settlers themselves.

The Tunisian crisis also marked a shift in the political use

[27] *Discours et messages: Dans l'attente*, pp. 625, 642; Astoux, *L'Oubli*, pp. 386-387.

[28] RPF, *Premières assises nationales*, Marseilles, 16-17 April 1948, motion adopted at the third plenary session, p. 192; *Conseil national*, Paris, 8 October 1948, "Rapport sur le problème indochinois," pp. 14, 33. Irving's judgment on the Gaullist role is accurate: they "must bear a heavy responsibility for the fact that concessions in Indochina were usually too little and too late" (Irving, *The First Indochina War*, pp. 142-143).

of the empire by the Gaullists. By late 1951, legislative elections had failed to award the RPF enough votes to overturn the regime. Its only hope was to undermine the regime and the parties which produced its governments directly, voting in such a way as to make the Assembly ungovernable, thus forcing the President of the Republic to call upon de Gaulle. As the threat from communism faded, the theme of resentful nationalism, centering on changes in the colonial empire, would provide the Gaullists with their principal weapon against the regime; its use would be reinforced by a changing political milieu and by the fragmentation of the movement after 1952. Ironically, this use of nationalism tied the Gaullists ever more tightly to a rapidly changing situation in the empire, ultimately threatening the unity of the movement itself and further impairing its ideological adaptation.

For both France and Gaullism the years from 1945 to 1952 were a time of lost opportunity in their dealings with the colonial empire. Despite the sensitivity of the movement to external threats to French status—a result of wartime experience and nationalist ideology—the RPF did not face a threat from either exit, given the weakness of political competition on the Right, or voice, since de Gaulle's ideological control of the movement was complete. The strategy of coalition-building through isolating the Communists pushed the movement toward ideological rigidity, however, and its unyielding attitude on colonial questions was reinforced by apparent quiet in the empire. The sole exception was Indochina, a conflict that only reinforced the link between anti-communism and resistance to colonial nationalism. After 1952, as one colonial crisis after another broke upon the French polity, the Gaullist movement which confronted them would no longer enjoy unity or the leadership of de Gaulle. As a result, adaptation to external change would be further impaired.

Fragmentation and intransigence, 1952-1958
The relatively secure position enjoyed by organized Gaullism under the leadership of de Gaulle quickly disappeared after 1952. Three changes produced an increasing attachment

to intransigent nationalism as the core of the movement's identity, with dire consequences for the colonial policy of the Fourth Republic. Domestically, the Gaullists faced greater competition from a resurgent traditional Right (the Indépendants or *modérés*) on one side and a Radical Party, revitalized by Pierre Mendès-France, on the other. The threat of exit, which had not been serious at the peak of RPF strength, became a central preoccupation and as fissures appeared in the movement, provided cause for the second change in Gaullist fortunes: the departure of Charles de Gaulle from active participation in the political life of the Fourth Republic. De Gaulle's departure combined with the third change—a surge in public attention and concern for France's international position—to reinforce those who clung to the traditional interpretation of Gaullism's role in France's external policy: resistance to change.

Competition and exit. With unification and organization the traditional Right (the *modérés*) posed the greatest threat to the RPF: they could provide a haven for those who desired exit from the ideological demands and the discipline of the Gaullists. Stabilization of the regime and an ebbing of the Communist threat increased the likelihood of such a transfer of support. A hierarchical and centralized RPF could not provide a permanent political home for many conservative politicians with strong local sources of support and a desire to participate in the spoils of the political system.

Defection to the Right, the first signal of Gaullist fragmentation, started with the rebellion of twenty-seven RPF deputies who voted to make the Conservative Antoine Pinay premier in March 1952. When the Gaullists attempted to impose discipline, all but one of the deputies promptly resigned from the RPF to form the group Action républicaine et sociale. With the fading of hopes for any change of constitutional regime, the temptations of participation in the governments of the despised Fourth Republic grew, even for loyal Gaullists.

RPF deputies voted for the Mayer cabinet in January 1953 as a way of blocking the ratification of the European Defense Community treaty; the next ministry, that of Joseph Laniel, marked the first participation of Gaullists in a cabinet. Despite

Gaullist mythology of inveterate opposition to "the system," they would be represented, at least initially, in each succeeding government of the Fourth Republic, save that of Bourgès-Maunoury in 1957.

De Gaulle departs. As the Rassemblement crumbled through defection and the temptations of the "system," Charles de Gaulle withdrew from leadership of the movement that he had called into being. Although final dissolution of the RPF was delayed until December, 1954, by the campaign against the EDC, leadership of the movement gravitated toward the parliamentarians, who were by now deeply involved in the once-abhorred regime. The hazards of the new situation would be faced without de Gaulle's ideological arbitration; his absence removed a source of unity in a heterogeneous group and left the movement with no recognized source of ideological adaptation. For Gaullist militants and electors, the departure of the General took from the movement its principal source of identity incentives.

Ironically, as de Gaulle left direction of the RPF, his own attitudes toward relations between France and its empire showed signs of increasing liberalism. From his speech at Neuilly-sur-Seine in October 1952 to his tour of Tunisia in the following spring (during which he refused to denounce the Neo-Destour nationalists) to his "final" press conference in June 1955 in which he suggested a type of federal arrangement with the North African protectorates and the inclusion of Algeria in "a community larger than France," de Gaulle sounded a different and far more accommodating note than had been heard during the Indochina War or the battle over the European Defense Community. His recognition of the force of nationalism in the region and his call for the substitution of association for domination should have pointed toward a conciliatory policy on the part of his followers during the Moroccan crisis that would reach its peak in late 1955 and the Algerian War that had begun in 1954. But his ability to command the remnants of the Gaullist movement was diminished, and the press conference of June 1955 marked the beginning of three years of public silence on his part.

Public concern turns outward. The leaderless Gaullists, facing increasing political competition, also confronted a domestic setting in which dramatic changes had occurred in the concerns of the French electorate. Since the end of World War II, questions of social and economic policy, such as inflation or labor disputes, had preoccupied the French population. In a single year, from August 1953 to August 1954, international questions suddenly assumed greater importance than domestic concerns in the public consciousness. Indochina, the European Defense Community, and disorder in North Africa all contributed to this heightened sensitivity to France's international situation; but the shift was not accompanied by pessimism concerning the threat of war: by early 1955, the fear of a new world war was at its lowest point since 1945.[29]

Gaullism, peculiarly sensitive to external change because of its nationalist orientation, would have to pursue its aims in a competitive political context now charged with concern for France's international position. The movement would find its anti-communist appeal of less and less use among a public not so preoccupied with the Soviet Union or the communist threat. To retain what remained of their political support, efforts at survival without de Gaulle reinforced ideological rigidity and the use of nationalist appeals to maintain a distinctive identity. De Gaulle's ambiguous cues were not followed: in the face of colonial nationalism, the Gaullists uniformly resisted compromise. Their chosen course was reinforced by the characteristics of the parliamentary group, a microcosm of Gaullism. Participation in the Resistance, a right-wing electoral clientele, and their career experience (a low representation of the traditional political professions) meant that these men would be sensitive to questions of national status and not given to party discipline or compromise.[30] Efforts to conserve what was left of the Gaullist political organization—particularly the support of RPF militants—imposed a further

[29] IFOP, *Sondages*, no. 4 (1954), pp. 5-6; no. 1 (1955), p. 23.

[30] The characteristics of the RPF deputies are given in Marie-France Chevrillon, "Les Républicains sociaux ou la traversée du désert, 1953-1958" (*Mémoire de maîtrise*, Institut d'Etudes Politiques, Paris), pp. 21, 37-38, 44.

ideological drag. In congresses of the movement (renamed the Social Republicans), the *pur et dur* viewpoint of Michel Debré pervaded the discussions; reports on the colonial empire might well have originated at Brazzaville in 1944.[31]

The Gaullists and the ministries: Playing and obstructing the "system." These political changes affected not only the Gaullists but, through them, the course of decolonization during crucial ministries of the Fourth Republic. The governments in which they served dealt with questions centering upon nationalism and France's place in the international order: the future of the colonial empire and European integration. Forced to confront these issues, which touched upon the core of Gaullist ideology, without a leader who could impose unity upon the group or a strong extraparliamentary movement to perform that task, the Gaullist group in the National Assembly began to fragment. To preserve their unity and conserve their ideological stakes, the Gaullists were likely to resist reform from within the cabinet or to withdraw their support. Duncan Macrae has confirmed that the Gaullists were the principal source of cabinet instability during the second legislature of the Fourth Republic.[32] During successive North African crises, and particularly at the culmination of the Moroccan crisis in 1955, Gaullists but, through them, the course of decolonization dur- which the movement had so often condemned. The Gaullists in Parliament would prove to be a threat to the regime whether resurgent or in decline. As the president of the Gaullist group in the Assembly declared when the group brought down the Mayer cabinet: "We are not dead then, for we can still destroy!" After each withdrawal of support, each display of intransigence, the Gaullists could feel satisfaction at confirming once again the vices of the "system."

[31] For example, the report prepared by Hettier de Boislambert for the 1955 Congress are reproduced in *La nation républicaine et sociale*, 2 December mention of any possibility for independence. The principal speeches at the Congress are reproduced in *La nation républicaine et sociale*, 2 December 1955.

[32] Duncan Macrae, Jr., *Parliament, Parties, and Society in France, 1946-1958* (New York: St. Martin's Press, 1967), pp. 177-178.

The two cabinets most beset by colonial crises, those of Pierre Mendès-France and Edgar Faure, demonstrated the importance of the Gaullists in thwarting decolonization and the positive role that they might have played in other circumstances. With the investiture of Pierre Mendès-France, whom the Gaullists supported overwhelmingly from the start, the pattern of instability induced by the former RPF deputies seemed to have been broken. In Mendès-France the Gaullists found a premier whose style of governing and combination of reformism with Jacobin patriotism fitted their own self-image well. They participated in his cabinet in key positions: Koenig at National Defense, Chaban-Delmas at Public Works and Communications, and, most important, Christian Fouchet at the newly-created Ministry of Tunisian and Moroccan Affairs.[33] The apparent support which Mendès-France enjoyed from the Gaullists was not unqualified, however: the Gaullist ministers used their power to slow the pace of change in North Africa, and those Gaullist deputies most sympathetic to the *modérés* on the Right offered less reliable support than the rest of the group.[34] In the final Assembly vote that brought down the Mendès-France cabinet, the Gaullist defection was not so great nor so dramatic as the instances which had preceded and would follow, but seventeen members of the group voted against the government, some because of the deteriorating situation in North Africa. (The opposition was greater by thirteen than it had been after the last debate on North African policy.)

Unlike Mendès-France, his successor Edgar Faure did not enjoy many advantages in dealing with the Gaullist parliamentarians. He was the quintessential man of the "system," and he constructed his coalition along the lines of conventional parliamentary arithmetic: the political coloration of the min-

[33] The other Gaullist members of the cabinet were Maurice Lemaire and Diomède Catroux.

[34] Christian Fouchet, *Au service du Général de Gaulle* (Paris: Plon, 1971), pp. 118-119. Koenig may also have threatened to resign: William S. Lee, "French Policy and the Tunisian Nationalist Movement, 1950-54" (D.Phil. thesis, Oxford University), p. 502.

istry and its support in the Assembly came from the Center-Right, in contrast to the Left of Center support gained by Mendès-France. Any decolonization would be politically even more arduous: the groups that formed the core of his majority, particularly the Conservatives (*modérés*) and the anti-Mendèsist Radicals, had defeated the previous government *because* of its efforts at change in North Africa.

The colonial issue that would dominate the Faure cabinet was Morocco, and the issue that would overshadow all others in Morocco was the future role of the Sultan Ben Youssef, who had been deposed by the French in August 1953, and had since become a symbol of Moroccan nationhood.[35] His feeble successor, Ben Arafa, was a puppet of the French Residency, unable to win popular legitimacy or to gain concessions from France. A stalemate ensued; counterterrorism met terrorism. Faure's intentions have been the subject of dispute, but most of the evidence suggests that he saw the necessity of an eventual return of the exiled sultan.[36] His political problem was one of convincing his right-wing supporters in the National Assembly of that necessity as well. In order to break the deadlock in Morocco, Faure, with canny political sense, chose a Gaullist, Gilbert Grandval, former French resident in the Saar, to become resident general in Rabat. Although the Right initially greeted his appointment with enthusiasm, the plan that Grandval eventually proposed to the government in Paris was far too liberal for his Gaullist colleagues in the cabinet.[37] A small band of Gaullist liberals supported the Grandval line, and one, Pierre Clostermann, resigned from the parliamentary group in disagreement with the position taken in its name. He asked bitterly, "The lessons of Indo-

---

[35] On the crisis surrounding the deposition, Stéphane Bernard, *The Franco-Moroccan Conflict, 1943-1956* (New Haven: Yale University Press, 1968), chap. 5; Pierre July, *Une république pour un roi* (Paris: Fayard, 1974); Georges Bidault, *Resistance* (London: Weidenfeld and Nicolson, 1967), pp. 182-189.

[36] July recalls Faure predicting in 1954 that all of North Africa would be independent in ten years. July, *Une république*, p. 3; Bernard, *The Franco-Moroccan Conflict*, pp. 243, 256.

[37] July, *Une république*, p. 68.

china, of Tunisia, have they not been enough? Will a new Dienbienphu be necessary, or other massacres, for you to open your eyes?"[38]

Apparently, the answer to his anguished question was yes. With the replacement of Grandval by General Boyer de Latour in Morocco, resistance to the directives of Paris grew: the foot-dragging Boyer de Latour was encouraged by the opponents of change in the cabinet, principally the Gaullists.[39] The unity and authority of the French government were seriously impaired, and the Gaullists were at the core of the disintegration. The parliamentary calculations that had made Gaullist support essential had changed by October, 1955, however: with the *Indépendants* (described below) on his side, Faure could finally dispense with the Gaullists and their efforts to paralyze a policy of movement in the protectorate.

The occasion was provided by a call for the constitution of a "government of public safety," made by the Comité national of the Social Republicans (the new Gaullist appellation) on 5 October. Perhaps the Gaullists thought the Moroccan crisis was that "external shock" which de Gaulle had named as the opportunity for his return. Whatever the reason for the call and the delegation sent to President Coty, the Gaullists had seriously miscalculated. Faure summoned the Gaullist members of the cabinet to the Matignon, demanded their resignations if they disagreed with his policy, and, after some resistance, received the resignations of all but one of the ministers. Only Corniglion-Molinier had been spared; he had declared, as a true Gaullist might, that "this was not the time to disown the Constitution nor to undermine hierarchy."[40] As the Algerian whirlwind grew, the vote of confidence which followed the Assembly debate on Faure's policy of evolution in Morocco pointed to the difficulty in decolonizing the French Right. Faure had won his gamble, but he was upheld in this instance by a *Center-Left* coalition: Socialists, Communists, and MRP

[38] *Le Monde*, 26 August 1955.
[39] Bernard, *The Franco-Moroccan Conflict*, pp. 308-309.
[40] *Le Monde*, 7 October 1955.

(Popular Republicans), as well as most of the Radicals with three-fourths of the Independent Republicans, led by Pinay, the foreign minister, and Duchet. The other right-wing groups, however, including the ex-Gaullist ARS and the Gaullists, opposed the ministry.

The embrace of Algérie française, 1956-1958

Efforts to preserve the electoral position that the RPF had won in 1951 utterly failed in the parliamentary elections of 2 January 1956. The French electorate replied that "Gaullism without de Gaulle was meaningless." The results were not a setback, they were a disaster: the Social Republicans lost over three million votes in comparison to the RPF figures, 78 percent of their former electorate. Only sixteen deputies were returned, from localities where the Gaullist deputies had strong ties and organization.[41]

Two sources may be given for this massive exit from the Gaullist standard: the retirement of de Gaulle, which left the Social Republicans without their principal source of identity, and ideological tension between the Gaullist parliamentarians and militants on the one hand, and the former RPF voters on the other.[42] The disadvantages of the Gaullists were compounded by the loss of many of the most secure constituencies to the Conservatives (through defection) and by the pattern of Left-Right competition in the 1955 electoral campaign. Espousing reformist rhetoric in domestic affairs and intransigent nationalism in external relations, the Gaullists were uncomfortable in either of the opposing coalitions, led on the

[41] François Goguel, "Géographie des élections du 2 janvier," in *Les élections du 2 janvier 1956*, p. 482; the importance of local strength is suggested in the particular studies of l'Aisne and Alsace, pp. 405, 415.

[42] The RPF voters were not vehemently opposed to the EDC; they were strongly attached to the Atlantic alliance, and, most important, they did not display strong hostility toward the regime. IFOP, *Sondages*, no. 3 (1952), pp. 33-34; no. 4 (1954), p. 14; no. 2 (1952), p. 8; no. 3 (1952), pp. 29-31. The election results are analyzed in François Goguel, "Géographie des élections du 2 janvier," in *Les élections du 2 janvier 1956* (Paris: Armand Colin, 1956), p. 482; the importance of local strength is suggested in local studies of the Aisne and Alsace contained in the same volume.

one hand by the proponent of colonial change, Mendès-France, and on the other by Edgar Faure, whose ministry they had attempted to destroy.

Such a massive defeat concentrates the mind wonderfully: for the small circle of Gaullists still committed to political action, early 1956 was a time for reconsidering political strategy. In the two years before the events of May, 1958 and the return of de Gaulle, four tendencies advocating different strategies would emerge in the much-reduced movement: those advocating participation in government, accepting the resilience of the Fourth Republic and espousing an electoral and parliamentary route to survival; those voicing a primordial hostility to the regime that the movement had always expressed, a hostility that grew with the Algerian War and led them to turn increasingly to direct action; a third group which reversed these priorities, placing the cause of *Algérie française* above all else, a commitment that would finally leave them outside the Gaullist movement; and last, a small band of liberals who were willing to accept looser ties between France and Algeria and who opposed the excesses of a policy of force. The groups were represented, respectively, by Jacques Chaban-Delmas, Michel Debré, Jacques Soustelle, and Edmond Michelet. For the first three tendencies, *Algérie française* would become central to their political efforts, although serving different ends for each.

Chaban-Delmas and regime politics. The rationale of the first group, who advocated continued participation in an apparently resilient regime, was presented in a memorandum analyzing for the Social Republicans the results of the election.[43] Describing the "lines of force" that emerged in the balloting, the report's author suggested utilizing the Mendèsist current by allying with the Republican Front, while resisting concessions on Algeria and other questions of national status. By becoming the "national wing" of the Republican Front, combining social reform and nationalist fervor, the Gaullists

---

[43] Centre national des républicains sociaux, "Étude des élections de 56 et leurs conséquences pour les républicains sociaux" (microfilm).

could reaffirm an identity that had become hopelessly ob-
scured after 1953, eliminating the conservatives in the movement at the same time. For those advocating participation,
Algérie française offered a critical element in the nationalist
identity of the Gaullists: by providing a criterion for supporting governments, the image of disunity that Gaullists had
presented in the preceding legislature could be avoided, and
the Gaullist claim to protect national interests within a corrupt
system could be maintained. Of course, participation also provided all the benefits of ministerial office for those, like Chaban-Delmas, with political fiefs to maintain. The position of
the Gaullists, as a small group at the Right-Center of the
political spectrum, offered substantial bargaining advantages
in the Assembly and lent support to the first tendency.

Michel Debré and the assault on the regime. If Chaban-
Delmas represented the moderated nationalism of political
survivors, the extremism of Debré reflected the sentiments of
Gaullist militants frustrated by electoral defeat at home and
national humiliation abroad. Gaullism after 1956 exemplified
the increased power of those most fiercely attached to a party
ideology in a movement that had just suffered massive exit
through electoral defeat. Discontent among party supporters
was manifest when Chaban-Delmas and Lemaire joined the
Mollet cabinet after the elections.[44] The harshness of their
attacks upon the regime grew over the next two years. They
placed their hopes in an external shock to bring down the
regime and to cause the return of de Gaulle. Algeria could
provide such a shock, and for these Gaullists, magnifying the
strain that the Algerian conflict placed upon the Fourth Republic became the core of their political strategy.

In explaining de Gaulle's later success in decolonizing the
movement, however, it is important to discern the *basis* for
this group's attachment to *Algérie française*. Michel Debré's
statement of Gaullist doctrine in *Ces princes qui nous go-
vernent*, published in 1957, makes clear that his principal concern is the *regime*. Algeria will probably be lost because the

---

[44] *Le Fait de la Quinzaine*, 7 March 1956, p. 1.

regime, dominated by a group of oligarchs without legitimacy or popular support, was "too far from all true authority, that which can reform without being overthrown by its own reforms." Debré's argument on Algeria, and in other realms, is orthodox Gaullism of the RPF period, based principally upon calculations of strategic and economic interest. However great the passion, there is surprisingly little sentimentality in this pessimistic and rationalistic view, and virtually no mention of the French settlers. Debré even implied that another regime, a different form for public life, might enable France to make the transition from the status of great power to a lesser rank without catastrophe: "The fact that a nation may no longer be a power of the first rank, and must limit its ambitions, does not signify its disappearance."[45] While the prescriptions that Debré offered, including his adamant refusal to consider independence ("secession") for Algeria, did not differ from those of other enthusiasts of *Algérie française*, his emphases—upon the regime, upon the strategic and economic ends which empire served—would provide the grounds for future divergence from his allies.

Soustelle and the Algerian connection. The most powerful of those allies was the third Gaullist tendency, led by Jacques Soustelle, former secretary general of the RPF. While Debré represented those Gaullists remaining loyal to the movement after the massive exit of 1956, Soustelle used the Algerian conflict to attract new sources of support, mobilized by the nationalist reaction to the war. Standing apart from the Social Republicans, he used his Union pour le salut et le renouveau de l'Algérie française (USRAF) to construct a parallel organization, one that he would ultimately use to challenge de Gaulle himself.

Despite apparent agreement among supporters of French Algeria, Soustelle reversed the priority of Debré and other Gaullists. For Debré, the probable "loss" of Algeria was a central symbol of the failure of the regime. The critical polit-

[45] Michel Debré, *Ces princes qui nous gouvernent* (Paris: Plon, 1957), pp. 81, 141.

ical lesson to be drawn was the absolute necessity for France to change the regime. For the Soustelle tendency, French Algeria was the final chance for France to remain France, to survive as a great power; its defense was *the* supreme goal to which all others should be subordinated. Most important, *Algérie française* was a test that could be applied to any regime, even a Gaullist one.

The disguised difference in emphasis found in Soustelle's arguments provided the basis for his future opposition to de Gaulle and other Gaullists on the question of Algeria. Those differences had a wider ideological and organizational source as well. Just as the question of the regime was foremost for Debré and most other Gaullist leaders, so they could not conceive of Gaullism, except as expounded and interpreted by de Gaulle. Soustelle saw the nature of Gaullism differently: in the formulation of Gaullist doctrine, at the foundation of the RPF, de Gaulle had played an active role, in his speeches and in the work of the RPF organs. Nevertheless, "the positions taken by the RPF did not come only from the thinking of its founder, but from the reflections, conducted together, of men from very diverse backgrounds."[46] In other words, when incorporated in a political movement, Gaullist ideology became part of the life of that movement; Soustelle challenged the position of de Gaulle as the sole or even the principal ideological arbiter of Gaullism.

Soustelle's notion of ideology fitted with his greater acceptance of political organizations and parliamentary forms. Soustelle, whose political career had begun on the Left, as the secretary general of an anti-fascist organization, viewed organized Gaullism on the model of a political party, with its militants, congresses, and parliamentarians. For de Gaulle, with his intense distrust of the "system" and his contempt for parties, this ideal was anathema: his political movements would be "rallies" or "unions," directly linking him with individual Frenchmen. Soustelle was also much less opposed to the par-

[46] Jacques Soustelle, *Vingt-huit ans de Gaullisme* (Paris: La Table Ronde, 1968), pp. 59-60.

liamentary regime than many *pur et dur* Gaullists, such as Debré: he believed that the possibilities for change from within were significant, and as president of the RPF group in the National Assembly after the elections of 1951, he chafed under the control exercised by de Gaulle, who was often in distant Colombey.

Gaullist liberalism. Almost forgotten in the extremism of Gaullist attachment to *Algérie française* were the small band of Gaullist liberals, who continued to assail the excesses of a policy of force in Algeria. René Capitant had protested the death of a former student, Ali Boumendjel, who had "committed suicide" between interrogations in March, 1957; Raymond Aron, after lending initial support to Soustelle, had penned a powerful critique of the integrationist thesis in *La tragédie algérienne*, drawing a bitter response from Soustelle. Three days after the fall of the Gaillard ministry in April, 1958, a group of liberal Gaullists issued a communiqué that urged the return of de Gaulle to power, not to preserve *Algérie française*, but to achieve the "peaceful resolution of the problems of Algeria, North Africa, and the Union française in the generous spirit of Brazzaville."

The political consequences of Gaullist strategy. These sources of future divergence were concealed in the final years of the Fourth Republic, however, as support for *Algérie française* among the Gaullists intensified, and the position of those who advocated participation in the governments of the regime steadily weakened. In the eyes of Gaullists, Algeria had become the last chance for France to remain a great power, a matter of "life or death": "The *idée fixe* of France today must be to maintain its ties with the overseas territories in such a way as to constitute with them a power on the international level. All else must be subordinated to this effort. . . ."[47] The maintenance of French Algeria became the most important criterion for Gaullist attitudes toward the governments in power: "Our position is without equivocation. To each government

[47] Centre national des républicains sociaux, *Note d'information*, December, 1957, pp. 2-3.

that asks for our help or our support, we will demand a clear definition of its position on two aspects of the French problem: reform of institutions, *Algérie française.*"[48]

As a result, the Gaullists, despite their small numbers, became a principal source of destabilization for the regime. Cabinet after cabinet was destroyed by the unyielding hostility of Soustelle and his followers to any compromise on Algeria. Soustelle acted to destroy the Bourgès-Maunoury cabinet in September, 1957, by opposing the *loi-cadre* (framework law) for Algeria that he had approved previously at a round table conference of party leaders; in his opposition he was able to carry the Social Republicans in the Assembly as well as a substantial number of *modérés.*[49] Gaullist intransigence was such that virtually any move toward reform in Algeria would encounter the opposition of Soustelle and the group in the Assembly. While they had voted for the amended *loi-cadre* presented by the Gaillard ministry, diluted to protect the position of the European minority, in the final vote of the *loi-cadre* (31 January-1 February 1958) most of the group abstained; Soustelle voted against; and only Chaban-Delmas and Liquard, the deputies from the Gironde, voted in favor of the government's proposal.[50] The final crisis of the beleaguered regime demonstrated the weakness of those Gaullists who favored a resolution of the Algerian crisis from within the Fourth Republic, now reduced to Chaban-Delmas alone. Once again Soustelle and the small group of Gaullists served as the spearhead and point of coalescence for those who shared their views on North Africa within the divided parties of the Right. In the vote of 15 April which ended the Gaillard ministry, all of the Gaullists, save the minister Chaban-Delmas, voted against the government.

De Gaulle's evolution. Organizationally the weakest of the

[48] CNRS, *Note d'information*, October, 1957.

[49] Roger Duchet, the leader of the Indépendants, recounts his surprise at Soustelle's destruction of the carefully arranged agreement on the *loi-cadre* in *La République épinglée* (Paris: Editions Alain Moreau, 1975), p. 197.

[50] *Année politique, 1958*, p. 14; Chevrillon, "Les Républicains sociaux," pp. 371-372.

Gaullist groups, the liberals did have an unsuspected ally: de Gaulle himself. The degree of change in de Gaulle's attitudes toward Algeria before 1958 should not be overestimated: at best he was groping for an alternative to the policy of force that permitted France to maintain a presence across the Mediterranean. Nevertheless, the transformation in de Gaulle's attitudes, those of a man over sixty years of age, can only be compared to the "conversion" of William Gladstone to Irish Home Rule in the 1880s. Sources for describing and explaining the evolution of de Gaulle's thinking after 1953 are limited: the testimony of his associates and his public statements, which were rare from 1955 to 1958. Because of the polemics that have surrounded de Gaulle's Algerian policy, each witness seems to have a different recollection of a different interview, which pointed, of course, in a different direction. The apparent contradictions rest upon an ideological combination that did not match any of the Gaullist tendencies described: de Gaulle's advocacy of a loosening of ties with North Africa—a willingness to negotiate with colonial nationalists and to consider a different framework for association with France—in combination with an unyielding hostility to the existing regime and condemnation of its inability to carry out the necessary reforms.[51]

In his *Memoirs* de Gaulle claims that on taking power in 1958, "on the essential point, therefore, my mind was made up. Whatever the dreams of the past or the regrets of today, whatever I myself had undoubtedly hoped for at other times, there was in my view no longer any alternative for Algeria but self-determination."[52] In April, 1970, he told Bernard Tricot that in 1958 he had thought for a long time that "Algeria would become, one day or another, independent," an observation that Tricot later confirmed with associates of de Gaulle.[53]

[51] Compare the accounts of Claude Estier in *France-Observateur*, 21 June 1956, p. 5 and Astoux, *L'Oubli*, p. 430.

[52] Charles de Gaulle, *Memoirs of Hope: Renewal and Endeavor* (New York: Simon and Schuster, 1971), pp. 45-46.

[53] Bernard Tricot, "La Décolonisation en Afrique du Nord" (Paper presented at the Institut Charles de Gaulle, Paris, 24 November 1972), p. 6.

While it is clear that de Gaulle had ruled out the integrationist solution advanced by Soustelle, the time span that he foresaw for independence was not clear. Tricot believes that de Gaulle had hoped to find "a solution founded on the personality of Algeria and on a close association, no doubt an institutional one, of that country with ours."[54] The framework for that association was to be the French Community, which was modeled on the structure that the Gaullists had been demanding since the war. The future for the African territories in the Community remained ambiguous, however: the colonies could remain in their present status, become departments of France, or transform themselves into states within the Community framework, which seemed a possible way station in the evolution of French-Algerian relations.[55] De Gaulle sought to preserve the Community, which all the sub-Saharan colonies save Guinea had joined, long enough to serve in the resolution of the Algeria conflict. French acceptance of African demands for independence with a much looser notion of the Community dashed these hopes and led de Gaulle to accept that Algeria would follow the same course.[56]

Soustelle's claims that de Gaulle's policies marked a sharp break with Gaullism of the RPF are correct: from a movement ideologically dependent upon a tenacious defense of every French position overseas, Gaullism was redefined as a nationalism of the "hexagon," exerting influence on a world scale, but not depending upon territorial control for that influence.[57] What had been the sources of de Gaulle's change of attitudes toward the empire?

First, while the war had implanted a colonial attachment

[54] Ibid.

[55] Paul-Marie de La Gorce, "De Gaulle et la décolonisation du continent noir," *Revue française d'études politiques africaines* 60 (December, 1970), pp. 47-48; de La Gorce, *De Gaulle entre deux mondes* (Paris: Fayard, 1964), p. 583.

[56] De La Gorce, "De Gaulle et la décolonisation," pp. 50-51; Alfred Grosser, *French Foreign Policy under de Gaulle* (Boston: Little, Brown and Co., 1965), p. 32; chap. 4.

[57] Soustelle's case is made most cogently in *Vingt-huit ans*, pt. 2, chap. 3.

in the movement, de Gaulle's career before the war pointed toward a continental conception of France. In the French Army's division between colonial officers and those of the metropolis, de Gaulle, like Foch and Pétain, belonged to the latter group: "For him, the military profession was not to be a matter of 'pacification.' . . . It would be firepower, modern techniques and the strategy of movement."[58] De Gaulle was stationed in the colonial empire only once before World War II, and the experience seems to have had little impact upon his thinking. Because of his career pattern, de Gaulle displayed little of that affection for the Europeans of North Africa that many colonial officers demonstrated. The political style of the Europeans across the Mediterranean, passionate and sentimental, was alien to the rational and bleak vision of the soldier from Lille.

De Gaulle's early career was not only metropolitan, it had been marked as well by a commitment to technological modernity as the core of military power. Willingness to accept greater autonomy and finally independence for France's overseas territories, including Algeria, was influenced by de Gaulle's return in the 1950s to this earlier conception. Immediately after the war, given the apparent military lessons of that conflict and the strategic conditions of the time, the colonial empire appeared to be an essential of French power, providing control of manpower, bases, and resources, all the military assets that had proven decisive, or so it seemed, in two world wars. The French political elite and the military remained attached to this image of international power far longer than the British or the American. But the colonial wars of the Fourth Republic demonstrated that efforts to retain the empire could result in a net *loss* of power, and new forms of international status and influence had appeared. Particularly dramatic in this regard was the Suez expedition: de Gaulle's close associate, Jacques Foccart, drew a lesson from the debacle that seemed to be shared by many: ". . . so long as France is not a military power in all senses, so long as she does not

[58] Lacouture, *De Gaulle* (New York: Avon Books, 1966), p. 208.

dispose of the atomic bomb, she will appear a tributary and a satellite."[59] The obsession of the French Army with Algeria was a bar to de Gaulle's efforts to obtain a new coinage of power for France in the form of a *force de frappe*. In adapting his personal conception of French strategy, de Gaulle remained a *nationalist*: the French Army could not be permitted to suffer another defeat; access to Saharan petroleum, critical to France's autonomy, must be secured.

De Gaulle and the UNR, 1958-1962: Surviving the loss of empire

De Gaulle's hesitant progress toward accepting change in Algeria remained hidden from those who worked to bring him to power in May, 1958. To speak of a Gaullist "plot" which reached fruition on 13 May 1958 would not only be incorrect, it would be beside the point. As Jacques Julliard notes, and as the account above suggests, since January, 1946, there had existed a "permanent plot, whose forms had varied."[60] The Gaullists had played a crucial role in maintaining the link between external success, defined as opposition to decolonization, and the legitimacy of the regime. Despite their efforts to increase pressure on the regime, however, the Gaullists could not produce the necessary external shock themselves. They lacked the necessary influence among the European population in Algeria, which, by 1958, had become the likely source of the fatal blow to the Fourth Republic.

Increased political mobilization among the French in Algeria, described in Chapter V, had been captured by the extreme Right and the Poujadists, many of whom were hostile to installing a Gaullist republic in Paris. The task of directing the discontent of the settlers and the military in Algeria to Gaullist ends was given to Léon Delbecque, a young Gaullist activist from the Nord. The minister for national defense, Jacques Chaban-Delmas, sent Delbecque to Algiers in December, 1957 as his "antenna." As Chaban-Delmas discreetly

[59] *Lettre à l'Union française*, 8 November 1956.
[60] Jacques Julliard, *La IVᵉ République* (Paris: Calmann-Lévy, 1968), p. 223.

covered in Paris, Delbecque was able to lay the groundwork for future Gaullist influence within the Army, the veterans' organizations, and the political groups in Algiers. All agree that Delbecque's work was critical for the outcome in May.[61]

After Delbecque, named a vice-chairman of the Algiers Committee of Public Safety, had succeeded in turning events toward an appeal to de Gaulle, the Gaullist strategy for the next two weeks became twofold: to encourage plans for a military invasion of the metropolis ("Operation Resurrection") in order to cause a collapse of resistance to de Gaulle's return, and, at the same time, to restrain such direct action to ensure that the transfer of power had at least a semblance of legality. Gaullist control over the pressure exerted was not complete, particularly over the military planning for Operation Resurrection in Algiers. In the metropolis, de Gaulle's message of 15 May, announcing his readiness to "assume the powers of the Republic," put the national network of Gaullists in a state of alert. Astoux, the former RPF militant, spent much of his time during these weeks restraining Gaullist militants in the provinces who wished to move immediately to direct action.[62]

Despite the risks, openly accepted by the Gaullists and by de Gaulle himself, of bringing the General to power on the points of bayonets,[63] the gamble succeeded: Charles de Gaulle was invested as the last premier of the Fourth Republic and given the mandate to create a new constitution. On his return to power, however, de Gaulle confronted many whose principal concern was not the construction of a new republic, but the maintenance of French rule in Algeria. Among the devotees

[61] Soustelle, *Vingt-huit ans*, p. 141; Louis Terrenoire, *De Gaulle et l'Algérie* (Paris: Fayard, 1964), pp. 64-65.

[62] Astoux, *L'Oubli*, p. 455. The tenuous situation in the southwest, as Operation Resurrection threatened, is documented by Jean-Paul Buffelan, *Le Complot du 13 mai 1958 dans le Sud-Ouest* (Paris: R. Pichon and R. Durand-Auzias, 1966).

[63] Philip Williams, "The Fourth Republic—Murder or Suicide?" in *Wars, Plots, and Scandals in Post-war France*, (Cambridge: Cambridge University Press, 1970), p. 156n; Soustelle, *Vingt-huit ans*, p. 147.

of *Algérie française* were not only the military, the French of Algeria, and the Conservatives, but also many Gaullists. To decolonize outside, de Gaulle had to decolonize inside. Despite his loathing for political parties the General needed to reestablish his ideological preeminence within Gaullism and to ensure the loyalty of the movement within Parliament and without as his Algerian policy evolved. In effect, de Gaulle had to construct a new political universe much closer in its outlines to the British one, with the same limits on exit and voice.

Limiting the power of parties: New institutions. Using the model illustrated in Table I, several explanations can be offered for de Gaulle's success in internal decolonization, despite the increased dedication of Gaullism to French Algeria before 1958. Since it was not clear how powerful organized Gaullism would be in the new regime, one strategy was limiting the power of those most committed ideologically to French Algeria within the new institutions of the Fifth Republic. The electoral system, a revival of the Third Republic's *scrutin d'arrondissement*, was designed in part to reduce the advantages of a right-wing electoral coalition that relied upon the popularity of de Gaulle. The tendency of the system was to localize and personalize the results and to resist the impact of new national movements.[64] But the device did not work: the legislative elections of November, 1958 resulted in an overwhelming victory for the UNR and the Conservatives; the parliamentary majority contained many who were eager to tie the government's hands in its efforts to move toward negotiations and a new status for Algeria.

The new deputies found themselves in a new parliament, however: "under the new regime the Parliament of France, once among the most powerful in the world, became one of the weakest."[65] The diminution of legislative power resulted

---

[64] Maurice Duverger, "Paradoxes d'une reforme electorale," in *Le Referendum de septembre et les élections de novembre 1958*, ed. François Goguel (Paris: Armand Colin, 1960), pp. 225-226.

[65] Philip Williams, *The French Parliament (1958-1967)* (London: George Allen and Unwin, Ltd., 1968), p. 21.

from a strengthening of the Presidency, particularly in the reserved sphere of external relations; in addition, the government had only limited responsibility before the Assembly. While the new institutions would not make the Debré cabinet invulnerable, the presidential system, combined with the UNR's dominance of the political Center, made it far easier for a President elected by the Right to govern from the Center. Only once was the ministry in serious jeopardy: during consideration of the *force de frappe* proposals, the left-wing opponents of the government's defense policies and the critics of its Algerian policy on the Right threatened to unite. At its peak, however, this opposition obtained only 215 votes.[66]

A third means of circumventing the power of the parties and those devoted to maintaining French Algeria was the referendum, skillfully employed by de Gaulle in January, 1961 and April, 1962 to win overwhelming approval of his Algerian policy. These new institutional mechanisms did not fully protect de Gaulle's ability to change course in Algeria, however. While those most attuned to ideological incentives exercised less power in the new regime, they could still attempt to thwart de Gaulle's efforts by the formation of an effective coalition across the Mediterranean, the type of military-settler-parliamentary coalition that had destroyed the previous regime. It was in this indirect sense that the dangers to the government from its own supporters were most threatening and the decolonization of the Gaullist movement most essential. The partisans within the UNR (the Union pour la Nouvelle République, the newest Gaullist appellation) of French rule in Algeria could seek to impose an *Algérie française* government upon de Gaulle; even if he retained control of the government, divisions within government or party could undermine his efforts to restore the authority of the republic over the military, the state administration, and the rebellious French of Algeria. Those who defended the French position overseas had learned long ago to play upon divisions in Paris in order to win freedom of action on the periphery. Both sides were

[66] Williams, *The French Parliament*, pp. 53-55.

aware of the role that the UNR might play; both sides struggled to win its loyalty.

The decolonization of Gaullism: A distinct identity and role. Before the legislative elections of November, 1958, the battle between those who favored leaving Algerian policy to de Gaulle and those who sought to commit Gaullism to *Algérie française* was fought on two questions: the establishment of a distinct identity for the Gaullist formation, the Union pour la nouvelle République, and the fixing of a role for the movement, that of *supporting* the government and de Gaulle, as well as the new regime. The UNR, founded after the referendum victory, was an uneasy coalition of two of the tendencies that had competed since 1956: those who were interested in gaining a share of the power in the regime, particularly the former Social Republicans, and those seeking to identify the movement with the cause of French Algeria. On the first central committee of the UNR were represented the Social Republicans (represented by Chaban-Delmas and Frey), the Union for French Renewal (committed to French Algeria and represented by Soustelle and Picard), the Republican Convention (also committed to French Algeria), and other, less important groups which tended to dilute the power of the *Algérie française* supporters. In successive pre-election decisions, Soustelle also failed to ensure an independent role for the movement and was prevented from forming electoral alliances with other supporters of Algerian integration, alliances that would have blurred its distinctive Gaullist identity. De Gaulle prevented Soustelle from becoming president of the new Gaullist organization: there would be no president, a figure who might try to reinterpret Gaullism against de Gaulle.[67]

Perhaps the most significant task for the UNR during this period, however, was the selection of parliamentary candidates, a procedure that was used to impose loyalty on the future legislators. Memories of the RPF and the threat of another schism led the leadership to employ a careful screening

[67] Jean Charlot, *L'Union pour la Nouvelle République: Etude du pouvoir au sein d'un parti politique* (Paris: Armand Colin, 1967), pp. 39-40.

process. Carried out principally by Roger Frey, the criterion used was past history as a loyal Gaullist. Here, once again, Soustelle was at a disadvantage, since many of the activists supporting French Algeria did not possess the necessary credentials. Not only would the new Gaullist candidates respond to identity incentives centered upon de Gaulle, the composition of the UNR group suggested that purposive incentives would play a role as well: the UNR deputies elected in 1958 were not ideologues new to politics, most had held office under the Fourth Republic.[68]

Thus, the UNR entered the electoral campaign as a movement of *support* for the government, a role similar to that of the British Conservative Party in relation to its leaders. For the moment the Gaullist movement did not claim an ideological role, and its key positions were held by loyalists and moderates on Algeria. After the 1958 elections, the pattern was reinforced: for the first time, a Gaullist party, led by de Gaulle, held the dominant position in a governing coalition. The supply of purposive incentives available to the leadership had grown enormously; with its electoral success, the number within the movement responding to such incentives would also grow. The scale of the UNR success suggested a revolution in electoral behavior that would only be confirmed in 1962: renewed attachment of a large part of the French electorate to de Gaulle, the Fifth Republic, and the UNR. The shifting electorate on the Right had found a political home that would continue to claim its loyalties over the next decade.[69]

Controlling exit and voice. After the elections, the threat from the advocates of French Algeria remained: exit on the parliamentary level was the most pressing danger, since the large contingent of Indépendants on the Right could once again serve as a pole of attraction for disaffected Gaullists. Voice could also be used to divide the UNR or to transform

[68] The preelection maneuvering is described in Charlot, *L'Union pour la Nouvelle République*, pp. 39-40; Williams, *The French Parliament*, p. 33.

[69] David R. Cameron, "Stability and Change in Patterns of French Partisanship," *Public Opinion Quarterly* 36 (Spring 1972), 19-30.

the electoral victory of Gaullism into a triumph for *Algérie française*. Within the parliamentary group of the UNR, strenuous efforts were directed to preventing exit and strictly controlling voice. A close relationship between government and the UNR group was guaranteed by the results of elections for a president and *bureau politique*. Louis Terrenoire, former secretary general of the RPF, defeated Jean-Baptiste Biaggi, an outspoken *Algérie française* extremist, for the presidency of the group, but only on a second ballot by 124 votes to 72. The first and most important test of the unity and loyalty of the group came after de Gaulle's speech of 17 September 1959, which proposed self-determination for Algeria. This significant and unmistakable turning from the advocates of integration seemed likely to produce defections from the UNR group. In response to the speech, a Rassemblement pour l'Algérie française was established in opposition to self-determination. Two UNR deputies, Biaggi and Battesti, joined it, testing the identity of the UNR. The *bureau politique* reacted quickly to oppose such double membership; the decision was supported by allies of Soustelle, who still hoped to conquer a unified movement.[70]

Efforts to control voice within the parliamentary group did finally result in some defections. Before the government's declaration on Algeria (13 October 1959), the UNR group met to designate speakers for the Assembly debate that would follow. In preparation for the debate the *bureau politique* had unanimously decided to appoint UNR spokesmen: the supporters of *Algérie française* were not among those named. With only three dissenting votes, the *bureau* announced its opposition to interventions in the debate by UNR deputies who had not been designated. The struggle over voice was transformed into exit: soon after the decision of the bureau, nine deputies announced their resignations from the UNR group.[71] Following the debate, four of the nine voted for the

[70] Terrenoire, *De Gaulle et l'Algérie*, pp. 134-135.

[71] The nine: Delbecque, Arrighi, Thomazo, Cathala, Brice, Grasset, Souchal, Biaggi, Battesti.

government nonetheless and requested readmission to the group. The premier, Michel Debré, demanded severity, and the rebels were denied reentry. The harsh sanctions imposed upon the dissidents doubtless had some deterrent effect upon other potential rebels during the "week of the barricades" in January, 1960, when the French of Algiers once again attempted to thwart change through direct action. The UNR group showed "remarkable unity of views": only one deputy opposed a resolution which affirmed total support for the President of the Republic.[72] In future tests, the group would respond with similar loyalty.

How had massive exit been avoided in a group that had included many partisans of French Algeria when elected in 1958? The selection process for UNR parliamentary candidates had undoubtedly been important; Jean Charlot has verified the greater degree of loyalty shown by those with past Gaullist affiliations.[73] Despite the local political attachments of many deputies, the elections of 1956 served as a warning of the probable fate of Gaullists without de Gaulle. Finally, the temptation of exit was reduced by the evolution of the Conservatives (Indépendants), the principal right-wing competitors of the Gaullists. As Conservative support for French Algeria evolved into opposition to the new regime, the barriers to Gaullist exit rose. Whatever their views on the future of Algeria, few Gaullists could have any nostalgia for a parliamentary regime that they had opposed for so long.

Opponents of the President's new course did possess a final arena for an embarrassing show of force: the extraparliamentary organization of the UNR. Their chances of success were greater, for the proportion of "new" Gaullists among militants was higher than among parliamentarians, and the sanctions available to the leadership were weaker. Struggle over the UNR position on Algeria assumed the form of a debate on its role and the relative powers of the leadership

[72] Terrenoire, *De Gaulle et l'Algérie*, pp. 136-137, 153; Charlot, *L'U.N.R.*, pp. 59-65.

[73] The incidence of dissidence was lowest for those with an RPF or RS background who did *not* have a Resistance past.

and the militants. At first, the Soustelle wing centered their attacks upon the secretary general, Albin Chalandon, who did not disguise his lack of sympathy for the integrationists.[74] The battle resumed in the form of a debate over the future of the movement at the first National Council in July, 1959.[75]

The most severe test of the organization, however, came, as it had for the deputies, after the self-determination announcement of September, 1959. Efforts were made to have the UNR declare itself in favor of *francisation* (integration). Unanimity in the Central Committee was only maintained by a motion which predicted the failure of any "separatist" solution.[76] Unable to carry the governing body of the UNR, the Soustelle forces turned their attention to the first national congress of the UNR, held at Bordeaux in November, 1959. De Gaulle made clear before the Congress that he did not wish the movement to commit itself to any position that foreclosed future evolution in Algeria.[77] Thus, the question was made a test of loyalty to the President of the Republic. Nevertheless, the reception given Soustelle at the Congress testified to the popularity of his position among the assembled militants. Only preparation of the Algerian motion in a small ad hoc committee that included the parliamentary leadership ensured that de Gaulle's wishes were respected. The new Central Committee also reflected the stronger position of the moderates: the loyalist federations of Paris and the Gironde elected nineteen of the fifty committee members; federations supporting French Algeria obtained fewer members or none at all.[78] The success of the moderates at Bordeaux, in this most "nonpolitical" of movements had been ensured by classic political techniques: the conquest of individual federations, particularly those of the Seine and the Gironde, and a backroom committee controlled by the leadership.[79]

[74] Charlot, *L'U.N.R.*, p. 50-54.
[75] Terrenoire, *De Gaulle et L'Algérie*, p. 131.
[76] Charlot, *L'U.N.R.*, pp. 58-59.
[77] Ibid., p. 68.
[78] Ibid., p. 73-75.
[79] Pierre Buchaillard and Bernard Contat, "L'Union pour la Nouvelle Ré-

The "revolt of the barricades" led to dismissal of Soustelle from his government positions on 4 February 1960; by that time the final defeat of the supporters of French Algeria within Gaullism had been assured. After his participation in the Colloque de Vincennes in April, Soustelle was excluded from the UNR; only four deputies followed him. Resistance from Army and settlers would continue, but Gaullism had been successfully decolonized. The course had not been an easy one, however. De Gaulle could witness the personal costs of loyalty in his own prime minister: Debré "adopted each of my initiatives with complete loyalty and was in any case aware that in matters of state reason must prevail. But he suffered and did not hide the fact."[80] The veteran militant, André Astoux, who had followed each rise and fall of Gaullist fortunes, felt disappointment, but it was soon forgotten: "The State has its reasons which reason does not always know. Like others, we had a bitter taste in our mouths, but what was that compared to the hope which filled our hearts?"[81]

De Gaulle's contribution, as Bernard Tricot has remarked, was not the decolonization of Algeria, which would have occurred in any case, but his ability to limit the effects on France of granting Algerian independence. A large measure of that success was owed to the successful decolonization of a sector of the French Right loyal to de Gaulle. Other political formations were not to enjoy such good fortune.

THE FRENCH CONSERVATIVES: ATTACHMENT TO EMPIRE AND THE DEMISE OF PARTIES

If Gaullist twists and turns during decolonization have been shrouded in the mythology of the Fifth Republic—Brazzaville, Algeria, and nothing between—the role of the French Conservatives (also known as Indépendants or *modérés*) has been largely forgotten. Lacking the ties to empire that the Gaullists

---

publique dans la Seine" (*Mémoire*, Institut d'Etudes Politiques, Paris, 1960), pp. 93-94.

[80] De Gaulle, *Memoirs of Hope*, p. 84.
[81] Astoux, *L'Oubli*, p. 465.

had forged in the World War, French Conservatives at first accepted decolonization, although with some equivocation. They later turned to a fierce commitment to what was left of the colonial empire. Riding a nationalist appeal, they achieved a dominant position on the Right; unable to divorce themselves from that appeal, they were divided and defeated in the new political world that developed after 1958, a world constructed in part to permit the decolonization of Algeria. The second largest group in the National Assembly elected in 1958, they had been reduced in five years to a fragment party, led by Valery Giscard d'Estaing, with only a weak national organization.

Before the Second World War, the French parliamentary Right had hardly possessed national organizations: Fédération républicaine and Alliance démocratique were appellations rather than political entities.[82] After the war, weakened by their involvement with Vichy, these formations seemed organizationally obsolete in the new age of monolithic parties that seemed to characterize the first years of the Fourth Republic. Given the parliamentary focus of the traditional Right, one might expect that initial efforts to unify the Conservative groups would take place among deputies and senators. The principal force in these efforts and those of the next decade was the senator from the Côte-d'Or, Roger Duchet. In early 1949 he gained the consent of other Conservative senators to the formation of a new point of affiliation, the Centre national des indépendants. The new Center would have no president, symbolizing the collegial nature of leadership among the *modérés*, but Duchet would serve as secretary general of the Center for the next ten years. The expansion of the Center owed much to Duchet's negotiating abilities, as one by one the other groups of deputies on the Right decided to ally under its aegis.[83] Affiliation did not imply fusion—some of the groups retained

[82] The political organizations of the prewar Right are described in Malcolm Anderson, *Conservative Politics in France* (London: George Allen and Unwin, Ltd., 1974), chap. 3.

[83] The first efforts at organization are described in Duchet, *La République épinglée*, p. 12.

considerable autonomy—but by 1955 the Conservatives had federated in a single formation to fight the parliamentary elections: the Indépendants et Paysans d'Action Sociale.

Even with greater unity at the parliamentary level, old-style Conservative politics continued in the clash of cliques (Duchet and Antoine Pinay on one side, Paul Reynaud and Joseph Laniel on the other), and in continued reliance upon a decentralized cadre form of organization. The Conservative electoral clientele, among the provincial bourgeoisie and rural property-holders, encouraged this style of politics, relying upon local notables rather than members or militants in the organization of the movement. The pattern of participation contrasted sharply with parties of the Left and even with the more urban Gaullists: apart from attendance at electoral meetings, the typical means of electioneering in rural areas, the *modéré* voter rarely took part in any other political activities.[84]

In 1951 Duchet could defiantly declare that the Indépendants were *not* a party; just as they reveled in that status, so the Conservatives also repudiated a formal ideology. A movement dominated by its parliamentarians, relying upon local notables for its electoral success, appealing to the bourgeoisie of rural and small-town France, was not likely to require ideological incentives. The low salience of colonial issues in French politics which affected the behavior of other parties before the mid-1950s was reinforced in the case of the Conservatives by the distance of overseas questions from the principal concerns of their provincial constituents.[85]

---

[84] Marcel Merle, "Les Modérés," and Mattei Dogan, "L'Origine sociale du personnel parlementaire français elu en 1951," in *Partis politiques et classes sociales en France*, ed. Duverger, pp. 250-254, 325; "L'Electeur modéré," in IFOP, *Sondages*, no. 3 (1952), pp. 40-42.

[85] The first *journées d'études*, the national gatherings that substituted for a party congress before 1954, reflected the domestic issues that were the principal concern of the *modérés* at this time: the commissions established dealt with local liberties, reform of the Constitution, peasant questions, and financial and economic questions. The Indépendant group in the Assembly in 1951 was formed on the basis of a program submitted by Paul Reynaud that contained no reference to foreign or colonial policy, except "rapid and efficacious efforts in matters of national defense." Somewhat more attention was paid to the colonial empire at the second *journées d'études* in March,

The ministries of Pierre Mendès-France and Edgar Faure marked the definitive reentry of the external and particularly colonial issues into French political life. The Conservatives could no longer avoid the divisive questions surrounding North Africa, but their behavior, at first glance, seems contradictory. Toward Mendès-France, initial hostility—forty of the forty-seven votes opposing his investiture came from the *modéré* groups—would grow during his months as premier. Opposition centered on North Africa, but the Conservatives, in contrast to the Gaullists, also resented the radically new style of leadership that Mendès-France introduced. The motion on North Africa of the first national congress of the Indépendants, held in December 1954 during the Mendès-France ministry, seemed a perfect expression of the die-hard position: calling for "pitiless repression" of any rebellion, it declared that "North Africa is an extension of France. France cannot be imagined without it."[86] The hostility of the Conservative leadership toward the Mendès-France cabinet and particularly its policy of limited reforms in North Africa was in part related to the unity in opposition that North Africa provided for a group that splintered on most other issues.[87] Their sudden discovery of ideological nationalism had been increased undoubtedly by

---

1952, but the emphasis reflected the fears of business interests facing threats to their protected markets in a world of increasing commercial competition.

[86] *France-Indépendante*, 14 December 1954; *Le Monde*, 4 December, 9 December, and 10 December 1954, are the principal sources for the proceedings of the Congress.

[87] In August, 1954, for example, the coefficient of cohesion within the Conservative group in the Assembly on the North African vote of confidence was .58; on a vote of confidence on the ministry's financial and economic program the same day (10 August) the coefficient dropped to .39. The *modérés* were even more splintered on the question of the EDC than other groups: while the Conservative groups on balance opposed the treaty, the coefficient of cohesion dropped to .28. In later votes on the North African policy of the ministry, after the outbreak of the Algerian rebellion, the *modéré* deputies displayed even greater cohesion, particularly in the vote of 10 December 1954 and the vote which ended the Mendès-France cabinet on 4 February 1955 (coefficient of cohesion .653). All voting statistics in this and other cases are taken from *Année politique*; the formula for computing the coefficient of cohesion from Stuart Rice; only positive and negative votes were used in the computation.

the addition of ex-Gaullist dissidents to the movement: they were consistently more hostile on North African questions than either the Indépendant or the Peasant components.

From die-hard opposition to decolonization under Mendès-France, the Conservatives moved to accept the decolonization of Morocco under the ministry of Edgar Faure, reversing the pattern of support and opposition displayed by the Gaullists. Their acceptance marked a temporary adaptation that the Gaullists had been unable to accomplish and provided a rare example of enlightened conservatism in colonial affairs during the Fourth Republic. Such an ability to change course suggested the freedom of action that the Conservative parliamentarians possessed, and the relatively weak hold that the ideology of empire had upon the movement. The key conversion was that of Antoine Pinay, Faure's foreign minister and the leader with the widest following in the group; the site of his conversion was the negotiations at Aix-les-Bains between members of the French cabinet and representatives of Moroccan opinion, including nationalists:

The striking contrast between the westernized nationalist leaders and the traditionalist delegates who seemed to have stepped straight out of the Middle Ages had helped considerably to persuade Pinay that the only persons with whom France could negotiate in Morocco were those who for two years had been calling so insistently for Mohammed V's [the exiled sultan] return to the throne.[88]

Roger Duchet, while more skeptical, followed Pinay's lead.

Since Faure's Moroccan policies depended on the support of at least one of the two right-wing groups (Conservatives or Gaullists), he used Pinay and Duchet to hold enough of their followers in support of his liberal policies to win approval by the National Assembly: "While the bulk of support came from the left, the right-wing backing essential to any decolonization policy had come from those Indépendants who followed Pinay."[89] As a result, the tenuous unity of the Conservatives was sacrificed, however: in the crucial vote of 8

[88] Bernard, *The Franco-Moroccan Conflict*, p. 291.
[89] Ibid., p. 327.

October 1955, the combined Conservative groups reached their greatest degree of division during the Faure cabinet. Opposition was particularly strong among the Peasants and the ex-Gaullists of the ARS, where personal loyalties to Pinay and Duchet were weakest and nationalist feelings strongest. Conservative efforts to appear as enlightened proponents of change in colonial relations persisted nevertheless in the electoral campaign of 1955. In contrast to the die-hard tone of their Congress only one year before, at the peak of opposition to Mendès-France, they chose not to emphasize the future of the colonial empire or the unrest in North Africa. Insofar as the topic was discussed the liberal views of Pinay were echoed.[90]

How is one to explain the shift in Conservative parliamentary behavior on colonial questions, and particularly North Africa, between the Mendès-France and Faure cabinets? Within the parliamentary group of a movement still dominated by its parliamentarians, the personal ties of Pinay and Duchet had served as a substitute for other, institutionalized means of gaining consent for Faure's policies in Morocco. Their influence was supplemented by the party's role in government rather than opposition: by excluding the principal *modéré* leaders from his cabinet, Mendès-France denied himself this means of leverage within the group.[91] The apparent adaptation of the *modérés* was also eased by their continuing weak attachment to the empire, for the historical and electoral reasons given above. In contrast to Gaullism, with a nationalist ideology implanted in an extraparliamentary organization and an electoral following, attachment to the colonial empire was not a central part of Conservative strategy at this time. Not only was reliance on ideological incentives low—the efforts to develop a "modern" political organization had hardly be-

[90] Georges Dupeux, "Les plates-formes des partis," in *Les Elections du 2 janvier 1956*, pp. 34-36; CNIP, Fiches de documentation, élections 1956, pp. 3-4, 8.

[91] As Duncan Macrae has noted, the opposition on the Right, particularly regarding North Africa, was similar for both the Mendès-France and the Faure cabinets. It was not identical, however: the issue of North Africa was combined with other grounds for opposition to Mendès-France.

gun—but an effort to compete with the Gaullists on nationalist terrain would have been difficult. The Indépendants could preserve their growing unity on economic and other issues only by reducing the salience of the colonial and North African questions within the movement: they simply agreed to disagree on the divisive Moroccan question. The Gaullists could not adopt this solution. More difficult to estimate is the influence of business interests, particularly during the Moroccan crisis: the acquiescence of at least part of those economic interests in the Faure strategy of decolonization is discussed in Chapter IV. Although the *modérés* had probably gained support from the *patronat* since Pinay's ministry in 1952, it would be inaccurate to assert that they were more attached to a business clientele than either the Radicals or the Gaullists in the Assembly: certainly the proportion of their deputies with such ties was no greater than among the other groups on the Right.[92] Any shift in the perceptions of business interests toward conciliation in late 1955 can at best be credited with strengthening the hand of Pinay and Duchet in dealing with their colleagues who had such connections.

A final permissive cause may be cited for the liberalism of the Conservatives during the electoral campaign: the party system seemed to permit them considerable flexibility. The disintegration of Gaullism and the alliance of many ex-Gaullists with the Centre national diminished the threat of exit. Perceiving no threat on the Right, the leaders of the Conservatives would pursue a strategy favored by their leaders—appealing to the Center. The results of the election of 2 January 1956 demonstrated that this estimate of the party system was a misperception. Their showing was far from the catastrophe experienced by the Gaullists—the *modérés* gained over half a million votes, as compared with their 1951 results—nevertheless, it was a "relative failure," given the disintegration of the Gaullists and splintering of Radicalism.[93] The dreams

[92] Merle, "Les Modérés," p. 256.

[93] François Goguel, "Géographie des élections du 2 janvier," in *Les Elections du 2 janvier 1956*, p. 484.

of the Conservatives to construct a "large conservative party on the British model" were thwarted principally by the success of the Poujadists, who not only claimed *modéré* votes, but also gained some of the former RPF votes that the Conservatives regarded as their inheritance. The weak hold of the Indépendants upon a part of the right-wing electorate and an electoral system based upon proportional representation raised obstacles to the Conservative quest for a dominant position on the Right, permitting exit in what was far from a two-party or even a two-coalition system. The response of the *modérés* to this setback quickly became apparent.

The discovery of Algérie française, 1956-1958

Immediately after the elections, the *modérés* ceased to be enlightened conservatives on North African questions. Despite the reticence of Pinay, Roger Duchet determined that the Conservative position on the empire would not be misinterpreted.[94] During 1956 the Conservatives reinterpreted their liberalism of the preceding year to the point of disavowing it. Not only did they turn against change in the colonial empire, they also began to link the future of France overseas with the future of the regime, a break with their previous repudiation of the extreme Right.[95]

How is one to explain yet another reversal, this sudden and fierce attachment to *Algérie française* on the part of the Conservatives, and their questioning of a regime that they had previously defended against the Gaullists? Three elements in their political situation can explain the about-face of the Conservatives: their exclusion from government; their need to construct an electoral coalition on the Right after the disappointment of the parliamentary elections; and their efforts to

[94] In May 1956 the *Comité directeur* of the Centre national approved a motion, with Pinay and Laniel in attendance, that endorsed the policy of pacification pursued in Algeria by Resident General Lacoste. The motion also condemned the "defeatism" of journals such as *Nouvelle Observateur* and *L'Express*, as well as the "treason" of the Communist Party.

[95] See Duchet's comment in *France-Indépendante*, 26 June 1956.

construct a "new model" political organization, relying upon militants and the ideological incentives that they required.

First, since the *modérés* were not participants in the Mollet and Bourgès-Maunoury cabinets (January, 1956-September, 1957), their position resembled that of the parliamentary group under Mendès-France, a state of opposition or quasi-opposition. The outcome was in many respects even more enviable for the Conservatives: with increased Communist representation and a new contingent of Poujadists in the new legislature, groups whose opposition could be taken as given, the added opposition of the Indépendants would prevent the formation of a government. The Conservatives could enforce resistance to nationalist demands in Algeria without assuming responsibility for the policies carried out by the government. Power without responsibility served to solve the "Pinay problem" as well. The former premier, by far the most popular leader of the *modérés*, was also among the most liberal on North African questions, diverging in an embarrassing way from the new course set by Duchet.

A second reason for renewed Conservative attention to the empire was an effort to attract an *electoral clientele* that had escaped them in the elections for the National Assembly. Duchet persisted in his goal of establishing a large conservative party that would compete with the Socialists *à l'anglaise*, despite the increased bargaining power of both extremes that had become apparent in the elections. The strategy that the movement took sought to ensure against exit to the Right; *Algérie française* was a principal instrument in that strategy.

A principal clientele that the *modérés* hoped to regain or win was the *Poujadist* electorate, whose size had provided one of the surprises of the balloting. Efforts to come to terms with the Poujadists had begun before the elections; after, the Indépendants were even more solicitous of their rivals. Duchet urged conciliation: "If the excesses of the Poujadists are to be condemned, some of their demands are perfectly justified and must be satisfied." The strident attacks of the Poujadists on decolonization during their campaign may have encouraged the *modérés* to become less moderate themselves in defending the colonial empire and using nationalist appeals. The attachment of the Poujadist movement to an aggressive colonialism seems to have been related to its *own* strategy of becoming a *national* movement (breaking out of its bastions south of the Loire); to infiltration by the extreme Right, notably the Algerian Paul Chevallet, who briefly became the chief ideologue of the movement; and possibly to financial support from the threatened colonial economic interests, particularly the Algerian settlers and the textile industry. The *electoral* importance of such appeals is doubtful, however. The results of a survey conducted in Paris (first *circonscription*) suggested strongly that even in such a normally nationalist setting, one whose Poujadist voters elected the *Algérie française* extremist, Jean-Marie Le Pen, the attacks upon the "gravediggers of empire" did not figure in the decision to vote Poujadist.[96]

A closer examination of Poujadism suggests that the Conservatives (and others) may have misread the importance of chauvinist rhetoric in Poujadist success. Although only part of Conservative opposition to greater Algerian autonomy derives from a process of "Poujadization" at the local level,[97] Poujadism did influence a shift in the center of gravity of the *modérés* nationally: the Centre national of the movement, directed by Duchet, increasingly emphasized nationalist ideological incentives. As the Poujadist parliamentary contingent disintegrated, many of its deputies, including such *Algérie française* extremists as Jean-Marie Le Pen, would affiliate with the *modérés*.

Other less important electoral constituencies were at stake as well; all would be tempted by the appeal of *Algérie française*. A resurgent extreme Right could not be the source of

[96] Jean Stoetzel and Pierre Hassner, "Resultats d'un Sondage dans le premier secteur de la Seine," *Les Elections du 2 janvier 1956*, p. 226.

[97] I. R. Campbell, "Political Attitudes in France to the Algerian Question, 1954-1962" (D.Phil. thesis, Oxford University, 1972), p. 463. Duncan Macrae finds a *negative* correlation between the intransigence of deputies on Algeria and the percentage of Poujadist votes in the department. One could argue, however, that anticipated *future* loss would affect the behavior of a deputy more than a past showing which had been overcome.

many votes (roughly a quarter of a million in the last elections of the Fourth Republic), but it could provide party activists, a tempting prospect for a group that still required a cadre of the ideologically committed. The Europeans of Algeria remained influential in Conservative political councils, despite their lack of representation in the National Assembly from 1956 to 1958. North Africa also entered *modéré* political calculations indirectly in the form of *rapatriés* who had left North Africa to settle in France. Many of these emigrants, fleeing political change across the Mediterranean, had settled in the southwest of France, the last regional stronghold of a Radicalism in decline and a likely area of conservative expansion.[98] The appeal of nationalism for the urban middle classes had been a feature of French political life since the late nineteenth century. Unlike the traditional constituency of the Conservatives—the rural and provincial bourgeoisie—this electorate was more volatile and demanded a higher degree of organization and ideological appeal. As the earlier success of the RPF had suggested, nationalism could provide the ideological incentives for this clientele. A final potential source of support for the Indépendants was a more surprising one. While the Conservatives attracted a high proportion of older voters, one survey suggests that they also won the support of a higher proportion of voters under thirty-five than *any* other political party.[99] *Algérie française* became a rallying cry and a spur to political activism for the young middle class. To attract and hold this elusive electorate on the Right and construct "un grand parti tory" in France was made even more difficult by the electoral system: by granting easy exit, it increased the bargaining power of the extremes.

The *modérés* were not merely responding to underlying

---

[98] The strategy of the *modérés* in this region is described in "La France a la recherché d' un grand party tory," *Entreprise*, 15 July 1957, p. 38; the geographical concentration of the *rapatriés* from North Africa is given in René Chiroux, *L'Extrême-droite sous la Ve République* (Paris: Librairie de droit et de jurisprudence, 1974), p. 101, map no. 5.

[99] "La France a la recherché d' un grand parti tory," p. 38; Stoetzel and Hassner in *Les Elections du 2 janvier 1956*, p. 221.

preferences in the electorate: the model outlined above suggests that parties are *actors*, shaping the attitudes and demands of their constituencies. Overlaying the search for a larger Conservative electorate and made necessary by that search, was the task of constructing a modern political party organization, a task undertaken by the secretary general of the Centre national des indépendants et paysans, Roger Duchet. It was an enterprise that, fatally for the Conservatives, would become intertwined with the cause of French Algeria. The Conservatives would remain a decentralized movement, a cadre party rather than a mass party. The notables would continue, even in Duchet's eyes, to form the principal apparatus of the movement.[100] Nevertheless, the utilization of subclass loyalties and local notables weakened after the Liberation as the agricultural sector contracted; urbanization would mean the nationalization of politics in both senses of the word.

To escape the regional and rural strongholds that had always provided the core of right-wing support in France, the *modérés* no longer repudiated the notion of becoming a party with a program and a greater degree of discipline. Endorsement by the Centre national became more important to candidates: the percentage of the vote won by candidates who had not obtained the imprimatur of Paris declined in the 1956 election, and a number of candidates without the CNIP label were beaten even *with* the support of local notables.[101] In the National Assembly the *modérés* continued to divide on many votes, and liberty of vote was retained. The 1954 Congress of the movement had instituted some collective control over participation in cabinets, however, and increasingly, deputies who disagreed with the rest of the group were willing to abstain rather than vote in opposition. Equally important, the volatile Conservative electorate seemed, with the disintegration of the Gaullists, to become somewhat more loyal to the movement.[102] As the coherence of the movement grew, Duchet

[100] Duchet, *La République épinglée*, p. 17.
[101] Philip Williams, *French Politicians and Elections, 1951-1969* (Cambridge: Cambridge University Press, 1970), p. 60.
[102] Survey cited in Merle, "Les Modérés," p. 274.

sought to ensure that French Algeria would become a symbol of its unity.

The nationalist strategy adopted by the Conservatives for these reasons seemed to be rewarded and reinforced in the by-elections of 1957; in one instance, the first sector of the Seine (Paris, Left Bank), they defeated Pierre Poujade himself. For Duchet, the lessons of electoral success were clear:

On the 13th of January, the voters of the first sector of the Seine indicated that France wished
—to affirm its rights in Algeria
—to combat the accomplices of Nasser
—to make defeatism fall back
—to refuse any extremist adventure[103]

The defense of French Algeria that was undertaken by the Conservatives after 1956, when combined with these electoral successes, made the group the principal source of cabinet instability in the final years of the Fourth Republic, a time when the survival of the regime required an active and coherent governmental majority. Since they sought to thwart certain types of reform in Algeria at a time when the political tide seemed to be running in their favor, the *modérés* could be less wary of overthrowing governments. The Conservatives caused the fall of the Mollet, Bourgès-Maunoury, and Gaillard cabinets; in the last two cases, Algeria was the issue in question.

The Fifth Republic and the decline of the Indépendants

Growing government instability and the apparent inability of the regime to deal with the Algerian question could only redound to the political benefit of the increasingly extremist *modérés*. The likely outcomes were either legislative elections, in which the Conservatives could hope at last to become the

[103] Louis Bodin and Jean Touchard, "L'Election partielle de la première circonscription de la Seine," *Revue Française de Science Politique* 7 (April-June, 1957), 281. The Conservative victory was labeled "a disaster for Poujade, but the triumph of Poujadism." Louis Bodin and Jean Touchard, "L'Election partielle de la première circonscription de la Seine," *RFSP* 7 (April-June, 1956), 286.

dominant party on the Right, or a government of public safety, grouping *Algérie française* forces across the political spectrum. Conservatives would form the core of such an alignment. The Conservatives had not counted on the intervention of Charles de Gaulle, however. While all of the Indépendants in the Assembly (save the inveterate *Pétainiste*, Jacques Isorni) had voted for de Gaulle's investiture, lack of enthusiasm among the *modérés* was evident. And prescient: having attached themselves to French Algeria, like many within the Gaullist movement, they were unable to detach themselves from their ideological commitment. A means of adaptation did not exist within the movement.

From the vantage point of the present, Duchet believes that the behavior of the *modéré* voters in 1958 sealed the fate of the movement: their exit to the Gaullists demonstrated the weak hold that the Conservatives had on their voters.[104] The evidence is hardly that clear, however. If the Indépendants had remained loyal coalition partners, there is reason to believe that they could have survived and prospered in the new regime, just as the rump of Républicains indépendants, led by Giscard d'Estaing, would flourish after 1962. Superficially, the results of the balloting in 1958 pointed to a continuing Conservative advance: their percentage of the vote increased, and their parliamentary group of 118 was second in size only to the Gaullists. While the *modérés* may have lost some of their former electors to the UNR, the success of the strategy pursued since 1956 seemed confirmed: the Poujadist voters whom they had cultivated were now part of their electorate.[105] The influence of the Conservative notables may also have been increased by the *scrutin d'arrondissement* and the tendency of the electorate to turn to established leaders in time of crisis.

Upon closer examination, the apparent success of the Indépendants also contained warning signs for the future. The Conservatives had benefited from the popularity of the Gen-

---

[104] Duchet's belief that the *modéré* voters simply became Gaullists in 1958 is expressed in *La République épinglée*, pp. 20-21.

[105] François Goguel, Alain Lancelot, and Jean Ranger, "Analyse des résultats," in *Le Référendum de septembre*, p. 372.

eral: when asked which party's objectives coincided best with those of the prime minister, the *modérés* were mentioned second only to the Gaullist formations among those responding.[106] The historical pattern in party loyalty on the part of the Conservative voters showed a steady strengthening of their attachment, *except* during the years of the RPF, when de Gaulle's hold on the right-wing electorate was demonstrated.[107] The Conservative voters were enthusiastic about the new regime, and they shared in the general disapproval of incumbent deputies and the parties of the Fourth Republic.[108] Another point of weakness for the Indépendants was the attraction which their Gaullist rival, the UNR, possessed for the urban electorate and the younger voters, those whom the Conservatives had been trying to attract with their nationalist appeal.[109]

These bits of evidence suggested that, in a choice between the Conservatives and either de Gaulle or the regime that he personified, the *modéré* voters would choose de Gaulle. The outlines of the new political landscape remained obscure, however, and a different reading could produce a different political strategy. The *modérés* had waged their campaign for the legislative elections in support of *Algérie française*, claiming that "for three years, the Indépendants had subordinated their entire policy to the salvation of French Algeria."[110] In sociological and political terms, the firmest supporters of French Algeria remained those on the political Right and those of higher social class and education.[111] The coalition that had supported the new regime and the government's majority in the Assembly substantially coincided with those who backed *Algérie française*. By emphasizing Algeria, the Conservatives would set themselves apart from de Gaulle and the UNR, but

---

[106] Georges Dupeux, Alain Girard, and Jean Stoetzel, "Une enquête par sondage auprès des électeurs," in *Le Référendum de septembre*, p. 143.

[107] Ibid., Table VII-1, p. 156; Table II, p. 181.

[108] Ibid., Tables II-1, II-2, pp. 151-152.

[109] Ibid., pp. 145, 160.

[110] CNIP, "Fiches de documentation, élections 1958."

[111] IFOP, *Sondages*, 1958, no. 4, pp. 23-25.

if the new regime operated like the previous one, those identity differences would prove valuable in carving out an electoral clientele. Such a strategy would prove particularly valuable if the Gaullists disintegrated as they had in 1952-1954. The Conservatives would then provide a haven for *Algérie française* sympathizers disillusioned by the shifting course of the new government.

These two sets of observations—the popularity of de Gaulle and the regime, the continued support of *Algérie française* by the *modéré* clientele—and the strategies derived from them pointed in different directions as de Gaulle moved away from an integrationist solution to the Algerian conflict. Divisions grew within the Conservative ranks between those who foresaw disaster in continuing to advocate resistance to Algerian decolonization and those who saw in *Algérie française* the movement's future, even as the movement as a whole opposed Gaullist policies for the economy, Europe, and the domestic political regime.

During the "week of the barricades" (24 to 30 January 1960), when the Algerian settlers placed the regime in question for the first time, Duchet and the Conseil national of the Centre national des indépendants seemed to condone the rebellion by sending a telegram of total solidarity to the deputies of Algeria and calling upon the President "to fulfill his constitutional role of arbiter and guarantor of the integrity of the Nation." The reaction by some of the parliamentarians to this apparent support for illegal acts was swift: Paul Reynaud and the Indépendant ministers broke their ties with Duchet's Centre. The National Congress of the movement, held at Paris in December, 1960, seemed to demonstrate the continued support of Conservatives for *Algérie française*, although the representative character of the gathering was questioned by some.

The opposition of the *modérés* to the Debré government on these issues—Algeria and Europe in particular—resembled the pattern of French politics under the former parliamentary regime: a party attempted to distance itself from its closest political rival, maintaining identity incentives for its followers. The combination of support for European integration, the

Atlantic alliance, and French Algeria also suggests the *ideological* weakness of the *modérés*. While this set of attitudes was characteristic of *Algérie française* die-hards within political and military circles, one can perceive its drawbacks as a nationalist appeal. Rather than the French "hexagon," so deeply engrained in the French public by the educational system, the *modérés* appealed to entities larger than France; they were supranationalists rather than nationalists. The common thread was anti-communism: the battle being waged across the Mediterranean was a battle on behalf of the entire West.

The first referendum on Algeria in January, 1961 revealed the weakness of electoral support for the cause of French Algeria and provided powerful ammunition within the Conservative movement for the supporters of the government. They seemed to succeed in 1961, when Duchet turned over his duties to Camille Laurens, an old colleague. The new model conservative party that Duchet had tried to construct seemed dead, killed by those that Duchet scornfully called "a club of parliamentarians." Sympathies for French Algeria lingered on. Even after Duchet's departure, the movement was the only group that failed to condemn the terrorists of the OAS.[112] Divisions prevented the Indépendants from taking a position on the second Algerian referendum, in which the electorate approved the Evian Accords ending the war. Even as the European settlers fled Algeria in 1962, the National Congress of the movement passed a resolution that condemned the policy of de Gaulle in Algeria.

Opposition to the government continued to grow among the Conservatives during 1962: the final split between movement and ministers came after de Gaulle's press conference of 15 May 1962, in which he scornfully dismissed certain concepts of European integration. The last straw was de Gaulle's proposal to revise the constitution in order to permit direct election of the President: the motion of censure that defeated

---

[112] Jean Charlot, "La Campagne des formations politiques," in *Le Référendum du 8 avril 1962*, ed. François Goguel (Paris: Armand Colin, 1963), p. 39.

the Pompidou government and brought legislative elections was opposed by only twelve Conservatives (who would become the core of the Républicains indépendants of Valéry Giscard d'Estaing) and was supported by 109 *modéré* deputies.

The 1962 elections were a catastrophe: only twenty-nine Indépendant deputies were elected; the vote for candidates of the Centre national fell from over four million in 1958 to less than two million, barely more than the resilient MRP. The most vehement partisans of *Algérie française* suffered the most, especially the twenty-four deputies who had voted for the Salan amendment. The *modérés* were effectively reduced to those rural and provincial bastions from whence they had come, enclaves in which the traditional politics of the notables were resistant to the appeals of the UNR.[113]

The end of French Algeria and the demise of the Conservatives

The reasons for the disappearance of the Conservatives do not lie solely in their inability to decolonize: opposition to de Gaulle sprang from more than one issue. In two ways, however, the effects of the political conflict over the future of Algeria contributed to their final disintegration. First, since a substantial and growing number of Conservative deputies were willing to support de Gaulle's course in Algeria, particularly after the referendum of January, 1961, the Algerian controversy exacerbated division within a perennially divided movement, blurring its identity in the eyes of the voters and causing it to appear sympathetic to extremists. Conservative supporters expect, even demand, unity from their representatives. The Gaullists were able to provide that appearance of unity; the Conservatives, on the other hand, appeared as the typical Fourth Republic band of squabbling politicians. Divisions persisted because the Conservatives had not completed the transition to a unified political party: they remained "half-organ-

[113] Janine Bourdin, "La Crise des Indépendants," *Revue Française de Science Politique* 13 (June, 1963), 443-445.

ized." The parliamentarians still exercised relative independence, yet they could not control those who opposed decolonization: the structure of power and the source of ideological control remained unclear. Activists brought into the *modéré* ranks by Duchet's efforts to build an organization were often drawn from the extreme Right; by creating an organization from the top down, the possibility that the organizational cadres would be unrepresentative of the Conservative electorate was increased.[114] This was particularly the case given the low level of political activity of Conservative voters.

Equally fatal to the chances for Conservative survival was the encouragement that Algeria offered to those who sought to play out a political strategy fitted to the old rules of the game. The ambiguous results of the 1958 elections, described above, encouraged Duchet and others to continue on the political trajectory that they had set in 1956, just as the Gaullists had reinforced their nationalism following the departure of de Gaulle and their 1956 setback. The choice of a strategy of opposition was influenced by the precedents of the Fourth Republic: How long before this Gaullism, like the RPF, would disintegrate, leading once again to de Gaulle's withdrawal from the political scene? Conservative behavior was governed by the preceding regime's rules: threatened with the possible exit of their voters, they *increased* their distance from the UNR, emphasizing ideological incentives to mark their distinctive identity. The *content* of Conservative ideology—a supranational support for the Atlantic alliance, European integration, and French Algeria—further complicated competition with de Gaulle. The *modérés* did not realize that the regime had changed, that the bipolarization induced by the presidential system meant their efforts to carve out an independent position on the Right were likely to fail. Their half-organized character also contributed to such misperceptions: the Conservative electorate was *not* in fact irreducibly loyal to the

[114] See for example, the description of the 1960 Congress in *Le Figaro*, 4 December 1960; the accusations of Paul Reynaud in the same journal on 16 January 1962.

movement. Despite the trappings of a political party, their willingness to exit would become apparent when forced to choose between the *modérés* and de Gaulle, between "chaos" and a painful decolonization.

An alternative strategy—non-ideological, supporting de Gaulle, relying upon the cautious notables to carve out a position at the *Center*—would be pursued with success by Républicains indépendants after 1962. Roger Duchet denounced this supple posture as opportunism and simple greed for office, an ironic inversion of the Gaullist critique of old-style Conservatives in the 1950s. Duchet had constructed a new model conservative formation vehemently attached to *Algérie française* just in time for it to be made obsolete by the new regime and the grant of independence to an FLN government in Algeria. He had endowed the movement with no means of maintaining its unity *and* adapting ideologically to its new milieu. Like the Gaullists of the Fourth Republic, the Conservatives continued along their previous trajectory. The former party of the notables had forgotten the first rule of behavior of that class: accept any regime that protects the social and economic position of the group and provides strong, even authoritarian, government. The value of that time-honored rule was demonstrated when a descendant of the loyalist *modérés*, Valéry Giscard d'Estaing, was elected President of the Fifth Republic in 1974.

THE BRITISH CONSERVATIVE PARTY: IDEOLOGICAL CHANGE AND POLITICAL SURVIVAL

In some accounts, the success of the British Conservatives in disengaging from their longstanding commitment to empire is easily explained: historical experiences of the Conservative elite had biased them toward accepting change in the colonial empire. While such an explanation points to significant advantages possessed by the Conservatives, one could argue just as plausibly that the party's longstanding attachment to empire made the likelihood of disruption *greater* than in the French cases. The ability of the Conservatives to escape the negative effects of decolonization requires additional explanations based on the content and role of party ideology, the party system, and the structure of power within the party. In all of these respects, the British Conservatives distinguished themselves from the French *modérés* and the Gaullists (pre-1958).

Both the content of Conservative ideology and its role in the party organization provided the Conservative leadership with flexibility in meeting changes in Britain's international environment. The existence of a dominion model and its transfer to Asian and African territories, after bitter struggle over India's future in the 1930s, meant that Britain possessed a crude theory of decolonization. Ironically, it was the more theoretical and ideological French who tended to muddle through from one colonial crisis to another. The assistance which the dominion model offered in decolonization should not be overemphasized, however: the question of *to whom* power would be transferred could be divisive, as the Conservative divisions over the settler colonies of Africa would attest.

The Depression years and the World War also pushed the attitudes of the Conservative elite in a direction favorable to decolonization. In opposition after 1945, a new political generation of Conservative leaders concentrated on internal affairs, convincing the electorate to return them to power by erasing their image as a party unconcerned with social welfare or full employment. Concentration upon domestic reforms and economic growth did not contribute to maintaining the imperial connection. The World War had confirmed British perceptions of their need for a continuing security relationship with the United States, which also tugged away from empire, particularly in the economic sphere. In marked contrast to the lessons absorbed by the Gaullist elite, the war had made clear that the Empire, whether the old dominions or the dependent territories, was a net *consumer* of security. The effect of these historical experiences (and here one is generalizing across a large number of individuals) was to push the British Conservative elite ahead of its French counterparts in the disengagement from empire.

Ahead, but by no means disengaged. Resistance within the party after 1945 would center upon three "empires," which, when threatened by changes in the international environment, aroused different points of resistance within the party:

The Empire as an economic bloc. The stimulus to resistance within the party would be postwar economic arrangements within the alliance with the United States, particularly the 1945 loan agreement, Bretton Woods, and General Agreement on Tariffs and Trade.

The Empire as a source of international status. With the end of British rule in India, Britain's empire of prestige centered upon the Middle East. The occasion for resistance within the party would be efforts made by Conservative governments to meet the demands of Arab nationalism, through concessions and, in the Suez invasion, by force.

The Empire as "kith and kin." This Empire included not only the Dominions of Canada, New Zealand, and Australia, but also those colonies in East and Central Africa with large settler populations. The latter cases, most comparable to French North Africa, aroused ideological resistance to African majority rule as well as opposition to decolonization by threatened economic interests.

Each tapped a different strand of those nationalist attitudes described in Chapter I, and the supporters of each would have to be circumvented for decolonization to succeed. Tracing the course of resistance in each case permits a better understanding of how the Conservative leadership was able to minimize the costs of decolonization to the party.

The Empire as an economic bloc: Last stand of the Tariff Reformers

Alliance with the United States affected many aspects of Britain's relations with the Empire, but few so directly as the economic relations between Britain and her dominions and colonies. In the postwar international economy, the American program meant opposition to all forms of preferential trading blocs, including that of the British Empire. Confronting the American demands were those within the party whose commitment to an imperial trading bloc had been reinforced by the experience of the 1930s and the war. British business and agriculture also remained attached to the system of controls and protection built up during the preceding decade.[115]

The pattern of resistance. In the debate on the American loan and Bretton Woods agreement, widespread opposition within the parliamentary party was apparent. The conditions attached to the loan seemed to commit Britain to dismantle imperial preference; these stipulations and the terms of the loan itself led to division within the Conservative parliamentary ranks that was not to be matched until the vote on Rhodesian oil sanctions in December, 1965.[116] Despite a two-line whip enjoining abstention, seventy-four Conservative M.P.'s opposed the financial arrangements and eight voted with the Labour government in their favor; a similar pattern of opposition characterized the Bretton Woods vote.[117]

At successive Annual Conferences in the postwar years, efforts were made to reinforce the commitment of the party to the Empire-Commonwealth as the principal organizing unit of Britain's external economic relations. At the 1948 Annual Conference, for example, two young imperial devotees, Julian Amery and Bernard Braine, tried to secure the denunciation of multilateral arrangements, such as GATT, to the degree that they limited imperial preference. The leaders of the party responded to this pressure with an image of Britain's external relations that symbolized the Conservative choice not to choose. Both Anthony Eden and Winston Churchill proposed "three immediate objectives" for British foreign policy, labeled the "three unities":

First, unity within the British Commonwealth and Empire. Second, unity with Western Europe. Third, unity across the Atlantic. These

[115] Richard N. Gardner, *Sterling-Dollar Diplomacy* (Oxford: Clarendon Press, 1956), pp. 18-19, 25, 32-33.

[116] Philip Norton, ed., *Dissension in the House of Commons* (London: Macmillan, 1975), p. 156n.

[117] Ibid., pp. 2-5.

three unities, I maintain—and I agree with my friend Mr. Amery—these three unities are not antagonistic, but complementary.[118]

Despite such efforts to appease those who favored maintaining the Empire as an economic bloc, disputes and amendments appeared at succeeding Annual Conferences, as some continued to urge greater reliance upon the Empire and Commonwealth rather than increased dependence upon the United States or closer economic ties with Europe.[119]

By the mid-1950s, such resistance had faded. Two developments account for this first and gradual decolonization of the party. The requirements of Britain's position in the international economy, as perceived by the Conservative leadership and most of the business coalition that supported the party, had changed in the decade after the war. The decision for multilateralism rather than a closed imperial economic system accorded with a resurgence of neo-liberalism within the party. The mercantilist requirements of managing an economic bloc and particularly the state intervention required were difficult to reconcile with the laissez-faire preferences of many Conservatives.

Just as the triumph of imperial preference in the 1930s had resulted from the intersection of changed economic requirements and the ideological attachment of a particular political generation, so the appearance of a new generation was a second reason for its decline within the party. The talented young men of "Butler's kindergarten" (Alport, Carr, Heath, Macleod, Powell), unlike the imperial ideologues of Milner's kin-

[118] National Union of Conservative and Unionist Associations. *Sixty-ninth Annual Conference* (Llandudno, 1948), p. 71.

[119] The motion by Duncan Sandys in favor of European unity was seconded by L. S. Amery in 1949, who made clear his perception of the limited Conservative commitment to Europe (*Annual Conference*, 1949, p. 63); in 1950 Amery moved an amendment that affirmed the need for economic cooperation in the Commonwealth (*Annual Conference*, 1950, pp. 34-35); in 1952 two motions were proposed, one urging amendment of GATT in those parts "injurious to Empire trade and development" (*Annual Conference*, 1952, pp. 50-51); the following year, Lord Balfour, chairman of the Commonwealth and Empire Industries Association, moved an addendum along the same lines (*Annual Conference*, 1953, pp. 61-63).

dergarten at the turn of the century, espoused a *domestic* strategy for the Conservative party: social reform was divorced from imperialism. In the parliamentary party, Berrington and Finer have discovered distinct cohorts in the 1950s that mark the shift from a Commonwealth to a European orientation: those M.P.'s who entered Parliament in 1950 or before were predominantly Empire supporters; beginning in 1951, the proportions begin to shift, and by 1955, the Europeans outnumbered the Empire contingent by nearly two to one.[120]

Effects on political outcomes. Lingering resistance by supporters of a Commonwealth economic stance by Britain could not force the party back from its commitment to the postwar multilateral economic framework, but it was able to hinder the substitution of Europe for the displaced Commonwealth. Leadership hesitation was apparent during the formulation of "Plan G," which argued for a European Free Trade Area.[121] By 1961, as African decolonization (and the resistance that it inspired) reached a climax, the Macmillan government moved toward negotiations for entry into the European Economic Community. The arguments for Europe that ultimately convinced Macmillan and his colleagues were those relating to Britain's international position, not the nation's economic well-being. The anti-communist appeal would prove useful in converting the party, just as it had served to justify the grant of independence to African colonies: "It is no longer a question of Europe or the Commonwealth or America—we need a united Free World."[122] Equally important was the role that Europe was expected to play in obtaining for Britain the status of a great power once again. Europe would become for the

[120] S. E. Finer, H. B. Berrington, and D. J. Bartholomew, *Backbench Opinion in the House of Commons, 1955-1959* (Oxford: Pergamon Press, 1961), p. 90.

[121] Harold Macmillan, *Riding the Storm, 1956-1959* (New York: Harper & Row, 1971), pp. 82, 85.

[122] Harold Macmillan, *Pointing the Way, 1959-1961* (New York: Harper & Row, 1972), p. 324.

Conservatives the substitute for empire, a new source of international prestige and influence.[123]

Despite these hopes for ideological adaptation, attachment to Commonwealth and Empire in the party remained the principal political obstacle to joining the Community:

> Certainly the Commonwealth aspects of the problem overshadowed all others—politically, economically and, above all, emotionally. The preferential trade arrangements, an important aspect of the Commonwealth link, had been a traditional part of Conservative policy for more than half a century.[124]

That part of industry and commerce represented by the Commonwealth Industries Association, as well as agriculture, the core Conservative interest that had destroyed the Peel cabinet in 1846, continued to oppose entry. Because of this ideological and economic resistance, the last stand of those who saw the Commonwealth as the principal external attachment of Britain, the government trod very warily: the splits of 1846 and 1903 were mentioned as possible precedents. Votes taken in Parliament on the question of application to the EEC (particularly that of 2-3 August 1961) demonstrated that opposition within the parliamentary party centered on those M.P.'s associated with the Commonwealth Industries Association. In the divisions of 8 November 1962 and 12 February 1963, there were no Conservative abstentions or cross-votes.[125]

Concern within the party continued, however, particularly

---

[123] As early as 1954, Julian Amery argued that Britain could draw together the Commonwealth and European systems to talk on equal terms with the superpowers; such an alliance would give Britain the opportunity "to lead the world once more." (*Annual Conference*, 1954, p. 30). See also memorandum from Lady Rhys-Williams to Macmillan in January, 1953 in *Tides of Fortune, 1945-1955* (New York: Harper & Row, 1969), p. 476. In the Central Office *Campaign Guide* (1964), this theme was prominent: ". . . a new unit of power has arisen in Europe in the shape of EEC, bound in the course of time to exert increasing political as well as economic influence" (p. 466).

[124] Harold Macmillan, *At the End of the Day, 1961-1963* (New York: Harper & Row, 1973), p. 7.

[125] Robert J. Jackson, *Rebels and Whips* (London: Macmillan, 1968), p. 175; Norton, *Dissension in the House of Commons*, pp. 189-190.

after the by-election reverses of 1962. Some Common Market opponents sought to organize the party rank and file to maintain the Commonwealth connection. The leadership prepared carefully, but the motions submitted to Annual Conference in 1962 suggest that their fears were overdrawn. Efforts by the Commonwealth die-hards Turton and Walker-Smith to amend the motion before the Conference in order to make it more favorable to the Commonwealth failed completely, attracting only about fifty votes of four thousand.[126]

A price had been paid, however, in this final effort to maintain the unity of the Conservative Party: the efforts to build in "safeguards" to appease domestic critics had not been carried out with sufficient attention to Britain's European interlocutors. Having surmounted the decolonization of his own movement, de Gaulle could afford impatience with the tergiversations of his British counterparts: he vetoed the British application. The party was left, between Empire and Europe, temporarily without an external ideological support.

The Empire of prestige: The Middle East and the Suez crisis

The Suez crisis of 1956 stimulated a different pattern of intraparty controversy, dividing the parliamentary party while solidifying the party outside Parliament in support of the government's intervention. It was in many respects an *elite* controversy; Suez also aroused the highest degree of conflict *between* parties of any episodes during decolonization. The Middle East imbroglio also tapped a different set of attitudes within the nationalist syndrome—those associated with international status and Britain's continued role as a great power. Brought to the fore were the dilemmas commonly associated with decolonization: the confrontation of colonial nationalism and national prestige.

Yet there was very little empire, in the strict sense of the word, in the Middle East. Apart from Cyprus and Aden, Britain exercised power through intermediaries and a web of dip-

---

[126] Macmillan, *At the End of the Day*, p. 140.

lomatic, military, and economic ties. Nevertheless, the challenge of Arab nationalism in this sphere of influence provoked one of the principal attempts at coercion in the history of British decolonization. As Anthony Nutting has remarked, "the more directly Britain exercised dominion over a vassal state, the readier it would seem were her statesmen to concede independence."[127] The unwillingness of the Conservative elite to concede change in the Middle East resulted from the coincidence of what remained of Britain's empire of prestige—that empire, formerly centered on India, which had assured British status as a world power—and an empire of interests which, in the case of petroleum, affected national autonomy and Britain's ability to play an independent role in world politics. The issue in 1956 was not the Suez Canal, but the future of an informal empire that had been carefully constructed in the Middle East, one that was now tottering under Nasser's attacks. The Middle East had become, in effect, an ideological substitute for the lost Indian Empire.

The pattern of resistance. At first, the willingness of the Conservative leadership to concede some of the narrowly military dimensions of the British position in the Middle East brought right-wing opposition. Negotiations to give up the military base on the Suez Canal led to the formation of a "Suez group" of parliamentary backbenchers. Their discontent with developments in Egypt found expression in informal organization, intervention in parliamentary debates, and statements of dissent at Annual Conference.[128] Final agreement on the withdrawal of British military forces from the Suez Canal Zone brought increased resistance from the group. Harry Legge-

[127] Anthony Nutting, *No End of a Lesson* (London: Constable and Co., 1967), p. 8.

[128] At the Annual Conference in October, 1953, Julian Amery had spoken in support of maintaining the base as the "hinge of our Imperial strength"; he claimed that "our mission in the Middle East is far from ended, and our responsibilities to its people as well as to the whole Commonwealth still require that British troops should remain in the Suez Canal" (*Annual Conference*, 1953, p. 31). On parliamentary resistance, Philip Goodhart, *The 1922* (London: Macmillan,1973), p. 172; Jackson, *Rebels and Whips*, p. 111.

Bourke resigned the Conservative whip on 14 July 1954; Charles Waterhouse resigned the chairmanship of the Conservative Defense Committee. Despite the appearance of Churchill, flanked by R. A. Butler and the secretary of state for war, Antony Head, before a meeting of backbenchers, the unity of the party was not preserved in the vote on the Suez agreement on 29 July 1954: twenty-eight Conservatives (including Legge-Bourke, now an Independent) voted against the government.[129] In the face of a unified cabinet and without the mobilized support of the party in the country, the immediate impact upon policy was slight, although limits to the tolerance of the parliamentary party had been set.

Growing Egyptian hostility to the Baghdad Pact—Britain's chief instrument of influence in the region—as well as the Egyptian-Czechoslovakian arms agreement in September, 1955, brought a pronounced hardening of the British position. The dismissal of General Glubb by King Hussein of Jordan on 1 March 1956, removing effective British influence over the Jordanian Army, seems to have been a turning point. Nasser came to be seen as a direct threat to the British position in the Middle East and her status as a great power.[130] The nationalization of the Suez Canal expanded the threat from the strategic to the economic realm—Britain's extensive petroleum investments. The precedent here was not the much-cited 1930s analogies of Eden, Macmillan, and others who opposed the "appeasement" of Nasser, but rather that of Mossadegh, overthrown with direct British and American assistance some years before.

The hard line taken by Eden after the nationalization brought

[129] Jackson, *Rebels and Whips*, pp. 111-112; Andrew Roth, *Enoch Powell* (London: MacDonald, 1970), p. 114; Norton, *Dissension in the House of Commons*, pp. 107-108.

[130] After the dismissal of Glubb, Eden noted: "Our general policy in the Middle East was founded on the need to protect British interests in Iraq and the Persian Gulf. The main threat to these interests was the growing influence of Nasser with his anti-Western ideology and collusion with Soviet Russia, especially in arms supply." Anthony Eden, *Full Circle* (Boston: Houghton Mifflin Co., 1960), p. 352.

no dissent in the cabinet: the full cabinet took the crucial decision of the crisis on 2 August: that force could be used if negotiations failed.[131] Second thoughts were expressed as Labour moved more clearly into opposition to the use of force, but most of the pressure from within the cabinet and the party during the crisis came from those urging coercion. Thomas described threats by Macmillan that his "own friends" in the party would not accept a negotiated settlement. The sentiments of the right-wing Suez group seemed to be accepted at the Annual Conference (11-13 October): an amendment proposed by Waterhouse, a leader of the Suez die-hards, was accepted by the assembled party members.

In the cabinet, the balance of opinion within the party made itself felt. Walter Monckton was the only open critic of Eden's course:

. . . I was the only member of the Cabinet who openly advised against invasion though it was plain that Mr. Butler had doubts and I know that Mr. Heathcoat Amory was troubled about it. Outside the Cabinet I was aware of a number of Ministers, apart from Mr. Nutting and Sir Edward Boyle who resigned, who were opposed to the operation . . . .[132]

At no point during the crisis did Conservative critics of Eden cross-vote with the opposition: resistance by the doves was confined to resignations (by two junior ministers, Anthony Nutting and Sir Edward Boyle), the communication of their opposition to the prime minister through the chief whip, and abstention. Eight of the opponents of the intervention ab-

[131] Hugh Thomas, *The Suez Affair* (London: Weidenfeld and Nicolson, 1967), p. 55; Lord Butler agrees that this decision was taken without dissent, despite his distaste for the hysterical analogies that were drawn with the 1930s: *The Art of the Possible* (Boston: Gambit, 1972), pp. 187-189.

[132] Lord Birkenhead, *Walter Monckton* (London: Weidenfeld and Nicolson, 1969), p. 308; Thomas, *The Suez Affair*, pp. 108, 116; Butler, *The Art of the Possible*, p. 189. Although portrayed as a "dove" in cabinet discussions, Butler's public statements took on the nationalist coloring favored within the party during the crisis; see, for example, *Our Way Ahead*, a party publication taken from a speech that he made on 11 October 1956.

stained in the vote of 8 November; on 28 November twenty-four M.P.'s signed an Early Day motion of criticism.[133]

The exercise of voice shifted from Left to Right with the decision to end British military action and withdraw the force engaged in the Suez Canal Zone: fifteen Suez group M.P.'s refused to vote for the government's withdrawal of British troops on 6 December.[134] Opposition continued into 1957, notably on 16 May, when the government announced that British ships would no longer be discouraged from using the Suez Canal. Of the fourteen die-hards who abstained on that occasion, eight also decided to resign the Conservative whip; some members of this irreducible core of dissidents would later reappear in more widespread opposition to African decolonization and joining the EEC.[135] The sympathies of the party rank and file were demonstrated by the disparity in treatment of the right-wing and left-wing Suez rebels. None of the former experienced serious difficulty with his constituency party, despite the extreme steps taken; critics of Eden's policy of coercion, however, did in many cases face hostility in their constituencies, and several were refused readoption.[136] The Suez group dissidents demonstrated the power that can be exercised by those who would find it most difficult to exit: by relying upon the attachment of the rank and file to core ideological precepts, such as nationalism, their position was secure.

[133] Thomas, *The Suez Affair*, p. 138; Harold Nicolson, *Diaries and Letters* (New York: Atheneum, 1968), p. 317; Jackson, *Rebels and Whips*, pp. 147-148.

[134] Apparently the number would have been larger but for bargaining by the chief whip: Andrew Roth, *Heath and the Heathmen* (London: Routledge & Kegan Paul, 1972), p. 111.

[135] Five of the eight who resigned the whip—Fell, Hinchingbrooke, Maitland, Maude, and Paul Williams—had also voted against the Anglo-Egyptian treaty in July, 1954; the other three were Biggs-Davison, Sir Victor Raikes, and Lawrence Turner. The course of right-wing dissidence is described in Jackson, *Rebels and Whips*, pp. 148-151.

[136] The contrast in constituency treatment of the two groups is discussed in Leon D. Epstein, *British Politics in the Suez Crisis*, (Urbana: University of Illinois Press, 1964), chap. 6.

Effects on political outcomes. Divisions within the party seem to have had little influence upon policy during the Suez crisis itself: the conflict over alternatives was played out in the cabinet; a turning point seems to have come with conversion of a number of the "war party" to support for withdrawal as international pressures mounted: ". . . the decisive point was reached when Mr. Macmillan was of the opinion that the United States would make our financial position impossible unless we called a halt."[137] Although defeated in the decision to withdraw, the Right did obtain the candidate for prime minister that it preferred in Harold Macmillan, the one-time hawk. And British policy in the Middle East did not change that dramatically after Suez, as later interventions in Jordan (1958) and Kuwait (1961) demonstrated. Macmillan felt the need to go slow on Cyprus in part because of the specter of right-wing dissent: "I have tried the Party pretty hard over Suez. I don't now want a panic about 'selling out in Cyprus.' Then there is 'disarmament.' . . . For all these reasons, I am not too keen on starting a new policy on Cyprus until *after* the House has risen."[138] A final influence on British policy can be detected in the development of nuclear weapons. In the spring of 1957 Macmillan noted the aid that Britain's first thermonuclear explosion gave in cushioning the impact of Suez: the new weapons seemed to guarantee, not only a "bigger bang for the buck" but also the continued status of Britain as a world power.[139]

The Suez crisis also affected the pattern of dissidence within the Conservative Party. The overlap of the Suez group with the proponents of Commonwealth trading arrangements had been slight up to this point: only four of the twenty-eight

[137] Birkenhead, *Walter Monckton*, p. 308; Thomas, *The Suez Affair*, p. 146; Macmillan, *Riding the Storm*, pp. 163-166.

[138] Macmillan, *Riding the Storm*, p. 661. Not until Makarios accepted British sovereignty over the bases was Macmillan able to breath a sigh of relief; see his diary entry for 18-19 February 1959, ibid., p. 237.

[139] Ibid., p. 237. Andrew J. Pierre, *Nuclear Politics: The British Experience with an Independent Strategic Force 1939-1970* (Oxford: Oxford University Press, 1972), pp. 176, 87.

Conservatives who voted against the Suez agreement in July 1954 had also voted against the American loan and Bretton Woods agreements in 1945. The coincidence of the Suez group with those who opposed the end of Britain's African empire would be greater: the Middle Eastern crisis gave birth to a "foreign policy Right" that would persist into the 1960s.[140]

An Empire of kith and kin: East and Central Africa

Before 1959 African policy had aroused little debate within the Conservative Party. West Africa in particular, although the scene of rapid political advance, remained outside domestic political conflict, as it had in France. Two areas within the colonial empire were marked as exceptions to the Westminster model of majority rule and self-government within the Empire, however. The fortress colonies, fragments of the axis between London and Calcutta, were now alleged to serve strategic ends in the eastern Mediterranean and the Indian Ocean. The future status of Cyprus, linked to the Suez debacle, aroused the greatest furor within the party, but Singapore, Hong Kong, Aden, Malta, Gibraltar, and even Kenya were placed in this category of dependencies.

Conservative policy foresaw two different sorts of obstacles to independence in East and Central Africa—the precondition of economic and social progress, and, most important, the European population: 60,000 in Kenya and about 300,000 in the Federation of the Rhodesias and Nyasaland. The doctrine of partnership became the proclaimed basis of Conservative policy in these settler colonies; the symbol of that doctrine was the Central African Federation. Partnership fitted well with Conservative ideology. Just as the party repudiated class conflict in Britain in favor of "one nation," so partnership was proclaimed as the solution to racial conflict in Africa. The concept acquired some of the power that integration possessed among the French partisans of Algérie française: a "liberal" solution that would benefit all members of the colonial population. The same fatal flaws marked the two doctrines:

[140] Finer, Berrington, and Bartholomew, *Backbench Opinion*, p. 106.

a failure to recognize equality among *collectivities* and a devolution of the interpretation of partnership (or integration) to the European population in Africa. In settler eyes, it came to mean, in the words of a prime minister of Southern Rhodesia, the "partnership of horse and rider." At best, partnership was equated with the dictum of Cecil Rhodes—"equal rights for all civilized men"—with the criteria for civilization set by the European settlers.

Should the British Government enforce partnership against resistance by the majority African population? The Conservatives answered yes with the foundation of the Central African Federation; the Labour Party answered no, splitting the postwar colonial consensus in British politics. The costs of the decision in the early 1950s were slight, and the backing given the Kenyan and Rhodesian settlers was seldom questioned; a West African model for political advance was rejected:

The [African nationalists] forget that conditions in British colonies on the West Coast are very different from those in the Rhodesias and Nyasaland where the European is almost entirely responsible for the economic development that has taken place, and most important of all, where he has made his home. He is not a bird of passage but is there to stay, and his children after him. . . . It is not on a basis of domination of one race by another that the future of Central Africa will develop but by a policy of partnership between the two races. No other course is possible.[141]

The response of the Conservative government to renewed African resistance after 1959 ended the party's unity on African policy. Violence in Nyasaland in early 1959, resulting in the deaths of fifty-two Africans and the detention without trial of over one thousand, suddenly forced the issue of the future of the settler colonies into British domestic politics. The report of the Devlin Commission, appointed by the Macmillan cabinet, demolished claims by the Federal government that Africans had contrived a "murder plot" and made other criticisms of the handling of the disorders. The cabinet's situation

[141] Conservative Research Department, *A Bi-Monthly Survey of Commonwealth and Colonial Affairs,* special issue (20 June 1952), p. 8.

was made more difficult by revelations in the same month of the deaths of eleven Africans at the Hola detention camp in Kenya, the result of beatings by prison guards.

Macmillan managed to stall on the future of Central Africa until the 1959 election gave him a larger majority in the House of Commons and added flexibility with the party. The most important element in the decisions of the Macmillan cabinet to accede to African demands for independence, demands that implied the end of the Central African Federation, was the risk involved in any coercive policy to support the European settlers in East and Central Africa. Macmillan had never been a devotee of empire; for the prime minister, the great struggle of the postwar era was that between democracy and communism: resistance to nationalism meant risking a turn by the colonial populations toward the Soviet bloc. It was this logic that he presented in his "wind of change" speech at Cape Town on 3 February 1960. An equally important justification for accelerating the pace of African decolonization, however, was the threat of violence. Sir Roy Welensky recalled Macmillan's refusal to support his demands that at least part of Northern Rhodesia be retained in the Federation, whatever the demands of African nationalists:

After all, many things can be put down by force. We could have held Cyprus if we had used German tactics—stringing men up in the villages and shooting people wholesale. In Algeria the French have a million men under arms, and they have now suffered a humiliating defeat. It is too simple a reading of history to think that you can exercise control simply by the use of power. Indeed, I cannot guarantee that British troops would undertake the kind of duties that would be necessary.[142]

Iain Macleod, the new colonial secretary who would oversee the change of course in Africa, agreed that "the heart of the argument" for the acceleration in African advance was that "any other policy would have led to terrible bloodshed."[143]

[142] Sir Roy Welensky, *Welensky's 4,000 Days* (London: Collins, 1964), pp. 323-324.
[143] Iain Macleod, "Trouble in Africa," *The Spectator*, 13 January 1964, p. 127.

The pattern of resistance. Others within the Conservative Party calculated the relative costs of coercion and accelerated change differently. As in the Suez case, resistance to Macleod's African initiatives was greatest among the parliamentarians; unlike Suez, the resistance was solely right-wing and was supplemented by the lobbying of the settler spokesmen and by those economic interests in Britain that feared the consequences of African rule. Their role is described in Chapters IV and V.

Despite the fears of Macmillan, Kenya proved the least divisive case in its effects on the party: the small size of the European population and the changing composition of the Kenyan economy produced local acquiescence, which was reflected in London. Kenyan Europeans responded to the release of the nationalist leader, Jomo Kenyatta, with less hostility than either Conservative parliamentary opinion or the colonial administration in Kenya. The future of the Central African Federation, with its far larger European population, and the repercussions of Katangan secession in the Congo stirred greater discord in the parliamentary party.

An African government in either Nyasaland or Northern Rhodesia was likely to demand secession from the white-dominated Federation. The secession of Nyasaland, an economic liability for the other partners, would probably have been conceded by Sir Roy Welensky, the Federal prime minister, but for the precedent set for Northern Rhodesia with its vital copper resources. The future of the Federation would be determined in February, 1961 by the outcome of the Northern Rhodesia constitutional conference, which would decide either for African majority rule or continued European predominance. Macmillan saw the crisis looming, though characteristically he exaggerated it:

If we lean too much to the European side:
1. [African] confidence in Her Majesty's Government will be undermined.
2. There will be serious disorder in Northern Rhodesia, perhaps spreading throughout the Federation.
3. [Some Ministers] will resign.
4. Our Government and Party will be split in two.

If, on the other hand, we make a decision which, without satisfying African demands, goes in their general favour:

1. Europeans will have no faith left in Her Majesty's Government.
2. Sir Roy Welensky will declare the Federation to be 'independent' and will try to take over the Government of Northern Rhodesia by force or bluff or both.
3. If the Governor defends his position, there will be civil war—Europeans versus British officials, troops and Africans.
4. [Other Ministers] will resign.
5. Our Government and Party will be split in two.[144]

The divisions within the parliamentary party that so worried the prime minister surfaced with an Early Day Motion tabled on 8 February 1961 by one of the most senior Conservative backbenchers, Robin Turton. The motion warned against taking a course in Northern Rhodesia that would lead to African majority rule. The usual die-hards were the first to sign, some of them former members of the Suez group—Paul Williams, Anthony Fell, John Biggs-Davison, Patrick Wall—but they were joined on this occasion by the center of the parliamentary party, an ominous development. These more moderate backbenchers were concerned with the long-standing British commitment to the Europeans of Central Africa and by the pace of change envisaged by Macleod. In two weeks, the number of signatures on the motion rose to 102, and then fell back to 87 (of 365 Conservative M.P.'s). Keatley attributes the success of the cabinet in avoiding an embarrassing defeat to the work of the party whips, as well as vigorous counter-lobbying by Macleod's liberal allies within the Party—Nigel Fisher, Humphrey Berkeley, Christopher Chataway—who tabled a motion of support attracting forty signatures.[145]

Before the Rhodesian imbroglio could be resolved, however, another severe internal crisis occurred, this time on the question of Katanga. The efforts of Tshombe's government to secede from the Republic of the Congo affected both the neigh-

---

[144] Macmillan, *At the End of the Day*, p. 309.
[145] Patrick Keatley, *The Politics of Partnership* (Baltimore: Penguin, 1963), p. 457.

boring Central African Federation and influential British economic interests. Both sought a regime in Katanga that was "stable, Westward-looking and friendly. Tshombe's provincial government seemed to represent all these things pretty well."[146] As early as 10 July 1960 Macmillan recorded pressure to support a declaration of independence by Katanga from Welensky, his allies in the Conservative Party, and the concerned business interests.[147]

The arrest of Tshombe on 28 April 1961 brought efforts by a familiar core of dissidents: an Early Day motion calling upon the British government to work for his release drew ninety-one signatures; the sponsors included Fell, Biggs-Davison, and Williams. The advance of United Nations forces against Katanga in the autumn of 1961 caused the greatest uproar, however: a British government seemed to be supporting the destruction of a friendly African government on the borders of one of its own colonies, endangering British investments at the same time. While Macmillan noted restiveness in the party after ten years in power, he could not have expected the resistance that was occasioned by the government's announcement on 8 December that it had decided to supply twenty-four 1,000-pound bombs to the United Nations forces. Macmillan's concern grew when the discontent spread, as it had in February, from "the small group of people who really hate me" to "the whole *centre* of the Party."[148] The absence of the foreign secretary aggravated the discontent, but Macmillan managed to quell the revolt. His technique on this occasion, which he compared to Suez in seriousness, was a model of the resources of the prime minister in controlling the exercise of voice: supplementary questions by the opposition permitted Macmillan to defend the government's actions; a meeting with the Executive of the 1922 Committee reestablished communication with the disgruntled backbench-

---

[146] Lord Alport, *The Sudden Assignment* (London: Hodder & Stoughton, 1965), p. 95.

[147] Macmillan, *Pointing the Way*, p. 263.

[148] Macmillan, *At the End of the Day*, p. 451; on the state of the party, p. 38.

ers; and finally, the behavior of the opposition in the parliamentary debate solidified the party, as it had during the Suez crisis.[149]

Parliamentary ferment at this time found little echo among the party rank and file. The Conservative Commonwealth Council, which had become a haven for Conservative activists interested in the colonial empire, was a source of opposition to the new pace of African advance. Its ability to influence the government was hindered by its organizational and financial dependence on the party, and the supporters of Macleod also prevented it from putting an authoritative stamp on its right-wing views.[150] A second group, somewhat outside the formal Conservative organization, would be of greater importance in the future: the Monday Club. The Monday Club broke with the pattern of Conservative groups concerned with external policy: it was not dominated by M.P.'s and remained primarily an extraparliamentary organization. Founded in January, 1961 by four young Tories discontented with Macmillan's policies at home and in the colonial empire, the Monday Club was transformed after 1964 from a ginger group into a mass organization, opposing the Labour government and its policies of sanctions against Rhodesia.[151] Despite its significance as a link between the right-wing opposition to decolonization and the future "new Right" within the Conservative Party of the 1960s and 1970s, their influence upon the course of decolonization, at least before Rhodesia's unilateral declaration of independence in 1965, was insignificant.

These Conservative groups allied with parliamentary resistance to Macleod's policies in Africa; they were less successful in mobilizing the party rank and file. The attitude of party activists, as represented at the Annual Conferences, is remarkable for its relative quiescence during the years of African decolonization. The two Conferences during Macleod's

[149] Ibid., pp. 451-452; Goodhart, The 1922, p. 181.

[150] David Goldsworthy, Colonial Issues in British Politics, 1945-1961, (Oxford: Clarendon Press, 1971), p. 285.

[151] Patrick Seyd, "Factionalism within the Conservative Party: The Monday Club," Government and Opposition 7 (Autumn 1972), 470-472.

tenure as colonial secretary (1960 and 1961) witnessed none of the uproar that the parliamentary party experienced. Macmillan's logic of anti-communism—concessions could prevent more radical and less desirable alternatives—pervaded the debates.[152] An analysis of the motions submitted to the Conference by the constituency parties from 1955 to 1963 confirms the impression derived from the debates. The attention paid to external affairs, including colonial affairs, was strikingly low. Only two related questions drew a greater response from the party activists: immigration, which was forced on to the party agenda, and the Common Market.[153]

Effects on political outcomes. Resistance within the cabinet and parliamentary party on the Northern Rhodesia question, as well as Kenyatta's release and the application to the Common Market, made itself felt in the constitutional plans for Northern Rhodesia. The June 1961 proposals differed significantly, and in favor of the Europeans, from those of February. But the effects of the final and powerful show of resistance in 1961 within the parliamentary party in the longer term were slight. Macleod was replaced at the Colonial Office by Reginald Maudling, but the new minister continued to press for the same policies. The decision taken in February, 1962 to propose a new constitution for Northern Rhodesia that would give a slight majority to the African population produced the expected burst of opposition from Sir Roy Welensky, who made yet another pilgrimage to London, and from his Conservative supporters. Forty M.P.'s signed a relatively mild motion tabled by Patrick Wall, but the cabinet held firm. Apparently Maudling threatened to resign if the constitutional proposals were not accepted.[154] The expected victories of African nationalists in Northern Rhodesia and the Rhodesian Front in Southern Rhodesia in the elections of late 1962 meant

---

[152] National Union, *Eightieth Annual Conference* (Brighton, 11-14 October 1961), p. 20.

[153] The data on conference motions was drawn from the National Union, *Programme of Proceedings* for each Conference.

[154] W. P. Kirkman, *Unscrambling an Empire* (London: Chatto and Windus, 1966), pp. 99-100; Macmillan, *At the End of the Day*, p. 320.

the end of the Federation. As the crisis over Rhodesia UDI in 1965 would demonstrate, however, it did not mean the end of the hold that "kith and kin" had upon the Conservative Party.

CONSERVATIVES AND THE DISENGAGEMENT FROM EMPIRE

Because of their ideological attachments to empire, all of the conservative political formations paid an organizational price during decolonization. Their sensitivity to changes on the periphery was transmitted into the metropolitan political order: in some cases, the result was severe (cabinet instability and ultimately change of political regime); in others, less so (a halting or compromised change of policy). In each case, party elites confronted colonial nationalism helped or burdened by certain domestic political facts, but ultimately their choices of strategy amplified or reduced the sensitivity of their organizations to external change and the secondary effects that it produced in the domestic political order and external policy.

A final comparison of the British Conservatives, the best example of political survival after disengagement from empire, with their French counterparts, permits an evaluation of the reasons for differences in domestic consequences. Changes in *ideological content* that had occurred before the years of decolonization were remarked upon above: they gave the British Conservatives certain advantages over their French counterparts, but did not eradicate the hold that the Empire had on the party. Ideological division did ease the task of the Conservative leadership in another way. The "Empire" was in fact several empires, each touching upon a different strand in the nationalist syndrome of attitudes—the Empire as an economic bloc, the Empire as a source of international status (the Middle Eastern sphere of influence), and the Empire as "kith and kin" (the dominions and settler colonies of Africa). Each of these facets of empire, when threatened by changes in the international environment, aroused different points of resistance within the party. Since the foci of opposition rarely over-lapped, the Conservative leadership faced a fragmented opposition. Finally, the *role* of ideology and ideological incentives was reduced in the life of the party after 1945; purposive rather than identity incentives were emphasized by the leadership, at least until a reaction by the new Right against this "end of ideology" appeared in the early 1960s.

The discussion of exit and voice suggested the value of the British *party system* in easing ideological adaptation, particularly in the barriers to exit that it imposed upon the ideologically committed. The presence of a clear opposition controlled the dissent of those who might resist changes by offering only *one* alternative government, and one that, on colonial issues, was even less acceptable to Conservative die-hards than the most liberal of Conservative cabinets. In the parliament of the French Fourth Republic, factions and parties could overturn cabinets and be assured that the succeeding cabinet would not differ greatly from the ministry just defeated; the new cabinet might well suit the dissidents better. As new political formations lacking the institutionalization of the British Conservatives, the French parties, for most of the 1950s, faced a highly competitive political milieu with low barriers to exit among their electorate. Struggling to imprint their identities upon potential supporters, the French Conservatives and the Gaullists relied upon identity incentives and particularly nationalist appeals. Unlike the British Conservative leadership, they lacked a reserve of loyalty that would have permitted a disengagement from ideological commitments and reduction in reliance on identity incentives.

Institutionalization also influenced another advantage possessed by the Conservative Party in overcoming the impact of decolonization: the *structure of power* within the party. The barriers to exit posed by the party system did not prevent the appearance of resistance within the party: as Hirschman has observed, the absence of possibilities for exit may lead to increased exercise of voice. The party had in the past been rent by conflicts inspired by changes in the international environment or differing external orientations. The typical portrait of a unified Conservative Party, dominated by its leadership, disappears when one turns from domestic policy to external questions. Before World War II, prime ministers were threatened, backbench revolts organized, and the party faithful mobilized on questions of international import: Tariff Reform, the only instance in recent history of the Conservatives putting forward "a major radical innovation"; the revolt over the promise of dominion status for India, led by Winston Churchill in the 1930s; and appeasement, which marked political careers for decades.[155]

These prewar examples suggest not only the indirect impact that international events could have upon the party, but also the power that the leadership possessed in controlling dissent, although not always without concessions in policy. As an institutionalized party, the pattern of power within the Conservative organization had been established in its essential features by the turn of the century; in the French cases, ambiguity characterized the roles and relative influence of the constituent parts of the organizations. Under Duchet, the French *modérés* remained "half-organized," with no clear sense of the locus of final ideological and strategic choice. Even the Gaullists saw the development of an alternative to the centralized and hierarchical plan of the RPF in the stance of Jacques Soustelle, apostle of a Gaullism without de Gaulle. Because the French parties were new organizations they lacked the numerous historical precedents undergirding perceptions of power within the British Conservative party.

Despite these advantages, one should not overestimate the security of the British Conservative leaders. As McKenzie notes

---

[155] The Tariff Reform controversy is discussed by Bernard Semmel, *Imperialism and Social Reform* (New York: Doubleday-Anchor, 1968), chaps. 4, 5, and 7; Blake, *The Conservative Party from Peel to Churchill*, chap. 6; and Robert J. Scally, *The Origins of the Lloyd George Coalition: The Politics of Social-Imperialism, 1900-1918* (Princeton: Princeton University Press, 1975), chap. 4. The best published account of the revolt over India is Gillian Peele, "Revolt over India," in *The Politics of Reappraisal, 1918-1939*, ed. Gillian Peele and Chris Cook (London: Macmillan, 1975), pp. 114-145. For the party conflict on appeasement: Neville Thompson, *The Anti-Appeasers* (Oxford: Oxford University Press, 1971).

in his revision of Lowell, "when appointed, the Leader leads, and the party follows, except when the party decides not to follow, then the Leader ceases to be Leader."[156] Determining the pattern of power empirically across a number of cases remains difficult: a "one-dimensional" view of power does not give an accurate picture of the party, since conflict is often disguised; the means of communication within the organization are such that the *anticipation* of resistance from a given quarter may cause certain issues to be avoided. In other words, the problem of nondecision complicates estimates of power distribution. *Bargaining within a coalition* is perhaps the best description of the character of a party's internal life; Richard Rose has described both British party organizations as "bargaining among barons."[157] Each member of the party coalition realizes (and here the party system is important) that, while refusing to compromise may bring temporary concessions, simultaneous refusal to compromise by several constituents of the coalition would bring great losses, in the form of probable electoral defeat. Nevertheless, at times, internal conflict has been forced, even at that cost: "while major conflicts . . . have occurred rarely, they have had cataclysmic consequences."[158]

Why then did the parts of the British Conservative party most committed to the imperial connection not push their expression of voice to the point of destructive internal conflict?

Apart from the effects of the party system in containing the exercise of voice and the power of institutional memory in recalling the costs of past strife, the opponents of change in the British party found themselves in a weak bargaining position. The principal pockets of resistance were found among the parliamentary backbenchers and the party rank and file;

---

[156] R. T. McKenzie, *British Political Parties*, 2nd ed. (New York: Frederick A. Praeger, 1963), p. 145.

[157] Richard Rose, *The Problem of Party Government* (London: Macmillan, 1974), p. 165.

[158] Michael Pinto-Duschinsky, "Central Office and 'Power' in the Conservative Party," *Political Studies* 20 (March, 1972), 12-13. This is an excellent account of the internal relations of power in the party.

from that base, they were unable to mount an effective campaign to thwart policies that they opposed.

Within the parliamentary party and outside it, one principal bargaining weakness was the lack of an alternative leader. Here, in contrast to the French Conservatives, the party's tradition of hierarchical organizations set one necessary condition for a successful opposition. Success or near-success of efforts in the past had resulted from the presence of someone of national stature, well-known in the party, at the head of the revolt, a Joseph Chamberlain or a Winston Churchill. The opponents of decolonization after 1945 lacked such a figure: the cabinet remained united throughout the Suez crisis and the acceleration of African decolonization under Iain Macleod. The nearest to a leader of resistance to the imperial retreat was Lord Salisbury, who resigned in 1956 upon the release of Archbishop Makarios, at a time when the party was still divided following the Suez intervention. As Lord Kilmuir discovered, however, his resignation, the only resignation of a cabinet minister on an issue of decolonization, was hardly a threat:

Earliest indications of Conservative reaction to the news were very startling. One area chairman, forewarned by telephone of the impending announcement, enquired, with genuine incomprehension, who Lord Salisbury was. The party as a whole, far from being dismayed, was blankly bewildered. Within a week the matter was virtually forgotten.[159]

Despite severe conflict within the cabinet during the decolonization of the settler colonies in Africa, the doctrine of collective responsibility held. The united front presented by the cabinet strengthened the bargaining advantages of the leadership vis-à-vis the outer parts of the Conservative coalition.

As the cases suggest—and the British party in this instance runs parallel to its French analogues—the most persistent and dangerous locus of resistance to decolonization was the parliamentary party, that stratum within the Conservative Party with a well-defined attitude toward external affairs but no

[159] Earl of Kilmuir, *Political Adventure* (London: Weidenfeld and Nicolson, 1964), p. 62.

responsibility for governing. As even the theoretician of prime ministerial government, Richard Crossman, admits, "the opposition that a Government really has to fear comes not from the official opposition on the other side of the House, but from those who are prepared to organize rebellion in the ranks behind it, and who can and do extort substantial concessions by the threat of withdrawing their votes."[160] Most of the disciplinary sanctions described in the textbooks—dissolution of Parliament, exclusion from the party, withdrawal of the whip—are seldom employed and probably would not work if they were used.[161] Exclusion from office in the future is probably the most effective weapon of the leadership; their principal task, however, is not the suppression of dissent with sanctions, but its anticipation, so that sanctions need not be imposed. The constituency parties did serve to keep some wayward M.P.'s in line, but the local associations function in relative autonomy, and they proved to be selective in their discipline: during the Suez crisis they acted against dissidents who dissented toward Labour even though their dissent was mild. The right-wing rebels, though taking such extreme steps as resigning the whip, experienced little difficulty with their local parties.

In dealing with voice within the parliamentary party, the Conservative leadership also possessed two additional instruments. Often, concessions were made, though seldom publicly. The influence of the right-wing M.P.'s was felt: after Suez, they caused Macmillan to delay a policy initiative on the Cyprus question; their threatened opposition to the European Common Market increased the cabinet's equivocation; repeated waves of rebellion in 1961, while not altering the aims of British policy in Africa, were able to slow somewhat the transfer of power. Perhaps the most significant bargaining counter in controlling the scale of dissent was in the hands of the opposition rather than the leadership of the Conservative Party: too great a show of resistance might cause the resig-

[160] Richard Crossman, *Inside View: Three Lectures on Prime Ministerial Government* (London: Jonathan Cape, 1972), p. 9.

[161] An evaluation of the sanctions available can be found in Jackson, *Rebels and Whips*, chap. 9, and in Pinto-Duschinsky, "Central Office," pp. 11-12.

nation of the government and the institution of a Labour cabinet. During the Suez crisis and the Conservative rebellion over Katanga in December, 1961, the intense opposition of Labour strengthened the hand of the Conservative cabinet against its own backbenchers.[162]

The Conservative Party outside Parliament is divided into two parts: Central Office with its network of constituency agents throughout Britain, and the National Union of Conservative and Unionist Associations, representing the party rank and file. Although the control of the leader of the party over Central Office has often been exaggerated, the possibility that Central Office would become a haven for ideological extremism like Duchet's Centre national des indépendants in France was very slight. The task of Central Office was winning elections; of all the parts of the party it was perhaps the most attuned to purposive rather than ideological incentives.

The party rank and file, on the other hand, *did* expect certain ideological incentives, and the Empire-Commonwealth had long been a principal part of Conservative identity. Despite the relative weakness of the party activists within the Conservative coalition—they possessed no mandate to direct the parliamentary party or the Central Office—activity by party members in the constituencies was necessary if the party were to remain in power. One technique employed by the leadership in gatherings of the party faithful was to reiterate their attachment to the Empire and Commonwealth, a statement of faith that had little to do with the operational realities of Conservative policy. This division between operational and fundamental ideology was noticed and criticized by a Commonwealth enthusiast in 1957: ". . . today, after six years of Tory rule all we get is the occasional platitude, the occasional remark by a Minister, 'I put the Commonwealth first,' but with no enthusiastic or practical policies."[163] While debates

---

[162] Macmillan comments on this point in *Pointing the Way*, pp. 451-452.

[163] National Union of Conservative and Unionist Associations, *Seventy-seventh Annual Conference* (Brighton, 10-12 October 1957), p. 104. The distinction between fundamental and operative ideology is made by Martin Seliger, *Ideology and Politics* (New York: Free Press, 1976).

at Annual Conference seemed to indicate a strong attachment to the imperial orientation, parliamentary rebels were never able to threaten the leadership with embarrassment at Annual Conference, despite repeated attempts on the question of Commonwealth economic ties and later the Common Market. After the mid-1950s, cross-pressures on the party rank and file grew as the issue of immigration became more prominent. Immigration, pointing to the politically unpleasant consequences of a closer Commonwealth tie, perhaps more than any other issue weakened the hold of Empire and Commonwealth upon the Conservative Right.[164]

As leaders of a mature political organization and one that was situated in a bipolar system of political competition, the Conservative elite could also shift the incentive structure of the party, reducing the use of ideological incentives dependent upon the symbolism of empire. The fact that the Conservatives held power from 1951 to 1964, a period that encompassed most of British decolonization, eased their task. The responsibility of governing not only speeded the ideological adaptation of the Conservative elite, it also offered them additional resources in their bargaining with those who resisted decolonization. Their success in dealing with the ideologically committed in the party is indicated by the absence of a significant extreme Right reaction to decolonization, a principal contrast with the French experience. Only the League of Empire Loyalists, whose roots lay in the British Union of Fascists and whose successors would include the National Front, could be described as springing from the crisis of decolonization, and their "unorthodox methods" only went as far as heckling, particularly at the 1958 Annual Conference of the party. After that widely publicized incident, pressure was applied to cause Conservatives to leave the League, and the group quickly declined.[165]

In the task of controlling voice within the party, the Con-

---

[164] Paul Foot, *The Rise of Enoch Powell* (London: Cornmarket Press, Ltd., 1969), pp. 37-38.

[165] George Thayer, *The British Political Fringe* (London: Anthony Blond, Ltd., 1965), pp. 58-660.

servative leaders enjoyed a final bargaining advantage: the attitudes of the electorate, which gave little sign of providing the raw material for resistance to decolonization. After the heavy by-election reverses of 1962, Macmillan checked with Central Office to determine the cause of the Conservative setbacks: "One thing that emerges with absolute clarity is that the popular reasons such as pensions, Schedule A, nuclear disarmament and Colonial policy, had nothing whatever to do with the result."[166] The 1959 election was marked by a lack of interest on the part of both Labour and Conservatives in the Empire: an analysis of election addresses shows that half the Conservative candidates said nothing about the Commonwealth.[167] The contrast with the state of the French electorate after 1954 could not be more striking: only the voters' attentiveness and concern with external affairs gave party dissidents the means of making their opposition stick. In Britain, the efforts of the Conservative cabinets to avoid costly efforts at containing colonial nationalism played an important role: prolonged conflict, causing inflation, higher taxes, or the death of conscripts might have changed the apathy of the electorate.

The possibilities for exit and voice posed more severe obstacles to the decolonization of the French Right, at least before 1958. The ideological givens—particularly the wartime experience of the Gaullists—made them less predisposed to concede a looser framework for the empire and more willing to interpret changes on the periphery as a Communist plot and a threat to the core of French national being. The party system, far from eliminating the prospect of exit, made it a constant threat to these poorly institutionalized parties, especially in the period between de Gaulle's withdrawal from public life and the institution of the Fifth Republic. A nostalgic nationalism seemed to offer some hope of differentiation from rivals and coalition building within a competitive political milieu. Finally, postwar efforts at organizing the French Right

[166] Macmillan, *At the End of the Day*, p. 63.
[167] D. E. Butler and Richard Rose, *The British General Election of 1959* (London: Macmillan, 1960), p. 132.

led to considerable ambiguity in the pattern of power and bargaining advantage within the coalitions of both the Gaullists and the French *modérés*. Antoine Pinay, by far the most popular leader of the French Conservatives, remained virtually isolated in his liberal attitude toward decolonization, despite the absence of an alternative leader; even de Gaulle was challenged by Soustelle in the name of French Algeria and a new conception of Gaullist organization. At the parliamentary level, collegiality of a nearly anarchic variety seemed the rule, and the party organizations outside parliament were, if anything, even more attuned to ideological incentives and resistant to concessions to colonial nationalism. It was very difficult to tell which party structure and which strategy might provide elusive electoral success for rivals on the French Right. Only de Gaulle, who "anglicized" the French system, finally settled the debate, and even he, to a degree that is often ignored, had to skillfully and at time deceptively deal with the protests of those who resisted the new course. The UNR's success, which approached the British case, was owed in large part to the peculiar position of de Gaulle in maintaining the loyalty of Gaullists and the conservative electorate in France, as well as to the institutions of the Fifth Republic, which reduced the influence of those most attached to *la plus grande France*.

The comparison of British and French parties calls into question the significance of French national sensitivity after the war. The French electorate *was* more sensitive to issues of national autonomy and status: the heritage of the World War and Resistance had left a residue that provided material for those who saw political opportunity in its use. The parties, as political organizations mediating the international environment, served to increase that sensitivity *and* to transform it into certain outcomes; the actions of British Conservative leaders directed attention to other issues. As the Empire disappeared, they proclaimed, "You never had it so good."

The divergent experiences of Conservatives in France and Britain during decolonization explode the myth that the Right is intrinsically better able to adapt a nation's external policies to new realities. The adaptability of the Right is itself dependent on the political variables described above. Richard Nixon may have been able to unfreeze American relations with China, as de Gaulle was able finally to decolonize Algeria; a look at their earlier careers suggests that at other times, political incentives pointed in a very different direction.

As ideological anchors for the colonial empires within metropolitan politics, the parties of the Right were inevitably affected by changes in that set of international relations. The transmission of that change to the politics of Britain and France, however, depended on domestic givens and strategic choices. Quite apart from this *indirect* impact, the parties also served as conduits of influence for colonial interests in metropolitan politics and represented a coalition of economic interests that was redefining its stakes in the continuation of colonial rule. The debate over party strategy and ideology coincided with a debate over the external interests of capitalism in these two countries, one which it intersected with the first debate, influencing it and being influenced by it. Before turning to those dimensions of decolonization, the fate of the parties on the Left, also shaped by the loss of empire, will be assessed.

CHAPTER III

French Socialists and British Labour: The Lure of Empire, The Benefits of Principle

THAT decolonization should have threatened a disorganized Right in France and even the governing Conservative Party in Britain is not surprising. Their ideological appeals were built around nationalism, defined in terms of a world role and a colonial empire; disengagement was likely to lead to disenchantment and revolt. Socialist parties, on the other hand, had, more or less ambiguously, been attached to anti-imperialism since the earliest years of the movement. Their principal electoral and organizational appeals were social and economic, not directly tied to international politics. One would hardly expect that disengagement from empire would threaten or divide them.

Yet the histories of the two Socialist parties in question—the French SFIO (Section française de l'internationale ouvrière) and the British Labour Party—might cause one to look again. In the 1930s and again after 1945, the parties were split more often over foreign policy than over domestic issues. Appeasement in the 1930s produced sharp battles within both formations, rendering the French Socialists powerless in the years after Munich and pointing toward the fateful vote of many French Socialist deputies for Pétain. Labour's reversal of its stand against rearmament led to the resignation of the party's leader, George Lansbury, and continued resistance to increases in the military budget.[1]

---

[1] The history of the Socialist Party in this period is documented in Nathanael L. Greene, *Crisis and Decline: The French Socialist Party in the Popular Front Era* (Ithaca, N.Y.: Cornell University Press, 1969). Labour's internal battles in the same period are described by Michael R. Gordon in *Conflict and Consensus in Labour's Foreign Policy, 1914-1965* (Stanford: Stanford University Press, 1969).

Although both the SFIO and Labour were racked by division over foreign policy after 1945—the European Defense Community for the French, nuclear disarmament for the British, German rearmament for both—decolonization presents a clear contrast in the domestic consequences suffered by the two parties. For the French Socialists, Algeria and the Mollet government's policy of pacification after 1956 would lead to a party split two years later. The British Labour Party, however, despite recurrent battles between traditionalists and revisionists, Bevanites and Gaitskellites, during the years of decolonization, did *not* fragment on this question. One could argue that, given the record of unity among the French Socialists during the Fourth Republic, far greater than any of its right-wing competitors, the Labour Party was the more likely candidate for disruption.

French Socialism, then, is the anomalous case within our expectations about Socialist parties and decolonization. Two questions concerning the SFIO reflect upon the course of French decolonization: Why did the Mollet government turn toward fighting a colonial war in Algeria in 1956? Why were those who opposed the policy within the Socialist party unable, through the exercise of voice, to force a change of course on the party? The pattern is different from that in the Conservative cases of Chapter II; here the resistance in the party does not result from an attempt to *disengage* from the empire. Rather, the dissidents protested Mollet's divergence from what they perceived to be the core of socialist ideology as applied to the empire—decolonization. Nevertheless, the framework of incentives within a political milieu (exit, voice, loyalty) can be employed to explain the contrast between the French and British cases.

Two parsimonious explanations have been offered for the contrasting outcomes on the British and French Left. Comparing the positions of the SFIO in opposition and then again when part of a governing coalition (until 1951 and after 1956), the simple fact of holding power might seem the best explanation for the shift of the Socialists toward conservatism and the protests that finally split the party. The British Labour

Party did not face the compromises of power in the years of decolonization between 1951 and 1964. Yet power *could* have unifying, or at least dissent-dampening effects—the experience of Gaullists, British Conservatives, and French Socialists would demonstrate as much—and parties out of power could be riven by conflict, witness the plight of the Labour Party during the 1950s.

A second, spare explanation in effect reverses the first: the Socialists were not *forced* to make the inevitable compromises of governing under the Fourth Republic, they were a part, from the beginning, of a "colonial consensus" extending from the SFIO to the Right of the political spectrum.[2] On this reading of the evidence, only the Communists stood apart from a widely shared set of attitudes, an official ideology with echoes in the popular mind, holding that France required a colonial empire and should resist efforts to dismantle it. The ideological distinctions between British Labour and French Socialists support this view, but Smith and others who judge the French Socialist record harshly overlook their liberalism from 1951-1955 (and in sub-Saharan Africa after 1955), and ignore the fact that the Socialists, even in the "homogeneous" Blum government of December, 1946, were incapable of governing without the consent of others. The sources and the political rationale of the Socialists' ideology also remain obscure. And, of course, if the Socialist Party were so firmly within the colonialist camp, then the fissure of 1956-1958 need never have appeared.

These simple and somewhat opposed explanations are powerful but incomplete. The reasons for the French Socialists' willingness to compromise their preferred colonial policies again and again while governing during the Fourth Republic must be made clear. The political dynamics that underlay their ambiguous ideology must also be examined. The different status of the British Labour Party can be used to throw in relief the reasons for the radically different effects that the

[2] This argument is made in most telling form by Tony Smith in *The French Stake in Algeria, 1945-1962* (Ithaca: Cornell University Press, 1978).

external shock of decolonization had upon the two political parties. For the failure of the politics of decolonization in France lay not only in a Right that would not or could not decolonize itself, but also in a divided Left, confused in its view of the French empire and unwilling to promote decolonization as a cause to rank with its old ideological favorites of social reform and anti-clericalism.*

In explaining the contrasting histories of these parties and the effect that decolonization had upon them (and through them upon the course of British and French policy), the framework of incentives and competition developed in Chapter II will be used to outline their political dilemmas. The French Socialists, whose choices were so intimately tied to the fate of the Fourth Republic, will be examined first and at greater length; the course of the Labour Party will be dealt with next; finally, the two cases are compared.

THE FRENCH SOCIALISTS: AMBIGUITY, LOYALTY, AND COLONIAL WARS

More than any other, one political fact influenced Socialist stands on colonial questions: since the Congress of Tours in 1920, the SFIO had ceased to be the sole claimant to the inheritance of French socialism. The presence of a Communist Party competing for the legacy of the prewar Socialist party forced the Socialists to pursue a strategy of reconstruction during the 1920s and 1930s that reinforced its already ambiguous position on colonial questions.

Even before the First World War, the party's generally anti-imperialist position, as expressed by Jean Jaurès, was conditional. Jaurès opposed imperialism, by and large, because it was regarded as a threat to *European* peace; on the other hand, the close association of the Socialists with the defense of republican institutions during and after the Dreyfus Affair had moved the party toward a more conciliatory attitude to-

---

* The Left considered in this chapter is principally the Socialists, but the Communist position, always a part of Socialist calculations, is also noted.

ward the *mission civilisatrice* of France overseas. As described in Chapter II, the French colonial empire was a construction of the Third Republic's *center*; thus, regime and empire were linked from the start.[3]

During the interwar years the Socialist Party, rebuilding itself under threat of Communist competition, deepened its confusion on colonialism. Opposition to colonial wars continued, and the Socialist mainstream, as represented by Léon Blum, continued to espouse a position on the colonies more reformist than its non-Communist counterparts. The final aim of Socialist colonial policy became increasingly obscure, however, as assimilationist ideas grew in popularity during the 1930s: granting political and economic rights to individual non-Europeans seemed to replace national self-determination as the end of colonial policy. Even reformist intentions were vitiated by the compromises of coalition politics: in this respect the Blum-Violette Algerian reforms of 1936 foreshadowed the fate of the Statute of Algeria in 1947. On the Left of a vague and ill-defined ideological center were the more resolute opponents of empire, grouped around the Gauche révolutionnaire of Marceau Pivert; to the Right were more convinced advocates of the colonial idea, especially the representatives of the European populations in North Africa.[4]

Like the postwar period, however, one should not view the 1920s and 1930s through the lens of the Algerian War. Most striking of all was the lack of interest in colonial questions on the part of the Socialist elite, particularly Léon Blum. At a time of economic crisis, threat of European war, and relatively weak challenges from colonial nationalism, one can

[3] The lack of clarity in Jaurès's position is evident in Harvey Goldberg, *The Life of Jean Jaurès* (Madison: University of Wisconsin Press, 1962), pp. 343-345; also Raoul Girardet, *L'Idée coloniale en France, 1871-1962* (Paris: La Table Ronde, 1972), pp. 107-109; Manuela Semidei, "Les Socialistes français et le problème colonial entre les deux guerres (1919-1939)," *Revue Français de Science Politique* 18 (December, 1968), 1118-1124.

[4] The best account of colonial policy is Semidei, "Les Socialistes français," pp. 1128-1153; also Tony Judt, *La Réconstruction du parti socialiste, 1921-1926* (Paris: Presse de la Fondation Nationale des Sciences Politiques, 1976), pp. 128-129.

comprehend the party's lack of attention. In fact, a lack of clarity in Socialist Party doctrine paralleled during these years in the British Labour Party. Elements of the conservative argument were missing, however, particularly any extended positive case for the benefits of empire in terms of French power and status. The French Socialists also displayed less interest in neo-mercantilist programs of imperial economic organization than such British trade unionists as Ernest Bevin.

The identity incentives developed by the Socialist Party for its militants and voters were not centered on anti-colonialism; indeed, while competition with the Communists pushed them away from the bourgeois parties to their Right on colonial questions, the need to distinguish themselves from the Communists as the "national" party on the Left pushed the Socialists into the arms of the Third Republic's colonial consensus. The party devoted few of its resources and best thinkers to examining colonial questions; as a result, party doctrine remained ambiguous on the ends of colonial policy and the appropriate attitude toward colonial nationalism. All of these contradictions would be carried into the Fourth Republic, where they would be complicated by changes wrought by the war itself and by a political strategy that reflected the disappointment of Socialist hopes for a dominant position on the Left.

The Socialists after liberation: Conservative strategy in radical guise

The political topography shaped in the first electoral and constitutional battles after Liberation served to set Socialist ideology and policy until the Fifth Republic. Internal party changes and the postwar structure of party competition soon impinged on the party's colonial program. The party's leadership and membership were purged of those implicated in supporting the Pétain regime (if there were no later mitigating circumstances), effectively eliminating most prewar supporters of the powerful secretary general, Paul Faure. This severe purge hardened attitudes on external policy. The Faure faction—pacifist, opposed to rearmament—had endorsed a type of "isolationism" for France in the 1930s. Eliminating this wing of the party could only emphasize the *nationalization* of the party. The postwar party leadership, particularly those who would assume office in the 1950s, was largely made up of those who had been Resistance leaders. The lessons that they had learned often resembled those of the Gaullists and others on the Right, particularly when the integrity of the French empire was threatened. The impact of Resistance experience should not be overstated, however, since some of the opponents of pacification in Algeria were active Resistance leaders, particularly Daniel Mayer, Robert Verdier, and Edouard Depreux.

Despite the elimination of one fraction of the old Socialist Party, the Socialists were also the political formation most dominated by Third Republic political figures and most resistant to absorbing *résistants* who sought a political home in the party's ranks.[5] The narrowing of Socialist personnel and the party's refusal to grant a larger share of influence for new recruits served to reinforce the ideological attachment to traditional Socialist doctrine, with all of its equivocations on colonial questions. That traditionalism was further reinforced by the changed structure of competition faced by the Socialists after the war.

Conservatism in leadership and cadres complemented the electoral strategy that the Socialists adopted in the face of their disappointing performance in the first three elections after Liberation. Despite their hopes to remain the dominant party on the Left, and perhaps to straddle a political Center shifted Left by war and liberation, the Socialists discovered in the aftermath of elections to the first Constituent Assembly (October, 1945) that they now trailed the Communist Party as the largest party on the Left, and had even fallen behind the new Christian Democratic entrant, the Mouvement républicain populaire. In the elections that followed, for the

[5] Philip Williams, *Crisis and Compromise: Politics in the Fourth Republic* (New York: Doubleday-Anchor, 1966), pp. 95, 104; Gordon Wright, *The Reshaping of French Democracy* (Boston: Beacon Press, 1970), p. 72.

Second Constituent and the first Assembly of the Fourth Republic (June 1946 and November 1946), the Socialists saw their parliamentary strength ebb further, with losses to both the Communists and to a resurgent Right.[6] While the Popular Front elections of June, 1936 had produced hopes for a dominant Socialist party within a dominant Left coalition, the postwar facts pointed to a more threatening future: the Socialists confronted a far stronger Communist Party within a Left on the retreat.

Their strategic dilemma was profound. In contrast to the strategy followed by the Italian Socialists, the Socialists found it difficult to contemplate a Popular Front revival, given the collapse of Radical strength and Communist gains. (Their decision would not be changed for twenty years.) Ideological conservatism made it impossible for the party to breach the sharp religious divide to its Right and appeal to the new Catholic electorate mobilized by the MRP. Faced with a threat of continuing hemorrhage of members and voters—the concern with *exit* described in the preceding chapter—the Socialists chose to maintain ideological barriers to exit on either side and reinforce the ideological incentives offered to party members. The culmination of this movement toward ideological conservatism to maintain an eroding electoral position came at the party Congress in Lyon in 1946: Guy Mollet led a successful attack on efforts by Blum and Mayer to transform the SFIO into a broader reformist grouping, a "workers party" based on "humanist socialism." Supported by a majority of the party faithful at the Congress, Mollet repudiated such an evolution and forced the party back, at least verbally, to a commitment to Marxist tenets.[7] With Mollet's victory, the

[6] The election results are summarized in Claude Leleu, *Géographie des élections françaises depuis 1936* (Paris: Presses universitaires de France, 1971), pp. 29-67.

[7] Accounts of the controversy are given in Daniel Ligou, *Histoire du socialisme en France, 1871-1961* (Paris: Presses universitaires de France, 1962), pp. 542-547; Roger Quilliot, *La S.F.I.O. et l'exercice du pouvoir, 1944-1958* (Paris: Fayard, 1972), chap. 10.

ideological boundaries of the postwar Socialist Party were set for some time.

The first election after the war, which produced an ideological rigidification among the Socialists, also pointed, paradoxically, to a change in electoral clientele that made a commitment to Marxist and revolutionary rhetoric seem even more outdated. The 1936 elections made clear the Socialist inroads in what had previously been rural bastions of the Radical Party south of the Loire.[8] The tendency to become the principal *laique* party in such areas, combined with the loss of working-class and left-wing support to the Communists, led many to argue that the Socialist party was becoming "Radicalized"* in the initial years of the Fourth Republic.[9] Although exaggerated—the import of "Radicalization" will be analyzed below—the tendency of the Socialists to behave like the "pivot party" of the Third Republic, a party attached only to anti-clerical and republican ideology and, above all, to power, was reinforced by more than a shift in electoral constituency. The greater weight in the party of representatives from the old Radical strongholds was linked to the importance assumed by Socialist leaders (often from that region) who were political managers in the best Radical tradition. Men such as Paul Ramadier (Aveyron) and Vincent Auriol (Haute-Garonne) consistently advocated participation in government coalitions; their attachment to Third Republic credos (such as the colonial idea) and their willingness to compromise with other parties in order to retain a share of power for the Socialists would have a pronounced influence on the Socialist response to decolonization early in the Fourth Republic.[10]

---

* "Radicalization" is capitalized to distinguish it from any connotation of movement to the Left. In this context, obviously, it has the opposite meaning.

[8] Greene, *Crisis and Decline*, pp. 66-70.

[9] Leleu, *Géographie*, pp. 63-64; François Goguel, *Géographie des élections françaises sous la troisième et la quatrième république* (Paris: Armand Colin, 1970), pp. 110-111.

[10] Williams, *Crisis and Compromise*, while noting the exaggeration of the "Radicalization" thesis, states that "many Socialist deputies and would-be deputies were really Radicals in spirit" (p. 104).

These changes in the Socialist Party after 1945 served to freeze the party in its prewar mold: reliance upon past personnel and past doctrine erected barriers to entry; a shift in electoral strategy, emphasizing traditional Socialist ideology, throwing up barriers to exit. Any ideological adaptation and reconsideration would have to come from within, but a final set of changes in party organization served to make the exercise of voice difficult and to foreclose such change. With the bitter factional quarrels of the 1930s vivid in their memories, Socialists at the first National Congress after Liberation (9-12 November 1944) decided to suppress organized factions and to centralize power within the party, strengthening the *Comité directeur* (previously the *Commission administrative permanente*) and directing that its elections be held from a single list, not by proportional representation. This change placed the dominant coalition in the party in a very strong position, since it could exclude at will the representatives of any minority from the principal representative bodies—power that would be deployed later during the Algerian War. The potential for internal control was reinforced by the regionalization of the party, which awarded a few large federations considerable power, particularly the normally united Pas-de-Calais, Nord, and Bouches-du-Rhône.[11] With such an arsenal for use against disruptive effects of voice, the Socialist Party in the Fourth Republic became one of the most disciplined groups in the National Assembly (far more disciplined than its British counterpart), but not a party characterized by ideological ferment or political experimentation.

Although the party leadership strengthened its hand in dealing with voice, the strategy employed against exit—reinforcing ideological incentives—and the Mollet victory in 1946, which seemed to signal a turn to a harder and more left-wing line in order to compete with the Communists, might have set the stage for a classic confrontation between the militant rank and file who had backed Mollet and the more pliable parliamentarians, the type of pattern that Michael Gordon describes

[11] Quilliot, *La S.F.I.O.*, pp. 29-32.

in the Labour Party at about the same time. Such pressure from the party rank and file was a feature of Socialist Party behavior after the war, but the fit was far from perfect. The ideological defeat of Blum and Mayer was by no means a clear victory for anti-colonialism, despite the inclusion of anti-imperialism in the insurgent program. As Mollet's later evolution would demonstrate, theirs was a *pre-Leninist* (or anti-Leninist) variant of Marxism, without the positive values attached to national self-determination and anti-colonial movements that could be found in Communist doctrine.[12] It soon became apparent that supporters of Blum were the most prominent liberals on colonial questions, together with members of the old revolutionary Left of the 1930s. At best the apparently "radical" reinforcement of traditional ideology would replicate the confused colonial doctrines of the prewar years; at worst, those doctrines that permitted the maintenance of French power would be reinforced, and dissidents would find less ability to challenge them.

The potential ideological strife between militants and leadership was also reduced by the changed political circumstances after 1946. With the departure of the Communists from the Ramadier government in May, 1947, possibilities for unified action on the Left virtually disappeared. With points of exit for dissatisfied Socialists closed, the SFIO could maintain itself by reiterating ideological formulae that had less and less relevance to France or to changes in the rest of the world. The Cold War, however, brought the dilemmas of sharing power in defense of the Republic and the first compromises that would lead Socialists to endorse colonial policies far removed from even their ambiguous precepts.

The Socialists share power, 1946-1950

Socialist formulas for the empire after Liberation were hardly radical. Their federative vocabulary resembled that of the

---

[12] Marx's own views, hardly sympathetic toward prenationalist or nationalist movements, including those in Algeria, are given in Shlomo Avineri, ed., *Karl Marx on Colonialism and Modernization* (Garden City, N.Y.: Doubleday-Anchor, 1969), especially pp. 47-48.

Gaullists, but the Socialists did emphasize "free association" of former colonies with France in the *Union française*. So long as free association was given a prominent place, the Socialists seemed to propose a French Union that resembled the British Commonwealth rather than the more tightly organized structure of the Gaullists.[13] The relatively liberal position of the Socialists was also demonstrated in Constituent Assembly debates and votes. At a time of heightened nationalism in France and in the colonies, they found themselves most often in coalition with the Communists and the overseas (non-European) representatives; the MRP and its leader, Georges Bidault, took a much harsher and resisting line toward colonial demands for autonomy and independence, spurred on by the Gaullist opposition described in Chapter III. The equivocation between individual and collective emancipation, the continued recitation of France's mission overseas, the protests that secession was not planned, served to place the Socialists within a "colonial consensus" of sorts, but the Communists found themselves there as well.[14] On a number of colonial questions, an unholy conservative alliance was struck between the Communists and the MRP, over the vigorous protests of the Socialists.[15] The Socialists were also held to a liberal position by prominent deputies from black Africa, such as the Senegalese deputy, Lamine-Gueye. As Marshall describes, however, such overseas deputies rarely challenged the dominant position of France within the empire.[16]

[13] The ambiguities of Socialist colonial doctrine are exemplified in the carefully hedged Article 85 of their constitutional project of November, 1945, cited in Quilliot, *La S.F.I.O.*, p. 147; and in the statement of the National Council, March, 1947 (*Le Populaire*, 25 March 1947, p. 2).

[14] As D. Bruce Marshall notes, "In fact, the Communist party did not press for increased colonial autonomy until after the Communist ministers were ejected from the government in May 1947. When there was still a chance that the PCF would control government policy, the French Communists were unwilling to endorse any reduction in French control over the colonies." D. Bruce Marshall, *The French Colonial Myth and Constitution-making in the Fourth Republic* (New Haven: Yale University Press, 1973), p. 245.

[15] Ibid., pp. 305-306; more generally on the difficult position of the Socialists, ibid., pp. 262-269; Wright, *Reshaping French Democracy*, p. 147; on the alignment of the Socialists and Communists, ibid., pp. 201-205.

[16] Marshall, *The French Colonial Myth*, pp. 162-166.

The battle over constitutional principles soon became a battle fought with more conventional weapons in Indochina, where open hostilities between the Vietminh, led by Ho Chi Minh, and the French had broken out in December, 1946. In Algeria, the power of the European settlers and the liberal will of the metropolis would be tested in the new statute enacted in 1947. These two episodes, which bridge the end of *tripartisme* and the collapse of cooperation with the Communists, serve as useful benchmarks for assessing Socialist colonial policy as the changes described above in party strategy and structure were instituted. These episodes are also a key part of the evidence for those who placed the Socialists within a homogeneous colonial consensus.[17] On closer examination, however, the record of the Socialist *Party* was not so illiberal as its critics have alleged, and the source of its compromises was not only ideological confusion. As Socialist ministers endorsed increasingly conservative colonial policies and the chances for a Left coalition slipped away, the party rank and file, as well as younger members of its leadership, protested the compromises made to guarantee a Third Force ministry in the National Assembly.

Indochina: The dirty war begins. Countenancing military repression in Indochina after the violence in Hanoi in December, 1946 was the most fateful decision of Léon Blum's transitory government, the last ministry before the institution of the Fourth Republic. Although Blum's ministry contained only Socialists, the party had to rely in the Assembly on support from their competitors, the Communists and the MRP. *Both* parties approved the Blum decision.[18] Blum hardly moved against the Vietminh with colonialist ardor; he seemed mortified that the decision had been thrust upon him, and his ministerial declaration made clear that self-government was the final aim of his government's policy.[19] At least part of the

---

[17] The strongest criticism is given in Smith, *The French Stake*, pp. 71-73, 77-78, 119.

[18] Georgette Elgey, *La République des illusions, 1945-1951* (Paris: Fayard, 1965), p. 171.

[19] Léon Blum, *L'Oeuvre de Léon Blum,* Vol. 3 (Paris: Editions Albin Michel, 1958), pp. 354-355.

explanation for this opening episode in a colonial war that would last eight years lies with the lack of control that Paris exercised over its representatives on the spot (a pattern of bureaucratic insubordination that is examined more closely in Chapter V). Elgey alleges that Marius Moutet, the Socialist minister for colonies, approved the bombardment of Haiphong, which touched off the spiral of violence. It also seems likely, however, that the military and bureaucratic forces in Indochina, led by Admiral Thierry d'Argenlieu, created such an incident to prevent a new government from opening negotiations with Ho after the elections of November, 1946.[20] When the government sent Moutet and General Leclerc to Indochina on a fact-finding mission, Moutet, shown carefully selected examples of Vietminh violence, became a convert to the policy of force. (McGeorge Bundy would follow in his footsteps some two decades later.)[21]

Paul Ramadier, the first premier of the Fourth Republic, did act to increase the control of Paris by replacing Thierry d'Argenlieu, but by early 1947, the Socialist ministers gradually wrote off any possibility of negotiations with Ho Chi Minh. The restoration of order was made a prerequisite to any negotiations.[22] The slippage in the Socialist position that occurred in 1947, from Blum's stated intentions to Ramadier's war policy, derived in part from the necessities of coalition politics, particularly after the departure of the Communists in May, 1947. After that break, the Socialists were forced to concede more and more to the MRP, which took a staunch colonialist position at this time (and would eventually mo-

[20] See the judgment by Philippe Devilliers, "Rapport: La guerre d'Indochine," in La Quatrième République (Paris: Librairie générale du droit et de jurisprudence, 1978), pp. 374-375.

[21] Quilliot, La S.F.I.O., p. 317; Elgey, La République, p. 253.

[22] A shift in the positions of both Moutet and Ramadier is clearest during Moutet's statement of policy in Indochina at the Council of Ministers on 5 March 1947. At this time, only a few days before the Truman Doctrine, Maurice Thorez expressed disagreement with most of Moutet's account, with one exception: "the maintenance of French sovereignty." Vincent Auriol, Journal du septennat, 1947-1954, Vol. 1 (Paris: Armand Colin, 1970), pp. 124-127.

nopolize the Colonial Ministry that oversaw the fighting). Coalition calculations were not the only explanation for Socialist endorsement of the policy of force, however. The key Socialist actors in these years—Paul Ramadier, Marius Moutet, Vincent Auriol (the new President of the Republic)—fitted the model of the "Radicalized" Socialists perfectly: all from the south of the Loire, all with a personal style of the political manager or "fixer." Their differences with cabinet colleagues on the Right were very often those of nuance.

But it would be inaccurate to leap from the behavior of Socialist ministers to an assertion that the Socialists belonged wholeheartedly to a "colonial consensus" from the beginning of the Fourth Republic. As their ministers adopted a policy of coercion in Indochina, the Socialist rank and file repeatedly made their opposition known. At the National Council of March, 1947, the party, while still endorsing the inclusion of Vietnam in the French Union, called for an immediate cease-fire and negotiations with "the government of Vietnam."[23] The policy of the Ramadier government was criticized harshly at a party Congress in the same year; the final motion called for the "abandonment of the colonialist policy which only maintains the unity of the French Union by using an apparatus of administrative and military coercion, both costly and inhuman, in flagrant violation of the Constitution."[24]

At first, Guy Mollet, secretary general and champion of the militants, pressured the Ramadier ministry for a policy of negotiation. By 1948, however, Mollet had adopted a "Third Force" logic in favor of Socialist participation to preserve the regime against a perceived Gaullist and Communist threat. Leadership of the opposition to Socialist membership in increasingly right-wing ministries shifted from Mollet to others, such as André Philip, Edouard Depreux, and Léon Boutbien. As late as 1949, the party Executive Committee (*Comité directeur*) had instructed Mollet to deliver a letter to Premier

[23] *Le Populaire*, 25 March 1947, p. 2.
[24] *Le Populaire*, 19 August 1947; Ligou, *Histoire du socialisme*, pp. 552-553.

Queuille (17 January 1949) that noted the failure of the Bao Dai effort and urged negotiation once again with Ho Chi Minh.[25] None of these efforts succeeded in reversing the successive steps toward deeper involvement in *la sale guerre*.

Algeria: reform aborted. Debate over the Algerian statute in the summer of 1947 elicited another episode of division within the party. Looking back at the arguments through the torment of war that would follow, the concessions that were debated seem pitifully small. Certainly, many of the Socialist elders held thoroughly orthodox views on Algeria: Vincent Auriol's conversation with Ferhat Abbas in 1947 was a dialogue of the deaf.[26] Others, such as Edouard Depreux, minister of the interior responsible for the new statute, did have liberal sympathies: within the very narrow constraints of the parliamentary coalition (made narrower by the vehement opposition of de Gaulle), Depreux viewed the statute as a first step toward increasing both the political rights of Algerian Muslims and the autonomy of Algeria.[27]

All of the many versions of the statute had hedges against "secession" or too large a political role for the majority Arab population; the principal ones were elections by two separate colleges (one European, one Muslim), equal representation in the Assembly for two communities very unequal in size, and limitation of the Assembly's powers to a very narrow range.[28] For the Socialist militants, however, the government's final proposal contained one concession too many to European

[25] The party Congress in July, 1949 declared for the "end of hostilities by negotiations with all elements of the Vietnamese people without precondition," but an effort by the Left to call for an immediate appeal to the United Nations and if unsuccessful, for the withdrawal of the Socialist ministers from the government, failed. (*Le Monde*, 20 July 1949). Also R.E.M. Irving, *The First Indochina War: French and American Policy 1945-54* (London: Croom Helm, 1975), pp. 65-66.

[26] Auriol, *Journal du septennat*, pp. 301-303.

[27] Edouard Depreux, *Souvenirs d'un militant* (Paris: Fayard, 1970), pp. 332-334.

[28] The best account of the passage of the statute and its implications is Thomas Oppermann, *Le Problème algérien* (Paris: Maspero, 1961), Chapter 4.

objections, particularly the inclusion of a nearly automatic two-thirds voting rule that would give the Europeans decisive blocking power. An intriguing element in Socialist opposition to their own ministers' proposal was the leadership of that opposition by Socialist representatives from Algeria. Their own more liberal version of the statute had been endorsed by the party's National Council, suggesting the influence that they could have in party councils on matters relating to North Africa. Liberalism fitted with calculations of Socialist political strategy: the elections of November, 1946, which had eliminated Socialists among the Muslim representatives and reduced their number in the European electorate as well, highlighted the danger that polarization in Algeria posed for Socialist political success. Their hope was collaboration with the Muslim moderates, represented by Ferhat Abbas and the U.D.M.A. (Union démocratique du Manifeste Algérien), a hope shared by Depreux himself.[29] The revolt against the Ramadier government's proposal at the Socialist National Congress succeeded: the Congress voted by a substantial majority to require Ramadier not to pose the question of confidence on the statute (thus permitting liberal amendments).[30]

The mildly liberal measures endorsed by the Socialists, which fitted both their political strategy in Algeria and their conflicting aims for the territory, were quickly vitiated by sabotage in implementing the statute. Edouard Depreux had defended the liberal governor general of Algeria, Yves Chataigneau, against repeated attacks by the leaders of the Europeans in Algeria. In February 1948, however, before the first elections to the Assembly, open insubordination by the Algeria prefects and a threat of resignation by the Radical minister René Mayer led the Socialists to accept Chataigneau's replacement by one of their own: Marcel-Edmond Naegelen, Socialist deputy from Alsace.

Under Naegelen, the first elections to the Algerian Assembly

[29] Quilliot, La S.F.I.O., pp. 259-260; Depreux, Souvenirs, pp. 332-333; Depreux's account seems to be confirmed by Abbas's interview with Auriol, cited above, n. 26.

[30] Le Populaire, 19 August 1947, p. 2.

in April, 1948 were blatantly rigged. Even Mollet later admitted that the Messalists (nationalists more radical than Ferhat Abbas) would have won 80 percent of the Muslim vote if the administration had not played so heavy-handed a role.[31] Naegelen's behavior was defended, however, by the new Socialist minister of the interior, Jules Moch. Socialists in the Assembly of the French Union did ally with the Communists to attempt an investigation of the elections, but they were told firmly that the question was not within their purview.

Naegelen's defense of his conduct before the Socialist parliamentary group on 6 July 1949 is a remarkable preview of the ideological amalgam that would later guide the policies of Guy Mollet and Robert Lacoste in Algeria. In it, one can see how Resistance-inspired nationalism, a bastardized Marxism, and anti-communism combined to produce opposition to liberalism and decolonization. Although Naegelen proclaimed proudly that he had carried out "a policy imbued with socialism," it is a fierce nationalism born of his wartime experiences in Alsace that pervades his remarks. He linked the "separatists" in Algeria (the followers of Messali Hadj and Ferhat Abbas) with the autonomist movement in Alsace that had displayed German sympathies during the Occupation, a "lesson" that he would not forget. Although his nationalism was conservative in flavor, Naegelen also put forward two tenets of policy that would characterize much of the moderate Left and Center in their attitudes toward North Africa: maintaining French presence and authority (no increase in *collective* autonomy) should be combined with the realization of equal *individual* rights for all those living in Algeria. And here a transformed and simplified socialism appears. Because of the emphasis on individual liberation, Naegelen also emphasizes economic and social reforms as a precondition to political development: "One does not give liberty to men in giving them a ballot but in eradicating ignorance, sickness, famine, thirst." Naegelen's nationalist opponents are

[31] Quilliot, *La S.F.I.O.*, p. 266; see also the evaluation by Oppermann, *Le Problème algérien*, pp. 94-103.

damned on two scores that would be convincing to many Socialists. In the context of an intensifying Cold War, they are linked to the *Communists*: he asked his audience what the international reaction would have been, just before the Italian elections, if the second college in Algeria had elected a Messalist majority. Arab nationalists are condemned for being *reactionaries* as well: they are guilty of the primal sin of the "use of religion for political ends" and a "narrow nationalism."[32]

Many of the themes of Socialist conservatism in colonial affairs were present in Naegelen's frank exposition. They were likely to be most appealing, among the Socialists and other groups, on the question of Algeria. Nevertheless, they were not uncontested; Naegelen, as his later opposition to the European Defense Community would demonstrate, was definitely on the nationalist right wing of the party. When Naegelen later attempted to fix partial elections for the Algerian Assembly in February, 1951 (a date chosen to reduce Muslim turnout), Borra and Rabier, Socialist deputies from Algeria, vehemently protested. Moch, however, once again backed Naegelen, and the Socialist group voted to accept the decrees, although a majority of deputies abstained.[33] In 1953, the conservative prime minister, Joseph Laniel, attempted to co-opt the Socialists for his status quo policy in Morocco by suggesting that Naegelen be appointed Resident General to replace General Guillaume. The Socialists had learned their lesson: the Executive Committee, with only three votes in favor of the proposition, advised Naegelen against accepting the position, and he complied.[34]

Dissent and division over decolonization, 1946-1951

The pattern of division that emerged in the Socialist Party under the impact of these first colonial crises bore some resemblance to foreign policy dissent in the British Labour Party

---

[32] SFIO, Groupe parlementaire, meeting of 6 July 1949, pp. 2-10.
[33] SFIO, Groupe parlementaire, meeting of 26 December 1950, p. 4.
[34] Quilliot, *La S.F.I.O.*, pp. 458-460.

at the same time: a split between *ministrables* committed to maintaining a traditional reading of French national interests, and the party militants, represented in National Councils and National Congresses, who repeatedly endorsed a Socialist policy toward the empire that, for all its ambiguity, was more amenable to negotiation with nationalists and to substantive reforms. The divisions, however, were never pushed to the point of rupture or even to the point of forcing Socialist withdrawal from cabinets during this period. The political consequences of the fissures that appeared within the party at this time were minimal.

Even within the ministerial group, splits along generational lines occurred: as early as 1947, André Philip and Edouard Depreux expressed concern at the replacement of liberal Erik Labonne as resident general in Morocco by General Juin; Ramadier, on the other hand, backed Bidault's choice, as he usually did on Indochina policy.[35] The parliamentary group, however, in contrast to the British Labour Party, remained remarkably united in its votes in the National Assembly.[36] Those islands of dissidence that persisted throughout the Fourth Republic were for the most part found in the party outside the Assembly.

Two strands of opposition centered on deputies and militants from the Federation of the Seine (the Paris region). Some had been part of Léon Blum's circle (Daniel Mayer, Robert Verdier, Oreste Rosenfeld), and thus had reason to criticize Mollet's apparent opportunism after 1946. Their opposition at this time, however, was directed to more than colonial issues: it embraced the question of faithfulness to Socialist principles within Third Force governments. A second element of opposition in the Seine Federation had an even longer history, tracing its roots to the revolutionary socialists of the 1930s, the Gauche révolutionnaire led by Marceau Pivert.

[35] Auriol, *Journal*, p. 279.

[36] The principal split came in September, 1948, over the question of legal proceedings against the Malagasy deputies accused of fomenting the 1947 uprising on the island. At that time a number of deputies, including some from African colonies or Algeria, resigned from the Socialist group.

This left group, which had ties to the Trotskyites during the 1930s, had taken a much stronger anti-colonial position than the party as a whole.[37] Pivert and some of his past associates, such as Jean Rous and Daniel Guérin, remained active in anti-colonial activities after the war. This group opposed the Indochina policy of successive Third Force governments, and, virtually alone among Socialist leaders, Pivert had established close ties to Messali Hadj and his Algerian nationalist movement in the interwar years.[38] Although Pivert and Rous continued to lead the fight for critical motions on colonial policy at Socialist Congresses, the party leadership had destroyed much of the Left's natural constituency by its measures to control voice by purging the Jeunesses socialistes (Socialist Youth) and to seal off exit by severing Socialist connections with independent Left intellectuals, such as those in Sartre's Rassemblement démocratique révolutionnaire.[39]

A third source of liberalism toward the colonial empire within the party should also be mentioned: academics concerned with colonial questions and representatives of the overseas societies themselves. Some of the colonial experts, such as Charles-André Julien and Andrée Viénot, had been part of Léon Blum's circle, and their influence declined with his death.[40] Representatives of the North African settlers, whose liberal criticisms were described above, tempered their advocacy of change after the outbreak of rebellion in the 1950s. Those who spoke for the majority populations, few in number, could at best force bad conscience on the Socialists; Lamine-Gueye, in exasperation at the Socialist unwillingness to defend Mad-

[37] For a description of the Pivertistes in the politics of the prewar party, Greene, *Crisis and Decline*, pp. 56-59; Jean-Paul Joubert, *Révolutionnaire de la S.F.I.O.: Marceau Pivert et le Pivertisme* (Paris: Presses de la Fondation Nationale des Sciences Politiques, 1977), pp. 82-83; Semidei, "Les Socialistes français," pp. 1136-1137.

[38] Joubert, *Revolutionnaire de la S.F.I.O.*, pp. 246-247; Fenner Brockway, *Outside the Right* (London: George Allen and Unwin, 1963), pp. 42-43.

[39] Quilliot, *La S.F.I.O.*, pp. 242-243. Ligou, *Histoire du socialisme*, pp. 552, 562, especially the statement by Jean Rous.

[40] Quilliot, *La S.F.I.O.*, pp. 442-443.

agascan deputies accused of inciting rebellion, cried out at one meeting of the Socialist group in the Assembly: "They are only being treated this way because they are black!"

Despite these early signs of division over compromise of Socialist principle in French colonial policy, rank-and-file dissent had few consequences for that policy. The Socialist ministers were willing to sacrifice such concerns for the demands of coalition politics, and, after 1947, the defense of the republican regime against its foes, Communist and Gaullist. For many of the older generation, the views expressed by Naegelen had become the new, conservative colonial orthodoxy. The strength of other parts of the party—especially the militants— had been permanently weakened by the postwar changes barring exit and weakening voice.

As Macrae has noted, Socialist unwillingness to compromise with Third Force governments was a principal cause of cabinet instability during the first legislature of the Fourth Republic (1947-1951), but economic and social issues, not the party's divisions over colonial policy, were the source of its resistance. Although the episodes described suggest a certain sensitivity of the Socialists to developments in the empire, anti-colonialism was simply not a core strand in their ideology, and, apart from the groups mentioned, colonial issues were not important enough for the Socialists to endanger an already shaky coalition.

The heightening of Cold War tensions after 1950 brought conservative tendencies to a peak before the 1951 parliamentary elections. At the party Congress held in May, a motion on Indochina took the "Cold War liberal" stand. Any mention of negotiations had disappeared; Indochina was simply "a theater of operations" in the "struggle against Stalinist imperialism"; a mention of modest reform was the only remnant of Socialist anti-colonialism. The declared policy on Algeria was also more Gaullist than Socialist in tone, suggesting one source of Socialist electoral fears.[41] To their critics, the party

[41] The Socialists committed themselves to complete application of the statute (ironic in light of Naegelen's tenure) and to policies to destroy "separatism" (*Le Populaire*, 19 May 1951).

had simply become an unprincipled cartel for the pursuit of power: "If today it no longer has the method of Marx nor the faith of Jaurès nor the austerity of Guesde, what is left? Power, no doubt: which is much—and nothing."[42] It would require a period of opposition and a different domestic and international setting for the Socialists to revert to a more enlightened, and less equivocal, interpretation of their ideology.

The Socialists back decolonization: 1952-1955

The elections of June, 1951 were another setback for the SFIO: losing 15 percent of its constituency, only the institution of the *apparentements* (designed to weaken the two extremes of the Communist Party and the Gaullist RPF) permitted the party to gain seats in the National Assembly. For many observers, the election confirmed the hypothesis of Socialism's "Radicalization": regionalization of the party into strongholds of the south and southwest; reliance upon well-known local figures rather than a national appeal.[43] These retrenchments in the party's electoral position had greater impact on the continued salience of the clerical issue than upon colonial issues, however.[44] This supposedly "Radicalized" party, reduced in size and geographic spread, moved back to a distinctively *liberal* policy toward decolonization, apparently belying the notion that it was only concerned with sharing power.

The key was another change in the Socialist position after 1951: a move to the "cure" of opposition that many opponents of Third Force policies had been advocating. In the new Assembly the balance of power was to the Right, though the first two ministries (Pleven, Faure) were supported by the Socialists and fell apart on economic and social questions (the clerical question loomed in the background), much like the preceding governments. The investiture of Antoine Pinay in

[42] Maurice Duverger, *Le Monde*, 4 October 1947.
[43] Leleu, *Géographie*, pp. 69-72; Goguel, *Géographie*, pp. 128-129.
[44] Philip Williams, "De Gaulle frustrated," in *French Politicians and Elections, 1951-1969* (Cambridge: Cambridge University Press, 1970), pp. 14-15.

March, 1952, described in Chapter II, was a watershed: it created the basis of a conservative coalition that would govern France until the next legislative elections. The Socialists, with a sigh of relief, were absolved of the burden of participation; they supported only one other government until 1956, that of Pierre Mendès-France.

Opposition quickly demonstrated that the Socialists could propose alternatives to the status quo tactics of conservative cabinets in 1952-1954. But their opposition stance and the turn toward liberalism also resulted from a new political constellation: an easing of polarization in both domestic and international politics awarded the Socialists greater freedom of maneuver. The concomitant decline of Communist and Gaullist threats to the republic eliminated the need to forge uneasy coalitions with conservative partners. The need to distinguish themselves from the Communists, particularly on Indochina, was no longer so essential, and Stalin's death held open for some in the party the possibility of future cooperation with their rival on the Left. The investiture of Pinay meant that the Gaullist threat faded on the Right; a decline in its ferocious nationalism, which had cost the Socialists some of their electoral support in 1951, also made a more conciliatory colonial policy feasible. In short, a widening of the center in French politics permitted a Left-Right division that would reach its peak in the 1956 parliamentary elections and within which Socialist liberalism on colonial policy would reach its peak. The changed international situation—in which the prominence of the Cold War receded somewhat—*eased* the position of the Socialists, while increasing the difficulties of Conservatives and Gaullists, whose organizations were far more sensitive to the threats to national status that originated in colonial nationalism and European integration.

The decline of the Cold War mentality quickly became clear in changed party stands toward Indochina in late 1952: at the National Council in November of that year, the party took a very critical tone toward existing policy, "recalling" that the party had never stopped asking for a search for negotiations with Ho Chi Minh (apparently forgetting the Congress motion eighteen months earlier). The party continued to repudiate the Communists' solution of simple withdrawal, which the party argued would lead to "bloody massacres" (a familiar theme in American debate over the Indochina conflict fifteen years later). The Socialists did, however, oppose the internationalization of the war, while arguing for an international solution in making peace.[45] National war-weariness had grown by the following year, and the first attempt to form a government under Mendès-France brought the issue to greater prominence. Despite the opposition of Guy Mollet (not on grounds of Indochina policy), the Socialists did vote for Mendès-France on this occasion and in his successful attempt in 1954. In discussions about the war in the parliamentary group, Mollet, always a sensitive political weathervane, sided with Alain Savary, a young deputy who had become a principal spokesman for the party on colonial questions. Mollet took at this time a position he would later reject in Algeria: "Any form of negotiation is desirable. The objective in the short term is to reach an armistice, with the treaty to be discussed later."[46] Even the nationalist Max Lejeune argued that the war had to be brought to a speedy conclusion; only Léon Boutbien, former spokesman of the far Left, took a resistant anti-communist line. Ultimately the Socialists endorsed the Mendès-France peace strategy, matching their own in large measure, and the party supported his government loyally from beginning to end.

In the successive crises of the French empire that followed, attention shifted from the "dirty war" in Indochina to North Africa. The nascent question of the future of the North African protectorates—Tunisia and Morocco—gave the Socialists further opportunity to demonstrate that they had an alternative to conservative repression. The two cases also demonstrated lingering shortcomings in their ideology, however, and, with the outbreak of rebellion in Algeria in November, 1954, the opening for a more nationalist and confrontational policy.

[45] *Le Populaire*, 18 November 1952.
[46] SFIO, Groupe parlementaire, meeting of 22 October 1953.

Tunisia showed the Socialists at their most liberal and conciliatory. Although they participated in none of the governments during the decolonization of the protectorate, their voices in the Assembly and at party meetings were consistently on the side of negotiation with the nationalist Néo-Destour led by Habib Bourguiba; the party repeatedly called for internal autonomy and a treaty of association with the protectorate that was based upon equality. Independence was skirted, but it would be the Mollet government that, while endorsing a policy of pacification in Algeria, negotiated treaties of independence with Morocco and Tunisia in 1956.

In contrast to the rest of North Africa, two aspects of the Tunisian situation reinforced the political impetus for liberalism. The nationalist movement in this case matched the party's image of what a democratic successor government should be. Bourguiba's Néo-Destour was above all *secular*, not Islamic in its appeal; he called upon the same Western principles, derived from the 1789 Revolution, that the Socialists could recognize in their own ideology. Bourguiba was also backed by a disciplined trade union movement. And he, unlike some nationalist groups, carefully avoided statements of hostility toward *France*, whatever his hostility toward the measures taken by particular governments.

The Socialists enjoyed uniquely close ties with the Néo-Destour, following a pattern that was characteristic of the British Labour Party and African nationalist movements. For the SFIO, Bourguiba's movement came to be seen as the *only* alternative in Tunisia. At the 1952 Congress of the party, Robert Verdier reported to the militants an argument that Bourguiba had used, which must have been as convincing to his Socialist audience as it would be to British Conservatives later in the decade: "If we fail, there will be room only for fascism, either religious, or communist."[47] Another key group, the Socialists among the Europeans of Tunisia, also endorsed a policy of liberalism, even moving in advance of the metropolitan party, just as the Algeria deputies had done im-

[47] *Le Populaire*, 26 May 1952, p. 3.

mediately after the war.[48] André Bidet, a member of the Council of the French Union from Tunisia, quickly became a spokesman for the party during the Tunisian crisis, consistently attacking repression by the government of the day and backing negotiations.

The importance of both the character of the nationalist movement and the attitudes of the Socialists on the spot was demonstrated by Socialist reticence toward the upsurge of nationalist discontent in Morocco. The nationalist movement there was less to Socialist liking: symbolized by a sultan and supported by the urban bourgeoisie. Although Socialists denounced the policy of repression pursued by the French Residency in Morocco, their denunciation stopped short of the same alliance with the nationalists that had appeared in Tunisia. The Socialist federation in Morocco had had less rapport with the nationalist movement and was suspicious of its Islamic and pan-Arab tendencies. Since in this case they lacked the direct information that they had received in Tunisia, the French Socialists tended to see the struggle between the sultan and el-Glaoui (the candidate of the Residency) as, in Quilliot's words, a battle of "grand seigneurs."[49] Even after the Socialist position hardened in opposition, the party's position lagged behind its stance toward Tunisia: the party recognized the right of Morocco to independence in stages, but also demanded the installation of a democratic regime and guarantees for French persons and goods.[50]

[48] Savary, in his report to the parliamentary group, estimated the membership of the federation at only 150, with about 10 non-Europeans. The *Force ouvrière* in Tunisia also opposed the policy of repression. Groupe parlementaire, meeting of 10 March 1953, pp. 2-4. Also William S. Lee, "French Policy and the Tunisian National Movement,1950-54" (D.Phil. thesis, Oxford University), p. 38; Quilliot, *La S.F.I.O.*, p. 448.

[49] Quilliot, *La S.F.I.O.*, pp. 452-454.

[50] At the 1952 Congress, Gauthier, a representative of the Moroccan federation, and Julien argued against a policy of force, but the Istiqlal was once again denounced (particularly by Gauthier) and the Congress only went so far as to demand internal autonomy, *after* France received assurances that Morocco had no wish for "separatism." *Le Populaire*, 26 May 1952, p. 3. For later positions, *Le Populaire*, 29 January 1953; 6 July 1954.

The Socialists' liberalism, then, was tempered by previous lack of concern with nationalist unrest in North Africa (which they shared with other parties), by their reliance upon local Socialists for information and program, and by the character of the nationalist movements. They still lacked a comprehensive policy toward the overseas territories or a clear sense of what the final result for the empire would be; the word "independence" was slow to appear in the party's manifestos and statements. Nevertheless, in the Assembly, they backed the principal decolonizing ministry of Mendès-France. Despite opposition from the supporters of European integration (notably Mollet), skepticism about his new political style—too critical of the "system" that they had built—and disagreements over economic policy, the Socialists made clear that the course pursued by Mendès-France in Indochina and North Africa was a principal reason for their support.[51] The Socialist deputies even relented in their opposition to the Faure ministry to throw their support behind Moroccan decolonization in October, 1955.

Following the Mendèsist experiment, the Algerian revolution widened and France faced the final crises in Morocco. The rapid rise of decolonization as a national political issue finally forced the Socialists to define a colonial policy, an effort that illuminated the differences among emerging factions within the party.

Incipient division in a time of unity: 1954-1955
Unrest in North Africa began to produce divisions among the Socialists, even in opposition, but the level of disagreement never matched that seen earlier, at the beginning of the Third Force period, or later, after the Socialist-led government of Guy Mollet had embarked on a policy of pacification in Algeria. Opposition continued to have its unifying and tonic effects on the party. Three currents of opinion soon became apparent within the parliamentary party, but there were no

[51] SFIO, Group parlementaire, 2 June 1953, p. 4; also 1 and 5 February 1955.

severe confrontations between them at this time, nor any factional battles at party meetings.

The initial response of the party to the outbreak of the Algerian uprising in November, 1954 was cautious and conservative. In discussion among the Socialist deputies before the debate of 9 December, the Algerian representatives no longer took a distinctly liberal line. Rabier, leader of the fight to make the Statute of 1947 less biased in favor of the Europeans, hastened to ask that the *ordre du jour* presented by the Socialists not group Tunisia, Morocco, and Algeria, since "the situation was completely different" in the Algerian case. The Muslim representative, Benhamed, claimed that the immense majority of the population had not followed the insurgents and that the press had greatly exaggerated the outbreak of violence. Only Coffin, a later liberal, stressed that the question was a *political* one that could not be met by economic and social reforms alone; he urged that a new formula and new structure be found for the French Union and the Republic.[52]

The Socialists were inclined to follow the lead of the Mendès-France cabinet in the early months of the revolt; as they moved into opposition under the Faure government after February, 1955, their position became more critical and the divisions within the party became more evident. Alain Savary led those attempting to set off a Socialist position on the liberal side of the Faure cabinet. At meetings of the parliamentary group in June and July, 1955, he was often supported by Robert Verdier, later to be a prominent opponent of Mollet's policies, and Savary usually succeeded in carrying the center of the group with him. His most vocal opponent at this time was a deputy who had been denouncing North African nationalism and concessions to "separatism" since the early 1950s: Max Lejeune, a leader of the second group, the "nationalists." Lejeune, a later leader of the "ultras" within the party during the Algerian War, was usually supported by Naegelen, Boutbien, and the deputies from Algeria. Although Savary and the

[52] SFIO, Groupe parlementaire, meeting of 9 December 1954.

liberals could usually rally most of the other deputies to their side, the attitudes expressed by those in the center, such as Christian Pineau, were often closer to the nationalist than the liberal point of view. Pineau, for example, stressed the essential support that the rebels were receiving from outside forces— the Arab League, the Communists, British and American firms. He claimed that "justice and force are at this time the two sole trumps of France."[53]

As France's position in North Africa deteriorated, confusions and oppositions within the parliamentary group found expression at the party's National Congress at Asnières in July, 1955. The hall was draped in red flags, and the slogan behind the tribune—"The unity of the workers makes world peace"—suggested the ideological fidelity of the party; the Congress itself confirmed that fidelity in continued equivocation on colonial questions. Even during preparations for the meeting the contradictions were clear: the Executive Committee had stated its intention to seek "a new definition of the French Union, putting aside both assimilation and independence to achieve a true association."[54]

Liberal arguments were put forcefully at the conference by André Bidet, who condemned the "regrettable fiction of the three departments of Algeria," and held up Tunisia as a model for the decolonization of North Africa. Oreste Rosenfeld, another of Mollet's future opponents, was more harsh, comparing the tone of administrative statements in Algeria to that of the Nazis during the Occupation. He emphasized the liberals' claim for politics first; social and economic reforms could not substitute for political change. The solution proposed for Algeria was no longer the statute beloved, if never implemented, by the party's ministers: Rosenfeld labeled it *dépassé*. Rather, he advocated an Algerian Assembly elected by a single electoral college (no mention of equal represen-

[53] The debates within the group can be found in the meetings of 22 June 1955; 29 June 1955 (for the Pineau comments), pp. 2-5; 19 July 1955, p. 3; 29 July 1955.

[54] *Le Monde*, 18 June 1955.

tation for the two communities), that would clearly exercise considerable autonomous powers—a substantial step toward home rule. The principal spokesmen in opposition to the liberals were the representatives of the Algerian settlers, though even their statements were qualified by condemnation of the sabotage of the 1947 Statute. They raised themes that would imbue Socialist discourse during the Mollet ministry, objecting to parallels between Tunisia and Algeria, affirming the complete attachment of the Algeria population to the metropole, and arguing that the *petits blancs* among the European population could be distinguished from the *gros colons*. These poor whites "who live with the Arabs are not our enemy," they contended.

The Socialist Congress witnessed little vacillation from any side on equality between Muslims and Europeans, and none of the stirring tributes to the history of French colonialism that one would hear at conservative and Gaullist gatherings. But the questions of how much autonomy would be granted and what the final relations between France and the overseas territories, including Algeria, would be, was sidestepped once again. The Congress did endorse more of the liberal argument than any other, however, by acknowledging that political advance had to accompany economic and social reform and noting that the end to be achieved "is to permit the accession of peoples to the direction of their own affairs and their free association to the French Community." As might have been expected, Algeria produced more hesitation than any other colonial question. The old solution of an Algerian Assembly, equally divided between Arab and European, elected by a single college, was endorsed once again. The "new forms of association" that would be permitted the territory, however, were left undefined, and Mollet's own speech to the Congress gave a conservative cast to that which had been decided, emphasizing "association" rather than "federation" and placing the solution of the party between "force" and "secession." The latter—independence—was labeled "a catastrophe for the

French working class as well as for the overseas populations."[55]

The Moroccan crisis of October, 1955 seemed to push the Socialists toward considering the future status of Algeria as a part of North Africa, rather than an inseparable part of France. Discussions in the Socialist parliamentary group demonstrate conclusively that, at this time, the future was open: Algeria was not the *exception* to decolonization. Even Naegelen admitted that the Statute of 1947 was outdated, and conservative members of the center, such as Pineau, could declare that the Socialists

must have the courage to state that the form of future Franco-Muslim collaboration, if French presence is maintained, will have no relation with the present system of Algerian departments. . . . We are moving toward forms of autonomy whose nature it is difficult to estimate, but we must not have any illusions on this point.[56]

But it was Albert Gazier, later a loyal ministerial supporter of the Mollet government, who put the crucial question most bluntly:

Is the current which, across the world, is in the course of pushing previously subject peoples toward independence going to spare Algeria or not? . . .

[Gazier] believes that it is an error to think that in the North African continent one will have an autonomous Morocco and Tunisia and an Algeria different from these two. If that is true, is it expedient to state it? Isn't it going to increase the nationalist feeling in Algeria? It is a great responsibility to take. . . . If one responds affirmatively to that question, that the current of independence will touch Algeria as well, then it is necessary to proceed to the study of the problems which flow from that acknowledgment. It will be necessary to study the forms to give to Algerian sovereignty and to concern ourselves, with much more care than we have done for Tunisia, with the safeguard and the preservation of the French population.

Mollet claimed to agree completely with Gazier, but in fact hastened to strike a center position (his typical strategy in the parliamentary group) between Savary and the liberals on the one hand, and Lejeune, the strident nationalist, who had argued that if France lost North Africa, "the regime would disappear." Mollet accepted the link between regime and Algeria made by Lejeune, an argument he would use in the future to discipline critics of his Algerian policy, but he rejected an attribution of the Algerian revolt to external aggression, claiming that "the French who had made Algerian policy for twenty-five years were solely responsible." He would forget his declaration one year later when the Suez intervention was authorized to halt "Nasserite aggression" in North Africa. Once again, Mollet sought to tilt the group consensus toward the status quo by giving the Socialist position as one between "pseudo-integration" and *"le départ."*[57]

The liberals continued to gain ground in the autumn of 1955, however. Savary won endorsement from the Socialist deputies for an *ordre du jour* that staked out an advanced position for the party: calling for the election of a new Algerian Assembly (without stipulating equal representation for each community), and, following those elections, discussions with Algerian representatives to define "the means and the stages toward an end to be fixed in these free discussions—regime of association or federal regime or *any other regime* permitting open ties between all elements of the Algerian population and establishing lasting, freely consented ties between France and Algeria [emphasis added]." Both Mollet and Naegelen thought it premature to mention elections, but the group adopted Savary's text with only Lejeune opposed and with eight abstentions. Several days later, in taking a position against the Faure government's *ordre du jour* (presented by Gaborit) on Algeria, the liberals again carried the day. Savary argued for a vote against, in order to separate the Socialists from the policy of force being pursued by the Faure ministry in Algeria. The party's Right (including Rabier, the Algerian deputy) argued for abstention or (in the case of Lejeune) voting in favor. Mollet, in a remark as ominous as his earlier declarations that elections were "premature," stated that he was basically for

[57] Comments by Gazier and Mollet in ibid.

a "bipartisan policy in overseas territories."[58] The final vote in the group suggested the relative weight of liberal support: only three votes were cast in favor (the far Right of Boutbien, Lejeune, and Doutrellot); thirty-six others voted for abstention; but the liberal opponents (seventy-nine) of the motion and of abstention carried the day.

The evolution of Socialist policy toward the colonial empire in the crucial years before Mollet's ministry makes clear that liberalism was gaining within parliamentary ranks and in the party outside parliament, and that that liberalism was based on an internal political strategy of *opposition*. The party followed Savary's course of setting themselves apart from the conservative coalition that governed France under Edgar Faure, despite Mollet's preference for a bipartisan policy. The clear Left-Right cleavage that characterized the election campaign in late 1955 confirmed the Socialists' support for decolonization, as did their alliance in the Republican Front with Pierre Mendès-France and the Radical Party. It was no longer necessary, it seemed, for the Socialists to save the regime by joining parties to their Right, and there was much less need to distinguish themselves from the Communists who competed with them to the Left. Philip Williams has described the effects that this *bipolarization* of the electoral battle would have on the Socialist strategy:

Apart from the perpetual Socialist-Communist duel, each party concentrated its fire on the opposing bloc and treated with sympathy (or ignored) the political groups who under P.R., or even in 1951, would have been its most dangerous and therefore most criticized competitors.[59]

Anti-colonialism became, more than it had been in the past, a part of Socialist Party identity, accentuated by the personal imprint of their ally, Mendès-France.

Their electoral platform borrowed extensively from party resolutions and positions taken in the National Assembly,

[58] SFIO, Groupe parlementaire, meeting of 18 October 1955.
[59] P. M. Williams, "The French Election of 1956: The Campaign," *Political Studies*, Vol. 4 (June, 1956), 163.

endorsing future ties between France and Algeria that could take any form wished by the populations.[60] And the Socialists did not ignore anti-colonialism in their campaign themes: a quantitative analysis suggests that their attention to such issues ranked below only the *Mendèsiste* Radicals and the Poujadists, their foes.[61] Even Mollet harshly condemned conservative policies in the French Union and took note of the British example of growing colonial autonomy; he condemned the "stupid and endless war" in Algeria.[62]

If there was a colonial consensus in the 1955 election campaign, it was (except for the Poujadists) a consensus in favor of peace and decolonization. With the electorate concerned over the situation in North Africa, and the press at last paying it full attention, "every national figure except M. Bidault was anxious to proclaim his liberal attitude."[63] And despite the fragmented National Assembly that emerged from the elections, the overall preference of the electorate was almost as clear-cut as the divisions between the two main blocs:

Whatever the complications of the parliamentary situation, the electorate expressed its views clearly enough. The 5 per cent increase in the Mendèsist share of the poll, while the Communists and Socialists held their own, amounted to a leftward 'swing' which would be considered remarkable in contemporary Britain. Since North Africa was unquestionably the main issue in the campaign, this amounted to a mandate—as plain as mandates can ever be—for a liberal attitude to a problem far harder to solve than Britain's in India nine years ago.[64]

Within a few months, that mandate would be forgotten, as the Socialist Party led France deeper into the Algerian War.

[60] Georges Dupeux, "Les Plates-formes des parties," in *Les Élections du 2 janvier 1956*, ed. Maurice Duverger (Paris: Armand Colin, 1957), p. 55.

[61] Alain Touraine, "Thèmes et vocabulaire d' une campaign électorale," ibid., p. 290.

[62] *Le Populaire*, 20 December 1955.

[63] Williams, "The French Elections," p. 167.

[64] Ibid., p. 175.

THE SOCIALISTS AND ALGERIA, 1956-1958: DISSENT AND FRAGMENTATION

Guy Mollet's Socialist-led government, which quickly moved to reinforce the policy of pacification in Algeria, soon faced fault-lines within the party that resembled those of the earlier period of Socialist power-sharing (1947-1951). The de facto center coalition that supported Mollet (with conservative support assured by a policy of force in North Africa) was challenged by Socialist dissenters in the parliamentary group (although visible divisions remained slight by British standards) and among the party rank and file. The divisions were deeper this time, however, although their effect on Socialist acceptance of coercion in Algeria remained slight. Only Mollet's decision to support the investiture of de Gaulle in 1958 and then to join de Gaulle's government and support the new constitution brought long-delayed rupture in the party in September, 1958. The division over Algeria, unlike earlier cleavage on colonial questions, was also fought over questions of political strategy, with Mollet's opponents criticizing not only his Algerian line, but the postwar closure of any opening to Communist dissidents on the Left or Catholic progressives on the Right. Given the costs to the party of Mollet's Algerian policy, two questions require answers: Why did Mollet pursue the course he did after 1956? Why did the expression of voice (and the threat of exit) in the party fail to reverse Mollet's Algerian policy?

Guy Mollet and the choice for pacification in Algeria

At least three explanations can be advanced to explain the actions of Guy Mollet, prime minister in the Republican Front government and secretary general of the SFIO: his own attitudes toward questions of the French Union and Algeria, attitudes that drew on the mélange that characterized Socialist ideology; Mollet's reading of the coalition possibilities in the new National Assembly; and finally, the effects of the party's stance on its electoral clientele and strategy.

Mollet's views on Algeria must be interpreted (since they

were stated most often to party groups) as part a strategy offering ideological incentives to the party faithful, as well as giving the party a means of interpreting the realities of the Algerian conflict. (Mollet did not resign as secretary general of the party when he became premier; he saw to it that his associate Pierre Commin was named interim secretary general.) He defended his Algerian policy as *socialist*, part of the great tradition inherited from Jaurès. At first, despite the cautions and concerns that he had expressed in 1955, it seemed that Mollet would pursue a liberal policy in Algeria, one that would match his government's forward-looking grant of independence to Morocco and Tunisia and the enlightened loi Defferre that set the territories of black Africa on the road to self-government. At the extraordinary Congress that followed the elections, Mollet was circumspect about plans for Algeria, given the necessities of coalition-building in the Assembly, but he did not retreat from the emphasis of previous Socialist statements—immediate elections to a new Algerian Assembly elected by a single college; the future of Algeria to be determined by negotiations; his "complete accord" with Mendès-France on this question. At the same Congress, the liberals kept firmly to their position on Mollet's Left: Oreste Rosenfeld denounced integration as based upon "an absurd myth: Algeria is France" and called for self-determination for the territory. It would be more than three years before a government of France (and it would not be a Socialist one) would accept Rosenfeld's program of self-determination. Even this confirmed liberal hoped for a federal solution in Algeria, "if it is still possible."[65]

The crucial shift in Mollet's attitudes toward Algeria has often been related to his disastrous visit to Algiers in February, 1956. He seems to have planned to replicate Mendès-France's surprise trip to Carthage (Tunisia) with General Juin in 1954, which had cut through the knot of the Tunisian crisis. Mollet, however, forgot the element of surprise, and appointed General Georges Catroux, an aging liberal, as Minister Resident,

[65] *Le Monde*, 17 January 1956, p. 3.

the newly elevated cabinet post for directing Algerian affairs. His reception in Algiers at the hands of the Europeans, infuriated by the appointment of Catroux, approached riot: as Mollet laid a wreath at the monument for the war dead in Algiers, he was abused with catcalls and pelted with tomatoes. In the face of such an apparently spontaneous (though in fact well-planned) resistance, Mollet conceded: Catroux was sacrificed to the mob.[66] With his resignation, a precedent had been set: the settlers of Algeria knew that they could participate in, even determine, the policy that Paris pursued in Algeria. For the Muslims of Algeria, on the other hand, any hope for a metropolitan government that would serve as a disinterested arbiter and peacemaker were dashed. And for the Socialist Party, the 6 February 1956 was a turning point, away from the course that it had taken, albeit haltingly, toward the loosening of colonial ties.

After Gaston Defferre (and some have said Pierre Mendès-France) had refused the Algerian responsibilities that Catroux had laid down, Mollet appointed the minister for economic affairs, Robert Lacoste, deputy from the Dordogne, a nationalist who had voted against the European Defense Community in 1954, a minister whose background as secretary general of the civil servants' union made it unlikely that he would take in hand the state apparatus in Algeria.

In public speeches and in private sessions before the Socialist parliamentary group, Mollet made clear the impact of the events of 6 February. His program for Algeria, shot through with ambiguity earlier, now tilted decidedly toward a policy of force rather than political reform or negotiation. Using his remarks to the Socialist deputies on 15 February 1956 and other statements, the outlines of the *Molletiste* view that would dominate the party's Algerian policy for the next four years becomes clear:

a) Mollet's analysis of Algeria found a vast center which could be recaptured for France: he estimated that the "great

[66] The incident is described in Alastair Horne, *A Savage War of Peace* (New York: Viking, 1978), pp. 147-152.

mass" of poorer *petits blancs*, who stood to lose everything if the French left Algeria, as well as 80 percent of the Muslim population, who were either passively sympathetic to France or actively hostile to the rebels.[67] A distinct alteration can be detected in Mollet's attitudes toward the Europeans in Algeria. Although Rabier and other settler spokesmen had taken this line in the past, Socialist statements in general painted lurid portraits of *gros colons* oppressing the Muslim population. Now, sympathy for and support of the European settlers would become more and more explicit, particularly as the weak Socialist ties to the Muslim population withered away.

b) Algeria is different: not only because of the large number of now-visible French citizens, but because historically there had not been an Algeria. The Algerian situation was no longer comparable to the rest of North Africa (as the party's liberals had argued and would continue to argue). While willing to concede an Algerian "personality," Mollet believed that an Algerian "nationality" did not exist.[68]

c) Denial of Algerian nationalism points to a resurgence of hostility to colonial nationalism that fitted well with Mollet's European orientation, an ambivalence that had marked the party's attitude toward Moroccan nationalism. The party's emphasis returns to Naegelen's old theme of *individual* liberation, to hostility toward a nationalism based upon "religious fanaticism," and to a final denial that decolonization, the accession of colonial peoples to independence, was in fact the inevitable historical trend that the party's Left perceived. In a remarkable address at the Pantheon in July, 1956 commemorating the death of Jaurès, Mollet placed his views within the grand Socialist tradition: against "an excess of blind nationalism," for "the total and complete liberation of each inhabitant of Algeria."[69] At the Toulouse Congress of the party in 1957, Mollet would argue that independence was "not a Socialist solution," that "the trend of the time is on

[67] SFIO, Groupe parlementaire, 15 February 1956, pp. 3-4.
[68] Ibid., p. 5.
[69] *Le Monde*, 29-30 July 1956.

the contrary to spare peoples the dangerous and useless step of xenophobic natonalism."

d) Given the unrepresentative, even phantasmagoric, character of colonial nationalism in Mollet's eyes, any acceptable negotiating partners had to be democratically elected: bearing arms, as Mollet never ceased to claim, did not give anyone the right to represent the people of Algeria. The elections, of course, could only follow the restoration of order: a position parallel to that taken by the Ramadier government in 1947 in the case of Indochina.

e) Since political solutions were pushed aside, the old Socialist emphasis on social and economic reforms once again came forward: correcting the injustices of Algerian society would win over that vast reservoir of uncommitted Arab sentiment. Political democracy could only be based upon a certain level of development—once again, echoes of bastardized Marxism.

f) Finally, as the war continued, two other themes would become prominent for Mollet and his allies. One was the old favorite of conservatives—the "bloodbath" that would result if the French left Algeria. The second, already mentioned during the Moroccan crisis of October, 1955, was the link between Algeria and the survival of the parliamentary regime. Particularly after the fall of the Mollet government in May, 1957, this argument would be used to good effect by Mollet to ensure Socialist participation in increasingly conservative governments. More than any other party, the Socialists saw their fate tied to that of the Fourth Republic, and even those who vehemently opposed Mollet's policies in Algeria were unwilling to see the regime succumb to nationalists of the extreme Right.

The essential elements of *Molletisme* were, in a peculiar looking-glass way, all drawn from the Socialist corpus, at least as defined in France: internationalism and anti-clericalism were redefined as hostility to Arab nationalism; social and economic reform was used to *replace* political change; sympathy for the working class became an attachment to *les petits* in Algeria (but *European petits*). The policies to match the *Molle-*

tiste views soon became apparent: a massive increase in the military forces available in Algeria and the formulation of Mollet's famous "triptych" of cease-fire, elections, and negotiations, which became the unshakable basis of the government's program. To the despair of the party's liberals, "cease-fire" was defined by Mollet and Lacoste as simple surrender by the FLN rebels. And independence, it also became clear, would never be allowed by Mollet, no matter what the views of the elected representatives of Algeria.[70]

Mollet's tenacious defense of his Algerian policy, even after the fall of the Fourth Republic, suggests his firm belief that it was the best course for France and his party. Nevertheless, his own well-established sensitivity to public opinion and his constant concern with threats to his own position in the party suggest political explanations for his behavior as well. The first and most obvious are the *demands of coalition formation* in the Assembly that was elected in January, 1956. The elections had produced an Assembly that looked nearly ungovernable: while the Socialists had made their first slight progress in share of vote since the war, they and their Republican Front allies were far short of an absolute majority. The gains that the Communists also made and the unexpected surge of support for the Poujadists on the Right complicated possibilities for alternative coalitions. Even if the MRP supported a Republican Front minority government, as it would in the case of Mollet's ministry, the Center-Left coalition would fall short of a majority. Leaving aside the Poujadists, a cabinet would have to rely either on Communist or on *modéré* (Conservative) votes to maintain itself.

At the Socialist Congress that followed the elections, Mollet had declared either the "popular front" or the "national union" solutions unthinkable, but he chose to accept Conservative support after the Communists moved into opposition. Although the Communists had gone so far as to vote special powers in Algeria for the Mollet government—arguing that

[70] Mollet makes his position clear as early as May, 1956 before the Socialist deputies (Groupe parlementaire, meeting of 23 May 1956, pp. 2-3).

they would be a prelude to negotiation—the party had drifted toward opposition by July, 1956 and the interventions by France against Egypt and the Soviet Union against the Hungarian uprising sealed the breach between the two parties. By late 1956, the Mollet government was at the mercy of the Conservatives, and the price for their support was a policy of force in Algeria: Guy Mollet was able to trade off a reformist domestic policy against an increasingly harsh Algerian policy.[71] The participation of the Conservatives themselves in the last cabinet of the Fourth Republic (that of Félix Gaillard) meant that the Socialists had reached a policy of effective support for a "national union" government, despite earlier protests.

A second political explanation derives the deepening commitment to *Algérie française* from the Socialists' *party and electoral goals*. The rise and final defeat of dissent within the Socialist Party, discussed below, suggests that Mollet was able to purchase support for his Algerian policy with the purposive incentives that tenure in office provided any party, incentives of considerable interest to the officeholders who were influential in the ranks of the party. Nevertheless, while the party's share of power helped to stave off discontent, it is difficult to see, particularly in light of the earlier record of liberalism, any push from below for pacification policies in Algeria. Even among colonial questions, Algeria did not at first possess the resonance for the party faithful that economic and social issues did.

The political strengths of the Mollet strategy seemed rather to lay with the electorate outside the Socialist organization. In early 1956, the Mollet government faced a fluid situation in French public opinion: Algeria had increased dramatically in importance in the public consciousness (probably because of the sending of conscripts) but this did not lead immediately to a hardening of attitudes. By July, 1956, only 23 percent of those surveyed backed a policy of force when given the choice

[71] Harvey G. Simmons, *French Socialists in Search of a Role, 1956-1967* (Ithaca, N.Y.: Cornell University Press, 1970), p. 73.

between military means or negotiation for independence; fully 45 percent backed negotiations. As Smith and others have noted, only the Communists consistently supported negotiations, but Socialist supporters were split fairly evenly, and the Right alone backed the policy of force by a large margin. The public mood had changed by late 1956, however, and the Suez intervention was supported by a substantial plurality.[72]

By-elections held in 1957 seemed to confirm popular support for Mollet's policies in Algeria. The election in the first sector of the Seine (Paris, Left Bank), which was marked by a surge in Conservative strength and reinforcement of their new electoral strategy, also implied that the Socialist Party could benefit from nationalist appeals. Mireille Osmin, the Socialist candidate, was a member of the anti-war minority in the party, but during the campaign she took a very orthodox line, including attacks on the *Mendèsiste* Radical candidate and other "defeatists." The Socialist campaign was also notable for its appeals to the ideological past of the party: confirming the argument that the party's postwar strategy had ossified its ideology and gradually destroyed it as an instrument for analyzing the questions that dominated postwar French politics.[73] Socialist strategy paid off in the Paris election: in January, 1956, the *Mendèsiste* candidate had overtaken the Socialist; in 1957, the positions were reversed.[74] The Communist candidate lost in comparison to the 1956 results as well. Overall, in the by-elections of 1957, the Socialists gained 3.6 percent against their 1956 election figures, while their chief rivals on the Left, those political formations most critical of the Algerian War—the Radicals and the Communists—each *lost* an equivalent amount.[75] As Mollet told his opponents within the parliamentary group just before the Suez invasion: "In the country, it is the people who applaud." The Algerian

[72] IFOP, *Sondages*, no. 3 (1956), p. 68.
[73] Louis Bodin and Jean Touchard, "L'Election partielle de la première circonscription de la Seine," *Revue française de science politique* 7 (April-June, 1957), 289.
[74] Ibid., p. 304.
[75] *Année politique*, 1957, p. 565.

strategy seemed to win the hearts and minds of the French electorate to the Socialist Party.

Despite the surge in popular and electoral support for the Socialists (or at least the absence of its erosion) it is difficult to argue that the results spurred the government on. Survey figures in *early* 1956, when the Mollet policy took shape, document that considerable public support existed for a liberal policy in Algeria, and that Communist support might have been forthcoming. Alternative courses did exist. The dissidents in the party proposed a different political strategy to match their own views on Algeria: the crisis within the Communist Party induced by de-Stalinization and the Hungarian revolt should have been used by the party to regain a position of dominance on the Left. As Edouard Depreux, one of Mollet's critics, remarked, in its 1957 electoral successes the party had too often made its gains on the Right. He regretted that the SFIO had not better "bitten into the clientele of the Communist Party."[76]

Mollet's Algerian policies thus fitted with the strategy that had been the party's since the beginning of the Cold War: to be Left *and* national—sealing off exit to either side. To Mollet's opponents, his Algeria policy was not only morally detestable, but also represented the choice of an obsolete political strategy. The dissidents saw, as they had in the past, that carving out a secure niche within the political spectrum would place the Socialists forever at the mercy of right-wing coalition partners in the Assembly. In place of this line, they urged an opening that resembled the old "travailliste" line of Blum and Mayer—a broad, democratic party on the Left that would be able to expand toward both the Left and the Center in the new circumstances of French politics. However, the apparent electoral success of the party in the last years of the Fourth Republic, the uncanny ability, remarked upon by Philip Williams, of Mollet to read public opinion, placed the longer-term view of the Algerian minority at a distinct disadvantage.

[76] Remarks at the National Council, May, 1957 (*Le Monde*, 14 May 1957, p. 7).

The failure of dissent, 1956-1958: Voice and exit

While the conservative parties described in Chapter II faced fragmentation in attempting to decolonize over the opposition of more ideologically devoted followers, the French Socialist Party, spared the costs of decolonization up to this point, now faced growing opposition from those who attacked Mollet's policies of pacification as a betrayal of Socialist principles. First in the parliamentary party, then among the party militants, the dissenters attempted to halt and reverse the deepening commitment of the Socialists to a colonial war. Their efforts at voice finally failed, and the party's decision to support the new constitution of the Fifth Republic brought a split that Mollet had managed to avoid for so long. What must be explained is not only the pattern of internal party opposition to the Algerian War, but why the opposition ultimately failed against a policy that seemed to be both unsuccessful *and* a violation of Socialist ideology.

Dissent in the parliamentary party, 1956-1958

Dissent within the Socialist group of the National Assembly appeared soon after Mollet's hardening of position in February, 1956. Evident early on in the records of the Socialist group, opposition took more time to become public. The traditional cohesion of the Socialist deputies, seriously violated on very few occasions in the Fourth Republic, withstood even the intense disagreement of the minority with government policy. While the dissidents moved from abstaining or voting against Mollet *within* the group, to public expressions of disagreement, to refusal finally to take part in Assembly votes, rarely did the dissident deputies violate the discipline of vote to vote *against* the group as a whole. Even abstention was extremely rare. Given this adherence to the rules of the party (in striking contrast to the attitudes toward dissent in the British Labour Party), the dissenters necessarily had to carry their fight outside parliament to the party at large.

By early March, 1956, in discussions of the Socialist parliamentary group, some of the Socialist deputies were voicing sharp criticism of Lacoste's policies in Algeria. Daniel Mayer, often a leader of the opposition to Mollet in the past, pointed out that Mollet was following a de facto policy of national union. Antoine Mazier was even more outspoken. At a time when the infant opposition was concentrating upon the necessity for negotiations, he went to the core of the matter: responding to Lacoste's arguments in favor of "dignity" for Algeria, Mazier remarked tartly that dignity for Algerians was independence, that with Tunisia and Morocco becoming independent, Algeria would not remain "indissolubly tied" to France.[77] In a first expression of disagreement with the government, the dissenting deputies abstained on a vote within the group that determined their collective position on special powers for the government in Algeria.[78]

Opposition increased in intensity in November, 1956, after the fight against Mollet and Lacoste had found expression in the party outside the Assembly. Edouard Depreux, disenchanted with the government's Algerian program, resigned as president of the Socialist group in the Assembly; he was replaced by Robert Verdier, another critic of Mollet. Heated discussions took place in the Executive Committee of the party and the parliamentary group over the proposed Algerian statute. Mollet's refusal to countenance a statute that might lead to independence, supported by "bloodbath" and "threat to the regime" arguments, did not convince the minority deputies.[79] They were further aroused by news that the military in Algeria had intercepted a flight carrying Ben Bella and other FLN leaders from Morocco to Tunisia, forced the flight to land, and arrested the leaders on board (22 October 1956). Mollet believed it impossible to reverse the action, which embittered relations with Tunisia and Morocco and thwarted once and for all secret peace negotiations between the Mollet government and the FLN. Following this incident, the minister for Moroccan and Tunisian affairs, Alain Savary, the last liberal in the cabinet (unless one counts Defferre), resigned.

[77] SFIO, Groupe parlementaire, 6 March 1956, p. 4.
[78] SFIO, Groupe parlementaire, 7 March 1956.
[79] Quilliot, La S.F.I.O., pp. 678-681.

The minority in the parliamentary group once again protested, and a core of twelve abstained when the group was polled for a vote of confidence (see Table II).

Army seizure of the FLN leaders took place during the deepening Suez crisis. In Socialist ranks the nationalization of the Canal had been greeted with hostility, and some of the harshest critics of Mollet, such as André Philip, were at first the most vehement opponents of Nasser.[80] The implicit threat to Israel, with its strong ties to the party, also explains a part of the reaction. In Mollet's own words, an "anti-Munich" reflex pushed the government toward intervention against Nasser; that emotional response was reinforced by the close connection (even cause) that many saw between Egypt and the Algerian revolution.[81]

While Mollet's government enjoyed a surge in popularity as an outpouring of nationalism swept the country, the intervention served to harden the opposition of Mollet's critics.[82] Their objections were made public outside of party meetings for the first time. A manifesto by André Philip combined criticism of the government's policies in Algeria and the Middle East with a new argument that the dissidents would brandish: that the party was becoming "nothing but an organ of propaganda in the service of government policy" and that freedom of discussion within the party was being stifled.[83] Philip's appeal to the party was followed by a letter to Pierre Commin, interim secretary general, signed by twenty-five Socialists (among them seventeen of the one hundred deputies) in support of Philip's criticisms, declaring that the government's policies did not reflect stated party positions and in any case were failures: the Suez intervention was labeled "cat-

[80] Ibid., p. 642.

[81] S.F.I.O., Groupe parlementaire, meeting of 3 October 1956, p. 5; although Mollet also discounts the notion that defeating Nasser would remove the Algerian problem altogether.

[82] The public mood in France during the Suez intervention is described in Herbert Luethy and David Rodnick, *French Motivations in the Suez Crisis* (Princeton: International Institute for Social Research, 1956).

[83] *Le Monde*, 20 November 1956, p. 7.

Table II. Dissenting Socialist Deputies: Algeria

Name	Abstention in group on vote of confidence, 25 October 1956	Letter to Commin December, 1956	Opposition to EDC	Minority motion Toulouse, June, 1957	Confidence, Algerian loi-cadre, 30 September 1957	Investiture, de Gaulle June, 1958
Arbeltier, René	X	X	—	X	—	Against
Berthet, Alix	X	X	—	X	Against	Against
Binot, Jean	X	X	X (+ Paris Agreements)	X	Against	Against
Cartier, Marcel	X	X	X	X	—	Against
Depreux, Edouard	X	X	—	X	Against	Against
Desson, Guy	X	X	X (+ Paris Agreements)	X	—	Against
Gourdon, Robert	X	—	X (+ Paris Agreements)	—	Against	Against
Mabrut, Lucien	X	X	X (+ Paris Agreements)	—	Abstention	Against
Mayer, Daniel	X	X	X	X	Against	—
Mazier, Antoine	X	X	X	X	Against	Against
Palmero, Jean	X	X	—	X	—	Against
Verdier, Robert	X	X	—	X	Against	Against
Briffod, Henri	—	X	—	X	—	Against
Bouhey, Jean	—	X	X (+ Paris Agreements)	—	—	For
Marguerite, Charles	Not taking part	X	—	X	Abstention	Against
Moch, Jules	—	X	X	—	—	For
Savary, Alain	—	X	—	X	Against	Against
Titeux, Camille	—	X	X (+ Paris Agreements)	X	Against	Against
			X	X	—	For

astrophic."[84] The letter to Commin marked not only a new step in *public* dissent on the part of the minority, but also a solidification of the group by those acts. Of signatories to the letter, a majority would leave the party to found the Parti socialist autonome when the split came in 1958.

Dissent spread among the deputies in early 1957. Members of the Center, such as Deixonne and Lussy, who normally supported Mollet, expressed their discontent with the tight control that the Executive Committee exercised over Socialist Algerian policy. The economic consequences of the war were also becoming apparent: some deputies supported a tax reform that Mollet considered politically dangerous.[85] Despite growing unease, however, those minority deputies who were willing to express their opposition before party Congresses and National Councils remained roughly the same: the minority motion submitted to the Congress of Toulouse in June, 1957 was signed by virtually the same deputies as the letter to Commin in November (Table II).

In July, 1957, however, following the Toulouse Congress, minority deputies took another fateful step. The fall of the Mollet government and the advent of a cabinet led by a right-wing Radical, Maurice Bourgès-Maunoury, added the issue of Socialist participation to the arsenal of the dissidents. Chances for gaining support on this broader issue and tapping weakened loyalty in the party were improved. A proposal to extend the government's existing special powers to metropolitan France for the first time concerned more than simply the Socialist group. The vote of confidence on special powers (19 July 1957) led twenty-six members of the Socialist group (including Robert Verdier, the president) to absent themselves from the vote; most of those not participating were past *minoritaires*. Depreux followed party discipline and then resigned from the Executive Committee of the party, since he could no longer

[84] *Le Monde*, 6 December 1956.
[85] SFIO, Groupe parlementaire, meeting of 14 March 1957, pp. 3-4; also 19 March 1957; 14 and 16 May 1957.

accept its decisions. Verdier resigned as chairman of the group, followed by two of the vice-chairmen, Charlot and Titeux.

By late 1957, the opponents of Mollet in the Assembly group seemed to have reached a plateau no higher than their strength one year before. But the *loi-cadre* proposed by the Bourgès-Maunoury government for Algeria added a new name to the list of critics, more important in the life of the party outside parliament than any of the others: Gaston Defferre, mayor of Marseilles, leader of the third-largest Socialist federation. Defferre's shift to more clear-cut opposition offered the minority its best hope of changing party policy and possibly replacing Mollet altogether. At the same time, disciplinary measures began to fall with increasing severity on those deputies who were most outspoken: Daniel Mayer, who alone among the Socialists voted against the renewal of special powers for Algeria and the metropolis under the Gaillard ministry (12 November), was suspended from the group until the end of the legislature. (Palmero, who abstained on the investiture vote for Gaillard, was suspended for only three months.) Mayer soon resigned from the Assembly.

In the last months of the Fourth Republic splits in the parliamentary party widened, but a certain fatalism on the question of Algeria also grew. Although Defferre had now joined the original group of Mollet's opponents in opposing participation in the Gaillard ministry and in rejecting the Mollet-Lacoste line in Algeria, the solutions that the two dissident groups proposed for resolving the conflict remained distinct.[86] Disenchantment grew: at a combined meeting of the Executive Committee and the parliamentary group in March, 1958, Mollet could only muster 63 of 101 deputies in favor of the government; 30 were opposed, and 8 abstained.[87] The final crisis, after the fall of the Gaillard cabinet in April, 1958, brought a temporary unity back to the group. Mollet softened his stand on Algeria, presenting Pierre Pflimlin, candidate for investiture as premier, as a "dove" on Algeria. After the seizure of the

[86] Quilliot, *La S.F.I.O.*, p. 733.
[87] SFIO, Groupe parlementaire, meeting of 7 March 1958.

Government General in Algiers on 13 May, the group's approval of Pflimlin, now tied to the defense of the Republic, became unanimous: Mollet's opponents, Mazier, Depreux, and Defferre, all argued forcefully that the group should accept the challenge that had been thrown down and back Pflimlin.[88] After Socialist ministers joined the Pflimlin cabinet, the deputies, with the exceptions of Felix Gouin and Max Lejeune (who was shouted down) seemed to be impervious to de Gaulle's appeals. At a meeting of the group and the party Executive Committee on 17 May, 111 of the 115 voting agreed that they would not rally under any circumstances to the proposed candidature of de Gaulle, "a challenge to republican legality."[89]

After the seizure of Corsica by paratroops from Algeria, Mollet's resistance to de Gaulle melted. The choice that Mollet saw was a stark one—de Gaulle's assumption of power legally or a government of the colonels. Mollet reiterated his argument just before the vote of the Socialist deputies on de Gaulle's investiture; no country in Europe had succeeded in removing a military dictatorship by internal opposition.[90] Mollet also tried to still the fears of those who viewed de Gaulle as an instrument of the "ultras" in Algeria by painting him as a liberal, "who goes far in the direction of an Algerian personality."[91]

On this occasion, though, Mollet was beaten: the group split in half, as did the Executive Committee of the party. The supporters of de Gaulle lost in both cases. Joining the long-standing Algerian opposition were many of those who had loyally supported Mollet in the past, but could not accept this violation of republican legality: Gazier, Pineau, Jacquet, and

[88] SFIO, Groupe parlementaire, meeting of 13 May 1958.

[89] Yet disagreements still emerged: Mollet was fearful of any appearance of an alliance with the Communists, which could play into de Gaulle's hands, while others in the group urged the building of bridges to the CGT and the Communist Party.

[90] SFIO, Groupe parlementaire, meeting of 31 May 1958, p. 5.

[91] SFIO, Groupe parlementaire (and Comité directeur), meeting of 30 May 1958.

Pierre Commin, Mollet's long-time ally in the party apparatus. Of the original core of dissidents who signed the letter to Commin in 1956, only Jules Moch and Jean Bouhey voted for de Gaulle's investiture. It appeared that the minority had at last found its majority, as the Fourth Republic collapsed around it.

But Guy Mollet would ultimately triumph, delaying a party Congress scheduled for the summer and winning over his most powerful foe, Gaston Defferre. The reasons for his success lay more in the party outside parliament, however. Before tracing the rise of dissidence among the rank and file in the federations, however, the group of minority deputies should be examined in order to explain the sources of their opposition.

The pattern of resistance to Mollet's policies resembled that of the late 1940s: its core was the Federation of the Seine, historically the center of Left dissidence in the party, a stronghold of the Gauche révolutionnaire and Bataille socialiste factions in the 1930s. The lineage of opposition continued directly in the persons of Marceau Pivert, Jean Rous, and others associated with the revolutionary Left in the 1930s, figures who opposed the Algerian War early on. The leaders of the Socialist group in the Assembly added a second strand of opposition, that might be called *Blumiste*, those associated with the former leader of the party in the 1930s or after the war. Daniel Mayer, Blum's heir apparent defeated by Mollet, was among Mollet's first and most tenacious opponents. The group also included Robert Verdier, Jules Moch, and, outside parliament, Oreste Rosenfeld, Charles-André Julien, and Blum's own son, Robert.

Other reasons contributed to Parisian leadership of the opposition to Mollet and Lacoste. Paris was the intellectual center of the nation, and intellectuals and students were prominent in opposing the Algerian War. Attention to foreign affairs was high; many of the deputies who opposed the war had international experience that made them sensitive to outside criticism from the Socialist International and the United States. (Moch had served at the United Nations, Philip at the Council of Europe.) And many of the dissident deputies had experience in colonial affairs, through parliamentary committees or the conduct of fact-finding missions for the party. Verdier, for example, had examined the situation in Tunisia for the SFIO; Savary had been the party spokesman on Indochina. Finally, the minority's concentration in the Paris region meant a greater opportunity to establish contact with other anti-war groups, ties that did not follow party lines in many cases.

Political explanations for the pattern of dissidence can also be advanced: the common characteristics of federations supporting the minority are examined below. Some overlap with other parliamentary divisions is apparent: a group of deputies on the Left that Macrae labels "Popular Front" were opponents of the European Defense Community and German rearmament in 1954; they were also (with two exceptions) part of the core group of antiwar deputies.[92]

Dissent outside the assembly: Voice denied

The leaders of parliamentary opposition to Mollet faced formidable obstacles in their efforts to change party policy. The balance between the party outside parliament and the deputies was tilted in favor of the former (in contrast to the British Labour Party) and Mollet was firmly in control of the party organization. Postwar changes in election procedures, described above, made it difficult for factions within the party to organize. Mollet was also backed by the largest federations in the party, particularly his own federation, the Pas-de-Calais, and the Nord, led by Augustin Laurent. Mollet's opponents possessed only two political assets: their stature as parliamentary leaders (although they lacked easy means of communication with militants outside their federations) and the fractious Federation of the Seine, the fourth largest in the party, but one which they could not win to their side.[93]

The battle for the party began soon after the appearance

[92] Duncan Macrae, Jr., *Parliament, Parties and Society in France, 1946-1958*, (New York: St. Martin's Press, 1967), p. 209, Table 7.12.

[93] On the governance of the party, Williams, *Crisis and Compromise*, pp. 98-100; on the power of the large federations, Simmons, *French Socialists*, pp. 170-172 and Appendix E, pp. 281-282. Party discipline was tightened further in 1956, with the National Council given final disciplinary power (Simmons, *French Socialists*, pp. 175-176).

of parliamentary opposition. Representatives of the Seine Federation led the way in criticizing the turn toward pacification at the National Council of the party in June, 1956. Mollet asked for support from the party, however, and he received it as the minority went down to crushing defeat. (The scale of minority support in party councils is given in Table III.) National Councils were meant to assess the fidelity of Socialist ministers to the decisions of the last party Congress; new policy was set at the Congresses, where the minority could organize more easily on the basis of an alternative motion.

At the National Congress (held at Lille, 18 June-1 July 1956), three principal motions were presented. The minority, represented in debates by Philip, Mazier, Rous, and Mayer, hammered away at the methods employed in Algeria under Lacoste; for some of the minority, such as Philip and Rous, the "Algerian national fact" had to be recognized and negotiations begun. Others (and the minority motion) sidestepped the future of Algeria and left it to negotiations with freely elected representatives of the population there. Mazier also put forward an alternative political strategy that the minority would continue to emphasize: the opportunities that de-Stalinization presented to the Socialists in making gains at the expense of the Communists. The Algerian conflict was an obstacle to establishing the party as the dominant force on the Left.

Motions from the Bouches-du-Rhône and the Nord were tepid criticisms of existing policy, easily incorporated into the leadership's motion, which urged the government to go further than it had in seeking peace in Algeria. The final motion thus became ambiguous enough to satisfy all but the hard core of dissidents (Mayer, Philip, and their supporters); even these were prepared to vote for the innocuous final paragraph of the motion. As party policy on Algeria, the motion passed at the Congress of Lille would serve as a future point of conflict. It easily covered the triptych of Mollet, by calling for restoration of peace, free elections, and then negotiations, as well as the maintenance of "indispensable ties with France." On the other hand, the motion assured Algeria "a wide autonomy

Table III. The Progress of the Minority, 1956-1958

Congress/Council	Majority	Minority	Abstentions	Absent	Percentage Minority Vote
National Council June, 1956	3,138	212	125	245	6.3%
National Congress, Lille June-July, 1956	3,308	363	44	5	9.9%
National Council December, 1956	3,247	270	78	0	7.7%
National Council May, 1957	2,997	401	435	79	11.9%
National Council June, 1957 (question of participation)	2,464	1,071	298	0	30.3%
National Congress, Toulouse June-July, 1957	2,547	779/498 (Defferre/Verdier)	45	43	20.4%/13.0%
National Council, March 1958 (Lussy amendment-participation)	2,650	1,121	83	58	29.7%
National Congress, Issy-les-Moulineaux September, 1958	3,370	611	43	0	15.3%

of direction, guaranteed by internal institutions partaking of executive and legislative power," and called in strong language for the negotiation of a cease-fire "with those whom we fight."[94] The party's will could be interpreted to mean continuing the effort at pacification or instituting a form of home rule as a first step toward independence. The motion was passed by a massive majority; having failed to swing any of the large federations to their side, the minority suffered another defeat. Two of their number were also dropped from the Executive Committee (Pivert and Rimbert). The Congress vote had demonstrated, however, that disenchantment within the party had spread beyond the sites of earliest discontent.

The outburst of parliamentary criticism that followed capture of the FLN leaders and the Suez intervention was greeted with a hardening of attitudes within the party in support of Mollet. Before the National Council of December, 1956, the large federations declared their total support for the Mollet government; Mollet's own federation of the Pas-de-Calais called for intraparty discipline as well. The party leadership was dealing firmly with expressions of voice: the list of publications to which Socialists could not contribute grew longer (including *France-Observateur*) and demands for a special National Congress were flatly refused. At the National Council, the minority spoke more clearly in favor of accepting Algerian independence than they had at the Congress of Lille, but their defeat was as complete as it had been at previous meetings.[95]

The party minority next advanced their rebellion by organizing more formally, creating the Comité socialiste d'études et d'action pour la paix en Algérie (29 January 1957). The bureau of the committee was dominated by the dissidents of the Paris region, combining both the *Blumistes* (Léon Blum's son played an active role) and the Left (Pivert and Rous). In the absence of the *tribune libre* demanded by Mollet's opponents, the committee would serve as a means of commu-

---

[94] *Le Monde*, 3 July 1956, p. 5; 30 June 1956, p. 5; 1-2 July 1956, p. 3.
[95] *Le Populaire*, 17 December 1956 and Claude Estier, "La Minorité socialiste peut-elle encore agir?" *France-Observateur*, 20 December 1956, p. 4.

nication with militants in other federations, helping to spread opposition beyond the Parisian base. Although the Executive Committee of the party called for the dissolution of the Committee, it continued its work, and proposed the minority motion at the Congress of Toulouse in 1957.[96]

Electoral successes by the Socialist Party (relative to their competitors on the Left) made the task of the Socialist dissidents harder in 1957, but the issue of participation in increasingly conservative cabinets after the fall of the Mollet government in May brought them new allies, as it had for the parliamentary opponents of the Algerian War. Early 1957 was also marked by widespread reports of torture and other crimes committed by French forces in Algeria and by government efforts to control publication of such information. Malaise grew with the subordination of the party to government requirements and the intensification of disciplinary measures against those who opposed the leadership position. The list of prohibited journals grew, and one dissident leader, André Philip, was expelled from the party following the publication of *Le Socialisme trahi*, in which he labeled the policy of pacification "a crime."[97]

The National Council held just before the fall of the Mollet government (12 May 1957) showed slender progress on the part of the minority, but the shift of the Bouches-du-Rhône federation from support to abstention indicated that Defferre's patience with the Mollet-Lacoste policies was growing thin. A few weeks later, a second Council (3 June 1957) demonstrated that the issue of participation added immensely to the minority's support, marshaling 1,071 votes against the successful leadership motion, which received 2,464.[98] With the question of supporting increasingly conservative governments at issue, both sides looked to the National Congress at

[96] Simmons, *French Socialists*, pp. 63-64; Depreux, *Souvenirs*, p. 467.

[97] Quilliot, *La S.F.I.O.*, pp. 725-728; André Philip, *Le Socialisme trahi* (Paris: Plon, 1957).

[98] Quilliot, *La S.F.I.O.*, p. 729.

Toulouse as a test of strength after more than a year of Socialist direction of the Algerian War.

Held in simmering heat, the Congress (27 June-1 July 1957) saw the harshest confrontations between supporters and opponents of Mollet and Lacoste. The conflict was heightened by the nationalist right wing of the party, in the persons of Robert Lacoste and Max Lejeune. Lacoste threw down the gauntlet to his foes early in the Congress, referring sarcastically to the Parisian and parliamentary base of the minority— "I believe that the master thinkers of this country are afflicted with what Karl Marx called parliamentary cretinism"—and declaring that independence was opposed by a majority of the party and the nation, hence no negotiations were possible. Lejeune's tone was even more hostile and bombastic, attacking the mildly critical motion of Defferre, the leaders of Morocco and Tunisia, and even the representative of the British Labour Party at the Congress, Aneurin Bevan. Bevan noted after Lejeune's speech, "I thought myself invited to be with the spiritual descendants of Jaurès. Instead, I find myself with those of Déroulède and Barrès."[99]

Although Lacoste's speech was greeted with "lively applause," the real contest at the Congress was one among the Depreux-Verdier minority, Defferre, and the Mollet-Commin leadership. The original band of *minoritaires* attempted to broaden their attacks on existing policy, emphasizing the economic and financial costs of the war, of concern to many outside the minority, and also the political opportunities foregone. The arguments of strategy that had been made earlier by Depreux and Mazier were reiterated; the barriers to exit had become barriers to the expansion of the Socialist electoral coalition in the face of Communist disarray:

The policy underway, if it brings in the short term some votes to the Socialist Party from the Right, prevents, on the other hand, an attempt to reconquer the workers, whose attachment to the Communist party has been profoundly shaken following the suppression of the Hungarian insurrection by the Soviet armies.

[99] Depreux, *Souvenirs*, p. 459.

The minority strategy was now clearly defined: measures to regain Muslim confidence, immediate recognition of the "national vocation" of Algeria, prenegotiations in the form of a "round table" conference, and guarantees for minorities, particularly the Europeans in Algeria.

The Defferre-Leenhardt motion, on the other hand, was a curious double condemnation of both the Mollet triptych and the round table idea of the Depreux-Verdier group, since both might *lead to independence* for Algeria. Although Defferre accepted the idea of prenegotiations from the minority, his refusal to accept the principle of self-determination made the liberalism of his position highly qualified. The leadership motion showed little change from Mollet's oft-stated triptych, although the cease-fire was made to sound somewhat less like unconditional surrender by the FLN. Mollet's speech to the Congress, however, made clear that independence was not an option for Algeria.[100]

Polarization in the party and the control exercised by the leadership was made clear in the treatment of the minority during the proceedings: when Mazier saluted Marceau Pivert and André Philip (the latter had been suspended for three years at this point) and criticized the intolerance of the party, the chair promptly cut him off, as if to prove the point. The relative isolation of the minority was demonstrated in the final vote: the Depreux-Verdier group made only slight progress (see Table III) although many more federations were divided or had joined one of the dissident factions. Mollet's setback at the Congress came instead at the hands of Defferre, who refused on this occasion the traditional *motion de synthèse* as a means of resolving the divisions within the party. It had become clear that an alliance between the Depreux-Verdier minority and the Defferre supporters could, with some additions, overturn the Mollet regime.

The issue of participation in the Gaillard ministry, which

---

[100] Motions are described in *Le Monde*, 1 June 1957 (minority); 2-3 June 1957 (Commin, Defferre), p. 5; motions are given in full in the *Bulletin interieur* of the party, no. 92 (June, 1957).

had brought Defferre into alliance with the parliamentary minority, also brought the two groups closer together outside parliament. At the National Council of December, 1957 they were together able to muster nearly a third of the mandates. The position improved only slightly by the March, 1958 National Council, but concern over Algeria had reached new proportions, even among former Mollet loyalists in the party. Mollet now tried to distance himself carefully from Lacoste by claiming that a cease-fire in Algeria would only require mutual guarantees, not surrender by the FLN. Nevertheless, he was forced to concede to calls by Savary, Moch, and surprisingly, Gazier for a National Council that would permit a "wide confrontation" of views.

Plans for such a National Council would be interrupted by the collapse of the regime in May, 1958. An even split in the parliamentary party, the entry of Mollet into the de Gaulle cabinet, the draft constitution—all seemed to provide an opening for overthrowing Mollet that the Algerian dissidents had been waiting for, despite the fact that many of their new allies, including Defferre, disagreed with them on the formula for peace across the Mediterranean. On 5 June, at a conference of information for the Seine Federation, minority leaders called for the resignation of Mollet, the expulsion of Lacoste from the party, and a National Congress to set a new course for the party. The Executive Committee, however, decided to retain Mollet as secretary general and to adjourn the National Congress planned for the summer until mid-September. Chances for success seemed high after assurances from Defferre that he would ally with the Depreux-Verdier group against the new constitution at the party Congress. After a conversation with de Gaulle, however, Defferre switched sides, claiming to support de Gaulle because of his liberal intentions in Algeria. Thus, Algeria (and the search for peace there) sealed the fate of those within the Socialist Party who had been fighting for liberal policies against the party leadership. The party not only voted its endorsement of the Constitution of the Fifth Republic; the minority also lost the support of Defferre on the Algerian motion, as he once again accepted the leadership platform, a slight revision of the worn triptych formula. Defferre was willing to sacrifice his mild liberalism in this instance in order to unite the party in time for the legislative elections.

For the beleaguered minority, now joined by those who opposed the new Constitution, the party Congress in September, 1958 was the occasion for long-delayed exit.[101] On 11 September 1958, at the Congress, the long-time dissenters announced the formation of the Parti socialiste autonome. Its leaders and the bulk of its members came from the Paris region and from other federations that had dissented from the leadership's Algerian stance. The new party opposed the new Constitution in the referendum, and fought the legislative elections of November, 1958 with other independent Left groups that were characterized by liberal views on decolonization: Pierre Mendès-France, François Mitterrand, and Claude Bourdet were among their allies. Despite the prominence of many PSA candidates for the Assembly, all twenty-two were defeated, though some (Mazier, Verdier, Desson, Depreux) outpolled the orthodox SFIO candidate.

The SFIO itself was largely spared by Mollet's deft change of course: by rallying to the new Constitution, it suffered little decline in its total vote, though the Gaullist advance caused it to lose over half its seats in the new Assembly. Despite the loss of his persistent opponents, Mollet's strategy for controlling exit and voice seemed to have preserved the party intact as it entered the new and unexplored political environment of the Fifth Republic.

Explaining dissidence

Trying to explain the pattern of dissent among the Socialist federations for an externally-induced fissure such as Algeria is difficult: like the issue of the European Defense Community, it cut across many existing lines of cleavage in the party, and

[101] On the final split, Simmons, *French Socialists*, pp. 88-93; Quilliot, *La S.F.I.O.*, pp. 737-750; Depreux, *Souvenirs*, chap. 17.

consistent explanations are difficult to perceive.[102] Three partially reinforcing explanations can be suggested, however: leadership by a deputy or local figure in the party; relative electoral success; and, most intriguing, given the linkage of party strategy with Algeria in internal debate, the relative threat posed by the Communist Party to the federation. In his study of foreign policy divisions within the Socialist Party during the 1930s, Greene suggests an explanation based on the attitude taken by a deputy or leading figure in the local party. Of the sixteen federations that voted for the Verdier motion at the Congress of Toulouse, the positions of at least seven can be explained in this way. But such an explanation assumes that the deputy influenced the federation's views, not that the deputy and the local militants might *share* a perspective that is based on some feature of the local political situation. Other drawbacks can be detected in the Algerian cases. The deputies of some federations (notably the Seine) could not bring their federations into the minority camp, however large the minority that they could muster; other federations took the minority position despite a leading figure (Paul Ramadier in the Aveyron, for example) who was firmly in the majority camp.

Greene supplies two additional explanations. One relates "electoral success with moderation in party politics, and conversely, the coincidence of electoral insignificance with a tendency toward radicalism."[103] Certainly there is some support for this hypothesis in the minority pattern of support: the large federations, until Gaston Defferre swung the Bouches-du-Rhône into opposition, uniformly supported the leadership position, with the single exception of the Haute-Garonne (not in the top five). But other federations that were resolutely *minoritaire*—Côtes-du-Nord, Ardennes—could hardly be regarded as electorally insignificant.

Both Greene and Macrae point to another, more intriguing

---

[102] Daniel Lerner and Raymond Aron, *France Defeats the EDC* (New York: Frederick A. Praeger: 1957), pp. 202-207.
[103] Greene, *Crisis and Decline*, p. 165.

explanation that is based on electoral competition and political strategy, one which supplements those already presented. Greene notes the tendency of Socialists in the 1930s to "resemble [their] most powerful regional or departmental adversary on the left of the political spectrum," which in the 1930s tended to "Radicalize" the Socialists.[104] Macrae, examining the Left of the Socialist Party during the Fourth Republic (a group that overlaps substantially with the Algerian dissenters), finds that political alliances and other characteristics of the departments explain little, but that there was some tendency on the part of the Left Socialists to be associated with a dominant Communist Party (supporting Greene's observation), though not an overwhelmingly dominant one. Support for the leadership and movement to the Center was associated with a dominant Socialist position in the department.[105] Table IV demonstrates, for the minority federations at least, that this explanation is quite strong. It also fits neatly with the *political* arguments that were being made by the dissidents during 1956-1957: that the Socialists could make gains at the expense of a Communist Party shaken by de-Stalinization and Hungary. Mollet rejected this left-wing strategy in favor of the line that had brought him to power: sealing off exit to the Left and the Right through nationalism and anti-clericalism, attracting new voters, largely from the Right, by pursuing policies both reformist and national. The success of Mollet's strategy after 1946 is in large measure the explanation for failure on the part of those who sought to reverse his policies in Algeria.

The failure of the dissenters: Explanations

In Roger Quilliot's words, "the failure of its Algerian policy remains for the SFIO the most sorrowful of its memories."[106] In assessing the reasons for that failure, the inability of the minority to change the party's course through the exercise of

---

[104] Ibid., p. 153.
[105] Macrae, *Parliament, Parties, and Society*, pp. 292-293.
[106] Quilliot, *La S.F.I.O.*, p. 760.

Table IV. Dissident Federations (Metropolitan France Only)

Federation	Minority support, Congress of Lille, 1956[1]	Minority support, Congress of Toulouse 1957[2]	Minority Deputy	PCF%/SFIO% (1956)[3]	Political orientation[4]
Côtes-du-Nord*	Unanimous	Verdier	X	20.2/18.3	Unclear
Haute-Savoie*	Unanimous	Verdier	X	15.9/8.2	Distinctly Right
Ardèche*	Majority	Verdier	X	21.1/6.1	Right
Ardennes*	Majority	Verdier	X	23.2/21.2	Distinctly Left
Cher	Majority	Defferre	—	28.5/8.1	Unclear
Nièvre	Majority	Verdier	—	23.1/14.4	Unclear
Calvados*		Verdier	X	15.5/11.1	Distinctly Right
Aisne*		Verdier	—	28.2/18.4	Left
Seine-et-Marne*		Verdier	X	24.7/10.5	Right
Marne		Verdier	—	22.6/8.1	Unclear
Meurthe-et-Moselle*		Verdier	X	22.5/12.5	Unclear
Vosges*		Verdier	—	17.2/8.6	Distinctly Right
Haute-Saône		Verdier	—	13.7/3.9	Distinctly Right
Isère*		Verdier	X	22.1/13.4	Unclear
Haute-Loire		Verdier	—	11.1/3.8	Distinctly Right
Aveyron		Verdier	—	9.7/13.9	Distinctly Right
Haute-Garonne*		Verdier	—	17.8/16.9	Left

KEY: * = "Left" federation (Macrae); Verdier = majority support for Verdier motion or Verdier/Defferre in equal proportions

[1] The federation of Ain also gave majority support to the dissidents at Lille but supported the leadership at Toulouse.

[2] Le Monde, 4 July 1957.

[3] Claude Leleu, Géographie des élections françaises depuis 1936 (Paris: Presses universitaires de France, 1971), pp. 263-264.

[4] Ibid., p. 271.

voice or the threat of exit is as much a part of the explanation as the original decisions for pacification in Algeria made by Mollet and Lacoste. For conservative parties, decolonization created fragmentation that *decreased* their ability to contribute to stable and decolonizing governments; for the Socialists in France, an *excess* of consensus within the party after 1956, the *ease* with which Mollet could control dissent, prevented the party from changing course and returning to the liberal policies of its immediate past. With Socialists presiding over a colonial war, there was also an excess of consensus within the political process as a whole; far more than before, the Fourth Republic did seem to have a colonial consensus after 1956. Both decolonization and the unity of the Socialist Party were least threatened when the Socialists were in opposition from 1952 to 1955, criticizing status quo policies and encouraging those, like Mendès-France, who sought change.

The failure of the minority after 1956 can be traced to the character of the party constructed since 1945. Specifically, their challenge to Mollet foundered on the ambiguities in Socialist anti-colonialism and its peripheral role in Socialist doctrine; the shift from ideological to purposive incentives, particularly in the third parliament of the Fourth Republic; the erection of barriers to exit; and, following from those barriers, the careful, even ruthless, suppression of voice.

Peripheral anti-colonialism. The ideological incentives of the party did not center on anti-imperialism in the same way that the empire formed the centerpiece for the nationalist ideology of the Right. The Socialist program for the empire had been unclear since the interwar years; not until the North African crises of the early 1950s did the party try to formulate consistent positions; ad hoc solutions continued to be endorsed in most cases. Experts on colonial questions, in striking contrast to the British Labour Party, did not play a significant role in defining the party's program.[107] More important than the confusion over Socialist colonial doctrine, however, was the *low salience* of anti-colonialism among Socialist ideolog-

[107] Philip, *Le socialisme trahi*, p. 197.

ical incentives: social and economic issues caused the party to withdraw its support from cabinets during the first legislature of the Fourth Republic; in the Fifth Republic, de Gaulle's program of economic austerity, not his Algerian policy, caused the Socialist ministers to leave the cabinet. When the minority attempted to mobilize the party against Mollet and Lacoste on the grounds that fighting a war of pacification in Algeria was not a Socialist program, resonance in the party was surprisingly slight, and Mollet's own "socialist" arguments in favor of his policies carried equivalent weight.

In part the party had been nationalized by the war, but the appeals of nationalism, while resurgent after 1956, should not be overestimated. Max Lejeune's strident "ultra" speech at the Congress of Toulouse was condemned by many outside the minority as wholly out of place at a Socialist Congress; while many of the arguments constructed by Mollet served the purposes of French nationalism, the *vocabulary* that they used was a Socialist one, particularly in party councils. To Mollet's critics, his was a debasement of Socialist ideology— Philip called it "a vulgar Marxism, badly digested, . . . come to legitimate a practical conservatism, scarcely concealed by the vague ideology of the solidarity of the little one against the big"—but even his critics were forced to attack Mollet's arguments as a misreading of Socialism, not as some other ideology.[108]

The incentives of power. The relatively minor part that anticolonialism played in the ideological identity of the party was reinforced by a shift within the party from *ideological* to *purposive* incentives. The role of purposive incentives raises once again the issue of "Radicalization" in the party. In terms of structure and discipline, the party remained distinct from those to its Right; even in terms of electoral clientele, the Socialists were more of a working-class party, particularly after the 1956 elections, when their gains were made in the industrial areas. Among party members, however, the picture was different.

[108] Ibid., p. 196; see also Oreste Rosenfeld's reply to Mollet's Toulouse speech, *France-Observateur*, 4 July 1956.

The party membership had shrunk year by year, with a brief reversal during the Mollet ministry; the proportion of civil servants among the rank and file was high. Party leadership, given the pivotal position of the party in many areas, was dominated by those with long experience in local and national politics. As Simmons notes, "For a party in which so many of the members make their living in politics, the reformer or innovator is not likely to win broad support."[109] The attitude toward power of the Socialist leadership and its rank and file, rather than shifts in its electoral clientele, made the purposive incentives offered by participation very tempting after 1956. Such effects were reinforced by the large-scale patronage dispensed by the party after 1956, welcomed after the lean years of opposition.[110]

Aging of the party membership also weakened the influence of the Algerian minority: the young in socialist and social democratic parties are typically more attuned to ideological incentives, and they were active during the Algerian War. But the Jeunesses socialistes had been in decline since the disbandment and reorganization of 1947; by 1957, it existed in only forty-eight of the ninety departments.[111] The Socialist student organization, led by Michel Rocard, was disciplined for its efforts to ally with Communist students against the Algerian War; its national bureau was disbanded as well.[112] The shift from ideological to purposive incentives within the party weakened further the ability of the minority to mobilize support on ideological issues such as Algeria among a rank and file more concerned with the benefits of governing than with challenging the first Socialist-led cabinet in nearly a decade.

[109] Simmons, *French Socialists*, pp. 205, 285-286, Appendix G (p. 287, on political experience); on the arguments concerning "Radicalization" of the party: Simmons, *French Socialists*, pp. 17-18, 210-211; Williams, *Crisis and Compromise*, pp. 101-103, 106-107; Goguel, "La géographie des élections du 2 janvier, in *Les Elections du 2 janvier 1956*, ed. Duverger, p. 492.

[110] Williams, *Crisis and Compromise*, p. 106.

[111] Ibid., p. 101.

[112] Ibid., pp. 101-102; Quilliot, *La S.F.I.O.*, pp. 185-190.

Barriers to exit. The long-delayed departure of the minority suggests that Mollet was also successful in sealing off exit to the Left or the Right—through nationalism, anti-communism, and anti-clericalism. The thickening of the walls of the "vieille maison" not only weakened the force of the dissidents' opposition within, but also made more difficult any contact with those outside the party who were opposed to the Algerian War. The decolonization coalition tended to split political groups, Left and Right, and many of those opposed to Mollet in the Socialist Party would have found their natural allies among Communist intellectuals and militants and those liberal Catholics, such as Jean-Marie Domenach or François Mauriac, who were beyond the pale of the party. It was such a coalition that was constructed when the PSA evolved into the Parti socialiste unifié in 1960: a combination of the socialist minority with Communist dissidents from the Tribune du communisme, *Mendèsiste* Radicals from the Centre d'action démocratique, and Catholic activists from the Union de la gauche socialiste.

Suppression of voice. A weak threat of exit itself reduced the power of voice, but the leadership of the party also sought to ensure that the dissidents remained isolated within the party or excluded from it. Debates within the party were carefully monitored through control of communication with the rank and file in the federations and discipline of those who attempted to use others means of communication. Until the foundation of the dissidents' own committee in 1957, their point of view could only be obtained through media controlled or approved by the party apparatus; hence their calls for greater intraparty democracy centered on the provision of a *Tribune libre*.

The weak threat of voice or exit that the dissidents could wield was also the result of their *own* acceptance of the rules and conventions that made the Socialists a disciplined and rarely divided party. Though the leadership wielded its disciplinary powers freely against critics of the government, few of the dissidents challenged the discipline of the parliamentary group. In similar circumstances in the British Labour Party, a backbench revolt of large proportions would probably have occurred. The concept of "loyalty" does seem to have some meaning here: that increment that heightens barriers to *both* exit and voice in certain organizations. The dissidents were themselves participants in that "patriotism of the party," that sentimental attachment to the group rather than its ideals, that André Philip used to explain Mollet's success.[113]

The Socialist Party finally suffered fragmentation in confronting the Algerian War, but the exit was much smaller than might have been feared. The damage to Socialist positions in the legislative elections of 1958 was small: not only were the PSA candidates defeated, but their electoral appeal seemed to lie with a *Mendèsiste* constituency, at least in Paris, than with the old Socialist clientele.[114] A closer analysis of the 1958 results reveals, however, a return to the pattern of "Radicalization" and regionalization perceived before the elections of 1956: a strengthening of the party's hold in the south and center of France and a loss (slight) in the Nord and the Pas-de-Calais and (greater) in other, more industrialized parts of France.[115] In the next elections (November, 1962) the pattern became even clearer, as the Socialists once again lost votes (as part of the opposition to de Gaulle on this occasion), although gaining seats in the Assembly. Its regional bastions became more accentuated, and the center of gravity of the party continued to drift toward the southwest of France.[116]

The Parti socialiste unifié, child of the Algerian dissidence, was the mirror image of its faded rival: as little concerned with power as its rival was with ideology, with appeal to groups shunned by the SFIO—students and the young, intel-

[113] Philip, *Le Socialisme trahi*, pp. 204-206.

[114] François Goguel, Alain Lancelot, Jean Ranger, "Analyse des resultats," in *L'Etablissement de la Cinquième République: Le Référendum de septembre et les élections de novembre 1958*, ed. Association Française de Science Politique, (Paris: Armand Colin, 1960), p. 335.

[115] Ibid., pp. 337-339.

[116] Leleu, *Géographie*, p. 127; François Goguel, "Analyse des resultats," in *Le Référendum d'octobre et les élections de novembre 1962* (Paris: Armand Colin, 1965), map on pp. 332-333; Simmons, *French Socialists*, chap. 8.

lectuals, and Catholics. The PSU was much closer in many respects to the "new" and highly successful Socialist party of the 1970s. Its strategy of a unified Left, in which the Socialists would regain the dominant position from the Communists, was precisely that of the opponents of Mollet in the 1950s. An analysis of the departments that had supported the *minoritaires* in 1956-1958 demonstrates that these were among those in which the new Parti socialiste would make its greatest gains (see Table V). Those departments in which the Socialists gained little or even lost ground after 1967 were, on the other hand, often part of the old Mollet majority. Guy Mollet had skillfully defended the "old house" of the SFIO while fighting a colonial war; the future belonged to his defeated opponents.

Table V. The New Socialist Party and the Old

Dissident federations (Toulouse Congress)	% increase in Socialist vote, 1967-1978*	Unanimous support for Mollet (Toulouse Congress)	% increase in Socialist vote, 1967-1978*
Côtes-du-Nord	> 15	Ariège	0-5
Haute-Savoie	5-10	Belfort	0-5
Ardèche	5-10	Corrèze	Decline
Ardennes	10-15	Creuse	5-10
Cher	5-10	Dordogne	Decline
Nièvre	Decline	Landes	0-5
Calvados	> 15	Loir-et-Cher	Decline
Aisne	5-10	Mayenne	15
Seine-et-Marne	5-10	Nord	Decline
Marne	0-5	Pas-de-Calais	0-5
Meurthe-et-Moselle	10-15	Tarn-et-Garonne	Decline
Vosges	10-15	Haute-Vienne	Decline
Haute-Saône	Decline		
Isère	10-15		
Haute-Loire	5-10		
Aveyron	10-15		
Haute-Garonne	0-5		

* From Jérôme Jaffré, "The French Electorate in March 1978," in *The French National Assembly Elections of 1978*, ed. Howard Penniman (Washington, D.C.: AEI, 1980), Map 5, p. 66.

THE LABOUR PARTY AND DECOLONIZATION:
UNITY IN A TIME OF DIVISION

Like the French Socialist Party, the Labour Party had a long history of division over foreign policy, particularly during the 1930s. Contention continued after 1945, particularly when Labour was in opposition from 1951 until 1964. German rearmament, the American alliance, the hydrogen bomb, and nuclear disarmament—the party repeatedly split, not only at the level of the parliamentary party, but quite often from leadership to rank and file.[117] Yet, unlike the French Socialists, colonial and near-colonial issues (such as the Middle East) did not add to fissures in the party; Labour confronted Conservative governments of the time united on colonial issues, particularly after Suez. A leader of the minority in the French Socialist Party captured the difference between the two groups: during the Suez crisis, the Socialist dissidents in France collaborated with the Labour Party across the Channel; opposing them were the British Conservatives and the French Socialist majority following Mollet.[118]

The absence of a split over decolonization, the ability of Labour, despite other internal battles, to use anti-colonialism in a unifying rather than divisive way was *not* due to the reduced importance of ideological incentives within the party. As Beer notes, "all accepted the necessity for a social philosophy with programmatic consequences. The opposing sides were at swords' points with regard to their respective ideologies, but they were united in their ideologism."[119] To depict

---

[117] Accounts of the party's divisions include Samuel H. Beer, *British Politics in the Collectivist Age* (New York: Knopf, 1965), chap. 8, for the point on vertical cleavage, pp. 230-232; Stephen Haseler, *The Gaitskellites* (London: Macmillan, 1969); R. T. McKenzie, *British Political Parties*, 2nd ed. (New York: Frederick A. Praeger, 1963), pp. 594-630; and, from the points of view of two opposing protagonists, Michael Foot, *Aneurin Bevan, Volume II: 1945-1960* (New York: Atheneum, 1974), especially chaps. 8-11, 15; Philip M. Williams, *Hugh Gaitskell* (London: Jonathan Cape, 1979).

[118] Depreux, *Souvenirs*, p. 122.

[119] Beer, *British Politics*, p. 234.

the battle within the Labour Party during the 1950s as simply a power struggle or a struggle for the succession to Clement Attlee would be a mistake. Nor does the structure of the party offer an obvious contrast to the French Socialists with one major exception: the central place awarded the trade unions in the party structure. The unions provided a certain ballast to the party enabling it to avoid permanent splits, but they could be divided themselves on many of the important questions—Clause IV or nuclear disarmament—that arose in this period.[120]

The Labour Party *could* be distinguished from its French counterpart in the content of its ideology with regard to colonial and international questions. During the 1930s, when divisions over foreign policy reached a peak, the same sorts of attitudes could be detected on both sides of the Channel: a neo-Marxist Left arguing for unity of action with the Communists and revolutionary struggle against imperialist wars; a pacifist Center only gradually converted to the necessity for rearmament and opposition to fascism; and a third group, based in the unions and the parliamentary party, that was far less reluctant to rearm in the face of the German threat.[121] Despite a resurgence of neo-Marxism in the 1930s, however, the tug of Communism and the importance of Marxist ideology within the Labour Party were much less important than in the SFIO. Typically, and this was particularly true after World War II, the Left in the Labour Party drew upon the tradition of one element in the original Labour coalition, the Independent Labour Party—socialist, internationalist, in many cases pacifist, but not Marxist. An unfriendly critic labeled this left-wing amalgam "a heteroclite mixture of adulterated Marxism, transposed Methodism and inherited liberalism."[122] Since many of the colonial specialists in the party were drawn from an ILP background—Fenner Brockway on the Left and

[120] Ibid., p. 240; Haseler, *The Gaitskellites*, p. 174, Table 4, gives the divisions within the union movement on the key issues of the 1950s.

[121] Gordon, *Conflict and Consensus*, chap. 2.

[122] Perry Anderson, "Origins of the Present Crisis," *New Left Review* 23 (Jan.-Feb., 1964), pp. 44.

Arthur Creech Jones, colonial secretary after 1945, in the Center—the ILP humanitarian and socialist approach to colonial problems filtered into the Labour mainstream.

Another ideological current that had no French parallel was the infusion from liberalism, a strand that grew during the 1920s as the Liberal Party declined and Liberal intellectuals moved to Labour. The Liberals brought with them a paternalist tradition of opposition to slavery and to mistreatment of colonial peoples (epitomized by E. D. Morel's campaign against forced labor in the Congo and Amazonia before World War I), an attachment to international organization, and, above all, opposition to protectionism in the form of imperial economic blocs.

A final ideological contrast with the French Socialists was the almost total absence of a vocal colonial Right in the party. In the early years of the Labour movement in Britain, the Fabians and certain Socialists, such as Robert Blatchford, had dabbled in imperialist commitments, but such intellectual ties dropped away quickly after World War I.[123] The positive attachment of the British working class to imperialism had always been slight. Despite allegations that the British labour movement had been incorporated as a "labour aristocracy" within the ruling order of Britain, in many respects, particularly in foreign affairs, it stood outside that order, and its ideology was formed in opposition to the national and imperial idea.[124]

Apart from the interest of a few trade unionists, among them Ernest Bevin, in schemes of imperial economic union during the interwar years, discussion of colonial questions was dominated by a non-Marxist Left and a humanitarian "Lib-Lab" center. Two other features were even more significant and closer to the French pattern: the low salience of colonial issues for the party at large and the relatively slight change

[123] Bernard Semmel, *Imperialism and Social Reform* (Garden City, N.Y.: Doubleday and Company 1968), pp. 54-73, 214-225.

[124] On early Labour opposition to imperialism, Bernard Porter, *Critics of Empire* (New York: St. Martin's Press, 1968), chaps. 4-6.

produced in colonial policy by the Labour coalition governments with the Liberals in 1924 and 1929-1931. While anti-
imperialism was part of the Labour ideology, it was hardly
the core of that ideology. As both the Left (Brockway) and
the Center (Leonard Woolf) discovered, it was an uphill struggle to win the party's attention for imperial questions, and
even harder to shift existing policy in a reformist direction.[125]

Whatever the party's influence on the management of the
colonial Empire, it had by 1945 set out a position of its own
on colonial questions that differed from the Conservative ideological credo: Labour displayed a decided lack of interest in
the empire of prestige, especially the Middle East, and very
little sign of attachment to the "kith and kin" of the settler
colonies in Africa. The Empire was not regarded, by and large,
as a security asset. Instead, the party's public positions signaled the triumph of the liberal humanitarian point of view.[126]
Contrasts with the French Socialists were not so clear as they
would seem through the historical lenses of the 1950s. Even
in the immediate postwar years, the Labour Party and a core
of experts at the Fabian Colonial Bureau were very reserved
about the question of political advance. The time-frame for
self-government (*within* the Commonwealth) appeared lengthy
and was conditional upon social and economic advance. As
late as 1946, for example, Rita Hinden, founder of the Colonial Bureau, could doubt whether "complete independence"
would be possible in the conditions of this century, a sentiment
often expressed by Mollet and others in France.[127] Nevertheless, a commitment to self-government *was* made by the party
as well as a commitment to reform the existing colonial system. The colonies were no longer to be subordinated to the

[125] Fenner Brockway, *Towards Tomorrow* (London: Hart-Davis, Mac-
Gibbon, 1977), pp. 78-80; Leonard Woolf, *Downhill All the Way* (New
York: Harcourt Brace Jovanovich, 1967), pp. 219, 236.

[126] David Goldsworthy, *Colonial Issues in British Politics, 1945-1961* (Oxford: Clarendon Press, 1971), p. 117.

[127] Partha Sarathi Gupta, *Imperialism and the British Labour Movement,
1914-1964* (London: Macmillan, 1975), p. 325; Goldsworthy, *Colonial Issues*, p. 121.

economic demands of the British economy and exploitation by private firms would be prevented.[128] It remained for the first Labour government with a clear majority in Parliament to convince the party that it was fulfilling its program.

The Labour government, 1945-1951: Experts and decolonization

Despite earlier hedging on political advance in the colonies, the Attlee government encountered surprisingly little opposition in the party on colonial policy. Unlike Socialist militants confronting the compromises of their ministers in Third Force cabinets at this time, the rank and file of the Labour Party did not rise up in revolt at the compromises of power. Labour was in control of its program, and the government did institute social and economic reforms that matched the program of the party and for the most part satisfied the experts who scrutinized them. The government also benefited from external circumstances, since no radical nationalist rebellion erupted immediately after the war to challenge the reformist path that had been chosen: Attlee and his colleagues faced no Ho Chi Minh. Instead, Labour supervised the violent, but politically accepted, decolonization of the Indian subcontinent; its relative ease set a pattern that could be transferred to other territories. The Labour Party was, of course, preoccupied with its daunting domestic plans; colonial issues were not mentioned in the election manifesto of 1945. Its agenda for reform in circumstances of economic austerity reduced conflict over decolonization, since the dilemma of "rising demands and insufficient resources" was compelling in reducing overseas commitments.[129] The deepest divisions in the Labour cabinet arose over the tension between domestic and international

[128] See "The Labour Party's Declaration of Policy for Colonial Peoples," Fabian Colonial Bureau Papers, 46/1, 57-62 (issued in 1940); radio address by Clement Attlee, in C. R. Attlee, *As It Happened* (London: Heinemann, 1954), p. 109.

[129] Harold and Margaret Sprout, "Rising Demands and Insufficient Resources," in *Economic Imperialism*, ed. Kenneth Boulding and Tapan Mukerjee, (Ann Arbor: University of Michigan Press, 1972), pp. 213-239.

demands—the budgetary consequences of Korean War rearmament, which brought about the resignations of Bevan, Wilson, and Freeman.

A low level of interest in colonial affairs left the shaping of
policy within the party to a relatively small number of experts
at the Fabian Colonial Bureau, the "main source of intraparty pressures on the Colonial Office."[130] The marshaling of
expertise at the Bureau, founded in October, 1940, sets the
Labour Party experience apart from that of the French Socialists. Originated by Rita Hinden, who was its secretary and
animator for ten years, the Bureau perceived its principal role
in research and publication on colonial questions. As the party's Imperial Advisory Committee faded in importance, however, it soon became a major clearinghouse for communications with individuals and groups in the colonial empire seeking
assistance from the party. It also provided information to
M.P.s who worked with the Bureau, as well as organizing
conferences, deputations to the Colonial Office, and letters to
the press.[131] Although some connected the Fabian Colonial
Bureau with the right wing of the Labour Party, the M.P.s
associated with the work of the Bureau included members of
the Bevanite Left as well, an important and early indicator of
the essential unity of the party in dealing with colonial questions.[132]

Points of potential conflict between the Colonial Office and
its interlocutors outside the government remained submerged,
for the most part. Efforts by the Foreign Office under Ernest
Bevin to maintain the Empire of prestige in the Mediterranean
did arouse Labour backbench opposition, though the question
of Palestine drew support from Zionist sympathizers rather
than an anti-colonial nexus. The Labour Government "proved
as reluctant as its predecessors to give up Cyprus," but the

[130] Goldsworthy, *Colonial Issues*, p. 124.
[131] For a good picture of the work of the Bureau at the peak of its influence,
see the Report of the Colonial Bureau to the Fabian Society Executive Committee, FCB Papers, 71/1 f 43, and Goldsworthy, *Colonial Issues*, pp. 123-
134.
[132] Gupta, *Imperialism*, p. 357.

full force of Greek demands for *Enosis* would not be felt until the 1950s.[133] The fact that a serious outbreak of violence did not occur on Cyprus during the Labour government may have spared the party a difficult choice between Bevin's view of interests in the Middle East and the party's commitment to eventual self-government in the colonies, a choice that the Conservatives initially made in favor of strategic aims.

Another point of potential conflict between government and party was the apparent subordination of the economic interests of colonial territories to the needs of the metropolis, particularly in the hard-pressed years of raw materials scarcity and dollar shortage. Elements of the Labour Party had toyed with protectionist ideas in the 1930s: for example, Bevin's willingness to consider a revision in Labour's long-standing attachment to free trade in favor of plans for imperial economic organization.[134] A need to spur dollar earnings and a commitment to planning prolonged Labour's attachment to mercantilist modes of thinking after the war.[135] Sterling balances held by some of the dependent territories provided an intragovernmental issue of contention between the Treasury, concerned that they not be drawn down in any way that would endanger the position of sterling, and a Colonial Office interested in the rapid economic development of the territories.[136] It took time for some within Labour to recognize the economic disadvantages imposed upon the colonies by the framework of imperial economic organization, and the economic corollaries of greater political autonomy were also slow in percolating into the party's positions: Hugh Gaitskell, then shadow chancellor of the exchequer, defended exchange controls and a strong sterling area in the early 1950s against the

[133] On dissension over the Middle East, Robert J. Jackson, *Rebels and Whips* (London: Macmillan, 1968), pp. 71-72; Cyprus: Nancy Crawshaw, *The Cyprus Revolt* (London: George Allen and Unwin, 1978), p. 34.

[134] Alan Bullock, *The Life and Times of Ernest Bevin: Volume I* (London: Heinemann, 1960), pp. 439-447.

[135] D. J. Morgan, *The Official History of Colonial Development*, 5 vols. (Atlantic Highlands, N.J.: Humanities Press, 1980), 2:21.

[136] Ibid., pp. 53-63.

238 — French Socialists and British Labour

Conservative government's moves toward convertibility and nondiscrimination. These compromises with the idea of the Empire as an economic bloc were regarded as necessary measures, given the weakness of Britain's external financial position after the war; little evidence can be found among the leadership or the rank and file for an ideological commitment to neo-mercantilism that would match that of the aging supporters of Empire Free Trade among the Tories.[137]

A third and most serious divergence between the ministerial and the party point of view did surface briefly at the end of the Labour government. As they had in the 1920s and the 1930s, the settler colonies demonstrated the most glaring disparity between Labour's proclaimed intentions and policy. In Kenya, the Colonial Office tacitly accepted the policies of a governor, Sir Philip Mitchell, who favored the European settlers; conflict developed with the Fabian Colonial Bureau as a result.[138] Another instance of compromise with white power in Africa brought the only instance of cross-voting by Labour M.P.'s on a colonial issue: the Seretse Khama case. Heir to the chieftaincy of the Bamangwato tribe in Bechuanaland, Seretse Khama married an Englishwoman, arousing opposition from the regent, his uncle Tshekedi Khama. To resolve the dispute within the tribe, the Labour government argued that Seretse Khama had to be exiled for five years, while his uncle would be forced to leave the Bamangwato reserve. Labour specialists in colonial affairs, inside the Fabian Colonial Bureau and without, suspected that the real reason for the government's action was opposition to the mixed marriage from the white settlers of Rhodesia and the new Nationalist government of South Africa. Later evidence seems to confirm their suspicions.

On 28 March 1950, seven Labour M.P.'s voted with the Conservatives against closure on the issue of Seretse Khama,

[137] On Gaitskell's defense, Williams, *Hugh Gaitskell*, pp. 317-318; Gupta, *Imperialism*, pp. 299-300.

[138] Goldsworthy, *Colonial Issues*, pp. 141-143; Gupta, *Imperialism*, pp. 328, 334-335.

and a number of others, including Fenner Brockway, were believed to have absented themselves from the House in protest.[139] The next year, in a Parliament with a far narrower Labour majority, the case of Tshekedi Khama was considered. Despite the personal intervention of the Prime Minister to ensure discipline, several Labour M.P.'s abstained; their protest was more than balanced by the support offered the government by imperialist Conservatives.[140] The backbench protests did not cause the commonwealth secretary, Patrick Gordon Walker, to budge; later, however, the party would intervene with a Conservative government to support the return of Seretse Khama to his homeland.

Thus, as the Labour Party entered opposition in 1951, issues of possible future conflict between those with a ministerial outlook and the colonial specialists, Fabian and Left, could be discerned. The most explosive, and one that would find a wider national audience, was the attitude that would be taken toward the European settlers of Africa; the decisive issue would be the Federation proposed among the Rhodesias and Nyasaland. Despite the opposition of the Colonial Bureau to federation, the ministerial position in the party seemed to be leaning toward acceptance. There was also likely to be disagreement over the timing of self-government in particular cases. Creech Jones had always resisted timetables for political advance, and his favored statement of the goals of colonial policy seemed to set steep political ("freedom from oppression from any quarter") and economic ("a fair standard of living") prerequisites for self-government.[141] The timetable implicit in the public statements of this period was a slow one: a Colonial Office working party in March, 1951 listed only a handful of

[139] Those voting against were all members of the Left, including several who had worked with the Fabian Colonial Bureau. Philip Norton, ed., *Dissension in the House of Commons* (London: Macmillan, 1975), pp. 82-83.

[140] An excellent account of the Khama affair is given in Goldsworthy, *Colonial Issues*, pp. 157-162.

[141] The full text of the Labour Government statement is given below, p. 343.

territories in which full membership in the Commonwealth would become a live issue "in the near future."[142]

Despite these potential pitfalls, however, only the issue of British Guiana seriously divided the party while in opposition, and that only briefly. While the Conservative leadership was forced to deal with repeated exercise of voice from opponents of decolonization, the Labour Party found a rare islet of unity in its attitude toward decolonization.

Labour in opposition, 1951-1964: Unexpected unity

The early years of opposition were not easy ones for the Labour Party, wracked by sharp conflicts over foreign policy—the Japanese Peace Treaty, defense spending, SEATO, German rearmament, the hydrogen bomb.[143] The Seretse Khama affair was evidence that the potent issue of race could stir the party beyond the small band of specialists at the Fabian Colonial Bureau and in the parliamentary party: resolutions submitted for the party conference in 1952 indicated an awakened rank and file.[144] And soon the Left had its own organization— the Movement for Colonial Freedom—to exert pressure on the leadership and mobilize support on the new colonial issues, particularly those surrounding the settler colonies.

Fenner Brockway had developed an interest in the colonial empire as a member of the ILP between the wars. He rejoined the Labour Party in 1947, and, with the expansion of the Left after the Bevan resignation of 1951, Brockway was delegated responsibility for colonial questions.[145] Brockway had already participated, in June, 1948, in the founding of the Congress

[142] Morgan, *Official History*, 5:56.

[143] In addition to works cited in n. 117; R. K. Alderman, "Parliamentary Party Discipline in Opposition: The Parliamentary Labour Party, 1951-1964," *Parliamentary Affairs* 21 (Spring 1968), 124-131.

[144] Of the resolutions received on colonial policy between July and October, 1952 from CLPs and trade unions, most dealt with South African racial policies, Seretse Khama, and the Federation. Labour Party, Commonwealth Subcommittee, Resolutions on Colonial Policy, 1951-1952.

[145] Brockway, *Towards Tomorrow*, pp. 163-165; Goldsworthy, *Colonial Issues*, pp. 276-277.

of Peoples against Imperialism, in which he had collaborated with the French Socialist Jean Rous. As the head of the London Committee of the Congress, Brockway had sponsored the Kenya Land Petition (which was viewed with skepticism by the Fabian Colonial Bureau); the Central Africa Committee, designed to coordinate the fight against federation (although his competitors, the Africa Bureau and the Fabian Colonial Bureau chose not to be coordinated); and a number of committees on Seretse Khama and British Guiana, before finally founding the Movement for Colonial Freedom in April, 1954.[146]

The response of the Fabian Colonial Bureau to this new organizational presence on its Left was chilly, even when the two agreed, as they did in opposing the Central African Federation. In part, friction stemmed from differences of style and image. As Goldsworthy notes, the Movement for Colonial Freedom "functioned less as a research body than as a crusade."[147] When Brockway, still leading the London Committee of the Congress, approached the Colonial Bureau in an effort to coordinate the campaign against the Federation, the Bureau decided that

the African cause would not be benefited if colour were given to the allegation that opposition to the federation was stirred up by 'extremists' in Britain and that the Bureau might do better to put its weight behind the campaign of the Africa Bureau, which had a wide appeal to all sections of the British public, particularly the churches.[148]

The two entities differed in their acceptance of the claims of colonial nationalists as well. The Movement for Colonial Freedom was much more willing to accept those claims at

---

[146] The Congress of Peoples Against Imperialism was noticed by the Labour Party: an internal report stated that it was regarded as giving a "widely distorted picture" of the policy of the Labour government, but it kept out Communists and the party determined it was not of sufficient importance to justify any action. (LP, Commonwealth Subcommittee, 50/20, "Note on South East Asia Committee and Congress of Peoples Against Imperialism," January 1951. Goldsworthy, *Colonial Issues*, pp. 271-273; Brockway, *Towards Tomorrow*, pp. 151-152.

[147] Goldsworthy, *Colonial Issues*, p. 324.

[148] FCB, 72/1 f 127, Advisory Committee Meeting, 11 June 1952.

face value, without the Fabians' careful research and insistence on democratic legitimacy. But ultimately a question of organizational competition also intervened. The surge of interest in colonial questions on the Left of the party, the renewed interest of the Labour Party organization under its Commonwealth officer John Hatch, the foundation of groups such as the Africa Bureau and the Movement for Colonial Freedom—all pointed to a relative decline in the position of the Fabian Colonial Bureau. Its influence on the government could not be sustained with Labour in opposition; its reformist program had largely been accomplished during the Labour government; its paternalism would not sit well with the colonial nationalists who were increasing their demands in step with their power. From within the Fabian Society itself came expressions of discontent, in the form of acerbic criticism by Margaret Cole, who declared that "the Bureau is failing to give the lead which once it gave to Labour thinking about the Colonies," criticizing the Bureau's journal, *Venture*, as "very dull reading."[149] In the Bureau's defense, its secretary, Marjorie Nicholson, was perhaps more accurate in describing the changing political context of colonial pressure group activity: "There are now many channels through which colonial opinions can flow into our own Labour Movement, and consequently less necessity for the Bureau, which used to be virtually the only channel, to undertake work of a 'non-Fabian' kind."[150]

Organizational rivalry, and particularly the challenge that the Left was mounting to the Labour leadership on issue after issue, might have produced a new front in the ongoing intra-party conflict. Surprisingly, only one colonial dispute brought the ideological differences in the party to the fore: British Guiana. It confronted the Labour Party with a dilemma that it had avoided: a democratically elected, radical socialist movement (the People's Progressive Party of Cheddi Jagan)

[149] Margaret Cole, "Notes on the Fabian Colonial Bureau," FCB 72/2 ff. 40-43. For the Bureau's own evaluation of the changes that came with opposition, "Future Policy of the Fabian Colonial Bureau," FCB 72/1 f 70, f 71, f 75; 10 November 1951.

[150] FCB 72/2 ff 72-74, letter of 11 December 1954.

that, when it achieved power in 1953, seemed to veer in anti-democratic directions. Its legitimacy was further questioned because of the Communist associations cultivated by some of its members. The Conservative government had few second thoughts: it moved in October, 1953 to dismiss the Jagan government and to suspend the colony's constitution, which had been granted by Labour, in a bloodless coup.

For the Labour Left, the issue was equally clear-cut: a radical movement that had begun to attack the existing structure of economic power in the colony had been overthrown by a government representing the interests of big business. For the Labour Right, the incident was not so easy to interpret. Rita Hinden made public her opposition to the PPP and its policies, which she believed were bent on establishing "a totalitarian state."[151] The trade unions resented the efforts of the PPP to sponsor a rival to their own Guianan protegé, a rival that was affiliated to the Communist-oriented World Federation of Trade Unions. The parliamentary party tried to bridge the divide by taking a middle position in the debate on 22 October, not expressing support of the PPP, but arguing that suspension of the constitution was too extreme a step in the situation.

Jagan and Burnham met with the Labour Party National Executive Committee in an attempt to sway the party, which they described as "our natural ally," in their direction. The hostility of the TUC , which had openly condemned the PPP on 28 October, made it unlikely that they would succeed, and the party maintained its position of 22 October. A subsidiary issue provided another test of strength between Left and Right—whether local parties should be advised not to hold meetings with PPP spokesmen on the platform. Here as well the Left (an amendment was moved in the NEC by Ian Mikardo, seconded by Barbara Castle) was defeated.[152] Mikardo retaliated in the pages of the *Tribune*, where he attacked the TUC position during the British Guiana crisis. The TUC and the Right

[151] Goldsworthy, *Colonial Issues*, p. 234.

[152] Labour Party, Commonwealth Subcommittee, 53/30; Labour Party, National Executive Committee Minutes, 3 November 1953.

forced a final contest in December: Sam Watson of the Miners moved the censure of Mikardo (carried after an amendment presented by Harold Wilson was defeated), and Herbert Morrison rubbed salt in the wound by adding a condemnation of Mikardo for speaking on the same platform as Jagan, which the NEC also accepted.[153]

During a year of relative quiet in the other battles that had divided Labour, British Guiana produced a new fault-line on a colonial issue where none had appeared before. On one side, a revived Left, with its sympathy for and support of radical nationalist movements, capable of mobilizing support in the constituency parties: the autumn produced a dramatic surge in motions submitted to the party concerning British Guiana. Eighty-one were critical of the NEC position to deny Labour platforms to the PPP; only two approved the NEC decision.[154] Ranged against the Left was a Right intent that self-government in the colonies would mean democratic self-government, and the trade unions, intensely anti-communist and suspicious of any effort at political control of the union movement.[155]

British Guiana could have been an ominous portent for Labour policy during the 1950s: a spilling over of Left-Right division from foreign policy into colonial issues; a party offering weak rejoinders to Conservative alternatives because of its own divisions. A second battle in 1953 provided a different pattern, however, one that would characterize Labour's colonial stance during the remainder of the 1950s: a unified party that carefully set itself apart from both the Conservatives and its own past equivocations. The question of the Central African Federation, endorsed by the Conservative Government, brought to the fore the question of settler power and racial inequality that had aroused the Labour Left during the Seretse Khama case. More significantly, it *unified* the Labour Left and Right in opposition.

[153] NEC Minutes (219), 16 December 1953.
[154] Labour Party, Commonwealth Subcommittee 53/32, "Analysis of resolutions on colonial policy received November 1953."
[155] The intense anti-communism among the trade union leadership is described in Haseler, *The Gaitskellites*, pp. 23-27.

In power, Labour's attitude toward the Federation had been equivocal. The Fabian Colonial Bureau had been alarmed at ministerial attitudes when the report on closer association of the Central African territories had been published in June, 1951. Patrick Gordon Walker, the Commonwealth secretary, had warned that Southern Rhodesia would turn to South Africa if federation were not achieved; James Griffiths, the colonial secretary, at first emphasized the view of Colonial Office officials that closer association would have economic advantages for the African populations in the proposed Federation, and also referred to the South African threat. At a later meeting with representatives of the Bureau, Griffiths drew back, assuring the Bureau that "African opinion would be the decisive factor in the final decision."[156] Griffiths's attachment of an important condition to support for the idea of federation would provide the focal point for unified opposition to the Conservative proposals in 1953.[157] While sacrificing bipartisan agreement on colonial policy, for which they were criticized by the Conservatives, the party leadership had taken a stance that united Left and all but a fringe of the Right. The colonial specialists of the Fabian Colonial Bureau, whether normally identified with the Right (Hinden) or the Left (Driberg) had determined as early as mid-1951 that the Federation plan should be opposed even if African consent could be won; the key issue was Southern Rhodesia's native policy.[158] In this instance, the specialists' paternalism set them to the Left of the Labour Party leadership, but they supported the party's opposition, even on narrower grounds. Right-wing opposition appeared among a few in the parliamentary party who accepted the arguments based on economic benefits and South African encroachment: they included Gordon Walker and trade union representatives, such as George Brown and Charles

[156] FCB, 72/1 f 50, f 59; 72/1 f 60, meeting of 10 July 1951.

[157] NEC Minutes (214), 17 December 1952; the resolution passed by the NEC on the Federation proposals in March, 1953 had taken precisely the same position. NEC minutes (215), 25 March 1953.

[158] FCB, Draft Policy statement, Advisory Committee meeting, 25 July 1951.

Hobson (the latter connected with the Joint East and Central Africa Board, described in Chapter IV). This small group abstained in two debates on the ratification of the Federation proposals.[159]

Right and Left had been accommodated on the slender grounds of opposition to any Federation imposed against African wishes. In earlier attacks on Conservative policy, the Labour opposition maintained unity on the questions of Malaya and the Mau Mau rebellion in Kenya by emphasizing the brutal methods that were employed in dealing with the rebellions and the need for attacking the underlying cause of discontent.[160] Malaya would appear once again as a point of dispute between the party leadership and the Movement for Colonial Freedom; like British Guiana, it touched on the question of anti-communism, the most sensitive point of difference between Left and Right. Kenya is a more interesting case: the Left did not force the issue in the way that it might have; as in the case of Malaya, the communal aspect (Kikuyu versus other African groups) served to dampen enthusiasm. Even those who identified closely with African demands and personalities, such as Fenner Brockway, were shocked by the brutality of the uprising.[161]

Kenya and the Federation both posed the question of the future of settler-dominated societies in Africa; the long time-horizon set for independence by the specialists in the party had permitted postponement of an answer to that question. Just as the French Socialists had vacillated when confronted with Arab nationalism in North Africa, so the Labour Party hedged for several years. The Fabian Colonial Bureau decided to emphasize democracy rather than "partnership" in its publication, *Advance to Democracy* (1952), breaking with the Conservatives' favored ideological prescription in the settler

[159] On the splits in the party, see Goldsworthy's excellent account, in *Colonial Issues*, pp. 226-230.

[160] Ibid., pp. 209-214.

[161] One person closely associated with the Africa Bureau during these years described the Labour Party's position on Mau Mau as "ambiguous," see for example, Brockway, *Towards Tomorrow*, p. 208.

colonies. In successive publications on East and Central Africa, however, the Bureau resorted to devices that were strongly reminiscent of those proposed in France during the debate over the Algerian Statute: multimember geographical constituencies, with reserved seats for minorities; a bicameral legislature with equal representation for the races, at least in one house. Admittedly, these were regarded as temporary measures.[162] The Labour Party lagged behind the Colonial Bureau, arguing in its 1954 statement, *From Colonies to Commonwealth*, for the anodyne formula of "genuine partnership based on racial equality."[163]

The party would not break finally with concepts such as partnership and clearly declare for political democracy in the settler colonies until the publication of *The Plural Society*, part of a series of four statements on colonial policy published in 1956. The party's shift to endorsement of one man, one vote was not induced by a particular crisis in the colonies or by rank-and-file pressure: when an attempt to consult the movement was made, only one local party in over 600 responded.[164] The party organization itself took the initiative. Its Commonwealth officer, John Hatch, organized the working parties under the Commonwealth Subcommittee; that on plural societies represented all factions within the party: chaired by Tom Driberg, its members included Rita Hinden, Fenner Brockway, and Arthur Creech Jones.[165] At no point in the official record is there evidence of conflict within the working party or its parent committees. The sharpest criticism of the

[162] FCB, 72/1 ff 112-116, Advisory Committee meeting of 2 April 1952.

[163] Labour Party, Commonwealth Subcommittee, 54/23/1, copy of letter from Creech Jones to the Commonwealth officer, criticizes the document; Goldsworthy, *Colonial Issues*, pp. 331-332.

[164] Goldsworthy, *Colonial Issues*, p. 334.

[165] The working party began with a statement of principle approved by the NEC in 1954, which was taken by Hatch on an African tour, and subsequently revised and approved by the Commonwealth Subcommittee in September, 1955 before work began on the policy statement. On the establishment and work of the working parties: LP/CSC 55/16 (Meeting of 8 November 1955); CSC 55/23, 8 May 1956; CSC 55/25, 12 June 1956; NEC Minutes, 27 June 1956.

draft, surprisingly, came from a member of the Left, Richard Crossman, who felt that the document ignored the persistence of racial and cultural differences: "I would be inclined to accept multiracialism as a final aim." He also noted the dilemma—most prominent in the British Guiana case—that the right of self-determination could be used for undemocratic ends, such as racial discrimination.[166]

Publication of *The Plural Society* meant that the Labour Party's goal in East and Central Africa was "scarcely distinguishable from that of indigenous nationalists in the plural societies: political power in indigenous hands, with no greater safeguard for immigrant minorities than a putative loss of racial consciousness among all concerned."[167] Only one symbol of settler power remained—the Central African Federation—and the Labour Party remained reluctant to prejudice its future: A 1958 statement by the NEC continued to argue that benefits could be derived from federation if the European minority convinced the Africans that the ultimate objective was complete democracy and equal rights for every citizen.[168] The party was slow to accept a right of secession by the African states at the time of constitutional review, scheduled in 1960.[169]

Any last lingering caution disappeared with the violence in Nyasaland in early 1959, which jolted the Conservative Party as well. When asked by Macmillan to participate in the review undertaken by the Monckton Commission, the Labour Party leader, Hugh Gaitskell, asked that the terms of reference of the commission be changed to include the right of secession. Since such a change would have been completely unacceptable to Sir Roy Welensky, prime minister of the Federation, Macmillan was forced to recruit Labour dissidents, such as Sir Hartley Shawcross. The prime minister was unable, however,

---

[166] The final draft did not accept multiracialism as the final goal. It is interesting to note Crossman's parallel: "On your argument we should regard Zionism as a wicked thing and aim at assimilating all Jews. Do you really mean this?" Labour Party, CSC 55/79, i and ii.

[167] Goldsworthy, *Colonial Issues*, p. 337.

[168] Labour Party, Commonwealth Subcommittee, 57/36, 38.

[169] Goldsworthy, *Colonial Issues*, pp. 339-340.

to prevent the commission from addressing the question of secession.[170] Gaitskell seemed prepared to use the threat of force to ward off white rebellion in Central Africa; he claimed that, had Labour won in 1959, he would have moved military forces into the northern territories of the Federation to face down Welensky. His long-term solution seemed to be buying out the settlers.[171] There is little evidence of any dissent within the party from Gaitskell's position on the crumbling Federation.[172]

The future of the racially divided societies of Africa had served to unify rather than divide the Labour Party in opposition. A second cluster of potentially divisive questions lay in the Middle East and the Mediterranean, the core of the Conservatives' empire of prestige. Bevin had accepted many of the traditional Conservative tenets in this region, while devolving others to the United States. The nationalization of the Iranian oil wells and refineries in 1951 raised many of the same issues that appeared in the Suez crisis five years later. Herbert Morrison, during his brief tenure as foreign secretary, combined Palmerstonian rhetoric with inaction in dealing with Mossadegh's challenge. The rest of the cabinet was more restrained; American caution also added to the balance in favor of negotiation.[173] The year in which the party set its course in Africa, 1956, also witnessed a demonstration that the Empire of prestige had little hold on it, in a crisis that split British political society almost perfectly along party lines: Suez.

The nearly unanimous opposition of Labour to the Suez expedition was not completely predictable. Foreign policy di-

[170] Williams, *Hugh Gaitskell*, pp. 484-485, 679-691.

[171] Ibid., p. 679.

[172] At a meeting of the Central African Policy Committee of the Labour Party on 13 April 1959, some lingering attachment to the value of federation was expressed by Arthur Bottomley and Sir Frank Soskice, but Griffiths argued that any conference should consider all proposals and posed the question of how Britain could keep the Africans of Nyasaland in the Federation if they were intent upon leaving.

[173] Bernard Donoughue and G. W. Jones, *Herbert Morrison: Portrait of a Politician* (London: Weidenfeld and Nicolson, 1973), pp. 497, 503-504; Williams, *Hugh Gaitskell*, pp. 271-274.

visions had characterized the early years of opposition, although these had been reduced by the reconciliation of Bevan and Gaitskell after the 1955 election. Many M.P.'s, particularly on the Left of the party, were supporters of Israel; few were sympathetic to Arab nationalism, and the nationalization of the Canal by Nasser elicited little initial sympathy in the party.[174] In the early weeks of the crisis, the party's right wing had given signs that it would support the Conservative government's hard line with Nasser. Herbert Morrison, an ardent supporter of Israel, continued the line that he had taken on Iran as foreign secretary, and, although it did not make its stand public, the General Council of the TUC had begun to mobilize behind the government. The first debates in Parliament, and particularly Gaitskell's intervention on 2 August, led some to believe that Eden might count on Labour's support of the use of force against Nasser. Gaitskell's use of analogies from the 1930s could have produced such an impression, but Philip Williams argues that the party leader's line did not vary during the crisis: drawing a distinction between nationalization and control of the Canal, a willingness to take action against Nasser but not to use force without additional justification, and a desire to have the Canal placed under United Nations control.[175]

After the government's intent became clear, the party mounted the "most intense parliamentary attack in British history," even as the nation conducted a military action abroad. The Labour Party displayed almost total unity in the crucial divisions and debates. Only the maverick M.P. for Wednesbury, Stanley Evans, abstained in a single division (1 November) and spoke against the leadership's position on the preceding day.[176] The substantial number of Jewish M.P.'s in the Labour

---

[174] Both Bevan and Gaitskell were highly sympathetic to Israel; Brockway, on the other hand, was a member of the Left who was anti-Zionist. As even Bevan's biographer remarked, Arab nationalism and Islam had little appeal for him.

[175] Williams, *Hugh Gaitskell*, p. 419; on opposition to Nasser, ibid., p. 428; Donoughue and Jones, *Morrison*, p. 456.

[176] Leon D. Epstein, *British Politics in the Suez Crisis* (Urbana: University of Illinois Press, 1964), pp. 128-132.

ranks followed the party's opposition to the intervention.[177] The constituency parties did not balk; the principal evidence of rank-and-file attitudes came earlier, when complaints were registered that the leadership seemed too supportive of the government.[178] Similar solidarity was maintained in later episodes in the region: the Lebanon and Jordan interventions of 1958, and Cyprus, where the party sympathized with the Greek cause.[179]

Only one incident marred the seamless consensus that the party had constructed on colonial policy, an incident of little importance, except as further evidence of the party's sensitivity when communism was mingled with colonial nationalism. The Movement for Colonial Freedom diverged on a number of occasions from the official party position on Southeast Asia. The status of the MCF added to the delicacy of the situation: although it pointedly dissociated itself from the Labour Party, claiming to be an independent organization, a large number of Labour M.P.'s (over 100) had become sponsors of the movement. The confusion between movement and party produced conflict; Brockway believed that the suspicions of the party were aroused because the MCF did not exclude Communists.[180] In 1958, a letter sponsored by the movement demanded the withdrawal of British troops from Malaya. It produced sharp reactions from the government of Malaya, from the People's Action Party of Lee Kuan Yew in Singapore, and within the Labour Party itself. Reporting on the incident, John Hatch traced the trouble to a "pro-communist" leader of the Southeast Asia Committee in the movement and urged further action by the party to prevent such incidents.[181] The party reacted mildly: in November, 1958 an agreement was reached with Brockway that a partial disclaimer should be printed above the sponsors of the movement and that the

[177] Ibid., pp. 173-198.
[178] Williams, *Hugh Gaitskell*, p. 425.
[179] Goldsworthy, *Colonial Issues*, pp. 352-356; Williams, *Hugh Gaitskell*, pp. 479-481; Foot, *Bevan*, pp. 1605-1606.
[180] Interview, Fenner Brockway, 22 January 1980.
[181] "The Movement for Colonial Freedom," Labour Party, CSC 1957-58/14; also CSC 57/48, Secretary's Report, June, 1958, ii.

movement would consult the Commonwealth Department of the party before issuing public statements.[182]

Hardly a heated confrontation, and virtually the last within the party on a colonial issue. Two related questions reinforced the unity that Gaitskell and the party found on the cluster of issues related to decolonization at a time of renewed division of Clause IV and unilateral nuclear disarmament. Immigration from the Commonwealth placed pressure on the defenders of the imperial faith within the Conservative Party. For Labour, the issue was not only one of attachment to the multiracial Commonwealth, but also one of racial discrimination, a return to the set of issues that had unified the party during the battle over federation. Gaitskell played upon the fact that the question was central to socialist ideology, insisting that the bill proposed by the Conservatives "like Suez, cut at the roots of the socialist faith and of belief in the brotherhood of man." The opposition, in this case, as over Suez, came from the Right, Gaitskell's normal base of support in the party.[183]

A second issue also saw Labour relatively united in opposition to a Conservative Party divided. The question of entering the European Economic Community served to attach the party, and particularly its left wing, to Gaitskell and the leadership. There were many reasons for rejecting the terms of entry negotiated by the Conservatives; attachment to the Commonwealth has probably been exaggerated as one of those reasons.[184] Even for Gaitskell, the attitude of the European Community toward the Commonwealth was more a test of its attitude toward the rest of the world—insular or outward-looking—than a sign of its willingness to accept a rival international bloc.[185] Although his biographer claims that consolidating the unity of the party after months of intense conflict was not the principal goal of Gaitskell's speech opposing the terms of entry at the party conference in 1962, there is no

[182] Labour Party, CSC 58/27; CD 1958-9/1, Secretary's Report, November, 1958; approved by the NEC on 17 November 1958.
[183] Williams, *Hugh Gaitskell*, pp. 679-680.
[184] Gupta, *Imperialism*, pp. 381-382.
[185] Williams, *Hugh Gaitskell*, pp. 704, 747.

question that the supporters of the Common Market were his usual allies in the party; as his wife remarked after his address to the conference: "Charlie, all the wrong people are cheering."[186] And on this occasion Richard Crossman summarized the effect of this and other colonial issues on the Labour Party: "Not since the Suez crisis has Hugh Gaitskell been so hated outside the Labour Party and so popular inside it as he is today."[187]

Explaining Labour's unity under pressure

Although Aden and Rhodesia would remain to challenge a future Labour government, Crossman's comment points to the paradox of Labour's position as decolonization drew to a close: the international divide of the Cold War had divided the party as well; the separation of Britain from its Empire provided a source of unity. One can understand this apparently anomalous outcome by examining the roots of division over foreign policy after 1945. They centered on the wisdom of dividing Europe into blocs and on perceptions of the two superpowers: "the real difference was over attitudes to the United States, and found expression over rearmament."[188] Outside the American alliance and the European theater, only Southeast Asia (and here the American effort to construct SEATO was the bone of contention) separated the Right and Left of the party. For *both* wings of the party, decolonization served an ideological purpose.

The Bevanite Left, with its hopes for British leadership of a nonaligned group between the two blocs, counted upon newly independent states, such as India, to provide a source of diplomatic support for their strategy. What has been called "an elaborate socialist version of imperial nostalgia" reinforced the other reasons for strong identification with colonial

---

[186] Ibid., p. 736; Gaitskellite support for the Common Market was not perfect, see Haseler, *The Gaitskellites*, pp. 227-231.

[187] Cited in Williams, *Hugh Gaitskell*, p. 730.

[188] Williams, *Hugh Gaitskell*, p. 323; Haseler, *The Gaitskellites*, chap. 6.

nationalism that lay in their reading of Socialist ideology.[189] The wholehearted support for decolonization of the Gaitskellite wing of the party, the apparent shift to the Left by Gaitskell on colonial and quasi-colonial issues, is more of a puzzle. The foreign policy rationale for such a position, however, is made clear in Gaitskell's Godkin lectures: an all-important American alliance and the opposition of the United States to repressive policies in the colonial empire, skepticism about the use of force as a foreign policy instrument in the Third World, and, above all, the belief that anti-colonialism was a principal weapon of the Soviet Union, that colonial nationalists could be won to the side of the West by progressive policies. In modified form, similar arguments were adopted by the Conservative Center and Left.[190] Thus, both Left and Right in the Labour Party could endorse decolonization for different reasons of foreign policy.

Unity was also maintained, as Gupta emphasizes, because there were "no more British Guianas."[191] Confrontation with another radical nationalist or communist-leaning movement could have split the party more seriously. Only Malaya provided a similar test, and there the communal conflict between Chinese and Malays made it difficult to view the struggle as a strictly anti-colonial one. The fact that Britain faced few nationalist movements that would tap the strong current of anti-communism in the party was in part the result of the pattern of economic development in the Empire, described in Chapter IV.

Reappearance of anti-communism as an issue in the colonies would also have mobilized the TUC; without that issue, the trade unions acted as an inert force on colonial issues, steadying the movement. The political engagement of the trade union movement in decolonization was very narrowly defined;

[189] Gordon, *Conflict and Consensus*, p. 259; on the foreign policy implications of the Third World, Foot, *Bevan*, p. 406 and Bevan's comments at the British Labour Party Commonwealth Conference, 27 May-6 June, 1957, Conference Report (mimeographed), pp. 43-46.

[190] Hugh Gaitskell, *The Challenge of Coexistence* (Cambridge: Harvard University Press, 1957), chap. 3.

[191] Gupta, *Imperialism*, p. 372.

one activist recalls it as "totally insular, worth a footnote, perhaps." Since 1937, the TUC had cooperated with the Colonial Office in establishing colonial trade unions.[192] After the war, it became absorbed in its competition with the Communist-affiliated WFTU, working closely with the American-led ICFTU, despite occasional friction over their respective roles in the British colonial territories. The TUC attitude toward colonial nationalists was often distant, since it objected to the use of trade unions as "political instruments," while nationalists saw them as among the first tools to employ against the colonial power.[193] Throughout the 1950s, the British trade union movement was content to maintain its monopoly in ties to colonial unions against all competitors; among its many objections to the Movement for Colonial Freedom was the suspicion that the movement would poach its preserve. Otherwise, though it would sometimes tilt to the Right of the leadership (on immigration, for example), colonial issues were simply not important enough to risk overt intervention.

Anti-colonialism provided ideological incentives that both wings of the party could employ; it gave the leadership a means of overcoming the residue of Bevanite battles over foreign policy. As Goldsworthy argues, however, the leadership did not adopt its partisan position in the early 1950s because of left-wing *pressure* to do so. Goldsworthy's rejection of this Conservative allegation, however, is beside the point: support for decolonization was a point of solidarity within the party and offered an easily perceived line of demarcation from the Tories. Its final advantage was *minimal electoral costs*, and possibly some electoral benefits. Evidence of the effect that Suez and other colonial issues had on the party's electoral fortunes did not provide a clear estimate. The report of the election subcommittee of the NEC in 1959 was adamant: the anti-British label used by the Tories "was terribly damaging.

[192] Marjorie Nicholson, "Government-Trade Union Cooperation in Colonial Labour Development, 1925-1945," Institute of Commonwealth Studies, London (mimeographed); D. I. Davies, "The Politics of the TUC's Colonial Policy," *Political Quarterly* 35 (January-March, 1964), 23-34.
[193] See Sir Vincent Tewson, "Trade Unionism in the Colonies," Labour Party Commonwealth Conference (see n. 189), p. 30.

It is likely that we lost votes on our attacks on Suez, Hola, and Nyasaland." An appendix to the report, however, argued that colonial policy was not an important issue in the election, although it had special political impact in Scotland (the Church of Scotland was active in Central Africa) and because it was an important part of the party's image, one that served to attract Liberal support. The implication was that anti-colonialism would have a *positive* net effect.[194] A questionnaire circulated by Morgan Philips to each Labour candidate after the election also contested the importance of decolonization as an issue: only 6 of 200 candidates believed that they had lost votes because of Labour's anti-colonial stand.[195] Epstein's study of Suez offers the same conflicting reading.[196] It seems likely that the benefits to the party from the increased ideological incentives that anti-colonialism offered to party activists and voters equaled or surpassed the losses from being portrayed as "anti-national."

Labour's unity has been contrasted to this point with its own record of division on other external issues. But Labour not only maintained its unity, the party also consistently supported decolonization. Guy Mollet nearly succeeded in preserving the unity of *his* party while pursuing a colonial war in Algeria. A more complete explanation of the effects of decolonization on the two parties can be obtained by comparing their organizational ideologies and political strategies during these years. And then it can be asked: did their divergent courses matter?

FRENCH SOCIALISTS AND BRITISH LABOUR: THE BENEFITS OF PRINCIPLE

An observer of the two socialist parties in 1954 would probably have been impressed by their similarities: the French

[194] Labour Party, NEC, "General Election 1959: Report of the Election Subcommittee, 28 October 1959, GE/E/Sub 2, p. 4 and Appendix, GE/E/Sub 1, p. 8.
[195] Williams, *Hugh Gaitskell*, p. 531.
[196] Epstein, *British Politics*, pp. 147-152.

Socialists at that time loyally supporting the decolonization program of Mendès-France; the Labour Party firmly committed to self-government for the colonies and unified in opposition to the Central African Federation. Both had made compromises in power, for reasons of Cold War foreign policy or, in the French case, coalition politics. Yet from 1956 on, the two parties parted ways: in the years of Labour's attack on Eden's intervention against Egypt and the resolution of lingering doubts about the future of the settler colonies, the Socialists under Mollet deepened their commitment to a war that Mollet had earlier labeled "stupid and endless."

For both parties, anti-colonialism was a significant part of their organizational ideologies; they, like the conservative parties, were sensitive to the course of change in the empires. For neither, however, was anti-colonialism a core element. In each case, crucial political and social alignments had occurred at the turn of the century that would shape their future ideological trajectories and explain the shakier attachment of French Socialism to anti-colonialism. At the time of the Dreyfus Affair and the bitter struggle between Church and State which followed, threatening, it seemed, the republican regime, Jaurès had led the Socialists to firm support of republican institutions. It was a momentous choice, further hardened by the split with the Communists after 1920; the colonial empire in France was a *republican* creation. Regime and empire were solidly attached and would remain so until the empire vanished. The attachment of the Socialists to the republican regime, which was even more deeply engrained by their prominent role in the birth of the Fourth Republic, implicated them in a tradition of empire and diluted their anti-colonialism.

British Labour's ideological attachments were formed at the same time, as the Labour Representation Committee and the Independent Labour Party emerged in the era of imperialism. Despite the flirtations of a few Socialist intellectuals with social imperialism, most of the Labour movement followed Keir Hardie in attaching itself to the existing Radical critique of imperialism; symbolic of this fusion of the Liberal Party Left and the new Labour movement was the "Lib-Lab" group around J. A. Hobson, whose economic analysis of imperialism would later contribute to the Leninist anti-imperialism adopted by the Third International. The Labour Party thus followed in ideological descent a part of the Liberal coalition that had stood outside the dominant ideological and political symbolism of British society—the monarchy, the landed aristocracy, the Established Church, and the Empire, particularly the Empire of prestige centered on India.

The fit of anti-colonialism with the underlying cleavage in British society meant that, in contrast to the French Socialists, rather than being drawn into the prevailing external consensus, the Labour Party tended to represent groups excluded from that consensus: the Nonconformist churches, the Celtic fringe, and the working class. The fusion of nineteenth-century Radicalism and socialism in foreign and colonial policy coupled with this subculture of exclusion gave the party its unique version of foreign policy, a socialist foreign policy, that would place it firmly on the side of decolonization.[197]

Specific differences in the ideological bundles that Labour and the SFIO brought to decolonization were also important. The *liberal* strand and that contributed by religious Nonconformity were central in Labour's attitude toward foreign and colonial questions from the start, and became the dominant attitude between the wars. The cluster of attitudes typical of the liberal humanitarian tradition gave the party a moral attitude toward international affairs, a commitment to anti-militarism and international organization (particularly apparent in the Suez crisis), a paternalist concern for the protection of the indigenous populations of the Empire (which derived from a long history of anti-slavery and aboriginal protection societies), and finally, emphasis upon the principle of national self-determination. The French SFIO lacked that inheritance from nineteenth-century liberalism. As Mollet remarked contemptuously during the Suez crisis: "Yes, but this

---

[197] For an argument that the Labour Party represents a deviant set of values and symbols within British political society, Frank Parkin, "Working-class Conservatives: A theory of political deviance," *British Journal of Sociology* 18 (September, 1967), 278-290.

[Britain] is a strange country. Here the Conservatives hold Socialist opinions and act accordingly; the Socialists are old-fashioned Liberals."[198] What the French Socialists did have was an attachment to Marxism almost wholly lacking in Britain. For the Socialist Left—Pivert and his allies—revolutionary Marxism implied anti-colonialism. In the vulgar and pre-Leninist variant endorsed by the party leadership, Marxism served as an unexpected justification for colonialism: its hierarchical view of societies (with Europe at the top of the hierarchy); economic and social determinism, used to deny the importance of political rights; hostility to nationalism, except, of course, French nationalism.

The gradual loss of class content in French Socialist ideology, its transmutation into what André Philip called no more than sympathy for the "little man," also led to a more solicitous attitude toward the settlers of North Africa. Here the bipolarity of the British polity was at work as well: the European settlers would never have considered turning to Labour for sympathy or political support in the metropolis. Labour's attitude toward colonial nationalist movements, described in Chapter V, was also more catholic than that of the French, who found only the Néo-Destour in North Africa as genuinely acceptable political partners.

Finally, the Labour Party had not been "nationalized" by recent history in the manner of the French Socialists. Despite the temptations that jingoism held for some of its members and voters and its deep-seated patriotism, the Labour Party always ran the risk of being condemned as "anti-national" by its opponents, during the Suez crisis and on other occasions. The French Socialists were almost unthinking nationalists after the experience of the Resistance, which marked the postwar leadership; many became as willing as the Gaullists to see concessions to change as defeat and treason. And those who had resisted the nationalist appeal most fiercely (and to such disastrous effect) in the 1930s had been largely eliminated

[198] Harold Macmillan, *Riding the Storm, 1956-1959* (New York: Harper & Row, 1971), p. 121.

from the party; in the British Labour Party, the old pacifist and anti-militarist strain continued into the Keep Left, Bevanite, and nuclear disarmament streams within the party.

Each of these differences in the *content* of socialist ideology and its political bases in the two countries reveal that anti-imperialism was a much clearer part of Labour's identity. Ideological uncertainty offered an opening for Mollet's policies in Algeria and the earlier compromises made by the party, but anti-colonialism had not been removed from the party's program, as the years from 1952 to 1955 demonstrated. The French Socialists in 1955 seemed to be moving toward dealing with Algeria as part of North Africa and not as the special case it later became. Certainly many expected power in 1956 to be used for peace, not a deepening of conflict.

Political strategy explains this divergence of the parties in the 1950s. For Mollet, the demands of parliamentary coalition (de facto support from the Right) combined with a past electoral strategy to seal exit to either side of the party (anticommunism) to produce a policy that resembled the National Union he had rejected immediately after the elections. The by-elections of 1957 seemed to demonstrate the advantages of nationalism in setting the Socialists apart from their competitors on the Left, the more anti-colonial *Mendèsiste* Radicals and Communists. Mollet's opponents, on the other hand, advocated a broader strategy, incorporating those discontented with the vagaries of the Communist Party line and Catholics with a social conscience.

For the Labour Party, in a different, bipolar system, such concern over exit did not weigh in the balance. Support for decolonization served as a slender means for obtaining a measure of party unity in a decade of almost endless strife. The discontent and grumbling within the trade union movement and on the party's right wing was more than balanced by the gains made in renewing the loyalty of the Left and reducing its exercise of voice. The losses electorally, as has been seen, were difficult to measure, but seemed insignificant compared to the gains to be made in presenting an image of unity when the Conservatives were likely to be divided. In any case, the appeals of anti-colonialism could attract ex-Liberals in the Center, who might not be as sympathetic to the economic programs of the Labour Party.[199]

Even if exit is controlled, for most democratic socialist parties, the problem of voice is a pressing one; as Beer notes, to be ideological *and* democratic is a recipe for ceaseless internal conflict.[200] Countering tendencies toward the exercise of voice were aspects of what Drucker calls the ethos of the Labour Party (and other socialist parties): loyalty to the leadership, a belief in "formal, explicit rules," and, on the part of the trade unions, an intense belief in solidarity, with the corollary of hostility toward those who would divide the party.[201] Electoral penalties imposed on a divided party also restrain an exercise of voice that goes too far.

On other issues, the Labour leadership had great difficulty in establishing discipline within the party given the tenacity of those on the Left who challenged the leadership in Parliament and among the party rank and file. Against a few dissidents discipline might be effective, against a large segment of the parliamentary party (nearly half on the question of German rearmament), most of the means available were hopelessly inadequate. Thus, the party turned to ideological incentives to unify the party and distance it from the Conservative opposition. On colonial questions—unlike almost every other issue of external policy—voice only became significant when coupled with the more sensitive issue of anti-communism or race.

Despite the opening provided by Socialist ideology, Mollet's turn toward repression in Algeria risked disruption of the party. Exit had been the principal dilemma for the Socialists immediately after the war, with two vigorous competitors to

---

[199] The importance of such issues for middle-class radicals is documented in Frank Parkin, *Middle Class Radicalism: The Social Bases of the British Campaign for Nuclear Disarmament* (Manchester: Manchester University Press, 1968).

[200] Beer, *British Politics*, pp. 234-239.

[201] H. M. Drucker, *Doctrine and Ethos in the Labour Party* (London: George Allen and Unwin, 1979), pp. 12-17.

the Left and Right. Mollet's strategy of anti-communism and anti-clericalism effectively raised insurmountable barriers to exit by the 1950s; Hungary and the weakening of the MRP did the rest. His principal task, then, became the control of voice within the party: barriers to exit reduced its force, and the powerful loyalty felt even by the dissidents did the rest. As Mollet's shift on the Algerian War became apparent, and the opposition attempted to organize, the dissidents discovered that their progress was hampered by two particular aspects of the party. Changes in party rules instituted after Liberation made it nearly impossible to create a *tendance* like those which had battled during the 1930s. The leadership possessed an array of disciplinary measures that it was willing to use against its opponents. A second feature was growing reliance upon purposive incentives; efforts to arouse ideological opposition against a wary policy that seemed to violate stated party tenets did not find a resonance in the party that might have been expected. Gains in economic and social programs (as well as simple political patronage) seemed more important to many in the party. Only the question of participation in increasingly conservative ministries, and finally de Gaulle's investiture, tapped a wider vein of discontent within the Socialist ranks.

Did the divergence make any difference? Both parties were in opposition for most the crucial years of decolonization; an equally important drama of decolonization was played out in the conservative parties that had more responsibility for policy. David Goldsworthy has carefully assessed the influence that Labour in opposition had on Conservative colonial policy in the 1950s.[202] Despite the claims of Labour spokesmen that the party could regularly influence the bargaining between government and colonial nationalists, Goldsworthy finds the opposition's impact more limited. In certain cases, its ties to colonial nationalists and its status as an alternative government could tip the balance: Cyprus is perhaps the clearest instance. In other cases, such as East and Central Africa, the

[202] Goldsworthy, *Colonial Issues*, chap. 10.

party's influence seems to have been more marked in the help that it offered in the political organization of African nationalist movements, an indirect way of influencing the costs and benefits weighed by Conservative governments.[203] Goldsworthy overlooks another aid that Labour could offer during decolonization, however: as the party's opposition during the Katanga episode suggests, widening the distance between the political parties eased the task of decolonization *within* that was faced by the Conservative leadership. Opposition attacks could be a useful weapon in internal party battles.

The results for French decolonization if the Socialists had maintained their support for decolonization in North Africa, in opposition if necessary, is one of the most intriguing hypotheses of the period. Certainly French decolonization did pursue its bumpy path most successfully when the Socialists were out of power, throwing their support to Mendès-France, maintaining links to the Tunisian nationalists, criticizing the standpat policies of conservative ministries—in short, behaving like a French Labour Party. After 1956, Duverger has suggested that they could have relied upon alternating coalitions (including Communist support) to carry out a more liberal policy in Algeria—other governments far more conservative had relied upon such support to survive. The fierce anti-communism of the party leadership made such a course unlikely; the risks of losing power to conservatives were also great.

The analogy to Labour quickly breaks down, however: the SFIO had no leverage over the FLN in Algeria and no friendly relations with it. It also lacked the hold over public opinion that the British parties could exert. Epstein documents the remarkable polarization that occurred in Britain after the two parties had staked out their opposing positions in the Suez crisis. The British parties did not simply respond to opinion, they helped to *shape* it; whether the tired and eroded SFIO could have exercised such influence to stave off the nationalist reaction that arose in late 1956 is doubtful.

[203] See Goldsworthy's assessment in ibid., pp. 359-360.

But the final insurmountable barrier to an opposition strategy and the final trump in Mollet's hand was the question of the regime. As D. Bruce Marshall has described, the regime may have been inseparably linked to the maintenance of French colonial rule as early as the years of constitution-making after 1945. In any case, the Gaullists and other right-wing critics of the republic amplified and strengthened the link in the 1950s. The danger was increased by the dissidence of the Algerian settlers (demonstrated on 6 February 1956), by the increasingly hostile attitude of the Army, and the insubordination of the state apparatus, which would become apparent in May, 1958. These features of French decolonization, examined in Chapter V, set the position of the SFIO apart from that of Labour. So long as the regime was in danger the Socialists would pay almost any price to save it, even the bitter cost of a colonial war in North Africa.

CHAPTER IV

Metropolitan Politics and the Economics of Empire

THE COLONIAL economies entered the politics of Britain and France by shaping the indirect ideological hold of the empires on the political parties and by directly penetrating and influencing the making of colonial policy. Even for those parties that represented business or capital, the external orientation of capitalist development was not a given, but a source of controversy: definitions of economic interest could not be separated from the ideological formulations of the political parties. Colonial interests sought in turn to shape those ideological appeals to fit *their* perceptions against competing sectors with lower stakes in the colonial status quo. Two important business organizations, for example, the Commonwealth and Empire Industries Association and the Joint East and Central Africa Board, were active in leading the resistance to the decolonization of the British Conservative Party; their French analogue, the Comité central de la France d'Outre-mer, engaged in fierce propaganda battles with the critics of colonial rule. These organizations, and individual firms, could also penetrate metropolitan politics more directly. Political parties, even pro-business parties, were not wholly reliable allies, and there were other avenues for influencing government policy— the bureaucracy, whether in London, Paris, or Africa, also offered access and a means of achieving their goals.

The goals themselves were not obvious. Not all businesses with interests in the colonial empires actively resisted decolonization. The stakes were potentially high, however: the end of colonial rule threatened the dismantling of complicated political arrangements protecting the colonial economy and more radical transformations in some cases. The settler colonies in particular faced the possibility of disruptive political change, an explosion of political participation, the threat of violence, and the installation of a political regime represented by different racial, social and economic interests.[1]

As a first step in analyzing the effects that colonial economic actors could have on the politics of decolonization, the attitudes of firms (or groups of firms) toward political change on the periphery can be related to characteristics of those firms. The investigation of resistance or accommodation across sectors and over time will be explored using the concept of political exposure. Linking political orientation to economic characteristics is only a first step, however. Political mediation through business organizations and the state was a crucial step in determining whether the impact of decolonization upon firms—inducing their resistance to change in existing colonial relations—could in fact arrest the course of disengagement.

The analysis is based upon data that are necessarily incomplete. Firms are reluctant to offer access to their archives to other than company historians; a detailed accounting across so many territories would be impossible in any case. Nevertheless, tentative conclusions can be drawn from published statements, company reports, contemporary observations, and internal documentation from two firms and two significant business pressure groups.[2]

POLITICAL EXPOSURE AND THE DETERMINANTS OF POLITICAL RESPONSE

The development of a market economy in colonial Africa was a political act, confirming Polanyi's claim that "the road to the free market was opened and kept open by an enormous increase in continuous, centrally organized and controlled in-

---

[1] These include the French cases of Algeria, Morocco and Tunisia and the British cases of Kenya, Tanganyika (now Tanzania), and the Central African Federation (now Zambia, Zimbabwe, and Malawi).

[2] The state of research on firms in the colonial empires is summarized in A. G. Hopkins, "Imperial Business in Africa, Part I: Sources," *Journal of African History* 17 (1976), 29-48.

terventionism."[3] To measure a firm's likely response to changes in its political environment—an environment whose importance was both magnified and uneven in colonial Africa—two dimensions of *political exposure* must be employed: dependence upon state policy (under the existing political system) for the firm's viability (*political sensitivity*) and an estimate of the probability of those political changes that would have an effect upon the firm (*probable political futures*). Political exposure can be expected to affect the attitude of the firm or sector toward political change; its relationship to political action is less clear. The discussion of political exposure which follows is directed to firms that had investments in the colonial empires; the concept will then be adapted for metropolitan companies that were dependent upon *markets* in the overseas territories.

Political sensitivity as a measure of dependence upon state policy

Colonial firms relied upon the state not only for the creation of markets; their dependence often extended to measures of state support that served to maintain their profitability in a hostile environment—tariffs, subsidies, and the like. The relative dependence of firms upon state policy can be viewed as deviation from the minimal political requirements of all firms, the policies labeled "magistracy" by Adam Smith (maintenance of public order and a system of justice, national defense, and the provision of public works or economic infrastructure).[4] Beyond these minimal requirements, certain economic actors had specific political needs of their own.

What characteristics of a firm might cause it to be concerned about changes in its political environment?

1. *Carrying out a "governmental" function.* Many colonial governments designated private firms as concessionaires in

[3] Karl Polyani, *The Great Transformation* (Boston: Beacon Press, 1957), p. 140.

[4] Charles Kindleberger, *Government and International Trade*, Essays in International Finance, No. 129 (Princeton, N.J.: Princeton University, International Finance Section, 1978), pp. 3-7.

such sectors as electricity, railroads, and public works. Even certain elements of magistracy were delegated by the metropolitan power in this way. A post-colonial regime would probably seek the capture of these functions for itself, using the model of other developing countries for the expansion of the state sector.

2. *Reliance upon the government for sales or capital.* The end of colonial rule threatened certain firms with loss of guaranteed sales or cheap investment funds. Some firms also relied upon the state for the provision of labor, but such policies had for the most part been ended before decolonization.

3. *Labor costs.* The importance of the wage bill in the cost structure of the firm might increase its sensitivity to political change. Change in a democratic direction (awarding greater political power to the working class) could increase the bargaining power of labor and reduce the profitability of the firm. Labor-intensive techniques also suggested greater vulnerability to substitution by the postcolonial state or by local entrepreneurs.

4. *Scale, size of investment, "prominence."* Moran and others have noted that large foreign firms are often likely to attract political attention; Moran has also suggested that a company with a large sunk investment is more vulnerable to pressure by the host country; if additional investment is required for expansion, however, the firm's position is likely to be stronger. Such an increase in political sensitivity was balanced by the new state's dependence upon large firms for much of its revenue and for the success of its development plans. This and other aspects of *state* dependence, for instance on imported technology and marketing, were shaped by the probable political future of the society, described below.[5]

5. *Metropolitan versus colonial base.* Was the firm part of a larger corporation based in the metropolis, or was it limited to the colonial setting? The subsidiary of a large international

[5] Theodore H. Moran, *Multinational Corporations and the Politics of Dependence* (Princeton: Princeton University Press, 1974), p. 160; Alfred Stepan, *The State and Society* (Princeton: Princeton University Press, 1978), pp. 242-245.

firm with only a minor interest in a given colony would probably respond differently from a local firm: not only was it less dependent on the colonial milieu, but its managerial personnel was probably more "metropolitan," with fewer ties to the political and social givens of the colonial regime. Decentralization, on the other hand, would probably produce political responses closer to those of locally-based enterprises. In either case, a subsidiary's links to the metropolis would also transmit its political response more effectively than the perceptions of its local counterpart.

6. *International competition.* Colonial systems were international regimes as well, often characterized by tariffs and other restrictive government policies that tied colonial areas to the metropolitan economy and ensured the viability of economic interests in the periphery. As a result, those firms that were less competitive internationally might be politically more sensitive to decolonization.

7. Finally, one characteristic difficult to assess: *attitude toward risk*. Compared to metropolitan firms, traditional colonial firms appeared more risk-averse after World War II, in part because of their controlled political and economic environment. The experience of a few firms, such as "Tiny" Rowland's Lonrho, suggests that it was possible for risk-takers to make gains during the breakdown of the colonial environment.[6]

The weight of these characteristics in determining political sensitivity can be tested against the responses of firms during decolonization. "Decolonization" could mean a number of possible futures, however, ranging from little change in existing political arrangements to radical demands that would threaten the existence of some firms. Political exposure, therefore, has a second aspect: the probable political future of the

---

[6] On the evolution of attitudes toward risk, A. G. Hopkins, "Imperial Business in Africa, Part II: Interpretations," *Journal of African History* 17 (1976), 281-283; cf. the conservatism of British firms in India, B. R. Tomlinson, *The Political Economy of the Raj, 1914-1947* (London: Macmillan, 1979), p. 52.

society and the likelihood that a particular political regime would take power following colonial rule.

Probable political future

Although few firms contemplated the future in systematic or probabilistic ways, this second element of political exposure should be treated as a cluster of possible outcomes. For a foreign corporation, the salient features in its calculations were the competing elites within the nationalist movement, their development programs (with implied changes in the postcolonial political economy), and the pressures that would be exerted upon the triumphant elite by its supporters—pressures that would vary according to the class, regional, and urban/rural composition of the dominant coalition. Contributing to the political probabilities, along with the *aims* of future elites, would be the *capabilities* of the eventual successor regime. These characteristics have been summarized by Alfred Stepan: the elite's commitment to control, its capacity to monitor foreign capital, and its marketing and technological capacities.[7] However radical its proclaimed development strategy, a weak state (or one low on the "host-country learning curve") would pose less of a threat to the expatriate investor. Even a weak state could impose certain costs, however, such as disorder and insecurity.

The outcomes feared by corporations included outright expropriation as well as "the risk of being forced out of business by deliberate government action, the risk of forceful government participation in the capital of a company, and the risk of future direct competition from a publicly owned company."[8] Firms with high political sensitivity could be affected by even less dramatic changes in government policies.

Thus, the political exposure of a firm (or sector) consists of its political sensitivity or dependence upon state policy, combined with the probable political futures that would change state policies essential to the firm's profitability.[9]

[7] Stepan, *The State and Society*, pp. 238-241.

[8] Lee Charles Nehrt, *The Political Climate for Private Foreign Investment* (New York: Frederick A. Praeger, 1970), p. 3.

[9] Stated more formally, $E = f[S(F_1)(P_1) + S(F_2)(P_2) + \ldots + S(F_n)(P_n)]$

The political exposure of firms dependent on colonial markets

Those metropolitan firms dependent upon colonial markets would calculate political exposure differently than investing firms, though their political action might be just as forceful. One element factored into the equation would be the *level of dependence* itself, a multiplier of the political exposure itself by a factor of the firm's trade with a particular colony (or the entire empire) divided by its metropolitan production. An exporting firm would be most concerned about those parts of political exposure that would affect the *likelihood of displacement* from colonial markets by international competition or indigenous producers, in the absence of the safeguard of the colonial relationship. On the side of political sensitivity, some of the firm characteristics listed above would be likely indicators of those exporters most sensitive to the end of imperial economic systems—labor-intensive production and international competitiveness in particular. In calculating the second term, probable political futures, the distinctions required would be less refined than those for investors: almost any independent state would try to revise existing trade relations in ways that would probably reduce imports from the former metropolis. Commercial autonomy was often the first exercise of power for a new nationalist coalition bent on industrialization through import substitution. Former colonial markets could be protected against international competition, however, through aid policies or currency manipulations.

THE RESPONSE OF FIRMS TO DECOLONIZATION: TRADE

For metropolitan political leaders and for particular economic interests, the colonial economic relationship had two aspects: an *external economic orientation*—a system of tariffs, exchange controls, and investment subsidies that channeled

---

where E is political exposure; S is political sensitivity; $F_1 \ldots F_n$ are political futures; $P_1 \ldots P_n$ are probabilities of given political futures. Although political exposure is only estimated here, indices could be constructed that would permit more precise measurement.

economic exchanges between metropolis and empire—and a system of *political control* exercised over dependent territories that permitted their economies to be shaped to suit metropolitan ends. In the case of France, the two halves of the colonial economic relationship fitted closely: political independence for African dependencies was believed to mean economic independence in the external sphere; in the British case, it was the Dominions, which already possessed economic autonomy, who were the principal international partners within the system of imperial preferences.

For both countries, however, postwar trade with the colonies was carried out within a carefully constructed political framework. After 1945 the British and French elites inherited economies that had become highly interdependent with the colonial empires (and the Dominions in the case of Britain). The postwar state of affairs had resulted not only from policy decisions taken in the 1920s and 1930s, but also from the peculiar economic environment of depression and war that had characterized the years since 1930. The economic concentration upon the empire that had occurred, however, was greater in the case of France. Although the percentage of Britain's trade taken by the Empire (including the Dominions) had been boosted by the adoption of imperial preference, the Empire was "nothing like a comprehensive economic system" at the end of the 1930s. In 1938 Europe still attracted more exports from Britain than India, Australia, New Zealand, Canada, the West Indies, and the United States combined, just as it had in earlier periods. World War II, which redirected Britain's sources of supply toward the Empire and Commonwealth and closed the European market, had accentuated the concentration of British trade; the postwar dollar shortage temporarily encouraged the continuation of this pattern.[10]

Encouraged by tariff legislation passed in 1928, French trade showed an even more emphatic shift toward the colonial em-

[10] J.D.B. Miller, *Survey of Commonwealth Affairs: Problems of Expansion and Attrition, 1953-1969* (Oxford: Oxford University Press, 1974), pp. 441, 268-269; Tomlinson, *The Political Economy of the Raj, 1914-1947*, pp. 133-138.

pire during the 1930s: imports from the overseas territories increased from 12 percent to 26 percent during the decade after 1925; exports grew from 16 percent to 32 percent in the same period.[11] Even in the 1950s, 26 percent of France's imports came from the *Union française*; 31 percent of her exports were destined for the empire.[12] In both the British and French cases, however, by the mid-1950s the impact of the mechanisms used to direct trade was eroding.[13]

More important politically, however, was the dependence of certain sectors upon the colonial empire for markets. A number of French industries stood out as particularly sensitive to the decolonization of trade in the mid-1950s: textiles (particularly cotton), beet sugar, petroleum products, tires, shoes, and certain products of the machine tool industry.[14] The highly protected character of the colonial market for these products is demonstrated by the surcharges which the colonial consumers paid above world prices: 3 percent to 105 percent for sugar; 23 percent for cotton textiles; 12 percent for petroleum products.[15]

Simple export dependence could multiply political exposure, but it is not the best indicator of it. In terms of displacement, given the strategy of industrialization followed by nearly every economy since Britain, the French textiles sector was likely to be the most threatened. Facing a deteriorating international competitive position, textiles were a labor-intensive

[11] Jean-Louis Miège, *Expansion européenne et décolonisation de 1870 à nos jours* (Paris: Presses Universitaires de France, 1973), p. 290.

[12] Pierre Moussa, *Les Chances économiques de la communauté franco-africaine* (Paris: Armand Colin, 1957), pp. 27, 34. These figures include Tunisia and Morocco. The best description of the complex combination of commercial and financial devices used to channel trade from France to its colonies is J. W. Saxe, "The Evolution of the Economic Structure of the French Union," (D.Phil. thesis, Oxford University, 1958), pp. 188-220.

[13] Moussa, *Les Chances*, pp. 46-49, 50; Miller cites a study by Harry Johnson that demonstrated the relative insignificance of the preference system in the British economy in the early 1960s: Miller, *Survey of Commonwealth Affairs*, p. 288.

[14] Moussa, *Les Chances*, pp. 246-247, Annex 12; p. 59.

[15] Ibid., p. 82.

industry, by far the largest (in numbers employed) among those dependent upon colonial markets: some 220,000 workers in the early 1950s.[16] The textile industry in France had every reason to resist decolonization, which threatened its last secure market in an increasingly competitive world economy. Spokesmen for one trade association, the Syndicat général de l'Industrie cotonnière, directly linked the end of the colonial empire with its economic distress. In listing the reasons for his industry's plight, the president of the association declared that "the first, and the clearest is the political break. In Indochina, in Morocco, and in Tunisia, the accession to independence has caused, more or less rapidly, a decline in imports of French products."[17] The principal baron of the industry, Marcel Boussac, was especially active in opposing political concessions in Morocco. Boussac had founded the Comptoir de l'industrie cotonnière: of its trade in cotton cloth in 1948, only 15 percent was sold in France; 35 percent was exported to the colonial empire.[18] His lobbying was supplemented by ownership of the right-wing newspaper, L'Aurore. Pierre July, minister for Moroccan and Tunisian affairs in the Edgar Faure cabinet, attributes Boussac's activities, at least in part, to his fear of being displaced in the Moroccan cotton trade by Arab competitors:

The installation of a nationalist government at Rabat would have severely thwarted, if not ruined, his projects to extend an important trade in cotton to Morocco: even more so, since, in Morocco, the Sebti, a great family of merchants, were ready to take his place.[19]

[16] On the international position of the European industry: Pierre de Calan, "Comment faire l'Europe cotonnière?" Société belge d'études et d'expansion: Bulletin bimestrial, no. 165 (March-April, 1955), p. 368; Le Monde des affaires en France de 1830 à nos jours (Paris: Société Edition de dictionnaires et encyclopédies, 1952), p. 363.

[17] "Défense des marchés cotonniers d'outre-mer," Perspectives, 23 July 1960, pp. 1-3; "Les Marchés de l'outre-mer français," Industrie cotonnière française (July, 1954), pp. 35-39.

[18] Le Monde des affaires, p. 645.

[19] Pierre July, Une république pour un roi (Paris: Fayard, 1974), p. 160; Boussac's opposition is attributed to "close ties with el-Glaoui" in Stéphane

In contrast to his earlier successful tactics in defeating the Franco-Italian Customs Union, however, Boussac was unable to construct a business coalition broad enough to block decolonization of the protectorate.[20] Textile interests found another political voice during the legislative campaign of 1955: the decline of the Vosges textile interests was linked by Pierre Poujade to the loss of empire. Whether the industry had provided financial support for the Poujadists is impossible to document.

In Britain those sectors with a high political exposure deriving from their dependence on Commonwealth markets found a voice for preserving and extending the system of Commonwealth preferences in the Commonwealth and Empire Industries Association (after 1961 the Commonwealth Industries Association), legatee of the Empire Industries Association founded in 1926 to promote imperial preference and a system of protective tariffs.[21] The association provided a core of leadership in battles within the Conservative Party to halt the trend toward multilateralism in the postwar period. At the Conservative Party Annual Conferences, the motions and amendments in favor of the preferential system were nearly always presented by members of the Executive Committee of the association.[22] Its parliamentary arm included members of both Houses of Parliament; the association provided speakers for and held meetings with local Conservative Associations, as well as publishing its monthly *Bulletin* designed for a larger audience.[23]

Bernard, *The Franco-Moroccan Conflict, 1943-1956* (New Haven: Yale University Press, 1968), pp. 263-264.

[20] Henry W. Ehrmann, *Organized Business in France* (Princeton: Princeton University Press, 1957), pp. 404-405, 411.

[21] The Empire Industries Association amalgamated with the British Empire League in 1947.

[22] Including the final effort to tie the hands of the Macmillan government at the Annual Conference in 1962: the amendment hostile to the EEC was moved by Robin Turton.

[23] A general account of the association's activities may be gleaned from the *Annual Report* and from "The Commonwealth Industries Association: What It Is and What It Does" (typescript, n.d.).

By the mid-1950s, however, the organization was in clear decline. As described in Chapter II, the failure of its efforts was owed in part to a change in political generations and the weakening of its ideological hold on the party, despite repeated Conservative professions of faith in the Commonwealth ideal. Membership in the Parliamentary Committee peaked in 1954 with 267 members; after the 1955 elections, membership dropped to 226, as a new political cohort entered the House.[24] The shifting of patterns of trade in the 1950s, in part the result of its earlier lack of success, reinforced organizational decline, as the association's financial support dropped.[25] Despite efforts at revival by younger members, when the battle over entry into the European Economic Community was joined in 1961-1962, the Conservative leadership faced an organizational foe that had lost much of its following within the party.[26] The preferentialist lobby was also afflicted by an ideological inconsistency that grew in the 1950s. As early as 1949, the association had been forced to widen its appeal to a general defense of free enterprise to obtain necessary support from industrial associations battling the Labour Government.[27] As the Conservative Party moved toward neo-liberalism in its economic policy, however, the neo-mer-

[24] The source for these figures is the *Annual Reports* for the relevant years; after 1955, membership figures were no longer recorded. The hold of the association weakened at the local level as well: the proportion of political (usually Conservative Party) meetings addressed declined. In the period 1953-1955, the number of such meetings dropped 25.5 percent and the number of people addressed at such gatherings declined by 30.4 percent. Empire Industries Association and British Empire League, *Annual Report*, 1955.

[25] In December, 1959, it was noted at a meeting of the Executive Committee of the association that it might be necessary to wind up its activities, since raising funds had become so difficult. (Commonwealth and Empire Industries Association, Executive Committee, 14 December 1959).

[26] See Chapter II above and Robert J. Lieber, *British Politics and European Unity* (Berkeley: University of California Press, 1970) pp. 204-205. At the meeting noted in n. 24, the discontent of younger members (Peter Walker, John Biggs-Davison, and Paul Williams) was evident.

[27] Empire Industries Association and British Empire League, Executive Committee, 22 September 1949.

cantilist arguments put forward by the supporters of Commonwealth preferences seemed increasingly out of step.

Finally, the very interests that had originally allied themselves with the association were shifting from under its banner as the Dominions and some of the colonies industrialized. The Dominion governments would have resisted efforts to impose a stronger set of commercial constraints, since their own efforts at industrialization would be endangered. On the question of Britain's entry into the Common Market, the Commonwealth countries' attitudes were of considerable importance: their open resistance would have immeasurably strengthened the position of the opponents of Europe within the Conservative Party. These Commonwealth members, particularly the "big five"—Canada, Australia, New Zealand, Pakistan, and India—did possess their *own* domestic political constraints in the form of interests that relied upon the access to the British market guaranteed by the preference system.[28] Despite their clear dislike for the 1962 terms of British entry into the European Community, however, the political repercussions were not severe.[29]

Just as the Dominion governments came to perceive negative dimensions to strengthened Commonwealth trading arrangements, so resistance to dismantling preferences by some sectors of the British economy was balanced by the cost of colonial ties for others. The contrasting political responses of the British and the French textile industries, for example, resulted in part from the greater degree of industrialization within British colonies and former colonies: industrial imports, favored by the system of preferences, met increasing opposition from beleaguered British manufacturers. In the case of textiles, a rising tide of cloth entered Britain from India, Pakistan, and particularly Hong Kong. As the minister responsible for defending the interests of the Crown Colonies, Lennox-Boyd tenaciously defended the free entry of his client's exports.

---

[28] Miller, *Survey of Commonwealth Affairs*, p. 288; Harold Macmillan, *At the End of the Day* (New York: Harper & Row, 1973), p. 114.

[29] Miller, *Survey of Commonwealth Affairs*, pp. 328-333.

Macmillan, however, was attuned to the domestic political consequences if nothing were done:

If we *force* Hong Kong to conform to an agreement which India and Pakistan seem ready to make, he [Lennox-Boyd] will resign. If we accept his point of view, we shall lose a lot of Lancashire trade . . . (perhaps inevitable) and nine (or even) fourteen Lancashire seats! This dilemma was *not* resolved by lunchtime.[30]

Disagreement between the colonial secretary and the president of the Board of Trade reached a point at which they "ceased to be on speaking terms—they are only on bawling terms."[31] All the while the party chairman warned of the political situation in Lancashire. The conflict between colonial and domestic interests was temporarily resolved by a three-year import limitation agreement reached in September, 1959, ancestor of the Multifiber Arrangement that governs the textile trade today.

Because the French colonies were by and large at a lower level of industrialization than the British, such industrial competition did not figure in the French case. Nevertheless, agriculture produced similar political juggling acts, an endless task of reconciling colonial, particularly North African, and metropolitan interests. Wine and wheat dominated European agriculture in Morocco and Algeria; both competed with French production, particularly wine, the principal export of Algeria. Thus, rather than supplying needed raw materials for the metropolis, this sector of the European colonial economy in North Africa offered only products that were not needed, at prices well above world levels.[32] Of course, when considered from the point of view of the agricultural sector in North Africa, this meticulously arranged effort to subsidize all parties *in-*

---

[30] Harold Macmillan, *Riding the Storm* (New York: Harper & Row, 1971), p. 740.

[31] Ibid., p. 741.

[32] Moussa, *Les Chances*, pp. 90-92; Charles F. Stewart, *The Economy of Morocco, 1912-1962* (Cambridge: Harvard University Press, 1964), pp. 89-90; René Gendarme, *L'Economie de l'Algérie* (Paris: Armand Colin, 1959), p. 17; Saxe, "Evolution," pp. 210-214.

creased their political exposure and their resistance to decolonization; at the same time, it prevented any alliance with agricultural interests in the metropolis.

THE RESPONSE OF FIRMS TO DECOLONIZATION: INVESTMENTS

In applying the model of political exposure to firms with investments in the colonial empire, one should note at the outset the generally greater dependence on state policy within the French Union as compared to the British colonies. Such dependence was encouraged by a higher level of protection against international competition, differing philosophies of colonial governance (direct versus indirect rule), and the larger role of the French state in economic development (although, as will be seen below, the state's entrepreneurial role could reduce political exposure). If this underlying contrast is taken into account, comparisons across sectors and firms are possible.

Metropolitan economic expansion in the colonial areas may be visualized across time in two waves, roughly divided by World War II. The first wave was dominated by agriculture, the production of primary products for the metropolis, and, to a lesser degree, mining. Public works and governance were in certain cases granted to chartered companies or concessionaires. Commerce in sub-Saharan Africa was dominated by large trading companies; however, the prominence of a few firms was more marked in West Africa than in East and Central Africa, the principal regions of British settlement. The second wave of industrialization was uneven; it was stimulated by the forced import substitution of World War II and the boom in prices of raw materials that continued up to the end of the Korean War; early industrialization was usually accompanied by an expansion of the commercial and banking sectors. The divide between the two waves of expatriate enterprises would produce a break point in later levels of political exposure.

The first wave: Concessionaires, agriculture, mining

Chartered companies and government concessionaires. Although these early enterprises had been overtaken by newer arrivals in the colonial economy, they survived in altered form to the years of decolonization. Their political exposure was high: the nature of their business activities raised their political sensitivity—they were highly dependent upon the government for setting rates, providing financing, and other support—and political futures were bleak, since all colonial nationalists desired their speedy replacement.

The political responses of British survivors in this group followed from their high political exposure. The British South Africa Company (often called the Chartered Company) had handed over its governing responsibilities in central Africa in the 1920s; it retained the mineral concessions that Cecil Rhodes had wrested from African tribes. As a *rentier*, claiming royalties from mineral development and lacking the protective role of an agent of economic development, the BSA had clashed with the European settlers of Northern Rhodesia.[33] Its strategy of opposition to rapid African advance, combined with efforts to strengthen its political position through diversifying its holdings and creating links, both to the larger and more secure copper multinationals in the territory and to the political elite in Britain, ultimately failed to halt or even slow the transfer of power. After inept eleventh-hour bargaining, the Chartered Company was left with the meager total of four million pounds for all its mineral rights in Zambia.[34] A second British con-

[33] Peter Slinn, "Commercial Concessions and Politics during the Colonial Period: The Role of the British South Africa Company in Northern Rhodesia, 1890-1964," *African Affairs* 70 (1971), 370, 378-379; Sir Roy Welensky, *Welensky's 4,000 Days* (London: Collins, 1964), pp. 32-33. Harry Oppenheimer sat on the board of directors of the BSA, Lord Robins, the president of BSA, in turn sat on the Anglo-American board; the BSA board also included Viscount Malvern, former prime minister of Southern Rhodesia and then of the Federation; Lord Salisbury, a central and senior figure in Conservative opposition to decolonization; and representatives of London banks.

[34] A good account of these negotiations is found in M.L.O. Faber and J. G. Potter, *Towards Economic Independence* (Cambridge: Cambridge University Press, 1971), pp. 40-61.

cessionaire, Tanganyika Concessions, Ltd. ("Tanks"), also opposed political change in Africa; its spokesmen vehemently backed law and order and paternalistic rule, a stand accounted for by its control of the Benguela railway and extensive interests in the Katanga copper mines. Even though its principal stakes were not in British territories, its connections in the Conservative Party were extensive, and the company's supporters were prominent in the Katanga lobby that tried to undermine the Macmillan government's assistance to United Nations suppression of Tshombe's rebellion. The prime minister himself bore witness to the firm's attacks:

Apart from the Congo, where U.N. forces—aided and abetted by U.S. forces—have defeated Tshombe and produced an internal crisis in the Tory Party, there has been a lot of routine work, ministerial meetings, etc. My chief hope is that the Union Minière will switch to Adoula—and that means [the interests which] are so heavily involved in Tanganyika Concessions, itself a large shareholder in Union Minière. Even in Africa *pecunia non olet.*[35]

Only one French concessionaire in North Africa ranked in historical importance with the British South Africa Company; in contrast to national patterns, its political exposure seemed lower than that of its British counterparts. The Banque de Paris et des Pays-Bas had been the dominant financial institution in Morocco before the imposition of the French protectorate. In addition to its central financial role (effectively controlling the protectorate's currency and supply of credit), the Banque de Paris served as an investment bank; it was involved in many sectors of the Moroccan economy through its holding companies, Omnium Nord-Africain and Compagnie générale du Maroc. Subsidiaries of the latter firm operated concessions in the public services, even though ownership in most cases formally resided with the Moroccan govern-

[35] Macmillan, *At the End of the Day*, pp. 283-284. The attitudes of the firm were clearly stated by the chairman in 1959, following the violence in Nyasaland that marked the beginning of the end for the colonial status quo in Central Africa: Tanganyika Concessions, Ltd., *Report and Accounts* (31 July 1959).

ment. Its prominence and quasi-governmental role made the Banque de Paris "a natural target for anti-imperialist and decolonizing forces."[36]

In contrast to the British concessionaires, however, the Banque de Paris does not appear to have been active in opposing decolonization in Morocco; the Moroccan government seemed to share its calculations of political exposure, treating its interests gingerly in the postindependence years.[37] The explanation may lie in its diversified activities and its size. The bank's Moroccan holdings were only part of its North African business; the very nature of its activities as a *banque d'affaires*—providing services to firms with only limited permanent interests in any one company—eased its adaptation. Its place in the Moroccan economy was so predominant, its ties to the French state so close, that its bargaining power with any successor regime was high. The second dimension of political exposure—its probable political future—seemed fairly bright so long as the conservative regime of the king channeled nationalist sentiment in harmless directions.

Agriculture. The core of resistance to decolonization could be found in the agricultural sector, despite variations in political exposure within it, particularly in the British colonies. Heavily dependent upon state policy, agriculture was subsidized by colonial administrations through the tax structure, provision of government services, and guaranteed markets in the metropolis. Settler agriculture lacked the ties to metropolitan enterprise that served to reduce political sensitivity; as individuals with the "long-term horizons of people pre-

---

[36] Nehrt, *The Political Climate for Foreign Private Investment*, p. 291. The most extensive account of the holdings of the metropolitan groups is given in Ayache, *Le Maroc*; a useful summary can be found in Stéphane Bernard, *Le Conflit franco-marocain, 1943-1956*, Vol. III (Brussels: Editions de l'Institut de Sociologie de l'Université libre de Bruxelles, 1963), pt. 3, chaps. 3-6.

[37] As late as the 1960s, Nehrt noted that the Moroccan government had not touched the holdings of Omnium Nord Africain; in the case of politically sensitive concessions, early terminations were negotiated, with indemnification (*The Political Climate for Foreign Private Investment*, pp. 291-293).

paring the way for their children," the sector sought control over a wider range of policy than other economic actors.[38]

The probable political future of settler agriculture was not promising. Land and land hunger were the driving forces behind nationalist movements from Rhodesia to Kenya to North Africa. The colonial state had carefully prepared the way for European agriculture; any successor regime was likely to threaten its property rights first. Few technological or other obstacles would prevent a successor government from substituting African or Arab farmers for Europeans. In Kenya, the White Highlands were a rallying point of opposition to colonial rule; the Algerian FLN, in its Soumman Declaration of 1956, had agreed upon the need for agrarian reform and land redistribution. The most extensive nationalizations in Tunisia and Morocco after independence involved agricultural land.

Agriculture's record of resistance to change in the colonial system confirms the prediction of high political exposure. Despite their relative prosperity (compared to the rest of the European community) and their generally greater familiarity with the Arab population, the *colons* of Morocco, organized in the Syndicats français d'exploitants agricoles, were a prominent part of the Moroccan lobby which opposed decolonization in Paris. The *grands colons* of Algeria, led by Henri Bourgeaud, had long dominated politics there and adamantly resisted political liberalization on behalf of a European population that was largely urban. Only in Tunisia did resistance on the part of the agricultural sector play a less prominent role: political power had shifted to other groups within the European population, and landholding was concentrated in the hands of large companies rather than of smallholders.[39]

[38] E. A. Brett, *Colonialism and Underdevelopment in East Africa* (New York: NOK Publishers, Ltd., 1973), p. 212.

[39] July, *Une république pour un roi*, p. 9; Ladislav Cerych, *Européens et marocains, 1930-1956: Sociologie d'une décolonisation* (Bruges: De Tempel, 1964), pp. 342-344; Gendarme, *L'Economie de l'Algérie*, pp. 143-144; Alistair Horne, *A Savage War of Peace* (New York: Viking, 1978), pp. 56-57;

Similar resistance was displayed by European settler agriculture in East and Central Africa. But here the sectoral response was more complex, because of the division of European agriculture into settler or proprietor-owned agriculture (predominant in Kenya) and plantation agriculture (the dominant mode in Tanganyika and Nyasaland). Plantation agriculture had usually developed in response to the world market, often with little government involvement in the early years. The European presence in plantation agriculture usually consisted of expatriate managers hired by the foreign owners, a group with fewer political requirements and a different response to political change. Even among locally controlled firms, ties to London were often close, especially in finance and shipping.

As a result, agriculture did not present a unified front in opposition to decolonization in British East and Central Africa.[40] In Kenya, the colonial government was able to endorse the land transfer program in the White Highlands as a means to remove nationalist pressure and to create an indigenous landowning bourgeoisie that would serve as an ally in defense of property. In Nyasaland, agriculture was even more dominated by large-scale expatriate enterprises, and therefore displayed the same split; only the die-hards of the Settlers' and Residents' Association of Nyasaland vehemently and unsuccessfully opposed any advances by African nationalists.[41]

Jean Poncet, *La Colonisation et l'agriculture européennes en Tunisie depuis 1881* (Paris: Mouton & Co., 1962), pp. 336-337, 636.

[40] Evelyn Baring, governor of Kenya, remarked on African perceptions of the different landholders: "The European population has small farmers as the strongest political element. It is the type resented most of all by the Africans. They give a greater appearance of permanency than the larger planter who may move capital elsewhere." Charles Douglas-Home, *Evelyn Baring: The Last Proconsul* (London: Collins, 1978), p. 271.

[41] The description of East African agriculture is drawn from Kathleen M. Stahl, *The Metropolitan Organization of British Colonial Trade* (London: Faber, 1951), pp. 218-273; on Kenya, Gary Wasserman, *Politics of Decolonization* (Cambridge: Cambridge University Press, 1976), pp. 136, 172-173; on Nyasaland, Robin Palmer, "European Resistance to African Majority Rule: The Settlers' and Residents' Association of Nyasaland, 1960-63," *African Affairs* 72 (July, 1973), 256-272. Also Hopkins, "Imperial Business, Part I," pp. 34-37.

Mining. In the case of mineral extraction, an analysis of political exposure does not point to a clear-cut outcome: size and impact on the local economy might ensure *or* endanger the firms during the transfer of power; large fixed investments and low technological requirements suggested vulnerability, while strong links to large international firms pointed in the opposite direction. Decolonization also held mixed prospects for the wage bills of these firms.

The multinational corporations that mined the copper of Northern Rhodesia also dominated the economy of central Africa. Because of their overwhelming economic importance, the attitudes of these firms toward African nationalism shaped the demise of the Central African Federation and European rule in the region. From the industry's beginnings in the 1920s, copper in Northern Rhodesia had been dominated by two groups. Rhodesian Anglo-American was a fiefdom in the vast mining empire constructed by Sir Ernest Oppenheimer in southern Africa; Northern Rhodesian copper was a strategic if small part of its diverse and contiguous interests. Rhodesian Selection Trust, the second copper giant, was a subsidiary of American Metal Climax, a firm with geographically scattered investments whose ownership was largely American and British.

Shared aspects of their political exposure did not prevent an initial divergence in the firms' reactions to African demands—divergence rooted in differing patterns of ownership, managerial ties, and regional corporate strategies. An explosion of violence in Nyasaland in 1959 brought the question of the Federation (and white rule) to the fore; the responses of the two firms, documented in statements by their chairmen, Harry Oppenheimer (Anglo-American) and Sir Ronald Prain (Selection Trust) illustrated their contrasting perceptions. Prain accepted the findings of the Monckton Commission and conceded the end of the Federation as well as eventual political control by the African population; Oppenheimer continued to espouse "partnership" and found it difficult to admit that the territories would follow a pattern set by the other African colonies to the north.[42] The differing strategies for reestablishing a secure political milieu can be traced to the ownership of the firms and their patterns of investment: Anglo-American had to be concerned about the effect of concessions upon its core in South Africa, and its mining and industrial holdings in Southern Rhodesia gave it a larger stake in the Federation.[43]

Ultimately, however, the two firms came to share a perception of relatively low political exposure, despite rapid evolution toward African rule and the prominence of their investments in Northern Rhodesia. Their managements' angle of vision remained distinct from that of the Rhodesian settlers and much attuned to metropolitan business. Despite apparent vulnerabilities, their political future seemed secure because of the enormous bargaining power they expected to wield vis-à-vis *any* successor regime. That bargaining power was founded upon their contribution to the export earnings and tax revenues of the territory and upon their indirect influence over the economic activity of the colony through the reinvestment of earnings. Some have argued that decolonization actually *increased* the power of firms of this scale—that acquiescence was simply another, clearer, perception of self-interest.[44] A

[42] For example, Anglo-American Corporation of South Africa, Ltd., *Chairman's Statement* (1959), p. 3. Despite the likelihood that his political preferences would not be met, Oppenheimer claimed that "we are not afraid of change and we believe we shall be able to work with the government of the future." Compare Oppenheimer's response to that of Prain: RST Group of Companies, *Statement by the Chairman (1959)* and 22 October 1960, p. 8. By late 1962, Prain expressed confidence in the future political status of Northern Rhodesia, accepting that "the wishes of the African people will prevail, and they will move progressively into a position in which they will be the controlling force in the government of the country." (*Statement by the Chairman*, 18 October 1962, p. 7).

[43] Rhodesian Anglo-American Ltd., Thirty-second Annual Report (30 June 1962); Rhodesian Selection Trust Group of Companies, *Statement by the Chairman, Sir Ronald Prain* (Salisbury, 15 October 1959). Richard Sklar considers the Wankie Colliery and the rental of Rhodesian Railways rolling stock from an Anglo-American subsidiary as the principal interests of Anglo-American in Southern Rhodesia: *Corporate Power in an African State* (Berkeley: University of California Press, 1975), p. 47.

[44] Their importance in the Federation is described by Colin Leys, *European*

final concern that might have stiffened the firms' resistance to political change was labor: the African trade unions were a powerful part of the nationalist coalition. But the companies had long been dealing with the unions, European and African, with little government assistance. After independence, the Zambian government tried to prevent an excessive differential between rural and urban wages; its development strategy thus coincided with the companies' interests.[45]

The mining firms in French North Africa did not match the political and economic power of the copper multinationals in central Africa. Rather, the mining sector was a variation on the familiar French theme of state intervention, a feature particularly evident in the postwar development of natural gas and petroleum reserves in Algeria. The discoveries of the 1950s were produced under the direction of the French state with the support of substantial private investments mobilized by the *banques d'affaires*.[46] Saharan resources proved to be one of the largest obstacles to the final negotiation of Algerian independence. Initially, France had demanded a special status for the region and a role in its development; the FLN insisted that the Sahara was a part of Algeria like any other.[47] The French government's last-ditch resistance should not, however, be seen as the result of pressures from those with private investments in Saharan petroleum. The state's own investment was at issue, together with the importance of these resources for the future autonomy and economic security of France. Ultimately, the French state's calculations of political exposure resembled those of the copper multinationals in Zambia: technological and financial dependence, combined with Algeria's desire for economic development, would assure a fu-

Politics in Southern Rhodesia (Oxford: Clarendon Press, 1959), p. 112; Sklar, *Corporate Power*, pp. 180-182.

[45] Elena L. Berger, *Labour, Race and Colonial Rule: The Copperbelt from 1924 to Independence* (Oxford: Clarendon Press, 1974), p. 225.

[46] Gendarme, *L'Economie de l'Algérie*, p. 255; "La Française des pétroles joue l'avenir du Sahara," *Entreprise*, 15 September 1957, pp. 20-26.

[47] Bernard Tricot, *Les Sentiers de la paix* (Paris: Plon, 1972), p. 258.

ture place for French interests. By the late 1960s, both sets of calculations had been proven false.

The second wave: Commerce, banking, manufacturing

Commerce and banking. Although included in the second wave of European economic presence, commercial enterprises were among the first to appear on the coasts of Africa. In West Africa their presence was nearly as dominant as the copper mining companies in the Federation; in East Africa, their place in the colonial economy was not so large, but they were significant purchasers of colonial products, from both European and African populations, and vendors of metropolitan merchandise.[48]

Large commercial firms with strong links to the metropolis did not make the same calculations of political exposure as the small merchants who were dependent upon the European population for sales and who faced immediate replacement in the aftermath of independence. A relatively low level of fixed investment by the large firms (who had often been criticized for not contributing to local industrialization) reduced their political sensitivity and their prominence in the colonial economy. The political future seemed relatively secure: as a principal link to the industrial metropole, their often-attacked monopoly position was difficult to undermine. While investments might be nationalized and operations on the periphery "localized," downstream bargaining power would remain intact.

These elements of political exposure suggested that commercial firms would not perceive a need to resist political change. From the early years of settlement in East Africa, their quiescence had been contrasted with the political activism of

[48] The West African role of these firms is described by A. G. Hopkins in *An Economic History of West Africa* (London: Longmans, 1975), pp. 198-204; Catherine Coquery-Vidrovitch, "L'Impact des intérêts coloniaux: S.C.O.A. et C.F.A.O. dan l'Ouest africain, 1910-1965," *Journal of African History* 16 (1975), 595-621. The structure of commerce in East Africa is described in Stahl, *The Metropolitan Organization of British Colonial Trade*, pp. 207-218.

the settlers: "The outlook of the mercantile community at any of the main ports, at Singapore, Colombo, and Mombasa alike, is notable for its detachment from local politics and its unsentimental preoccupation with trade."[49]

The political sensitivity of the shipping industry, at least in the French case, induced a conservatism typified by Laurent Schiaffino, a leading shipping magnate and longstanding opponent of liberalization in Algeria. The threat to this heavily protected industry was principally international, however: it did not come from the resistance of Algerian consumers or the threat of substitution by local entrepreneurs, but from the hostility of French exporters to a web of restrictive regulations and from the possible encroachment of foreign merchant fleets. British shipping interests, who had long been exposed to a more competitive environment, were less likely than their French counterparts to anticipate catastrophe in the dismantling of the colonial system.[50]

The banking sector was an early arrival that enjoyed new growth in the postwar years. The principal private banks in the French colonies were the *banques d'affaires*, long active in developing sources of raw materials for the French economy. As the case of the Banque de Paris et des Pays-Bas has illustrated, their political exposure was lowered by limited participation in any single enterprise. A network of ties within the metropolitan "group" also served to reduce risk: any threat to interests so important in the French economy could lead to disinvestment, and thus to destabilization of a newly independent economy. And political exposure could be reduced, once again, by partnership with the state, which, after 1945, had become a *banquier d'affaires* in its own right in the overseas territories, "undertaking risks in the national interest."[51]

In British Africa, portfolio investments by banks played a less prominent part, even though the commercial banks had

[49] Stahl, *The Metropolitan Organization of British Colonial Trade*, p. 295.

[50] Gendarme, *L'Economie de l'Algérie* p. 168; Stahl, *The Metropolitan Organization of British Colonial Trade*, pp. 204-205.

[51] Jean Bouvier, *Un siècle de banque française* (Paris: Librarie Hachette, 1973), pp. 149-150.

assumed roles (such as central banker) that were not typical of their business in Britain. During the banks' postwar growth in increasingly complex colonial economies, these more "political" functions were eliminated, and the political sensitivity of the banks came to resemble that of commercial firms.[52] Banking operations could, of course, be seriously affected by political instability and disorder, as Barclays discovered in Egypt in 1952 and in other locales.[53] The banks' prosperity depended on the level of economic activity and on confidence in the future government's capability of managing the economy. Such considerations could lead to caution in handing power to nationalists, particularly those who were dependent on coalitions that would press for inflationary programs. On the other hand, a desire to end damaging political uncertainty might induce the banks to lend their support to liberalization in order to forestall more damaging disruptions.

Although colonial banks were dependent upon the European sector of the colonial economy, their expansion in East and Central Africa relied upon rising African incomes as well.[54] Other characteristics also reduced political exposure during decolonization: capital investment in fixed plant was low; branches were spread throughout the colonies, cushioning losses in a single territory; labor was not a major concern.[55] Postwar expansion had brought decentralization, permitting easier adaptation to local conditions, and later easing the transition to greater local control of banking operations.[56] Like commercial firms, the banks could adapt to conditions of increased economic power for Africans; as nationalism advanced, banks

[52] For example, the Standard Bank in the Central African Federation: J. A. Henry, *The First Hundred Years of the Standard Bank* (London: Oxford University Press, 1963), p. 294.

[53] Sir Julian Crossley and John Blandford, *The DCO Story* (London: Barclays Bank International Ltd., 1975), pp. 182-183, 185-190.

[54] W. T. Newlyn and D. C. Rowan, *Money and Banking in British Colonial Africa* (Oxford: Clarendon Press, 1954), pp. 85-95.

[55] Hopkins, "Imperial Business, Part II," p. 276.

[56] Henry, *The First Hundred Years*, pp. 318-319; Crossley and Blandford, *The DCO Story*, pp. 180-181. Susan Strange, *Sterling and British Policy* (London: Oxford University Press, 1971), pp. 164-174.

became "good citizens" by investing more on the periphery and by "localizing" operations. Throughout, their aim, like that of the commercial firms, remained access.

Manufacturing. Banking and commerce owed a part of their postwar growth and ultimate political posture to the growth of manufacturing, core of the second wave of expatriate business expansion after World War II. Manufacturing and its ancillary sectors of commerce and banking, which had grown more rapidly in some territories than in others, changed the political exposure of metropolitan firms in the colonial economies. The shift was particularly apparent in Kenya, and, with certain variations, in the Central African Federation and Morocco.

Following World War II, agriculture lost its claim to exclusive representation of European economic interests in Kenya. Industry and commerce grew rapidly: by 1955, the value of manufactured goods produced in Kenya was greater than European-run or -owned agricultural production. The balance within manufacturing shifted toward expatriate—principally British—firms that were increasingly engaged in production for the African consumer.[57] As African demands for political change grew, these aspects of the Kenyan economy gave rise to a new calculation of political exposure. The managerial class, like its mercantile predecessors, at first chose to remain aloof from the political strife of the 1950s.[58] Later in the decade, however, the "new men" pursued a more activist role; they provided a base for the New Kenya Group (formed in April, 1959), which split from the majority of the settler community and supported multiracialism as the goal of Kenyan political evolution. Despite its minority status within the Kenyan European community, the New Kenya Group exercised a disproportionate influence through its relations with the colonial government and through financial resources that have

---

[57] D. S. Pearson, *Industrial Development in East Africa* (Nairobi: Oxford University Press, 1969), pp. 14-17; A. H. Amsden, *International Firms and Labour in Kenya: 1945-1970* (London: Frank Cass and Co., 1971), pp. 50-51.

[58] Amsden, *International Firms*, p. 53.

been traced to "British-tied commercial sources."[59] This political strategy, in contrast to that of the die-hard settlers, was classically conservative: it aimed to construct a coalition in defense of property across racial lines, thereby preserving intact the key features of the colonial political economy.

Morocco alone among French North African territories displayed a similar shift toward the second wave and a reduction in resistance to political change. The *colons* of the agricultural sector were, like their Kenyan counterparts, gradually being overshadowed in the booming Moroccan economy by those engaged in banking, manufacturing, and commerce. The postwar years witnessed a surge in investment and industrial development: overall industrial production tripled between 1939 and 1955, growing 80 percent from 1948 to 1955; in these years, the rate of investment reached levels that were typical of highly developed economies. The size of firms in the European sector of the economy also grew, as evidenced by a low ratio of *patrons* to employees or wage-earners within the European working population.[60]

Behind the barricade to change mounted by the *petits blancs* and the administration itself, the businessmen of the Moroccan new wave were able to avoid overt participation in the conflict between Moroccan nationalists and those who resisted their demands. A choice between resistance and acquiescence was required only when that barricade was breached during the tenure of Gilbert Grandval as Resident General in 1955. Some French businessmen (among them Jacques Lemaigre-Dubreuil, who was assassinated by counter-terrorists), had supported the small groups of liberals sympathetic to demands for Moroccan autonomy; but their influence cannot be compared to that of the New Kenya Group. Some connections can be made between particular business ties and political stance. Greater resistance was offered by firms which were partly owned by el-Glaoui, the pasha of Marrakech, inveterate enemy of the sultan and his nationalist supporters.

[59] Wasserman, *Politics of Decolonization*, pp. 38, 40.
[60] Cerych, *Européens et marocains*, pp. 137-138, 155, 173-175, 329.

A more significant point of division was the metropolitan connection: firms with a solely Moroccan base were among the leading opponents of moves toward autonomy. A prime example was the Banque Mas, which owned *La Vigie Marocaine*, a newspaper that consistently expressed the most conservative views.[61]

In general most French businessmen in the newer sectors seemed to believe that political disengagement and adaptation were the wisest course, proving that they "were not, in principle, opposed to independence for Morocco."[62] Even such tacit acceptance of political change proved a boon for the Faure cabinet as it confronted Moroccan decolonization. The stance of Moroccan business interests may have moved the conservative ministers, Antoine Pinay and Roger Duchet, to accept the course set by Prime Minister Edgar Faure; the ministry could also face the political risks of decolonization without a concomitant threat of economic catastrophe.[63] The hopes of the new wave of French business were based upon the reconciliation of conservative French nationalism with conservative Moroccan nationalism—hopes fulfilled in large measure in the 1960s.

The two components of political exposure clearly reinforced each other in Morocco and Kenya. New metropolitan economic interests were less dependent upon the colonial polity for survival, and economic development had helped to shape a nationalist coalition that favored only limited changes in the colonial political economy. With a European economy at the opposite end of the sectoral spectrum—favoring those that were most threatened by any change in the colonial relation-

[61] Ibid., pp. 352-353.

[62] Ibid., p. 354.

[63] The attitudes of businessmen were captured at the time in interviews, recorded in Bernard, *Le Conflit franco-marocain*, pp. 246-247. French capital voted on the future of Morocco in its continued high level of investment: although slowing after 1953 as the political situation in the protectorate worsened and some flight capital left the country, the investment level was higher in 1955, the year of greatest disturbance, than in a number of postwar years. (Cerych, *Européens et marocains*, p. 350).

ship—Algeria's economic stagnation and political immobility brought forth an increasingly radicalized anti-colonial movement.[64] Although it was not a doctrinaire movement, nor one given to lengthy manifestoes on the future Algeria for which it fought, the FLN represented the most radical nationalist alternative among those that would eventually assume power in the African colonial territories. Did this radicalism significantly affect the behavior of firms, particularly manufacturing firms, that were active in Algeria and North Africa?

An answer to this question would illuminate the weight attached to each of the dimensions of political exposure—the political sensitivity of a firm and its probable political future. The responses of two French firms of the new wave, both based in North Africa, provide the beginnings of an answer: the probable political future they envisaged in the three North African territories provides a critical case for comparing the two aspects of political exposure. The firms, Verreries de l'Afrique du Nord (VAN) and the Société Commerciale et Minière pour l'Afrique du Nord (SOCOMAN) were subsidiaries of major French industrial enterprises, respectively Saint-Gobain Industries and Pont-à-Mousson. The activities of the parent firms were not concentrated in North Africa or the colonial empire; their principal international interests were in Europe.[65]

Although these companies were part of the new wave of postwar economic expansion in the French empire, they exhibited a high degree of political sensitivity. VAN's operations

[64] Metropolitan investment was not absent, but private investment in Algeria concentrated in real estate and commerce, and efforts by the French state to encourage industrialization after 1945 were largely thwarted by competition from metropolitan industry. The tax structure, biased in favor of agriculture, further stifled industrial development. (Gendarme, *L'Economie de L'Algérie*, pp. 144, 169-170; Pierre Moussa, *Les Chances économiques*, chap. 9.)

[65] The archives were made available through the courtesy of the management of the parent firms, joined since 1971. A brief history of the parent firms and a description of present activities can be found in P. Allard et al., *Dictionnaire des groupes industriels et financiers en France* (Paris: Seuil, 1978), pp. 103-106.

centered on a glassmaking factory near Oran; it had been established under a complicated political regime designed to ensure the economic viability of small-scale manufacturing in a competitive industry.[66] SOCOMAN's business activities were more diversified: as a supplier of cast-iron pipe, contractor for public works, and manufacturer of cement pipe in North Africa, its dependence upon state policy lay not so much in protection and guaranteed markets as in government expenditures on public works and the level of economic activity in the region.

Although the future of French North Africa grew more uncertain during the 1950s, one is struck in both cases by a persistent note of optimism in political evaluations of the period. For instance, a proposal to expand VAN's factory, offered in 1956—a year of great insecurity—took note of the political risks surrounding VAN's small, protected market in North Africa. The report did not foresee insurmountable political changes, however: one scenario cast Algeria's future in the image of Morocco. The company's prosperity was not linked to a die-hard defense of the colonial order; on the contrary, the government's efforts to increase economic development in favor of the Muslims was seen as yet another incentive to remain.[67] VAN continued business operations to the end of French rule and beyond. The factory closed only in December, 1962, after demands by the new Algerian government that it hire additional workers had made the situation impossible in the eyes of its managers.

[66] VAN began as a creation of perceived political need under Vichy: the regime saw such subsidiaries as a means of easing economic discontent in North Africa and assuring a French future for those territories. The political concessions made to ensure the viability of the firm included customs preferences to permit penetration of the Tunisian and Moroccan markets and a complicated set of subsidy arrangements agreed after the war, guaranteeing that the Government General of Algeria would cover any losses (as well as providing credits and loans) in exchange for holdings in the firm.

[67] VAN, Correspondance de la Délégation Générale de l'Algérie, 1954-1963, "Situation des verreries de l'Afrique du Nord en 1956," 6 July 1956, especially pp. 6-8. Also letter from Le Corre to Franci, 21 January 1957, in the same dossier.

The tenacious optimism of VAN might be attributed to the security of the Oran region during most of the Algerian War; SOCOMAN's role in building natural gas and petroleum pipelines placed it in the front line of the conflict. The optimistic attitude of SOCOMAN may have been influenced by its decision—taken before the onset of political upheaval in North Africa—to diversify into areas as distant as Uruguay, South Africa, Ceylon, and Kuwait. Growth in business from the Algerian War, however, offset the effects of diversification; the share of the company's business derived from North Africa actually increased as the conflict deepened.[68] For each of the firms, political turmoil and the threat of regime change brought certain opportunities: the possibility of a protected Algerian market for VAN; the expansion of public credits for SOCOMAN; the side benefits of an expanded French military presence in both cases. As one executive of SOCOMAN remarked in 1955 after a visit to North Africa: "our activity will benefit (we should not rejoice in it, but we should make note of it) from the present crisis, which had made necessary growth in government credits and public works in general. . . ."[69] The firms' perceptions of political risk were carefully separated from the fate of small businesses and the European population. At no point did the managers who recorded their views express opposition to political evolution, despite its less desirable consequences—labor unrest and the possibility that a hostile nationalist faction would take power.[70]

[68] In 1956, for example, Algeria provided 25 percent of the company's business; by 1960, the share had grown to 39 percent. SOCOMAN, Conseils d'administration, 23 October 1956; 17 June 1960. The reasons for the start of diversification have not come to light, although the political situation in North Africa clearly speeded it.

[69] SOCOMAN, Report on the *tournée* of M. L. Giboin, 12 December 1955.

[70] In 1956, one SOCOMAN manager noted Arab hostility toward the French population in North Africa, but foresaw improvement if "the composition of the population in North Africa were modified in part . . ." (Conseil d'administration, 25 June 1956). In the report cited above, rumors of an "Algerian Republic" are mentioned: although surprise is registered, at no point is it suggested that such an outcome would be a disaster; instead, the model of Morocco was again used as the likeliest image of Algeria's future.

Although the two firms examined here are only a small sample, their calculations of political exposure, even in the case of Algeria, suggest that probable political futures were not carefully defined and played a less important role in their calculations than political sensitivity. The vague ideology of the FLN and the absence of information on the nationalist organization contributed to imprecise analogies with Tunisia and Morocco, and thus to relative optimism. Even more important was the peculiar way in which their political sensitivity (usually adding to political exposure) lowered perceptions of political exposure in certain ways. The concept of political sensitivity requires refinement: a firm could be dependent upon the state in its role as *protector* (characteristic of earlier colonial firms under the Third Republic) or as *entrepreneur* (more typical after World War II). If the state's *own* interests were involved, as in the development of Saharan petroleum or the construction of public works, the private interests that cooperated with it would feel more secure. The wary businessman would need to determine the state's hierarchy of interests, which in turn produced a rough hierarchy of political risk. The new role taken on by the French state in the colonial empire affected not only the politically sensitive among the second wave of colonial enterprises, but also the *banques d'affaires* in Morocco—those meldings of the oldest parastatal forms of colonial involvement and the newest, most politically supple economic actors.

The determinants of political exposure

The determinants of political exposure can be estimated and ranked in a rough way by using the political responses of sectors and firms during decolonization. As expected, the high political sensitivity of those firms with parastatal roles (concessionaires) did produce a high perception of political exposure. The case of the Banque de Paris suggests that the scale of the enterprise or the relatively small share of such concessions in total revenue could lower political sensitivity. In general, an increasing scale of operations, which might either have raised or lowered sensitivity, in most cases seems to have reduced political anxieties. For the copper companies of Northern Rhodesia, the economic vulnerability of the successor government was of greater importance than the prominence of the firms within the local economy.

Although the guaranteed market provided by the colonial system was vital for much of the European settler agriculture, potential international or indigenous competition was not a prominent concern for most investors. Many foresaw the successor regimes' attempts to pursue import substitution and thereby to protect infant industries (even those with colonial ancestries); in the British case, declining levels of effective protection made the question moot. For metropolitan firms dependent upon the colonies for an export market, this dimension of political sensitivity was far more important. For SOCOMAN and VAN, labor relations were of concern as discipline broke down and expatriate personnel left for the metropolis. But fear of future labor strife or higher wage bills was not central in the estimates for the longer term—perhaps, once again, because a successor regime was expected to enforce labor discipline in the manner of the old colonial government.

One highly significant distinction that separated much of the first wave of colonial enterprises from the postwar newcomers was a subsidiary link to a metropolitan parent. Multinational patterns of organization gave many of the new firms a different angle of vision on political conflict and change; they also permitted reduction of political exposure through diversification. In such cases, decisions to remain in troubled areas could be influenced by fears that less risk-averse competitors might replace the departing firm. The contrast between a local base and a subsidiary's ties to the metropolis was particularly important in the cases of Kenya and Morocco, reinforcing other aspects of lowered political exposure. New forms of political dependency also reduced political exposure as the colonial state undertook certain entrepreneurial functions, sharing directly in political risks rather than providing a protective setting in which such risks were reduced.

All of these determinants of political sensitivity were con-

ditioned by the second facet of political exposure: the political
futures foreseen by the firms in question. Despite certain parallels between these firms and contemporary multinationals,
one contrast is of vital importance: nationalization was still
unusual in the late 1950s and early 1960s, and the expatriate
firms and their governments seemed to hold most of the cards
in bargaining over their futures. No clear estimate existed of
a learning curve for successor governments; in general, the
loss of European managerial and technical personnel was
thought to be a crippling obstacle to any effort at exercising
national autonomy. The capabilities of the new regimes, and
their ability to obtain alternative expertise (from the socialist
countries if necessary) were often underestimated. Businesses
of the new wave also counted upon the desire of most post-
colonial regimes to industrialize, and thus on temporary acquiescence in a foreign manufacturing presence.

The optimistic political evaluations of the firms were often
shaped by the metropolitan governments, which tried to convince businesses that power was being transferred to those
who would ensure a capitalist political economy, one fairly
close to existing colonial reality. By trying to provide guarantees of this sort—through aid agreements, entrenched clauses
in constitutions, and other means—the metropolitan governments were often able to widen the splits within expatriate
business interests, thereby bringing the second wave of expatriate business to accept the new order tacitly. The governments could also reduce the anxiety produced by the breakdown of order in North Africa and Kenya—cases in which
business showed remarkable sang-froid, since firms could rely
upon the state to maintain a minimal level of security necessary for the pursuit of its own interests.

POLITICAL EXPOSURE AND POLITICAL OUTCOMES

A tentative relationship between particular characteristics
of firms and sectors and political exposure (as measured by
attitudes toward political change) can be discerned in the firms'
response to decolonization. These differences were reflected

in the contrasting courses of British and French decolonization and in differing histories of territories within each of the empires. Because of a greater propensity for British business to invest in the Dominions and colonies, the new wave of manufacturing, banking, and commerce—often with metropolitan ties—tended to be more advanced there than in French North Africa (with the possible exception of Morocco). The relative weight of the sectors most likely to resist change in colonial political arrangements, whether international or internal, was reduced. A quickened pace of economic development also assisted in the creation of nationalist elites that were not so likely to alter the colonial political economy in a radical way, thus shifting perceptions of probable political futures. In certain instances, the economic development taking place on the periphery even led to competition with metropolitan industry, producing a political sensitivity in Britain that militated *against* continuing links to the colonial empires.

On all of these counts, the French empire differed from the British. Because of the low level of French industrial investment in most of the overseas dependencies, the French empire resembled much more closely the traditional view of the "colonial pact": the metropolis supplied manufactures; the colonies raw materials.[71] Metropolitan business interests in the French colonies were heavily biased in favor of those that would be most threatened by colonial nationalist movements—in particular agriculture; the nationalist groups in Algeria, Indochina, and elsewhere often were peasant movements with radical aims. Because industrial development had been discouraged or undercut by metropolitan industry, there was little competitive threat from within the empire to weaken the colonial relationship. Overall, the political exposure, and the political resistance, of the French colonial economic interests were generally higher than those of the British.

By producing a set of givens that confronted metropolitan political elites, the contrasting sectoral compositions of the

[71] Only a small part of France's commerce with the empire deviated from this pattern; Moussa, *Les Chances*, pp. 27-28, 34.

French and British colonial economies did influence the course of decolonization. But could the structure of the colonial economies be said to *determine* the political outcomes—among colonial territories, or between the British and French cases? Three obstacles barred the direct translation of economic response into political outcome. They point to the limitations of a purely sectoral analysis: the gap between political exposure and political action on the part of firms; alternative explanations for the behavior of firms; and the mediation of the political system, which could amplify or (more frequently) diminish the efficacy of political actions.

The ambiguity of political response. Even firms or sectors that perceived high political exposure did not automatically take action to penetrate the metropolitan political system and arrest undesirable change. If the costs were low, the potential benefits high, *and* the likelihood of influencing policy significant, action might be countenanced. Even then, hurdles remained: it was difficult to calculate political futures, firms were often poorly equipped to influence the metropolitan arena, and the costs in future hostility could be enormous if efforts failed.

In any grouping by positive political action, therefore, firms clustered around a policy of *attentisme*; they did not present a clearly demarcated spectrum according to political exposure. An apolitical attitude—already deeply engrained in certain sectors—coupled with an emphasis upon contributions to economic development, often seemed the wisest course for those firms that could convince themselves of some future in the colony. Two types of firms were at the extremes of any distribution by political activity. At one pole were the firms whose political exposure made a policy of wait-and-see impossible (or suicidal). The British South Africa Company pursued a combination of strategies typical of such firms: cultivation of ties with metropolitan political and economic figures who would speak on its behalf; economic insurance through interlocking relations with larger and less threatened firms; diversification of operations and fields of activity. At the opposite pole were a few firms that capitalized on political change:

political risk-takers. Lonrho, created by Roland W. ("Tiny") Rowland, exemplified the firm that flourished on the divisions accompanying decolonization. It had originally been based in the white-dominated Central African Federation; by the end of 1967, Rowland had extended business operations to fourteen countries. He cultivated personal contacts with the new governing elites, "Africanized" operations, and sought out activities that would contribute to economic development and greater autonomy.[72]

Alternative explanations for political action. Although a relationship between the metropolitan political strategy of a firm and its political exposure is to be expected, the characteristics of a firm or sector were not the only explanations for its attitude toward decolonization. Personal or ideological features of the firm's management often reinforced its expected position. Members of the French business community contributed to the cause of *Algérie française*: was such support the result of the political exposure of their firms in North Africa, or of political connections that made them sympathetic to right-wing causes? The strident opposition to African decolonization by Lord Salisbury (British South Africa Company) and Captain Charles Waterhouse (Tanks) may have been the result of their positions in first-wave colonial firms, but the ideological baggage of their political generation meshed with the interests of the firms. A more recent illustration of the intertwining of corporate and personal world views may be found in the American multinational, ITT. There certainly were sectoral reasons for the political sensitivity of its operations in Chile (its concession to operate the Chilean telephone system), but the personality and ideology of Harold Geneen seem to account just as well for the company's activities in that country.[73]

Organizational and political mediation. Between firms with

[72] Suzanne Cronje, Margaret Ling, and Gillian Cronje, *The Lonrho Connection*, (Encino, Ca.: Bellweather Books, 1976).

[73] Anthony Sampson, *The Sovereign State of ITT* (New York: Stein and Day, 1973).

their own evaluations of the costs and risks of political change on the periphery, and national policies that could arrest or thwart that change, were organized interest groups and the state itself. These mediating entities made a direct translation on the firms' preferences into political outcomes even more unlikely.

Although firms could deal directly with governments (and often did in the colonies), semi-official business associations played a prominent role in transmitting their views. Two of these specialized organizations—the Joint East and Central Africa Board in Britain, and the Comité central de la France d'Outre-mer in France—illustrate the effects of aggregation upon the firms' responses to political change.[74] The Joint Board, which had long enjoyed a quasi-official role in representing East African business and settler interests, began to voice a new political line during the 1950s, as the settlers were submerged in the second wave of British enterprises, and overall political exposure, changed. The turning point came after the unexpected and violent uprising in Kenya; the broad outlines of the new strategy were intended to preserve the essential features of the colonial political economy by forging an alliance between "progressive" business elements (Michael Blundell of the New Kenya Group was a favorite of the Board) and moderate nationalists. Its political aims, which reflected the growing influence of the new wave of metropolitan business within the organization, was "political stability" through support for "moderates of all races."

But opinions on which Africans were "moderates," and thus acceptable to the business interests represented by the Board, could change quickly. Julius Nyerere, whose nationalist rhetoric had been anathema to those with an economic stake in Tanganyika, became, within one year, a cooperative leader who offered the grail of political stability. Political acceptability had limits, however, if the necessary assurances were

[74] In investigating the activities of these two groups, the complete records of the Joint Board were available; the archives of the Comité central were being catalogued, and records of the constituent sections, which may have been more active, were not available.

not given to "existing interests" or if political intransigence shaded into economic radicalism. In early 1961 the Board reflected prevailing sentiment in the Conservative Party that Kenyatta's release and possible leadership of Kenya was unthinkable:

Clearly the power to order Kenyatta's release lay in London and not with the Governor, and the general feeling was that if H.M.G. were faced with a revolutionary situation in Kenya they would give way, in which case there would be resignations in Kenya Government circles. Feeling was, however, strong among Conservative back-benchers, both in the House of Lords and the House of Commons that H.M.G. would be faced with a very difficult situation if they did give way. A very definite pledge had been given about Mau Mau irreconcilables. If there were any question of Jomo Kenyatta taking office, the Joint Board would protest and would make the Government well aware of its attitude through its friends in the Conservative Party.[75]

Resistance to Kenneth Kaunda's nationalist U.N.I.P. in Northern Rhodesia was also intense, since its victory would have meant the end of the Central African Federation. The chairman, Lord Colyton, suggested a rival African formation, the African National Congress, as a "possible and acceptable alternative to U.N.I.P." Citing Kaunda's recent statements, he declared his belief that "it is [not] possible to do business with U.N.I.P and if the new Northern Rhodesian constitution is so designed as to bring them to power it would be disastrous for the whole people of Northern Rhodesia, black or white."[76] The Executive Committee of the Joint Board found the initial constitutional proposals for Northern Rhodesia "quite unworkable" in February, 1961, and specific note was taken of the Turton motion opposing African majority rule in the territory.[77]

As the pace of change in Africa was accelerated under Macleod, the Board tried to fashion new instruments of resistance.

[75] Joint East and Central Africa Board, minutes of the Executive Committee (19 January 1961).

[76] Joint Board, Chairman's Letter, no. 65 (28 February 1961).

[77] Joint Board, Executive Committee, 28 February 1961.

Earlier, Board members, if not the Board itself, had offered financial assistance to "multiracial" alternatives in an effort to block the nationalist advance.[78] In London, the Board continued to rely upon its old techniques of lobbying the Colonial Office. Increasingly, however, the colonial secretary, Iain Macleod, came to be viewed as the chief obstacle to the solutions sought by the Board in Africa; the new colonial secretary, unlike his Conservative predecessors, did not respond exclusively to the perceptions and the advice of settler and business interests.

Under a new chairman, Lord Colyton, the Board shifted to new tactics. Tapping the connections that the Joint Board enjoyed in the Conservative Party, members of the Council and the Executive Committee were aware of and often supported campaigns within the party to oppose the government's policy in Kenya, Northern Rhodesia, and finally Katanga. What Colyton called "the reckless and almost criminally foolish activities of the United Nations in Katanga" led to the backbench revolt, described in Chapter II, that so alarmed Macmillan in December, 1961. Following that display of resistance within the Conservative Party, the chairman virtually threatened the government in his letter to members of the Joint Board in December:

It is no wonder that those who are concerned for the future of the Federation—including a large block of the British Conservative Party—are deeply concerned. No announcement has yet been made, but it must be taken as certain that any such changes [in the Northern

[78] In discussion following an address by the director of the United Tanganyika Party (the weak opponent of Nyerere's TANU), note was taken of the relatively small European agricultural sector and its limited resources: "financial assistance must come from the big firms. Some firms were nervous and said 'this is politics' but in fact the funds of all political parties were mainly subscribed by the larger firms and trade unions." A similar appeal for financial support was made on behalf of KADU, the rivals of Kenyatta, before the Kenyan election of 1963: "The business world had very strict reservations against contributions to any political party but it was noted that KADU had made several appeals to firms and plantations operating in Kenya." (Joint Board, minutes of the Council, 29 March 1957; 10 April 1963.)

Rhodesian constitutional proposals] will be strongly resented—and resisted—in Parliament.[79]

The Joint Board's involvement in Conservative Party resistance to the government's policy in Africa was a departure from the quiet and effective lobbying that had characterized the Board's activities in the past. Despite the support that it was able to marshal in both Houses of Parliament, these expressions of voice failed to do more than delay somewhat the transfer of power to African nationalists that the Board opposed. The reasons for the Board's failure were both internal and external. Within the Board itself, the aggregation of colonial economic interests led to less than wholehearted support for resistance; the lower political exposure of some members and their concern for the future tugged toward *attentisme*: ". . . as the possibility was seen of certain political leaders coming into power in African states, individuals, companies, etc., became afraid to express their views for fear of subsequent persecution."[80] Also, the organization had no alternative strategy with which to replace the policy of the British government; the corporate representatives were no more willing to countenance massive coercion than the Macmillan cabinet. Perhaps the most important explanation for the failure of the Board's efforts at resistance in 1960-1962, even when it joined forces with other opponents in the Conservative Party, was the changed political milieu. The old reliable methods of penetrating the metropolitan political process began to fail as colonial questions became a source of intense partisan controversy; the government, usually attuned to business interests, was able to survive its attacks in favor of a wider definition of national interests.

A similar shift occurred in French politics during the 1950s, as the ideological hegemony of the colonial consensus was challenged. The French counterpart of the Joint Board, the Comité central de la France d'Outre-mer, began in an even weaker position: fragmentation of the colonial lobby offered

[79] Joint Board, Chairman's Letter, no. 63 (31 December 1961).
[80] Joint Board, minutes of the Executive Committee, 14 September 1961.

competing avenues of approach to government and administration, thereby contributing to the financial woes of the organization. Its influence was further limited by a political strategy that reflected its narrow economic base. Its political stance displayed little of the evolution toward support for moderate conservative solutions that characterized the Joint Board at about the same time. The business ties of those directing the Comité central explain its conservative, colonialist position. In those cases where connections can be traced, they lead back to colonial firms of the "first wave": the old mercantile firms of Bordeaux, the Ligue maritime et coloniale française, concessionaires of public utilities, plantation owners, and certain banks. The longtime president of the Comité symbolized this bias: he was president of that most prominent of colonial concessions, the Suez Canal Company. In short, the Comité represented those firms and sectors whose political exposure was highest—a segment of the French economy even less representative than its British counterpart; the organization included only a few companies that could also be considered large metropolitan firms.[81]

The political preferences of the economic interests that resisted political change were diluted by organizational aggregation or thwarted by changes in political environment during decolonization. But the final and decisive filter of political preferences resided in *the state and the political elite*. Even when the business organizations found themselves in unified opposition to rapid transformations in the colonial order— as the Joint Board did in 1960-1962—their efforts, while slowing change, could not halt it. Alternative explanations, dependent on the autonomy awarded the state in setting external economic policy, can be advanced for this failure. A Marxist

[81] Parallel with the Moroccan crisis, which saw Pinay and Duchet swing to support of decolonization, one can detect a liberalization of line among some of the officers of the organization. See especially Conseil d'administration, 8 July 1955; 18 November 1955. By early 1956, it had also become apparent that the channels to the metropolis for business were so numerous as to call into question the role of the Comité (Conseil d'administration, 13 January 1956).

account might emphasize the declining status of the colonial sectors as a fraction of the metropolitan economies—a decline that necessarily offered less and less political influence to colonial interests. A structural variant of the Marxist model might add that the political elite in fact perceived the long-term interests of the colonial firms (often over their resistance) in creating moderate (and weak) successor governments. A political or statist explanation would point to the relative independence of the political elite in shaping international economic strategies, often for reasons of national security or overall economic success. Those strategies, once chosen, would reinforce the decline of older and less adaptable colonial interests.[82]

With the evidence at hand, it is not possible to decide conclusively among these competing models. It appears, however, that the political elites of Britain and France, through a logic of *unintended* consequences, responded to the weakened position of those economic interests intent on maintaining the old colonial system and at the same time further eroded the position of those interests by altering the international orientation of their economies.

In his study of the defeat of the Lancashire textile lobby and the grant of tariff autonomy to India after World War I, Clive Dewey has traced a model for change of economic orientation that would be replicated later for the colonial empire as a whole. Even before World War I, Lancashire and its textile industry had declined relative to other export sectors in the British economy: coal and engineering had surpassed it. The World War also brought an increase in the bargaining power

---

[82] A recent exposition of competing Marxist theories of the state is Bob Jessop, *The Capitalist State* (Oxford, Martin Robertson, 1982). For an excellent application of the Marxist perspective to an important historical episode, emphasizing the conflict among fractions of capital, David Abraham, *The Collapse of the Weimar Republic: Political Economy and Crisis* (Princeton: Princeton University Press, 1981). For these approaches as applied to American foreign policy, see Stephen Krasner, *Defending the National Interest: Raw Materials Investments and U.S. Foreign Policy* (Princeton: Princeton University Press, 1978), chap. 1.

of the still-dependent Government of India and a questioning of the dominant free trade consensus. Finally, the political instruments of the lobby proved less and less effective in new political circumstances: "The eclipse of the Lancashire lobby in English political life was part and parcel of the decline of the provinces in British politics, and the emergence of a highly-centralized class-based political system. . . ."[83] Not only had Lancashire and its empire-dependent industry failed to adapt economically, it had failed to innovate politically. As would be the case with colonial economic interests during the 1950s, the first steps in decline rapidly became cumulative: as political advantages were lost, economic wounding followed, and with it, the loss of financial resources necessary for organizational survival.

Dewey's model of economic and political decline can also be applied to the decisions taken by political elites in Britain and France in the 1950s:

a) Reduced economic importance. With the restoration of peacetime economic conditions, the *relative* importance of those sectors in the metropolitan economies dependent on the colonial empire shrank for two reasons: a return to "normal" patterns of trade after decades of depression and war, and postwar growth in the metropolitan economies, which outstripped the lagging colonial sector.

With the revival of the European and Japanese economies, an older pattern of trade reappeared for Britain:

In retrospect, it is easy to see that, once Britain and its European markets and suppliers had recovered from their wartime exhaustion, the siege economy would be neither practicable nor tolerable, and that the overseas countries, while wishing to retain their markets in Britain, would also be eager to try other sources of imports and investment.[84]

[83] Clive Dewey, "The End of the Imperialism of Free Trade: The Eclipse of the Lancashire Lobby and the Concession of Fiscal Autonomy to India," in *The Imperial Impact: Studies in the Economic History of Africa and India,* ed. Clive Dewey and A. G. Hopkins (London: University of London, Athlone Press, 1978), p. 56.

[84] Miller, *Survey of Commonwealth Affairs,* p. 442.

After reaching a peak in importance for France in 1948-1949, exports to the overseas territories slumped as a contribution to manufacturing growth, while the domestic economy surged ahead.[85] Even the large overall share of French exports directed to the French Union in the 1950s were concentrated in a few sectors (sugar, cotton, and silk cloth) and represented less that 10 percent of industrial production.[86] The British and French patterns in trade followed those of other industrial economies: the enormous growth in world trade from 1950 to 1970 was concentrated in trade *among* North America, Europe, and Japan, not in trade between these economies and the colonial empires or formerly dependent territories.[87]

b) Economic calculations and ideological shifts. The relative decline in importance of the colonial empires for the metropolitan economies, the increasing evidence that the future of Britain and France lay in intensified exchanges with other industrial economies, gave political elites the autonomy to make a new calculation of costs and benefits. The macroeconomic benefits of the colonial system were rapidly declining along with its aggregate importance. During the years of dollar shortage in the late 1940s and early 1950s, both colonial empires were meant to be a source of a dollar surplus (through exports outside their currency blocs) that would benefit the metropolis and, in the British case, the members of the sterling area as a whole. The French overseas territories did not provide the foreign exchange benefits that had been hoped; at least a part of the French deficit with the rest of the world

[85] Saxe, "Evolution," pp. 346, 347.

[86] François Caron, *An Economic History of Modern France* (London: Methuen & Co., Ltd., 1979), p. 216.

[87] By most measures, the contribution of the developing countries to world trade stagnated during these two decades. For example, their share of world exports was 27.0 percent in 1953 and 23.2 percent in 1970. Kathryn Morton and Peter Tulloch, *Trade and Developing Countries* (London: Croom Helm, 1977), Table 1.1, p. 35. The dynamics of such diversification away from former colonial patterns after decolonization is traced, in terms similar to those used here, by Michael Lipton, "Neither Partnership nor Dependence," in *Decolonisation and After*, ed. W. H. Morris-Jones and Georges Fischer, (London: Frank Cass & Co., Ltd., 1980), pp. 158-191.

economy was owed, in fact, to the exports diverted to colonial markets and the resources committed to producing for those markets.[88] The British were more successful in their use of the dollar-earning capacities of some of their colonies, but the economic side effects of relying upon the discriminatory currency bloc were the same as in France: exporters were encouraged to rely on "soft" markets; resources in the metropolitan economy were tied up in providing for those markets rather than being released. In any case, Britain did not require political control to retain the perceived financial benefits of the sterling bloc, even though the road from Master Currency to Negotiated Currency was a bumpy one.[89]

Increasing costs were an important element as well: maintaining the colonial system in the face of rising nationalist resistance would mean a commitment to permanent coercion. The military burdens weighed particularly heavily for France. Although only a portion of the French military effort was devoted to colonial theaters, military expenditures had more than a direct budgetary effect: defense procurement competed with the needs of domestic investment.[90] By the time that the Second Plan was formulated, the French Union had come to be seen as an economic burden.[91] In Britain, when Prime Minister Harold Macmillan asked for a careful accounting of the costs and benefits of the colonies for Britain in 1957, it was concluded that "the economic considerations were fairly evenly matched. Consequently, it was felt that the economic interests of the United Kingdom were unlikely in themselves to be decisive in determining whether or not a territory should become independent."[92]

[88] Saxe, "Evolution," pp. 114, 574-575.

[89] Susan Strange, *Sterling and British Policy*, pp. 62-70. The contribution of the colonial territories to the sterling area's reserves was boosted by the Korean war raw materials boom: D. J. Morgan, *The Official History of Colonial Development*, Volume 2: *Developing British Colonial Resources, 1945-1951* (Atlantic Highlands, N.J.: Humanities Press, 1980), p. 31.

[90] Saxe, "Evolution," p. 151.

[91] Ibid., p. 127.

[92] Morgan, *Official History*, Volume 5, p. 102.

Calculations of aggregate benefits and costs were shaped by the ideological debates described in previous chapters, and here as well changes worked against the opponents of decolonization. The ideological arguments of those who viewed empires as economic blocs and important power resources in international competition failed to carry the day. Mercantilist justifications were swept aside; the proponents of empire appeared solely as protectors of particular economic interests and were condemned as exponents of Malthusianism in an era of economic growth.

In the 1950s, political choices were made against increased autonomy (as defined by the mercantilists) and in favor of economic growth and efficiency. Those choices were reinforced by changes in the international environment: pressure from the United States for a multilateral system of trade and payments, and, for France, the establishment of the European Economic Community. As the proponents of reinforced colonial ties lost on the international level, economic development in the empire further reduced their political influence; finally, a calculation of national interests permitted the dismantling of the formal political framework of colonial rule, with the acquiescence of at least a fraction of the European economy in the colonies.

c) Political obsolescence. Finally, the fate of the colonial lobbies demonstrates that, like the Lancashire textile lobby earlier, those economic interests committed to the colonial status quo lost their political efficacy in the metropolitan political arena. Their slipping political leverage led to an irreversible decline, as financial support for their organizations dried up, further reducing their capacity to influence events in Britain and France. Thus, the once powerful Commonwealth Industries Association was reduced to shifting its political appeals in an effort to win financial support from increasingly skeptical businessmen.

POLITICS AND ECONOMICS IN DECOLONIZATION

The uncertainty of direct political action, alternative explanations for that action, and, most important, the mediation of political exposures by interest groups and the state, all served to qualify the translation of firm perceptions and preferences into political outcomes at the center. Although these political elements distorted and diluted the reading made by firms on the periphery, the comparative structures of the colonial economies did confront the political elites in Britain and France with different levels of resistance to decolonization and with different risks. For, even if the direct intervention of firms or their representative organizations in metropolitan politics was more limited than the spectrum of political exposure might suggest, firms on the periphery still had the power, through disinvestment and simple cessation of activity, to turn decolonization into an economic debacle. The actions of the French government during Moroccan decolonization and the British during the transfer of power in Kenya made clear how important this concern was in shaping political moves at the center. These were capitalist economies, after all, and many of the most important economic decisions remained in private hands, even if those private actors had failed to change policy in Paris or London. The political elites in Paris and London thus attempted to lower political exposure by constructing a more favorable political future, by insuring firms against adverse political changes, or, in the eyes of some, by constructing the bases for a neo-colonial political economy on the periphery.

The assumption of a direct and unmediated relation between economic structure and political outcome also fails to explain at least one of the cases on the periphery as well, the anomalous case of Southern Rhodesia, the dominant economy in the Central African Federation. Like Morocco and Kenya, Rhodesia had begun its industrialization after World War II.[93] Despite this shift in the economic balance, the Europeans of

[93] The share of the European work force employed in industry in Southern Rhodesia (the core of European settlement) increased steadily until 1956; the proportion in the tertiary sector (commercial and government services) also increased. William J. Barber, *The Economy of British Central Africa* (Stanford: Stanford University Press, 1961), pp. 115, 141; Table IX, p. 113 (high rate of investment); D. J. Murray, *The Governmental System in Southern Rhodesia* (Oxford: Clarendon Press, 1970), p. 17.

Rhodesia declared unilateral independence in 1965 and continued to resist decolonization (black majority rule) in a bloody guerrilla war for fifteen years. How can this failure of the model of political acquiescence be explained?

A bias toward accepting political change could certainly be detected within the Rhodesian business community during the months that preceded the unilateral declaration of independence. Before the elections that would be used by the Rhodesian Front to justify its demands for independence, the major economic associations of Southern Rhodesia published reports on the consequences of illegal independence. Sensing their dependence upon the international economy and upon Britain, the peak organizations of industry and commerce were pessimistic regarding the country's prospects.[94] In the negotiations that preceded the final break, the British prime minister, Harold Wilson, testified to the conciliatory attitudes of business: "The businessmen in general were, of all the groups I saw in Rhodesia apart from the churches, the most insistent on the need for a settlement, the most ready to make concessions from the European hard line, and the most ready to criticize Rhodesian Front intransigence."[95]

Acquiescence by the industrial and commercial sectors was not translated into political power, however. First, the sectoral shift was diluted politically: despite a rapid drop in the importance of agriculture as a source of European employment (from 25 percent in 1925 to 5 percent in 1965), the political system of Southern Rhodesia continued to award disproportionate power to the agricultural sector.[96] More important, the power of the economic elites had been displaced by political mobilization on the part of the Rhodesian Front, which attracted not only agricultural interests but also such groups as government employees who were threatened by decolonization. Combined with the unwillingness of the British gov-

[94] Larry W. Bowman, *Politics in Rhodesia: White Power in an African State* (Cambridge: Harvard University Press, 1973), p. 79.

[95] Harold Wilson, *The Labour Government, 1964-1970* (Harmondsworth: Penguin, 1974), pp. 209-210.

[96] Murray, *The Governmental System in Southern Rhodesia*, p. 17.

ernment to employ coercion, these elements undercut a "Kenyan solution" to Rhodesian decolonization. White Rhodesians making *individual* calculations of political exposure confounded predictions based on economic change and were able to translate their political resistance into power through the Rhodesian Front. As the settlers sensed that their old means of penetrating metropolitan politics were slipping away, a new form of politics took command. The dynamics of that new politics, that finally separated the Europeans in Rhodesia and in Algeria from the metropolis, is described in Chapter V.

Colonial Populations, the State and the Politics of Britain and France

IT IS A commonplace of the history of decolonization that Europeans resident in the colonial empires were among the most vociferous and effective opponents of the transfer of power to African or Arab majorities. Combining certain advantages of metropolitan citizenship with the immunities of a foreign domicile, the settlers resisted both in the sphere of metropolitan politics and in the colonies. Examining a number of British and French cases, similarities appear in the conduct of settler politics. Their impact upon the metropolis and its efforts to enforce changes in the colonial relationship was determined by three elements: the intensity of resistance by the European population (and their ability to transmit that resistance effectively to the metropolis); the representation offered to the European populations as compared to their non-European opponents in the metropolitan political system; and finally, the ability of the settlers to forge an alliance with the means of implementing metropolitan policy—the military and the colonial administration—thereby thwarting change and gaining a new avenue of access to the metropolis.

THE DETERMINANTS OF SETTLER RESISTANCE

Three possible explanations can be suggested for the degree of resistance offered by the European colonial populations to decolonization: the relative size of the population; its sense of permanence; and its collective political exposure. As Table VI demonstrates, the *size* of the settler colonies in comparison to the non-European populations varied widely from territory to territory. Examining the figures given in the table, a "critical

Table VI. European Populations in Africa

Territory	Size of Population	Ratio of Non-European to European Population
Algeria	984,031 (1954)	9:1
Tunisia	239,000 (1946)	14:1
Morocco	325,271 (1951)	22:1
South Africa	2,641,689 (1951)	4:1
Federation of Rhodesias and Nyasaland	287,300 (1958)	26:1
Southern Rhodesia (Zimbabwe)	207,000 (1958)	13:1
Northern Rhodesia (Zambia)	72,000 (1958)	31:1
Nyasaland (Malawi)	8,300 (1958)	328:1
Kenya	67,700 (1960)	93:1
Tanganyika	22,300 (1960)	408:1

SOURCES: Gendarme, *L'Économie de l'Algérie* (Paris: Armand Colin, 1959), p. 116; Georgette Elgey, *Histoire de la IVe République: La République des contradictions, 1951-1954* (Paris: Fayard, 1968), p. 348n; Ladislav Cerych, *Européens et marocains, 1930-1956* (Bruges: De Tempel, 1964), p. 313; T.R.H. Davenport, *South Africa* (Toronto: University of Toronto Press, 1977), p. 297; L. H. Gann and P. Duignan, *White Settlers in Tropical Africa* (Harmondsworth: Penguin, 1962), pp. 159-166.

NOTE: Non-European population for South Africa = African and Coloured populations. Non-European population for British territories does not include Asians.

mass" theory of settler resistance could be posited: resistance increased as the ratio of non-European to European population decreased. Algeria and Kenya would represent poles on the spectrum of resistance and acquiescence. The reasons for the relationship between size and resistance were the perception of the community as a self-contained and self-sustaining entity, increasing the likelihood of successful opposition; size would also reflect upon the second element in resistance, the permanence of the settlement. While Table VI does point to a significant relationship, the ambiguous middle cases lead to a search for more refined explanations.

Measuring the second explanation for resistance, *permanence* (the French word *enracinement* is perhaps more precise) is a difficult task. One index would be the proportions in the population owning different types of property, data that are difficult to obtain. An alternative measure would compare the proportion of those born in the territory to immigrants. Here, from available statistics, a few interesting comparisons appear: about 83 percent of the French Algerian population was born in Algeria, as compared to 34 percent among the Europeans of Morocco.[1] Even this measure is questionable, however: recent immigrants were often the most ardent defenders of the colonial status quo, in part because of their economic insecurity. The connection between extremism and new immigrants was often remarked upon in Kenya and Rhodesia; in the latter case, it was compounded by the influx of settlers from South Africa, who brought with them exclusionist racial attitudes.

A more reliable supplement to the factor of size in explaining resistance is the notion of political exposure. In Chapter IV certain economic sectors or business interests were singled out as possessing low or high exposure and an accompanying low or high propensity to resist political change. The groups dealt with—farmers and businessmen—formed a small, though important, portion of European society. What of the other members of these populations? If the *stakes* of Europeans are examined, wide differences among the European colonies become apparent. Moroccan Europeans had an average income that was nearly 40 percent higher than the French average; Algeria, on the other hand, displayed an average income for its European population that was 20 percent lower than the metropolitan average.[2] The income of the Kenyan Europeans, even more elevated than that of the Moroccans, was accompanied by a relatively high social status. Although the social composition changed after 1945, there was still truth in the observation that a considerable part of the Kenyan colony

---

[1] "Qui sont les Français d'Algérie?" *Entreprise*, 9 November 1957, p. 43; Ladislav Cerych, *Européens et marocains, 1930-1956* (Bruges: De Tempel, 1964), pp. 320-321. Cerych notes that the Moroccan figures include immigrants who were born in Tunisia and Algeria.

[2] Cerych, *Européens et marocains*, p. 329; "Qui sont les Français d'Algérie?" p. 44.

was made up of "public school men, younger sons [of peers], and retired army and navy people."[3]

One could argue that higher incomes and status, a larger stake, should make the likelihood of resistance higher. The second term of political exposure points to the importance of future expectations, however. The highly paid manager in a firm would not be directly threatened by a change in political regime: like the firm itself in many instances, his skills would not, in the short-run at least, be replaced by an African or Asian competitor. Thus, higher incomes combined with a larger industrial or commercial sector would be likely to produce a *lower* propensity to resist. This crude relationship is not a perfect predictor; the structure of the working population must be examined carefully. Although Europeans in the Central African Federation had average incomes higher than those in Kenya, their social status and occupational structure were not the same. As Leys notes, the skilled artisan was the "real center of gravity" in the European community of Southern Rhodesia; despite their high incomes, many felt economically insecure and threatened by African advance.[4]

Among the occupational groups most threatened by decolonization were unskilled workers, service employees, and above all, the lower-ranking civil servants. All of the colonies in North, East and Central Africa were characterized by a level of urbanization and a large tertiary sector that contrasted sharply with the metropolitan image (and the colonists' self-image) of farmers and miners.[5] The inflated tertiary sector in the French cases, however, owed much more to a large governmental contribution. In Algeria, there were two and one-half times more civil servants than *colons* (farmers).[6] The

[3] Marjorie Ruth Dilley, *British Policy in Kenya Colony*, 2nd ed. (London: Frank Cass & Co., Ltd., 1966), p. 35.

[4] Colin Leys, *European Politics in Southern Rhodesia* (Oxford: Clarendon Press, 1959), pp. 80, 86.

[5] Cerych, *Européens et marocains*, p. 321; "Qui sont les Français d'Algérie?" p. 44; L. H. Gann and P. Duignan, *White Settlers in Tropical Africa* (London: Penguin, 1962), p. 160.

[6] Cerych, *Européens et marocains*, p. 328; René Gendarme, *L'Économie de l'Algérie* (Paris: Armand Colin, 1959), p. 147.

preponderance of the *petit fonctionnaire* was found in exacerbated form in Tunisia: Lee cites one estimate that 70 percent of the French population there was made up of civil servants and their dependents.[7] Significantly, the leadership of the European colony in Tunisia passed from a *colon* before World War I to a businessman-lawyer in the interwar decades to the *petit fonctionnaire*, Antoine Colonna, during the years of decolonization. Despite the growth of the government sector in the British colonies during the postwar years, a similar preponderant political role for the civil servants did not result, in part because of the "lighter" administration preferred by the British and in part because the colonial civil servants did not identify with the European community, for reasons discussed below. This pattern was broken in Southern Rhodesia, which, as a self-governing colony, possessed its own local administration.[8] The place of the government sector within the European working population was likely to be directly related to opposing change in the colonial relationship: not only did these workers depend directly upon the metropolitan tie (and thus have a higher political sensitivity), they were also likely to be the first replaced under a successor nationalist regime.

SETTLER POLITICS AND METROPOLITAN POLITICS

These elements of the colonial societies—size, permanence, and political exposure—shaped the degree of resistance that the European populations would display to decolonization. The *effectiveness* of their resistance, however, would depend upon other characteristics of settler politics: the unity of the community and its elite, its political skill in negotiating the corridors of metropolitan politics, and finally, the relative degree of influence in the metropolis possessed by its rivals, the African and Arab populations.

The unity of the settler elite was closely related to the degree

[7] William S. Lee, "French Policy and the Tunisian Nationalist Movement, 1950-54" (D.Phil. thesis, Oxford University), p. 10.

[8] D. J. Murray, *The Governmental System in Southern Rhodesia* (Oxford: Clarendon Press, 1970), chap. 3.

of economic development and industrialization in the colonial economy, as described in Chapter IV. On this criterion, Algeria, with little industrialization and a small business class, may be distinguished from Morocco, Kenya, and the Federation. Not only was the number of businessmen small (the same number as Morocco for a population three times the size), the business class was not entrepreneurial in its outlook.[9] Algeria's European society represented a transfer across the Mediterranean of the static economy of southern France: the imitation was perfect, even to the central place of wine and cereals in the agricultural sector.[10] The pervasiveness of the agrarian ethos, symbolized by the leadership role awarded to the *grands colons* in this highly urbanized society, and the absence of an industrial or commercial elite with powerful alternative visions of the economic or political future, all produced a homogenous European community united to a cohesive social and political elite: the divisions that appeared in Kenya, Morocco, or the Federation were not apparent in Algeria; no large band of "liberals" argued for adaptation to majority rule.

Settler influence and the politics of the notables

To maintain the colonial status quo, the Europeans pursued political activities on two fronts: first, in the colony or protectorate itself, they sought to "capture" the administration in order to protect their position; second, they influenced the politics of the metropolis so as to obtain the necessary economic and political support and to prevent unwanted metropolitan intervention in local affairs. As Pierre Nora describes, "collective local inertia demands toward the metropolis a destructive activism and an incessant political mobilization."[11]

Before the threat from colonial nationalism became over-

[9] Gendarme, *L'Économie de l'Algérie*, pp. 141-143.

[10] The pattern of emigration from France to Algeria confirmed the hold of the declining regions of France: after 1875 the largest groups of French emigrants came from south of the Loire. Aveyron alone in certain years provided one-tenth of the total ("Qui sont les Français d'Algérie?" p. 43).

[11] Pierre Nora, *Les Français d'Algérie* (Paris: René Julliard, 1961), p. 98.

whelming, the politics of settler societies throughout Africa was usually the politics of notables, a peculiar combination of the apolitical and the intensely political. In Algeria, as Parodi's analysis makes clear, the apolitical tendency was confirmed by the large number of electoral abstentions (usually about 30 percent in the postwar elections and referenda) and by the decline of left-wing parties—the Communists and the Socialists—that required a high degree of political participation from their members. Instead of the politics of participation, the Europeans of Algeria turned to a personal style of politics, supporting the *gros colons* who served as their emissaries to the metropolis.[12] In Kenya, the once-powerful Convention of Associations declined, and a similar pattern of political activity emerged, one that would persist until the renewed threat from African nationalism in the 1950s.[13] In Rhodesia as well, "public affairs to a considerable extent remained a matter of local 'notables.' "[14] Conflict between the business elite and the Rhodesian populace did occur, particularly over the question of joining larger political units (South Africa in the 1920s, the Federation in the 1950s), but such strife was episodic; persisting cleavages did not develop. A principal reason for the apparent unity of the settler societies behind their notables was discussed in Chapter I: the principal division, that between colonizer and colonized, lay *outside* the effective political system. The fact that settler politics was conducted against the backdrop of a surrounding hostile majority explains the fading of class cleavages, the weakness of left-wing parties and organized labor, and the apolitical quality of political discourse.[15] The absence of significant conflict within the settler societies also permitted the settlers' repre-

[12] Jean-Luc Parodi, "Le 13 Mai 1958: Les Algériens d'origine européenne et la politique" (*mémoire*, Institut d'Études Politiques, 1960), pp. 26-29, 31-32.

[13] Gary Wasserman, *Politics of Decolonization* (Cambridge: Cambridge University Press, 1976), pp. 28-29.

[14] L. H. Gann and M. Gelfand, *Huggins of Rhodesia* (London: George Allen and Unwin, 1964), pp. 88-89.

[15] Leys, *European Politics*, pp. 174-175.

sentatives in metropolitan politics to act in a unified fashion to protect the colonial status quo. They became "technicians of political manipulation" in Paris and in London.[16]

Since the days of Eugène Etienne and the *parti colonial*, the representatives of North Africa had held positions of great influence in the French parliament: Algeria, a part of the Republic, sent both deputies and senators to Paris; the French of Morocco and Tunisia, senators only. In their political activities, the Algerian parliamentarians supported the interests of their North African allies.[17] Like economic interest groups, the North African settlers seldom attempted to involve the French public in their cause; indeed, that would prove one of their fatal political weaknesses. Like the *parti colonial* they relied upon lobbying government ministers; in the Fourth Republic they also infiltrated political parties of the Right and Center. Their lobbying activities, intensifying at those times when concessions to their nationalist opponents appeared imminent, were usually successful—so long as maintaining the status quo was not costly and had not become a matter of partisan dispute.[18]

The effectiveness of the settler lobby was in part dependent upon their success in infiltrating the metropolitan political parties. The role of the Gaullists, the *modérés*, and even the Socialists, in forwarding the aims of the Tunisian and Moroccan settlers has been described in earlier chapters. The principal haven for the North African lobby, however, was the Radical Party, which virtually became a pressure group for the defense of European interests in Algeria and the protectorates.

The alliance of the Radical Party and North African settler interests was not based upon an ideological commitment to empire by the party: any nostalgia expressed for the Third

[16] Nora, *Les Français*, p. 98.

[17] Lee, "French Policy," p. 33.

[18] Ibid., pp. 37, 134, 213. A journalistic account that must be used with some caution: "Le Fonctionnement du 'lobby' marocaine," *France Observateur*, 2 September 1954; also Georgette Elgey, *Histoire de la IVe République* (Paris: Fayard, 1968), p. 349.

Republic's colonial achievements was purely residual. Indeed, the ideological decay of the Radicals, as the Church-State issue faded in importance, and the decline in their political fortunes after World War II made them ideal political partners for the North African settlers. Despite their weakness (they obtained only forty-three seats in the First Legislature of the Fourth Republic), the Radicals, at the center of the political spectrum, were essential to governing coalitions. Represented, at least initially, in every government of the Fourth Republic after 1947, the Radicals provided that permanent access to metropolitan power desired by the French of North Africa. The Radical monopoly on the Ministry of the Interior (responsible for Algeria) was an added boon for the North African lobby.[19]

Under the hegemony of conservative "Neo-Radicals" the party pursued an opportunistic political strategy; one speaker at a party congress defined the "main task of a great party" as "the same as that of a good stomach: not to reject, but to assimilate."[20] The North African interests were assimilated with little question by the party: their influence derived in large measure from their generous funding of the party machine and their provision of electoral support.[21] Prominent North Africans were also prominent Radicals: Henri Borgeaud, the "unofficial governor-general of Algeria," chaired the senatorial group that included the Radicals; the party also claimed Antoine Colonna, the principal spokesman for the Tunisian French, and an influential Moroccan affiliate headed by Pierre Mas, a leading opponent of liberalization in the protectorate.[22]

In return the Radical Party became a perfect example of Finer's "Esau phenomenon" by which an interest group at-

[19] Between July 1950 and the final ministry of the Fourth Republic, only one non-Radical—François Mitterrand—was minister of the interior.

[20] Cited in Francis de Tarr, *The French Radical Party from Herriot to Mendès-France* (London: Oxford University Press, 1961), p. 9.

[21] Ibid., p. 83; Lee, "French Policy," p. 214.

[22] De Tarr, *The French Radical Party*, pp. 83-84; Jean-Thomas Nordmann, *Histoire des radicaux, 1820-1973* (Paris: Editions de la Table Ronde, 1974), pp. 359-360.

taches its particular program to that of a political party.[23] The North African representatives at Radical Party congresses set the program of the party in this sphere.[24] From within cabinets, Radical ministers saw to it that North African political arrangements were not endangered.[25] When Pierre Mendès-France offered Tunisia internal autonomy in 1954, Léon Martinaud-Déplat, the party's administrative head, opposed the premier, who was also a Radical, in the National Assembly.[26] The final defeat of the Mendès-France cabinet in February, 1955 was owed principally to the defection of Radical deputies led by the Algerian deputy and former premier, René Mayer. When another Radical premier, Edgar Faure, moved to break the stalemate in Morocco in 1955, a prominent businessman, Emile Roche (vice-president of both the Radical Party and the Conseil économique) figured prominently among those who opposed the return of the deposed sultan.[27]

The ability of the North African settlers to intervene directly in French politics is usually contrasted with Britain's exclusion of the colonial populations from its political life: the Europeans of Rhodesia, Kenya, or Australia were not represented at Westminster; representation had, after all, been one of the issues that led to the American Revolution. This view seriously understates the ability of the settlers to influence British politics, however. The House of Lords provided direct representation for the European colonies in Africa in much the same way as the French Senate. It fulfilled this role in part through the ennobling of colonials, such as Lord Malvern (the former Godfrey Huggins, prime minister of Southern Rhodesia and then the Federation), and in part by its overrepresentation of the right-wing of the Conservative Party, which was closely

[23] S. E. Finer, *Anonymous Empire* (London: Pall Mall Press, 1966), pp. 55-56.

[24] De Tarr, *The French Radical Party*, pp. 112-117; the records of the party congresses also demonstrate the prominent place awarded the North Africans.

[25] Elgey, *Histoire de la IVᵉ République*, pp. 361, 368.

[26] Lee, "French Policy," pp. 503-504.

[27] Pierre July, *Une république pour un roi* (Paris: Fayard, 1974), pp. 9-10.

tied to the settlers, especially those in Kenya.[28] The House of Lords was the scene of some of the fiercest attacks upon Macleod, including Lord Salisbury's bitter condemnation of the colonial secretary in March, 1961 as being "too clever by half." While the formal political powers of the Lords were not great, sentiment in the upper House was a significant indicator of the attitudes of the Conservative establishment.

Settler lobbying also took place within the Conservative Party in the House of Commons: indirectly, through such intermediaries as the Joint East and Central African Board; directly, in the hearing given to settler representatives by the parliamentary party and its backbench committees. A principal practitioner of these political tactics was Sir Roy Welensky, the prime minister of the Federation; he repeatedly played upon the special status granted the Europeans in Africa by Conservative circles: "kith and kin" entitled to a special hearing. At the peak of the crisis in Central Africa during 1961-1962, Welensky flew regularly to London to undermine Macleod's policies from within the Conservative Party:

I assumed that he intended to appeal over the heads of the British Government to public opinion in Britain and that he was being encouraged to do so by some of his influential supporters at Westminster. These provided him with a constant flow of gossip and advice. He often claimed to me that he had inside information from sources close to the Cabinet and from senior members of both Houses of Parliament which contradicted the advice and views which I offered him.[29]

Macmillan was aware of the close relations of Welensky with the right wing of the party; he noted at one point Welensky's meeting with backbenchers: "I heard that he had addressed two hundred or more Conservative MPs, making a bitter attack upon the Commonwealth Secretary."[30] Welensky's per-

[28] C.J.M. Alport, *The Sudden Assignment* (London: Hodder & Stoughton, 1965), p. 221.

[29] Ibid., p. 61.

[30] Harold Macmillan, *At the End of the Day* (New York: Harper & Row, 1973), p. 312.

sonal efforts were supplemented by a more professional campaign: since the 1950s, the Federation had employed the Conservatives' own public relations firm, Colman, Prentis, and Varley (and its subsidiary, Voice and Vision, Ltd.) to shape a favorable image of the Federation in Britain.[31]

A new politics: Exclusion from the metropolis

The influence that the settlers exerted in metropolitan politics rested upon a fragile set of relationships: maintenance of the dominant political position of the Europeans on the periphery at relatively low cost to the metropolis; a secure political position for settler notables both in Africa and in London or Paris. In the 1950s these conditions for success disappeared, and a new pattern of colonial politics was born. Colonial issues became topics of political controversy in the metropolis; colonial nationalism raised the cost of maintaining the status quo; a threatened settler population opted for new forms of politics that ended the role of the notables.

French North Africa suffered a setback when it lost its principal metropolitan political foothold, the Radical Party. Radical premiers, first Mendès-France and then Faure, began to reform the relations of France with the North African territories; the neo-Radical allies of the North African lobby were routed in May, 1955, when Martinaud-Déplat was removed as the administrative president. Shortly after, most of its prominent leaders were expelled from the party by the Mendèsists. Although the settlers could still find a political home among the Gaullists and the Indépendants, Mendès-France had taken colonial issues out of the back rooms of party negotiation and placed them in the arena of political controversy: the North African settlers were no longer the undisputed interpreters of African affairs for the metropolis.

The outbreak of the insurrection in 1954 had also changed the outlines of Algerian politics. After dissolution of the Na-

[31] Patrick Keatley, *The Politics of Partnership* (Baltimore: Penguin, 1963), pp. 447-448.

tional Assembly in December, 1955, the French of Algeria were no longer represented in the lower chamber (elections were postponed); only their representation in the Senate continued. The Algerian Assembly was dissolved on 12 April 1956; the *conseils généraux* and the municipal governments in December of that year. The old politics of the notables and of metropolitan political manipulation was finished.[32] When Algerian deputies once again appeared in Paris under the Fifth Republic, they represented new means of political organization among the European population; their influence, like that of the National Assembly as a whole, was greatly reduced under the new regime.

Although Welensky noticed "an inexplicable hardening of attitude toward ourselves" in the mid-1950s, the influence of the settlers within the Conservative Party declined less dramatically than that of the North African lobby in France. Less concern for "kith and kin" in Africa was displayed by the new political generation within the party, a change that was particularly evident after the 1959 General Election. Michael Blundell, the leader of the New Kenya Group, records his shock at the new attitude: "At an explosive dinner in the House of Commons, where I met a number of the younger ex-Bow Group Tory MPs, one of them exactly expressed the prevailing mood by saying: 'What do I care about the f . . . ing settlers, let them bloody well look after themselves.' "[33] Welensky's tactics boomeranged decisively; Alport has described the role of British domestic politics in reducing his access to the Conservative Party:

The inevitable attempts of the Opposition to exploit the Government's embarrassment would cause the Conservative Party to close its ranks around the Ministers concerned. Whatever might be the rights and wrongs of the case, the Government could not allow public pressure from Welensky to appear to cause them to deviate in the smallest degree from their proclaimed policy . . . it would be under-

---

[32] Parodi, "Le 13 Mai 1958," pp. 36-40.

[33] Sir Michael Blundell, *So Rough a Wind* (London: Weidenfeld and Nicolson, 1964), p. 226.

standable if those who remained friendly to the Federation concluded that, even so, they could not accept indefinitely such a political liability in terms of the balance of power in British politics.[34]

A supporter of Macleod recalls advising Hastings Banda, the Nyasaland nationalist leader, to avoid direct attacks upon Welensky, permitting the settler leader to make the Africans' case, a strategy that succeeded.[35]

The elevation of colonial issues to a prominent place in the domestic politics of Britain and France ended the monopoly of interpreting colonial reality long held by the settlers and made their lobbying activities, like those of the economic interest groups, less effective. The hold of the settlers in metropolitan politics was further weakened by their own ambivalent attitudes toward the mother country, a combination of oft-proclaimed attachment and scarcely disguised contempt.[36] The misunderstandings that occurred were all the more painful, since the metropolitan and colonial societies seemed superficially so similar. The settlers were not willing to concede genuine metropolitan intervention in their affairs: they sought a guarantee of their dominant position on the periphery, but not meddling by British or French outsiders. They were outraged when their justifications were questioned, as Alport discovered:

The thing that bewildered and infuriated most Europeans in Southern Rhodesia was the fact that people in Britain appeared unable to grasp the justice of their point of view. . . . The British could help them to safeguard their standards if they wished, and their failure to do so was shocking betrayal. Britain of the 1960s was decadent. . . . It was even rumoured at a later stage that a British minister himself had admitted that Britain no longer had the will to rule.[37]

---

[34] Alport, *The Sudden Assignment*, p. 62; later Alport warned that Welensky risked becoming a bore to those in London (p. 171); cf. Gann and Gelfand, *Huggins of Rhodesia*, p. 260.

[35] Sir Nigel Fisher, interview, London, 18 October 1976.

[36] Nora, *Les Français*, p. 133; cf. Gann and Gelfand, *Huggins of Rhodesia*, p. 266.

[37] Alport, *The Sudden Assignment*, p. 143.

A new politics: Mobilization on the periphery

The inability of the settlers to influence metropolitan politics and maintain the colonial tie derived from political changes on the periphery as well. Old-style settler politics, the politics of notables that had provided these societies with their metropolitan emissaries for many years, ended, further increasing alienation from the colonial powers. Under growing threat from the African and Arab populations, the mass of the European population was mobilized to resist changes in the status quo; the new variety of settler politics not only overthrew the old notables who had dealt with the metropolis but also served to further obstruct decolonization. The mobilization of the European population took place most dramatically in the larger colonies, Rhodesia and Algeria. In Kenya, Morocco, and Tunisia, despite increased political involvement, the metropolitan government was able to circumvent the old system of settler influence and transfer political power to the majority population. Even in these cases, the appearance of extremist organizations, such as *Présence française* in Morocco, made clear that the metropolitan elite was racing against time in establishing a new political regime.

In Algeria and Rhodesia in the 1950s, European politics assumed new organizational forms, mass movements that expressed local particularism combined with attachment to the metropolis, heightened political activity married with suspicion of "politics." For French Algeria the new metropolitan allies were those apolitical and intensely nationalistic movements that found analogues in the colonial milieu. Veterans' associations, long a political force in the European colony, were principal participants in the demonstrations of 6 February 1956 that caused Guy Mollet to turn from the liberal promises of the Republican Front. The veterans, whose activities would become increasingly important in the next two years, were joined by the students, who became the "first defenders of *immobilisme*," and by the Poujadists. The apolitical extremism of Pierre Poujade and his strident defense of France's colonial empire were highly successful on the southern shore of the Mediterranean; the Poujadist appeal, born in the economically declining regions of France, was likely to find a substantial following in the similar social structure of French Algeria. By the end of 1955 Poujadism could claim an estimated 100,000 adherents in Algeria.[38] The Algerian settlers also began to affiliate with movements that had more subversive aims, such as the *Union française nord-africaine*. A society threatened by demands for majority rule was fertile ground for ideologies that repudiated democracy and republicanism.

Despite the loss of Algerian representation in the National Assembly, these movements and their metropolitan allies, such as Soustelle's USRAF, were at first able to defeat attempts to change the status quo in North Africa. From 6 February 1956, when the Algerian mob caused the Mollet government to back down from promises of peace in Algeria, until the climax of the new politics in 1958, it seemed as if the Algerian tail was indeed wagging the French dog. The peak of political influence was reached by the French of Algeria in 1958 following the return of de Gaulle, after Committees of Public Safety, linking the Army and the settlers, assured the local position of the European population. At the same time their allies among the Gaullists and the *modérés* provided guarantees in France.[39]

De Gaulle's speech promising self-determination for Algeria in September, 1959 threatened separation from France and inclusion in a much larger Arab population. To arrest change the French of Algeria resorted to direct action, as they had in the past. During the "week of the barricades" in January, 1960 the settlers attempted to reconstruct the local and met-

---

[38] Parodi, "Le 13 Mai 1958," p. 62. Parodi offers an excellent account of the growth of these organizations, pp. 43-66.

[39] Descriptions of the events in Algiers in May 1958 are given by Philip Williams, "The Fourth Republic—Murder or Suicide?" in *Wars, Plots and Scandals in Post-war France* (Cambridge: Cambridge University Press, 1970); and in George Armstrong Kelly, *Lost Soldiers* (Cambridge: MIT Press, 1965), chap. 11.

ropolitan coalition that had overturned the previous regime. De Gaulle had weakened the settlers' ties to their allies, however: the military on this occasion did not take the side of the Europeans, whose leaders they distrusted; the dismissal of Soustelle after the episode and the outrage expressed at Roger Duchet's attitude confirmed the weakening position of the settlers in French politics.

After the failure of the "Generals' putsch" in April, 1961, settler resistance in Algeria moved to its final and most extreme phase, an expression of a society under siege: the Organisation de l'Armée Secrète (OAS). Including both settler and military members, the strategy of counter-terrorism pursued by the OAS only emphasizèd the weakness of the European position in Algeria; although its sympathizers in the metropolis were widely spread, the OAS operating in France found itself in an "alien milieu," and its actions were "isolated and unsustained."[40] Its acts of violence against civilians in the metropolis severed the remaining ties of sympathy for the settlers.

The counter-terrorism of the OAS, widely supported among the French of Algeria, stands in contrast to the British settlers of the Federation: the French of Algeria did not possess the option of independence. Their dependence upon France—for security and for economic survival—was too great. While that dependence made their political exposure high, it left them no possibility for an existence separate from France. When the decision for disengagement came from Paris, the European population of Algeria had little choice but to return to the metropolis as well.

The politics of mobilization among a threatened settler population drastically changed the configuration of power in the Central African Federation too. Conflict between the settler elite and at least part of the Rhodesian white population had been a recurrent aspect of politics in the colony: on the question of union with South Africa in the 1920s and later in deciding for federation with Northern Rhodesia and Nyasa-

[40] Kelly, *Lost Soldiers*, pp. 332-336.

land, the economic aims of the business elite clashed with settler fears of being submerged in a larger African population.

The campaign for the Federation was successful, but the links to the northern territories were not universally popular: many of the less prosperous members of the European population, who foresaw fewer benefits from the federation and possible loss from African advance, opposed the federal relationship.[41] The engine of success in the referendum, the United Central African Association, had been established by the Southern Rhodesian prime minister, Godfrey Huggins, in close alliance with the Rhodesian Federated Chambers of Commerce and the Federation of Rhodesian Industries. It provided the basis for the "party" that would govern Southern Rhodesia and the Federation for the next nine years.[42]

Never well-financed, the Federal Party was a cadre organization, supported by the economic elite but lacking grassroots support. It owed its political success to the conservative interpretation that it placed upon partnership and to the economic benefits that the white population gained from the new federal structure in the 1950s. After the eruption of African nationalism in 1959, however, the Federal Party did not have the organizational strength to counter its more extreme opponent, the Dominion Party, which sought Dominion status outside the Federation for white-ruled Southern Rhodesia. As white fears grew, the dynamics of increasing intransigence took hold, exacerbated by the superior political skills of the Dominion Party:

In contrast to earlier parties, the Dominion Party and the Rhodesian Front [its successor] have had a continuing existence. These two sought to raise the temperature of party politics and thus maintain a constant interest in its activities; and by doing this they aimed at the same time to counter the governing party's technique of lowering the intensity of feeling so as to be able to operate through economic associations.[43]

[41] Gann and Gelfand, *Huggins of Rhodesia*, p. 227.

[42] Murray, *The Governmental System in Southern Rhodesia*, pp. 193-197; Gann and Gelfand, *Huggins of Rhodesia*, p. 228.

[43] Murray, *The Governmental System in Southern Rhodesia*, p. 362.

In contrast,

> The Federal Party, an old-fashioned type of oligarchic organization, lacked both the men and the money to set up branches in the villages or to conduct popular propaganda; it lacked a social programme for the disinherited; it maintained no more emotional contact with the people than did the Department of Income Tax.[44]

The success of the Rhodesian Front in the 1962 General Election demonstrated the efficacy of this strategy of political mobilization. The organization of the population *against* the notables and the old style of politics was clearer than in Algeria, where the old parties had been even weaker. The mobilization of the Rhodesian settlers had a point and a program—Dominion status—which contrasted with the Algerian case. Facing the possibility of becoming a minority in a polity dominated by the formerly subordinate Arab population, the French of Algeria could only turn to counter-terrorism and direct action, tactics that would ultimately weaken their attachment to France. The Rhodesian Front aimed to make relations with the metropolis less critical to the European population of Southern Rhodesia; it could successfully set this goal since the white population of the colony (which had been self-governing since 1923) possessed its own means of maintaining its internal position. As early as 1949 Welensky had threatened forcible resistance if the British government demanded the paramountcy of African interests. In early 1961, when the British government seemed prepared to introduce majority rule in Northern Rhodesia, threats of force were once again made; in this instance an attempt by the Federal government to seize control of the northern territories was feared.[45] The political prerequisites for severing the ties to Britain were not in place until the consolidation of the Rhodesian Front's power after 1962, however.

[44] Gann and Gelfand, *Huggins of Rhodesia*, p. 264.
[45] Sir Roy Welensky, *Welensky's 4,000 Days* (London: Collins, 1964), p. 34; Harold Macmillan, *Pointing the Way* (New York: Harper & Row, 1972), pp. 297-298; Macmillan, *At the End of the Day*, p. 311; Alport, *Sudden Assignment*, pp. 33-34.

While the outcomes in Algeria and Rhodesia were different, determined by differences in the governance of the two colonial empires, the characteristics of settler politics in the British and French colonies were remarkably similar. The principal differences in the political behavior of the settler communities, apart from those resulting from developments in metropolitan politics, came from the factors described earlier: size, permanence, perceived political exposure, and the unitary or divided character of the European elite in the colony. In Morocco and Kenya these elements biased the situation to permit the metropolitan power to win its race against the political mobilization of the settler population; in Algeria and Rhodesia, that race was lost: France confronted a uniformly hostile but completely dependent European population in one instance and Britain an uncontrollable move toward independence in the other.

COLONIZER AND COLONIZED IN THE POLITICS OF THE METROPOLIS

The pace and outcome of decolonization was also determined by another characteristic of the relations between metropolis and empire: the disparity between the means of political influence possessed by the settlers and the possibility for intervention in the metropolis by the non-European population. On this score, the populations in the French North African territories were at a significant disadvantage as compared to the Africans of British Kenya or Central Africa.

Algerian nationalism, for example, found no voice in the French political system, despite the incorporation of the Algerian departments in the Republic. The Statute of 1947, although compromised to protect the status of the French population, seemed to promise significant representation for the Arab majority in both the Algerian Assembly and the National Assembly in Paris. The possibility of balancing settler penetration of metropolitan political parties was destroyed by the banning of nationalist organizations, the enforced exile of their leaders, and the blatant rigging of elections held under the statute.[46] In a dialectical fashion, Algerian nationalism turned to its own mobilization of the Arab population and the use of violence; just as the Europeans would later develop a new form of politics to defend their threatened position, so the nationalists first threw off the old leadership and its methods of seeking to influence French policy. The leaders of the insurrection that began in November, 1954—young and unknown members of the Comité révolutionnaire pour l'unité et l'action (CRUA)—were no longer interested in manipulating metropolitan political alignments, given past failures. Their commitment to winning the battle in Algeria rather than Paris, symbolic in itself of their anti-colonialism, would frustrate the efforts of French governments seeking *interlocuteurs valables* of the older and more familiar sort.

Moroccan and Tunisian nationalists did find a limited number of allies in French politics, despite their status as foreign nationals. As described in Chapter III, Bourguiba and the Néo-Destour maintained good relations with the French Socialist Party, which offered support for liberal positions during Tunisian decolonization. Since the Socialists did not participate in any of the ministries between 1951 and 1956, the predominance of the French settlers within the governments of the period was assured. The liberal allies of Moroccan nationalism benefited from a presence in both France and Morocco. Not connected to a particular political party, their center of gravity was the Catholic Center and Left; the focus of the liberal movement in Paris was the Comité France-Maghreb, presided over by François Mauriac. The political power of the liberals was slight given the means of obstruction possessed by the settlers at the center and on the periphery. Nevertheless, they provided a means of breaking the monopoly of information that had been held by the Europeans and their allies in Paris. For example, after the brutal repression of December, 1952, the liberals (using Catholic informants in Morocco) chal-

[46] Thomas Oppermann, *Le Problème algérien* (Paris: Maspero, 1961), pp. 94-102; Dorothy Pickles, *Algeria and France* (New York: Frederick A. Praeger, 1963), pp. 26-30.

lenged the Residency's interpretation of the violence and its estimates of the loss of life.[47]

Despite these limited means of representation in French politics, the North African Muslims could not hope to exercise the degree of influence captured by the omnipresent settler lobbyists and their right-wing political allies. The case of the French territories in sub-Saharan Africa illustrates the difference that genuine and direct representation in the metropolis could make. The second Constitutent Assembly had demonstrated the power that could be wielded by a unified colonial bloc within a closely divided legislature.[48] As Algerian nationalists lost their representation in the Assemblies of the Fourth Republic, it was the representatives of black Africa who came to play the balancing role, even though divided between two groups: the Rassemblement démocratique africaine (RDA) and the Indépendants d'outre-mer. The RDA, like many other nationalist formations, at first affiliated with the Communists in the Assembly; they soon perceived, like the representatives of the North African settlers, that their most effective strategy would be a centrist one. In 1950, the RDA affiliated with the Union démocratique et socialiste de la Résistance (UDSR) of François Mitterrand and René Pleven, "the chief of those marginal formations whose support every ministry needed."[49] The African deputies then proceeded to bargain for desired reforms with their parliamentary support: their importance is suggested by the presence of at least one African deputy in every ministry after that of Mendès-France.[50] Their strategy was successful: ". . the electoral law was mod-

[47] Stéphane Bernard, *Le Conflit franco-marocain, Vol. III* (Brussels: Editions de l'Institut de Sociologie de l'Université libre de Bruxelles, 1963), pp. 187-197; Hervé Bleuchot, *Les Libéraux français au Maroc (1947-1955)* (Aix: Editions de l'Université de Provence, 1973), pp. 220-221.

[48] Gordon Wright, *The Reshaping of French Democracy* (Boston: Beacon Press, 1970), pp. 189-190, 204-205.

[49] Philip Williams, *Crisis and Compromise* (New York: Doubleday-Anchor, 1966), p. 185.

[50] Philippe Guillemin, "Les Elus d'Afrique Noire à l'Assemblée Nationale sous la Quatrième République," *Revue Française de Science Politique* 8 (December, 1958), p. 824.

ified by their pressure as early as 1951, and from 1956 their views were decisive in policy-making for the tropical territories."[51]

This pattern of metropolitan representation was permitted to develop only for a region that was likely to present few obstacles to decolonization in any case. In British politics, which tended to polarize colonial issues between the two parties, African nationalists, even (or perhaps *especially*) in territories dominated by the Europeans, were able to find domestic spokesmen and allies, particularly in the Labour Party. Their avenues of access replicated the indirect means of influence that the settlers exerted within the Conservative Party.

During and immediately after World War II, the interest of the Labour Party in colonial questions had been stimulated by the Fabian Colonial Bureau, described in Chapter III. Sir Charles Ponsonby, a member of the Conservative colonial establishment and chairman of the Joint East African Board at the time, recalled with some distaste the complications which the new Labour activism produced:

This procedure [one of forwarding questions from the colonies to be put to the colonial secretary] resulted in a number of clever people overseas, especially West Africans, sending in questions to the Fabian Society. Grievances which could and should have been dealt with locally took up the time of Parliament, but (what was worse) a certain amount of *Kudos* attached to a person three or four thousand miles away. . . . In this way during the war, Messrs. Creech Jones and Sorenson, both sincere men, were also built up as the protectors of the Africans.[52]

As it accepted the goals of the African nationalist movements, the Labour Party assisted them in influencing both public opinion and government policy in Britain. Because of the Labour Party's activities, the advantages that the settlers possessed in Conservative circles were in part countered by similar representation of the African position.

[51] Williams, *Crisis and Compromise*, p. 188.
[52] Sir Charles Ponsonby, *Ponsonby Remembers* (Oxford: Alden Press, 1965), pp. 115-116.

THE STATE IN THE EMPIRE:
THE ADMINISTRATION AND THE MILITARY

The Europeans in the empire possessed one final resource in their efforts to maintain the colonial status quo: the colonial administration and the military, instruments for implementing metropolitan policy. Through the state apparatus the Europeans could exert additional influence upon metropolitan policy; by winning the administration to their point of view, they could obstruct efforts to change the balance of power on the periphery. The administration and the military had their own reasons for resisting change, of course: their attachment to governing the colonial empires would prove a principal obstacle in the transfer of power to other hands. In this crucial sphere of political action, the contrast between British and French experiences is once again striking. While apparent administrative insubordination contributed to the trials of French governments that attempted to decolonize; the British government could count upon obedience to its instructions, even in areas of considerable settler influence.

The explanation for this difference in bureaucratic behavior does not lie in the administrative structures of the colonial empires: both were, of necessity, marked by a large degree of decentralization. Even Algeria, despite the claims of the integrationists, had never been governed precisely like the French departments, because of its large Muslim population and because the Europeans did not want to be governed in that way. The 1947 Statute noted in its first article the "civil personality, financial autonomy, and particular organization" of this group of departments: the presence of an Algerian Assembly and a governor-general, as well as the double electoral college, marked the distinctive status of Algeria.[53] By treaty France exercised indirect control over Morocco and Tunisia, but despite their protectorate status, the realities of French administration approached the Algerian model. The indigenous administrations

[53] The statute text is reproduced in Oppermann, *Le Problème algérien*, pp. 287-298.

became a façade as the inflated French bureaucracy assumed more and more governmental functions. By the postwar years, the only means that the bey or the sultan possessed to thwart the French resident general was a "strike": his refusal to sign decrees desired by the French.

The resident general in Morocco or Tunisia was "representative of all the powers of the Republic" in the protected states; a similar proconsular role was awarded the governor-general of Algeria. In the British colonial empire, the clear lines of authority from the colonial secretary to the governor of each colony and the institutions of local representation that each governor faced seemed to imply a more limited role than that enjoyed by the residents of French North Africa. The British colonial governor retained a significant area of discretion, however:

> However tightly the legal department defined his powers of dissolution or suspension, he held the balance between conflicting forces; he could hardly obstruct the official policy of granting self-government, but he was in a strong position to modify the actions of the Secretary of State.[54]

The latitude built into the two systems could be expanded by the careful use of that most precious resource of the man on the spot: information. Control of information available to the metropolis was the most potent and least risky means that the administrator in Africa could employ in thwarting official intentions. Those in Paris and London frequently complained that they were misinformed or not informed at all of the situation on the periphery.[55]

Given the decentralized character of both empires, an explanation for the failure of metropolitan control in the French case must be sought in other features of the political situation. First, of course, one must demonstrate that the politicians at the center did give clearly stated and adequately communi-

[54] J. M. Lee, Colonial Development and Good Government (Oxford: Clarendon Press, 1967), p. 231.

[55] Viscount Chandos, The Memoirs of Lord Chandos (London: The Bodley Head, 1962), p. 393; Elgey, Histoire de la IVe République, p. 402.

cated orders that were disobeyed. The former foreign minister of France, Robert Schuman, has put the politicians' case most bluntly in several pages of special pleading that appeared in 1953.[56] According to Schuman, as foreign minister he possessed only limited control over the men who represented France in the North African protectorates. The Residents were inclined to present him with *faits accomplis*; the prerequisite for reforms, in his view, was "a return to precise notions of responsibility and of hierarchical subordination." In response to this hand-wringing, Alfred Grosser has pointed out that proof of the disobedience claimed by Schuman requires evidence of precise instructions, not a hallmark of French cabinets during these years.[57]

Cases that are often used as examples of administrative insubordination suggest that a principal cause of the independent policy pursued by French administrators was lack of clarity in the political signals emanating from Paris. One reason for this confusion in political course was the influence exerted, through effective lobbying, by the settlers. In other instances, rapid change of governments produced inconsistent directions. In January, 1952, for example, the Faure cabinet revived a liberal policy of progress toward internal autonomy for Tunisia, one that stood in contrast to the course set by the preceding cabinet in December, 1951. The Resident General, de Hauteclocque, "played the game loyally," according to Faure. The Faure ministry fell on 29 February, however, and it had not rescinded the instructions issued to the Residency by the previous cabinet. As a result, the Resident General in Tunis had *two* courses from which to choose. He interpreted the contradictory instructions according to his own conservative attitudes and in line with the broad discretion granted to his office: disregarding the Faure ministry as a brief interlude, he removed the Tunisian ministers sympathetic to the nationalist cause and sought to create the conditions for

[56] Robert Schuman, "Nécessité d'une politique," *La Nef* 10 (March, 1953), 7-9.

[57] Alfred Grosser, *La IVe République et sa politique extérieure* (Paris: Armand Colin, 1961), pp. 53-54.

an agreement with "good" Tunisians.[58] The politicians in Paris were only too happy to declare his action an unauthorized *fait accompli*, since a resolution of the Tunisian question threatened the ministry's parliamentary coalition.

The weak political lead given by the center to the French administration was aggravated by the division of political responsibility for the empire. Only the territories of sub-Saharan Africa and Madagascar were the responsibility of the minister for overseas France. The North African territories were administered by ministries whose principal tasks lay elsewhere: Algeria by the Ministry of the Interior, Morocco and Tunisia by the Ministry for Foreign Affairs. Robert Schuman, foreign minister from July, 1948 until January, 1953, was principally absorbed in European affairs; neither his interests nor his political priorities dictated devoting much attention to French North Africa. This neglect continued until the appointment of a minister for Moroccan and Tunisian affairs by Pierre Mendès-France in July, 1954. The divided attention of ministers responsible for the overseas territories of France can be contrasted with the single task of the colonial secretary in the British Cabinet. His area of responsibility narrowed over the years: in 1925 relations with the self-governing Dominions were hived off to the Dominions (later Commonwealth Relations) Office; the India Office was extinguished with the independence of the subcontinent. The Colonial Office was left with sole responsibility for nearly every overseas dependency and responsibility for very little else.

The question of divided responsibility touches upon another explanation for the greater success of British political leaders in resisting capture of the colonial administration by the European populations in Africa: the definition of the *task* of the colonial administration. Certainly the ministries responsible for French North Africa rarely defined their role as ensuring the political advancement of the Muslim population. From its responsibilities in metropolitan France the Interior Ministry would be particularly attuned to the wishes of the French in

[58] Elgey, *Histoire de la IVᵉ République*, pp. 368-369.

Algeria and willing to leave most administrative decisions to the governor-general. The Quai d'Orsay defined its role as the defense of the interests of France and of French nationals abroad; in North Africa this meant maintaining the colonial status quo and protecting the French settlers. It was particularly ill-equipped for carrying out Lyautey's original aim of creating autonomous Arab states in Morocco and Tunisia.

Just as the dominion model had provided a theory of decolonization for the British political elite, the concept of trusteeship offered a clear definition of the task of the Colonial Office. Jeffries cites with approval Creech Jones's summary, which "crystallized the purpose of the whole work of the present-day Colonial Office":

> The central purpose of British colonial policy is simple. It is to guide the colonial territories to responsible self-government within the Commonwealth in conditions that ensure to the people concerned both a fair standard of living and freedom from oppression from any quarter.[59]

This definition of task had a second function. The Labour Party served as the principal representative of African interests in the political arena; within the cabinet, even Conservative cabinets, the colonial secretary played a similar role. Conflict between his colonial secretary and his commonwealth relations secretary, so irritating to Macmillan, merely reproduced the growing conflict between their respective administrative charges in Africa.

Authoritative decisions, clear administrative responsibility at the center, and a well-defined organizational task contributed to the ability of British governments to maintain the loyalty of the colonial administration. British colonial policy in East and Central Africa did show signs of bending to its best-organized and most familiar clientele, however. Although British policy and the Colonial Service were devoted to the eventual goal of self-government, the question remained: self-

---

[59] *The Colonial Empire, 1947-1948*, Cmd. 7433, June, 1948, para. 3, cited in Sir Charles Jeffries, *The Colonial Office* (London: George Allen and Unwin, 1956), p. 38.

government by whom? Southern Rhodesia had gained effective internal self-government in 1923, a "liberal" concession that excluded the African population from participation in government. In Kenya the settlers pressed for greater local control and sought to capture the energies and the sympathies of the colonial administration. As Margery Perham noted, "Remember that the officials, who never cease to hear and read the settlers' case, and who, being of the same race and social type are in natural contact and sympathy with them, hardly ever hear the opposite case."[60] Their partial success was attested by Kenyan development policy, which neglected the native reserves and proclaimed the central economic role of the Europeans of the "White Highlands."[61]

Despite such bending of policy to meet the demands of the settlers, when the test of decolonization came, the Europeans in British-ruled Africa discovered that they had not constructed a closed administrative system impervious to metropolitan initiatives. In contrast to French practice in North Africa, the Colonial Office employed certain techniques that ensured accountability to the center rather than responsiveness to local interests. Thus, in the tug of war between center and periphery for the loyalties of the servants of the state, the center was far more likely to win.

In the appointment of the powerful proconsular officials in the overseas territories—the residents and governors—the French governments permitted the settler groups and their allies to exercise a veto over most appointments. Thus, the principal intermediary between metropolitan politics and colonial politics was typically a sympathizer of the Europeans on the periphery, an "old hand." The residents general of Morocco after 1945 in particular fit this mold. The reformer

[60] Elspeth Huxley and Margery Perham, *Race and Politics in Kenya*, 2nd ed. (London: Faber, 1956), p. 153.

[61] Ibid., p. 71; Michael McWilliam, "Economic Policy and the Kenya Settlers, 1945-48," in *Essays in Imperial Government*, ed. K. Robinson and F. Madden (Oxford: Blackwell, 1963), p. 192; Carl G. Rosberg, Jr. and John Nottingham, *The Myth of 'Mau Mau': Nationalism in Kenya* (Stanford: Hoover Institution, 1966), pp. 205-206.

Erik Labonne was replaced by General Alphonse Juin, who had served in Morocco under Lyautey. In early 1951 Juin gave cover to the first attempt to overthrow the sultan of Morocco, whose sympathies with the nationalist Istiqlal were regarded as a threat by the French administration. The government urged Juin to accept a command with NATO, but the general refused to leave his post and threatened to resign if forced out before mid-1951. The cabinet in Paris was infuriated by his blackmail, but yielded—his prestige in Paris was too great to be overcome.[62] After finally relinquishing the Residency in August, 1951 Juin continued to be a vociferous opponent of liberalization in Morocco. He was succeeded by General Auguste Guillaume, another "old Moroccan," and the pattern continued with the appointment in June, 1954 of Francis Lacoste, a diplomat who had been deputy minister and secretary general of the protectorate under Juin. The last appointment of this type was General Boyer de Latour, appointed in 1955 by the premier, Edgar Faure, as a gesture of appeasement to his right-wing critics. The instructions from the government to Boyer de Latour remained those issued to his predecessor, Grandval, but the general obstructed them with all the persistence of previous residents. Finally, two subordinate members of the Residency staff were ordered by Paris to circumvent their superior, obtain the abdication of the incumbent sultan, and thus resolve the crisis.[63]

The appointment of colonial governors under the British system was governed much less by politics, more by bureaucratic procedures. Occasionally, an old hand would have an impact upon colonial policy: Sir Philip Mitchell, who had spent most of his career in East and Central Africa, proved particularly insensitive to African unrest in Kenya during his tenure in the years before the Emergency. More often, governors were chosen from outside the Colonial Service to guarantee loyalty to London and received strong metropolitan

---

[62] Stéphane Bernard, *The Franco-Moroccan Conflict, 1943-1956,*(New Haven: Yale University Press, 1968) p. 80.

[63] Ibid., pp. 299-300; Pierre July, *Une République pour un roi*, chap. 9.

support: Sir Evelyn Baring, the governor of Kenya during the Emergency, is a case in point; Gilbert Grandval's role in the decolonization of Morocco further illustrates the mark that such an "outsider" could make upon a rigid and conservative bureaucracy.[64]

Even with an administration directed by a governor or Resident willing to carry out metropolitan instructions, the colonial administration could and did balk. Here once again, British policy served to overcome resistance and ensure that London's wishes were in fact carried out. The recruitment and training programs of the Colonial Service contributed to administrative loyalty. Under the direction of Sir Ralph Furse, the Colonial Service recruited young men of "good family," ensuring through close ties with the public schools and the ancient universities (particularly Oxford) that these men shared the same governing ethos as those who entered the Home Civil Service or filled Parliament: "By the age of twenty-one basic assumptions were so deeply ingrained that everyone knew what to expect. Few written rules were necessary. Everyone was an Old Boy."[65] Being an Old Boy, caught in a web of loyalties that were focused upon the metropolis, helped to prevent one from becoming an old hand, attached to a given colonial milieu.

Apart from recruitment procedures, administrative practice in Africa loosened the hold of the European population there. Colonial Service officers were rotated frequently within a given colony and among colonies. They were strictly prohibited from engaging in local politics or expressing their own political views in public, whether on behalf of Africans or Europeans. Finally, African representation was at least indirectly guaranteed within the administrative structure. In Kenya, for example, the chief native commissioner sat on the Legislative

[64] On the record of Sir Philip Mitchell: Rosberg and Nottingham, *The Myth of 'Mau Mau,'* pp. 198-203; on Grandval: Bernard, *The Franco-Moroccan Conflict*, pp. 252-293.

[65] Robert Heussler, *Yesterday's Rulers: The Making of the British Colonial Service* (Syracuse: Syracuse University Press, 1963), p. 103.

Council and headed a network of officers stationed in the African areas.

The French administration in North Africa was not tied to the metropolis by any of the techniques employed by the British. The *fonctionnaire* in Morocco and Tunisia often considered himself a settler first and a civil servant second: Julien described the North African territories as *"colonies des fonctionnaires."*[66] The members of the French administration were not of high social standing like the members of the British Colonial Service; the status that they enjoyed in North Africa could not be replicated in the metropolis. Finally, the sheer numbers of French colonial administrators in North Africa were far greater than in the British colonial territories. A certain "critical mass" was reached beyond which the *petis fonctionnaires* perceived certain corporate interests in opposition to the wishes of Paris: preventing Muslims from obtaining positions that they wished to hand on to their children, constantly extending the range of the French administration rather than devolving responsibilities upon the Arab population. The French administration, possessing these interests of its own and identifying closely with the rest of the European population, proved an unreliable instrument in carrying out political change:

The French colony did not actually outnumber the administration; it would be more exact to say that the administration identified itself with the colony. The most influential notables were all playing the same game, whether they were civil servants, businessmen, or wealthy settlers.[67]

Thus, a perverse form of bureaucratic democracy was created in what appeared to be a rigidly hierarchical structure.

French efforts to decolonize faced not only the powerful resistance of the European populations in North Africa, but also an administration often captured by that population. The administration was not only unresponsive to metropolitan

[66] C. A. Julien, *L'Afrique du Nord en marche* (Paris: Plon, 1952), pp. 58-60.
[67] Bernard, *The Franco-Moroccan Conflict*, p. 68.

commands (when they were clearly stated), it also provided an additional avenue of access to policy-making in Paris for the Europeans. Administrators who had retired or left the government service would often appear as settler spokesmen in Paris, assisting such lobbies as the Comité central de la France d'outre-mer or seeking to represent electorally the French of North Africa.

The contrasts between the British and French colonial administrations are clear enough; the role of the military in the French empire is a critical element that scarcely had an analogue to the British case. The Army (and to a lesser degree the other services) raised in aggravated form the same obstacles to controlling the state bureaucracy. An alliance with the military also provided the settlers' surest guarantee of their local position as well as their most powerful means of influencing the politics of the metropolis.

The historical pattern of military influence upon metropolitan France was a long one: military pressures for expansion had appeared in most regions of French influence during the nineteenth century, but Algeria and the Western Sudan in particular had provided extended episodes of military activity that were virtually free of metropolitan supervision.[68] Lack of political oversight after the start of hostilities marked French experience in both the Third and the Fourth Republics:

... the resort to force followed upon a decision of the Premier or Minister of Foreign Affairs to have recourse to warlike measures to achieve a diplomatic objective, often on the advice of the military authorities. Once military action gets underway, control of the whole diplomatic situation tends to pass into the hands of the generals or admirals, usually with the acquiescence of the ministers.[69]

After a decision for coercion rather than negotiation with colonial nationalist movements, the military's role expanded

---

[68] The military expansion in the Western Sudan is described in A. S. Kanya-Forstner, *The Conquest of the Western Sudan: A Study in French Military Imperialism* (Cambridge: Cambridge University Press, 1969).

[69] Frederick L. Schuman, *War and Diplomacy in the French Republic* (New York: McGraw-Hill, 1931), p. 347.

as did its impact upon metropolitan politics. The part played by the French Army in decolonization has been well-documented; here the sources of its intervention in the politics of the metropolis will be briefly discussed as well as the reasons for its eventual acceptance of the end of its colonial role.[70]

The key to understanding both the activities of the French Army during these years and the success of de Gaulle in regaining control of the military is the strong corporate identity that has always defined the intervention of the military in French politics (although not always the intervention of military men). The overriding fear of dividing the ranks, strengthened by the experience of Vichy and the Free French, usually dampened any impulse to political activism.

The transition from an unwillingness to accept close civilian supervision in the colonial empire, characteristic for some time in the French Army, to a more radical desire to influence the politics of metropolitan France, can be traced to two sources: one external, one internal. First, the experience of World War II, in which Charles de Gaulle summoned the French Army to insubordination in order to continue the battle against the German invader, caused a crisis of obedience that would scar the postwar years. Officers were now expected, it seemed, to make political judgments, to concern themselves with the legitimacy of decisions taken by apparently transitory political regimes, a sharp break with the apolitical stance of the military since 1815. Although no direct connection can be found between the dissident officers of 1940-1945 and those who questioned decolonization during the Fourth and Fifth Republics, the historical precedent in responding to an external shock certainly weakened civilian control.[71]

Perhaps more important was the *type* of colonial war that the French military fought. Isolated from the civilian political society by a succession of overseas conflicts, a new ideology

[70] The two best accounts are John Steward Ambler, *The French Army in Politics, 1945-1962* (Columbus: Ohio State University Press, 1962), and Kelly, *Lost Soldiers*.

[71] Robert Paxton, *Parades and Politics at Vichy* (Princeton: Princeton University Press, 1966), pp. 426-427.

of military action began to override old predispositions: *la guerre révolutionnaire*.[72] Although it reinforced the old sense of isolation, the new ideology added a novel ingredient in its sense of mission toward metropolitan politics, rarely displayed by the old army. The temptation to intervene derived from two aspects of the new warfare that pushed the Army in explicitly political directions. First, postwar colonial conflicts caused the military to take on new, political responsibilities on the periphery that had not been characteristic of their role in the past. As Ambler describes, "The objectives of war have always been political. Now the means as well had become deeply political as each officer—indeed, each soldier—was called upon to be a government propagandist and a jack-of-all-trades."[73] The *guerre révolutionnaire* also demanded a clear setting of political goals, a task which the governments of the Fourth Republic often failed, as earlier accounts of bureaucratic insubordination make clear. The military quickly perceived a political vacuum at the center, and, in 1958, moved to fill it.

The new activism was focused upon Algeria, the last great colonial war and the first great testing ground of the new military strategy.[74] Although the new ideology of the *guerre révolutionnaire* encouraged intervention in politics, it did not provide an ideal basis for an alliance between the Army in Algeria and the Europeans. While some elements in the Army identified with the North African settlers, particularly the paratroopers and the Foreign Legion, others, particularly those soldiers who dealt with the Muslim population, viewed European intransigence and conservatism as an obstacle to the more equitable Algerian society that they envisaged.[75] A common attachment to *Algérie française* temporarily disguised the possible rift between soldier and settler; the movement of *13*

[72] Kelly, *Lost Soldiers*, chap. 7.

[73] Ambler, *The French Army*, p. 184.

[74] Tunisia and Morocco had been sacrificed without severe military resistance in part because the Army realized that it had insufficient resources to wage campaigns in the protectorates: Lee, "French Policy," pp. 482-487.

[75] Ambler, *The French Army*, pp. 286-287; Kelly, *Lost Soldiers*, p. 147.

Mai and the formation of the Committees of Public Safety marked the high point of their collaboration in opposition to the politics of France. Those months in 1958 also marked the apogee of their success in influencing the metropolis—the end of the Fourth Republic, under threat from Operation Resurrection, a military invasion staged from Algeria.

The coalition of settlers and Army was potent, but the solution to the crisis—de Gaulle—also sealed the fate of that coalition for the future. After several months of tolerating collaboration between settlers and military, de Gaulle set about breaking an alliance that could once again threaten the regime. While he decolonized the Gaullists and weakened the partisans of French Algeria in metropolitan politics, de Gaulle also moved to split the Army from the settlers: in October, 1958 military men were ordered to cease participation in any organization of a political character, in particular the Committees of Public Safety. The most political officers were replaced: Salan, who had cried "Vive de Gaulle!" in Algiers in May, was now "promoted" to become inspector general of defense; Jouhaud was retired at his request; and many other activists of lower rank were transferred to posts outside Algeria.[76]

Despite continuing complicity between some officers and the civilian *ultras* in Algiers, the Army refused to join actively the settlers' cause during the "week of the barricades" in January, 1960; in April, 1961 the attempted putsch by the generals failed to rally most of the Algerian armed forces. The split between Army and settlers widened when European demonstrators were fired upon on 5 March 1962; the breach was sealed by OAS attacks upon unsympathetic officers.[77] De Gaulle's success was explained in part by the new tasks that he offered to the French armed forces in place of the colonial role that had consumed their energies for a century, especially the development of the *force de frappe*.[78] As an explanation of indiscipline in the Army, however, the "modernization cri-

[76] Ambler, *The French Army*, p. 253.
[77] Ibid., p. 261.
[78] Kelly, *Lost Soldiers*, p. 293.

sis" accounts for the behavior of only certain units, such as the Foreign Legion.[79]

The impact of a colonial milieu in shaping the political orientation of an army has been apparent in other cases: the Nationalist forces that began the Spanish Civil War originated in Spanish Morocco; more recently, the Portuguese Army learned both left-wing politics and an interventionist role from its unending colonial war in Africa. Britain, however, faced no military obstacle to decolonization and no military impact upon its society that even remotely resembled these cases or that of France. The role of the British Army in the colonial empire was limited: its tasks overseas were not political in the manner of either the old or the new French colonial army in North Africa. The British Army suffered no external shock that might have produced a crisis of loyalty after 1945: like members of the Colonial Service, the military officer was typically well-integrated into the prevailing ethos of civilian political life. The British did produce their own theories of counter-insurgency and guerrilla warfare, but they stood in sharp contrast to the French tradition of the *guerre révolutionnaire* in their explicit separation of military and civilian responsibilities (particularly police work) and their clear demand for political guidance of the military mission.[80] Military resistance to decolonization centered, as one would expect, upon the empire of prestige that once stretched to India, and specifically upon Cyprus and Aden. Even in these instances, the attitudes of civilian politicians were at least as important, and, of course, British expatriate populations were insignificant. In the single British case of military counter-insurgency combined with a substantial settler population—Kenya—the attitudes of the military officers were hardly sympathetic to settler demands. General Erskine, commander of British forces in Kenya, once remarked, "I hate the guts of them all, they are all middle

[79] Ambler, *The French Army*, p. 298.

[80] For example, Robert Thompson, *Defeating Communist Insurgency: Experiences from Malaya and Vietnam* (London: Chatto & Windus, 1966), chap. 6; Brigadier Richard L. Clutterbuck, *The Long Long War* (New York: Frederick A. Praeger, 1966), p. 178.

class sluts. I never want to see another Kenya man or woman and I dislike them all with few exceptions."[81] Such hostility prevented even the tenuous alliance that army and settlers forged in Algeria. A final contrast with French military experience was the speed with which the British Army adjusted to a predominantly European and nuclear role that both Conservatives and Labour had endorsed. The lingering place given to defense policy east of Suez seems more a wasteful bit of nostalgia than a serious inability to adapt to new strategic realities.[82]

Two contrasting portraits emerge from examining the impact of colonial populations upon metropolitan politics. On the one hand, France: a coalition among settlers, administration and military to thwart temporarily efforts at change; solidarity on the periphery and fragmentation at the center. On the other hand, Britain: a metropolitan political elite that was able to maintain control of political change in Africa (apart from Southern Rhodesia) by separating its instrument—the administration—from the Europeans resident in the colonies; cohesion in London and fragmentation on the periphery. A second pattern also emerges: the conflict between European and non-European in the Empire was reproduced indirectly in British politics; in the case of France, that conflict was stifled in the center as it had been on the periphery, until the Algerian conflict brought it home in the brutal form of OAS and FLN terrorism.

[81] Charles Douglas-Home, *Evelyn Baring: The Last Proconsul*, (London: Collins, 1978), p. 242.

[82] The best account is Philip Darby, *British Defence Policy East of Suez, 1947-1968* (London: Oxford University Press, 1973).

CHAPTER VI

Conclusion: The Decolonization of British and French Societies

As THE Algerian crisis deepened, a Socialist deputy remarked that it seemed France had been colonized by its empire. That a nation could be so constrained by a set of international relations carefully constructed over time sums up the contrast between Britain and France and points to the source, it has been argued, of many of the differences in their pattern of decolonization. Three sets of links, three dynamics, indirect and direct, by which the colonial empires could influence the politics of Britain and France have been investigated.

Ideology served not only as a means of interpreting the course of events on the periphery, but also as an organizational asset used in the pursuit of power. Only after Liberation, when the Communist Party had achieved the dominant position within a powerful Left coalition, did modern party organization begin to take hold on the French Right. The Gaullist Rassemblement du Peuple Français tried to unify an electoral clientele that demonstrated its volatility in each postwar election. In building a new national organization, both the Gaullists and, later in the 1950s, the Indépendants had to deal with the threat of exit by their party members and electorates. To strengthen the weak identities of their formations (with the exception of Gaullism *with* de Gaulle), the parties turned to nationalism (and opposition to decolonization) to provide the necessary ideological incentives; through a process of competition, intransigence on colonial questions was reinforced. The critical years were the mid-1950s. French conservatives moved to accept decolonization during the Moroccan crisis in late 1955, only to swing sharply toward a policy of support for *Algérie française* after 1956, a turn owed in part to the electoral success of the stridently colonialist Poujadist movement. After the withdrawal of de Gaulle from active leadership of his movement, the Gaullists reinforced their existing nationalism to maintain themselves against growing competition on the Right. Fragmentation and electoral defeat in 1956 made attachment to the existing trajectory of resistance even more likely, as a means of separating the now tiny party from its coalition partners in the Mollet government and as a means of hastening the external shock that might bring de Gaulle back to power.

If party competition by organizations early in their life cycles prompted an ideological attachment to empire as the empires came under threat, the lack of a clearly defined organizational structure hindered ideological adaptation. For the Gaullists, the RPF years were a lost opportunity, a time when a hierarchical organization guided by de Gaulle could have begun the difficult task of ideological disengagement. The electoral strategy of polarization pursued by the RPF thwarted that possibility, however. After de Gaulle's retreat from leadership, in the years of the "wandering in the desert," only a small band of liberals argued in favor of more conciliatory colonial policies, without the knowledge that de Gaulle himself was closer to their views than he was to the majority of the rump party. Only de Gaulle's return to power, as focus of loyalty and an ideological arbiter at the head of a revived Gaullist movement could, when combined with the change to a presidential regime under the Fifth Republic, permit the final, painful decolonization of French politics. The French Conservatives, on the other hand, using their attachment to French Algeria to distinguish themselves from the Gaullists, chose their identity incentives unwisely. Their electors, when offered a choice between de Gaulle and *Algérie française*, would choose de Gaulle. The *modérés* were divided and defeated in a new political order whose outlines they did not comprehend.

The relative ease with which British Conservatives surmounted decolonization could not have been predicted immediately after World War II. The persistent intraparty battles over Indian decolonization and imperial protectionism demonstrated the importance of the party's long attachment to empire and the central role played by the Empire in the party's incentive structure and electoral appeal. Countering its organizational attachment was the greater institutionalization of the party, an awareness of the advantages of organizational loyalty at all levels of party organization; the British Conservative Party, a national party since the nineteenth century, no longer needed the identity incentives required by organizations at an earlier point in their life cycles. The bipolar party structure also impeded exit: the ideologically committed could find no other political home within a polarized political system; defection would, in any case, have risked bringing to power a Labour government whose colonial policies were even less acceptable.

As it moved to sever the ties to empire, *voice* rather than exit threatened the unity of the party. The discontented could express their dissent—in Parliament, in the party conferences, and in the myriad colonial pressure groups. In overcoming resistance to final ideological detachment, Conservative governments possessed certain assets in their party ideology: a dominion model of decolonization that could be applied, increased emphasis upon domestic affairs after 1945, and the fact that the "Empire" was in fact several empires with different constituencies in the party. The leadership also benefited from a favorable structure of power within the party: weighted heavily toward the top, which remained united with few exceptions throughout the course of decolonization, the distribution of power offered little hope of success to the discontented backbenchers who formed the core of resistance to the disengagement from empire. The bargaining advantages of the leadership also included acquiescence of the party rank and file and of the Conservative electorate.

When compared to their conservative counterparts, the parties of the Left had few ideological connections to empire, but they maintained an equally fierce attachment to "socialist foreign policy," whatever the disputes over its definition. That attachment, which had repeatedly divided their parties in the past, also reflected on their attitudes toward colonialism and the dismantling of the empires. In a mirror image of the differences between the French and British Right, the bipolar party structure in Britain and the divisions of the French Left lay at the source of the different political strategies pursued by French Socialists and British Labour, strategies that would have profound consequences for decolonization.

Division on the Left posed the Socialists in France with formidable dilemmas after Liberation; the solution chosen was that of Guy Mollet, best described as anti-revisionism. Against Blum and Mayer, who endorsed a "workers' party," Mollet led the party rank and file in a revolt that fixed an apparently radical course for the SFIO, one that would fend off its two larger partners—the MRP on the Right and the Communists on the Left—in order to maintain a distinct identity and carve out a place for itself in the political spectrum. The ambiguities and contradictions in Socialist ideology toward the colonial empire were confirmed. The combination of ideological conservatism, the barrier of the Cold War (preventing cooperation with the Communists), and the pull of Third Force coalitions in defense of the Fourth Republic, gradually pressed the Socialists toward support for war in Indochina and the status quo in North Africa. The Labour Party was faced with its own dilemmas while in power after the war, but none that forced it away from support for decolonization. The decolonization of the Indian subcontinent, without a large European population or the threat of Communist intrusion, was, for the most part, a bipartisan affair.

After 1951, as both parties entered opposition, their political strategies and their orientation toward decolonization converged. As colonial issues erupted into the wider political arena, the two parties set themselves apart from the conservatives and their status quo policies. Both hedged on the future of the settler colonies in Africa, which were likely to be the most contentious cases. Both condemned excesses of repression by conservative governments, but were willing to endorse military measures against radical nationalist movements that sought power through forceful means—the Labour Party in Kenya and Malaya, the SFIO in Algeria. For both parties, an easing of the domestic political effects of the Cold War meant that colonial questions could be considered more easily apart from the overall international and military balance; a Communist threat made decolonization more difficult to countenance, as the Socialists had discovered in Indochina and the Labour Party in British Guiana.

The temporary bipolarity that had appeared in both political systems disappeared after 1956, however, as the two left-wing parties diverged once again. As the Labour Party resolved its last doubts about the future of the settler colonies in Africa and sharpened its opposition to the Conservatives' informal empire in the Middle East, French Socialists instituted grants of autonomy or independence in sub-Saharan Africa, Morocco and Tunisia, while turning to repression in Algeria and intervention at Suez. After the British Guiana episode, which temporarily divided the Labour Party between the trade unions and a newly active anti-colonial Left, the Labour leadership found in decolonization a rare point of unity in a time of division. The gains to be made organizationally, among the party rank and file, seemed greater than any potential losses among the electorate.

Guy Mollet and the leadership of the SFIO reversed these calculations. Internal party dynamics provided no strong impulse for resisting the decolonization of Algeria, although settler representatives and a vocal nationalist Right, absent from the Labour Party, did oppose party liberals. Attachment to anti-colonialism proved to be weak as well, however, and the leadership could turn to a policy of force without the danger of division that might have threatened the Labour Party in similar circumstances. When rupture finally came, Algerian dissent had been swelled by opposition to the new Gaullist constitution. Mollet's success in countering voice within the Socialist Party was owed to aspects of the party that had enabled the British Conservatives to *decolonize* without rupture, as well as to some that were unique to the Socialist case. Institutionalization and the instinctive loyalty that it engendered—producing a barrier to exit and voice—enabled the leadership to deepen France's military involvement in Algeria untroubled by its opponents within. The incentive structure of the party had been altered after 1946 to emphasize purposive incentives, as the party's personnel, with its heavy weight of political experience, indicated. Even more than the British Conservatives, however, Mollet had internal weapons to channel dissent into easily controlled arenas and to prevent cross-party alliances by the supporters of decolonization. Ironically, those instruments had been awarded the leadership because of the disastrous effects of another international shock—German rearmament and aggression in the 1930s—on the SFIO.

Two sorts of *direct* avenues can be discerned in the pattern of linkage politics during decolonization: transmission of the attitudes of firms and the programs of colonial populations into the metropolitan political arena, through interest group and parliamentary channels, and the reaction of the state itself to changes in the colonial empires.

In the French colonial system, an enlarged role for the state, a heavier layer of protection from the world market, and a slower pace of economic development on the periphery combined to shift the weight of French capitalism in the empire toward those sectors with relatively high political exposure. The second wave of economic penetration in Africa was more fully developed in the British Empire. Firms with characteristics that produced lower political exposure—larger scale, a more competitive international position, and, perhaps most important, a subsidiary relationship with metropolitan enterprise—had begun to crack the political dominance of earlier economic actors, particularly settler agriculture. France's North African territories displayed similar variation, but only Morocco had enjoyed substantial economic growth based on manufacturing and services. The Algerian economy represented the opposite pole, with its heavily protected agricultural sector (wine and grain) and a market so open to metropolitan exports of manufactures that the growth of indigenous industrial production was stunted. Patterns of economic development influenced perceptions of the political future in the empires as well. Kenya and Morocco produced a relatively conservative nationalist elite willing to preserve the essential outlines of the existing political economy; Algeria's FLN, however, represented a more radical and threatening alternative.

Perceptions of political exposure, which biased firms against political change or induced them to acquiesce in it, had to be transmitted to metropolitan politics if policy were to be affected. The old forms of political penetration and influence became less and less successful in a new political climate. Both the Joint East and Central Africa Board and the Comité central de la France d'Outre-mer whose political repertoires dated to the era of high imperialism, saw their hold on policy disintegrate along with their monopoly in representing colonial economic interests. Not only had the opponents of colonial rule now mobilized, firms also had many other channels of influence, particularly those companies with a subsidiary link to a parent firm. The ability to influence was further weakened by the growing heterogeneity of their clientele, particularly in British Africa. And the political elites of Britain and France, whatever their balancing of costs and benefits in the harsh economic circumstances of the 1930s and 1940s, made different calculations of national interest in the decade that followed. The international system of depression and war that had produced a concentration upon the colonial link began to disappear. As France started its latest and most prolonged period of industrialization and Britain enjoyed high growth rates, the metropolitan economies simply outstripped the ossified set of colonial relations. As the costs of coercion rose, the empires came to seem not only superfluous to national economic well-being, but positively detrimental to a global orientation in external economic relations. Economic growth meant that the old mercantilist pattern of economic relations lost their base of support in the metropolis, reducing in turn the resources available to those attempting to resist the economic trends through political means, a cycle of decline that doomed those irreversibly attached to the colonial status quo.

The state also reduced the ability of economic interests to resist in another way. Even in the more protected and state-centered French system, new state roles undertaken in the colonial empire after World War II served to reduce political exposure and to increase, particularly through public investment, the leverage that the state had over economic activity on the periphery. But the state was not always a neutral arbiter in the process of decolonization. A final contrast between the French and British patterns lies in the ability of the French state to thwart the implementation of metropolitan decisions on the periphery and involve itself actively in the process of decision itself. The state *itself* could serve as a transmission belt for the political shocks of decolonization, a role dramatized by the threat of paratroops descending on Paris in May, 1958. While the British elite could, by and large, rely upon a colonial administration closely tied to the metropolitan political context, French cabinets, even when they were able to send clear signals to the administration, would often find that it had been captured by the periphery. Military and civilian bureaucracies were adept at playing politics in Paris, as were the European settlers, undercutting the abilities of successive governments to impose a clear political line for decolonization. Such obstruction, however, even in the most severe instance of Algeria, was finally undermined by the absence of a firm alliance between the European population and the military, the lack of a feasible colonial political program (apart from continued military repression), and the political mobilization of the settlers, which *severed* their ties to metropolitan politics, while, at the same time, increasing their capacity to resist. The British state did not face the threat of such a state-settler alliance, since the military were never so deeply engaged in the politics of colonial rule. Their dilemma lay elsewhere: in conceding the means of coercion to the settlers of Central Africa, their state remained intact, but the settlers *could* produce an alternative to decolonization—the seizure of power by a minority regime.

The domestic political consequences described *did* have an effect in turn on the course of decolonization and the content of colonial policy. The indirect hold that the empires exercised through the political parties in both countries raised the potential political costs during disengagement. In the French case, parties fragmented, preventing the formation of coherent governing majorities (as in the final ministries of the Fourth Republic) or sought to preserve their unity by withdrawing support from decolonizing ministries (the pattern of Gaullist behavior during Moroccan decolonization). Attachment to empire had an even more damaging effect on the domestic political regime after 1956. The Gaullists amplified the strain that the Algerian War placed on the Fourth Republic not only in the Assembly, where Jacques Soustelle brought down governments, but also outside the parliament, where Michel Debré and others tightened the connection between the fate of Algeria and the legitimacy of the regime. Although the consequences were not so grave, the British Conservative leadership took into account resistance to decolonization among the party's parliamentary membership and its rank and file. The result was hesitation over Britain's economic links to Europe, a continued attachment to a British role in the Middle East and east of Suez, and a pattern of small retreats during the decolonization of Africa.

On the left, decolonization had an impact as well, but the costs were imposed for *not* disengaging. The strategy adopted by the Labour Party, one of unified and distanced opposition to colonialism, speeded decolonization and preserved the party. Although the Algerian War split the Socialist Party, Mollet managed to sustain the party's electoral support through the changes of the first years of the Fifth Republic. The consequences for decolonization in his "success," however, had been a further blow to the legitimacy of the political regime that the party had helped to found and longer term erosion in Socialist support.

The direct means by which the empires intervened in metropolitan politics also affected the shape of colonial policy. If decolonization proceeded too swiftly, balky economic interests could threaten the metropolitan government with chaos on the periphery; acquiescence by those interests could give a shaky government another valuable card to play against its opponents. Business groups could also act more directly: the best documented cases are the contributions made to "moderate" African parties by British firms in East Africa and the alliance between the Joint Board's leadership and other opponents of Macmillan's accelerated decolonization in 1960-1962. Finally, the resistance of the French state presented Fourth Republic governments with *faits accomplis* that could halt progress toward decolonization. The most dramatic examples were the deposition of the Moroccan sultan in August, 1953 and the seizure of the FLN leaders in October, 1956. Alternatively, actors on the periphery, settlers, or bureaucracy, could ally themselves with domestic political opponents of decolonization. Roy Welensky and successive Moroccan proconsuls are the best illustrations, not only adding obstacles but also directing an additional political threat against a decolonizing government.

SUPPLEMENTARY AND ALTERNATIVE EXPLANATIONS

What has been presented here is admittedly only one perspective, a particular angle of vision on decolonization that attempts to explain important differences in these national cases: domestic political consequences that resulted from change (or threatened change) in a particular set of international relations altered the course of policy toward the empires during the years of disengagement. This viewpoint must, however, be weighed more systematically against other explanations for the contrasting courses of British and French, both those that supplement and strengthen the account given here and those that claim to offer alternatives.

Some French political formations have been omitted, particularly the Communists, mentioned in Chapter III, and the Center parties, the Radicals and the MRP. Both deserve full-scale studies of their own, since two of these groups, the Communists and the Radicals, provide additional evidence of the ways in which international change can place strains on party structures. In the Communist case strain came less from the South—the colonial empires—than from the East—the process of de-Stalinization and Soviet intervention in Hungary—which cost the party considerable intellectual and electoral support. The Radicals were another casualty of decolonization: after the war, as described in Chapter V, the Neo-Radicals turned the party toward economic conservatism and support for North African settlers. The ascendancy of Mendès-France deepened the divisions within the party, particularly on colonial questions. Of the omitted groups, only the MRP was spared the consequences of international change in France's penetrated society; Bidault alone among its leaders persevered in a die-hard colonialist posture. None of these cases, however, contradicts the approach taken here or the argument that the domestic consequences of international politics were important in explaining outcomes.

Another set of explanations also reinforces the general argument. At least two international actors pressed for an end to colonialism; they served as external allies to the domestic opponents of imperialism and were figured into the internal political calculus. Often self-interested, the role of the United States in urging decolonization has been well-documented for the war and immediate postwar years, particularly American relations with the declining hegemonial power, Britain.[1] British and French economic dependence upon the United States gave the alliance leader considerable leverage over the survival of the colonial empires. Nevertheless, American interests were framed principally to favor the dismantling of imperial barriers to freer trade and the end of discriminatory currency blocs. Persistent economic weakness and the onset of the Cold War further tempered American anti-colonialism, since some efforts to resist decolonization fitted the anti-communist strategy of the United States. Growing American support for French military efforts in Indochina was the most prominent example.

[1] Richard N. Gardner's *Sterling-Dollar Diplomacy* (Oxford: Clarendon Press, 1956) was cited in Chapter II; Gabriel Kolko offers a revisionist view of inter-alliance relations in *The Politics of War* (New York: Vintage Books, 1968), especially chaps. 12 and 19; also Christopher Thorne, *Allies of a Kind: The United States, Britain, and the War against Japan, 1941-1945* (London: Oxford University Press, 1978); William Roger Louis, *Imperialism at Bay* (New York: Oxford University Press, 1978).

In the 1950s a more critical American attitude reemerged. In Britain, the political elite, particularly the Right of the Labour Party and the Center and Left of the Conservative Party, was sensitive to opinion across the Atlantic. (The more ideologically committed wings of both parties were far more anti-American, though for different reasons.) French alliance relations with the United States were less close, and, though the record has yet to be examined fully, the pressures exerted by the United States seemed to be less effective. American actions during Suez could force a turn in the British government's policy and provide useful ammunition to the Labour opposition; in France, political gains could be made on both the Right and the Left by *resisting* the importunity of the North American ally: the Fourth Republic's final crisis was opened by an Anglo-American offer to intercede in France's dispute with Tunisia.

A second international actor also influenced metropolitan politics, though seldom with the same effect as the United States. The United Nations, increasingly attuned to the views of the newly independent and non-aligned nations, publicly pressed for accelerated decolonization. Very different receptions were offered to such expressions of international opposition or condemnation in the cases of Britain and France. International organization has never been a favored panacea of the French political elite, particularly in the sphere of security; little devotion was expressed to the League of Nations or the United Nations, although more hope has been placed in organizations with limited aspirations, such as the European Community. For the British Labour and Liberal parties, however, an attachment to international organization has long been an article of faith. The call of the Labour Party for recourse to the United Nations destroyed an initial political consensus in Britain during the Suez crisis. This domestic audience for the views of the United Nations and the nonaligned countries (many of them members of the Commonwealth) made at least a part of the British polity sensitive to international opinion.

Incomparability

Arguments of incomparability are not alternative explanations; they simply reject any effort to generalize from a comparison of these two national cases of decolonization. One such argument suggests that different models for colonial rule and the eventual transfer of power, particularly the availability of the dominion models as a template for postwar policy in Britain, provides the best single explanation for differences in the course of decolonization. The advantages that the dominion model offered to British Conservatives in critical cases such as India were noted above; the hedges, however, were not. As Tomlinson notes, in the 1920s and 1930s, dominion status foreseen for India was never quite the same as that envisaged for the "white" Dominions; dominion status was only acceptable "so long as India's commercial, currency and military policy options were predetermined by other influences over which British interests had the whip hand."[2] Recent evidence on official resistance to Labour's postwar plans for East Africa suggests that the level of conservatism was high, and that the dominion model was not viewed as immediately applicable.[3] In other words, the British "model" was much closer to the French model endorsed by the Gaullists and others than to complete independence. India was in any case a relatively clear-cut case; its future was never to be the same as that of the colonies of settlement. In Africa, however, the future was more ambiguous. The Central African Federation, at least, aspired to eventual dominion status. In this case, the dominion model cut against decolonization based on majority rule, as it had earlier in South Africa.

French historical experience provides a second argument for the incomparability of these cases of decolonization: occupation and defeat in World War II necessarily made France more sensitive and resistant to decolonization. Such an ar-

[2] B. R. Tomlinson, *The Political Economy of the Raj, 1914-1947* (London: Macmillan, 1979), p. 145.

[3] John W. Cell, "On the Eve of Decolonization: the Colonial Office's Plans for the Transfer of Power in Africa, 1947," *Journal of Imperial and Commonwealth History* 8 (May, 1980), 235-257.

gument fits well with a theoretical approach based upon the domestic consequences of international relations, but when stated in such general form, applied to the whole of French postwar experience, the argument is hard to credit. Taken to its logical conclusion, such an argument would have predicted that France could not decolonize (in this respect, it resembles the colonial consensus argument described below), but, in fact, France did. The internal effects of war and resistance were concentrated in French society—the Gaullists in particular epitomized the "nationalization" of French politics that resulted from the war. In other political groups, such as the SFIO, only a fraction of the party took a firm nationalist position. As the SFIO case also demonstrates, nationalization was less than complete and less than perfectly related to resistance to decolonization: *opposition* to the Algerian War was also led by Resistance leaders such as Daniel Mayer and Edouard Depreux. Nationalist sentiment seemed to fade over time: all of the parties were willing to trumpet their attachment to *la plus grande France* after Liberation, but differences among the parties grew from the late 1940s, as traditional ideologies reasserted their hold.

If French wartime experience cannot be used to explain all or most of the contrast between French and British decolonization, a final variant of the incomparability argument centers, not on historical distinctions, but on the cases chosen. Algeria is taken as a special case, not to be likened to any British colony, with the possible exception of Ireland. One theme of this study has run directly counter to this argument: that French decolonization should not be viewed solely through the lens of Algeria and the failure that the Algerian conflict represents for many French. Even in the terms of this analysis, Algeria was bound to be a difficult case of decolonization: its indirect effects upon the logic of party competition were the greatest; the direct impact was large, since access to metropolitan politics was less restricted for a territory that was juridically part of France itself. Despite the legal fiction, however, until 1956, both the opponents and the proponents of decolonization regarded North Africa as a bloc. The election campaign of December, 1955 was not fought in the hysterical rhetoric of French Algeria that would later become dominant; as discussions in the Socialist parliamentary group (Chapter III) and the responses of French firms (Chapter IV) indicate, Algerian decolonization was not regarded as inconceivable. The raw materials for an attachment to French Algeria existed, but Algeria was in large measure a *created* special case. The assertion of the integrationist position in its extreme form came with the acceleration of the military conflict after 1956 and campaigns by *Algérie française* activists in the metropolis.

Few of these challenges to the comparison of Britain and France are convincing, though some could be incorporated in the frame of analysis employed in this study. More important are the *alternative* explanations that have been advanced for the contrasting patterns of decolonization in Britain and France.

The impossible coalitions

Alfred Grosser has advanced an appealing explanation for the immobilism of French policy based on multiple divisions within the French political spectrum. Grosser argues that a decolonization majority on the Left was rendered impossible by the Cold War. To decolonize required the Communists; to defend liberal democracy against the Communists required a majority that refused decolonization. As Grosser points out, in contrast to France, Italy had no colonies after the war, and Britain had no Communist electorate.[4] (A secondary effect, not described by Grosser, was the dilemma that a dominant Communist party posed for the Socialists, described in Chapter III.)

Grosser's argument fails on two counts. First, in 1954 and 1955, parliamentary coalitions were constructed, with some difficulty, that were able to take important steps in decolonization. Despite Gaullist mythology about the Fourth Republic, the Mendès-France and Faure cabinets demonstrate that a political base for liberal policies could be found. A

---

[4] Alfred Grosser, *La IVᵉ République et sa politique extérieure* (Paris: Armand Colin, 1961), p. 398.

"Mendès-France coalition," which relied upon the Gaullists for necessary right-wing support, became impossible after Gaullist setbacks in the 1956 elections. The hostility of the MRP toward Mendès-France on the question of Europe, excluding a group with increasingly liberal attitudes on colonial questions, was another weakness in this possible coalition. More likely after 1954 was a "Faure coalition," but the votes on Moroccan decolonization in October, 1955 illustrated its drawbacks: support from the Socialists or Communists for a coalition so conservative on social and economic issues was unlikely; their votes in 1955 were given to a motion that approved the outcome in Morocco without approving the government's general policy.

Although both coalitions became far more difficult to construct in the Third Legislature of the Fourth Republic, the critical changes were those that took place *within* each potential coalition. On the Left, the Socialist Party turned from conciliation toward repression in Algeria. Partly as a result of the Algerian conflict, the Radical Party disintegrated, leaving Mendès-France without a significant base of political power. Grosser's argument implies that decolonization in Britain was carried out by the *Left*; in fact, although the Labour Party's position was helpful, decolonization was largely accomplished by a conservative party that could decolonize itself. Its French analogues could not, until de Gaulle returned to power; the greatest barrier to any decolonizing coalition lay in that continuing attachment to empire among French conservatives.

Public opinion and the colonial consensus

In Chapter III, Tony Smith's argument that French colonial policy was based upon an unchanging colonial consensus was questioned in light of variation in the Socialist Party's record on colonial policy. Although every party, except the Communists, did have defenders of empire among its leaders (Lejeune and Lacoste in the Socialist Party, Bidault in the MRP, Morice in the Radicals, and many on the Right), the balance shifted away from the nationalists as one moved to the Left of the political spectrum. Any argument for a colonial consensus also runs against evidence of French public opinion toward the colonial empire. That data suggests that even Algeria was not an object of intense attachment on the part of the French population. On the question of the future status of Algeria, nearly half of the French population at the time of the 1956 elections preferred its continued status as a department of France; by mid-1956, however, after a dramatic leap in salience (Algeria became the "most important problem for France" for 63 percent of the population), those surveyed chose negotiations with the rebels rather than military repression when given a simple choice. Even after Suez, when a hardening of support for integration occurred, the proportion willing to accept looser ties also grew: by July, 1957, 52 percent of those surveyed chose to give Algeria either considerable internal autonomy or complete independence; 36 percent opted for integration with France.[5] In the best analysis of the public opinion data, Charles-Robert Ageron notes that the perceived support for a revival of nationalism after 1956 was not evident among the public at large. There, apathy and underlying pacifism colored attitudes toward the use of force in Algeria.[6]

Although arguments for an unchanging consensus against decolonization cannot be sustained, the concept of a colonial consensus is consistent with the thesis presented here if interpreted more narrowly. At the level of the political class a greater degree of consensus did appear, particularly during the "Third Force" period of 1947-1951, and again after 1956. As Duncan Macrae remarks, while the parties were pulled away from governing coalitions by their followers, the governments that succeeded one another suffered from "an excess of somewhat misplaced consensus": "The function of a responsible opposition—proposing an alternative policy and providing an alternative set of persons to carry it out—was

[5] *Sondages*, no. 3 (1955), pp. 20-21; no. 2 (1957), p. 41.
[6] Charles-Robert Ageron, "L'Opinion française devant la guerre d'Algérie," *Revue française d'histoire d'outre-mer* 63 (1976), 256-285.

missing."[7] As Macrae notes, however, the system did approach such a model during the Second Legislature, with the investiture of Pinay and later of Mendès-France. As the closest approach to a British pattern of competition, these were also the years of greatest achievement in French decolonization. Thus, consensus, colonial or otherwise, did seem to produce immobilism in the face of colonial nationalism, while division produced movement. Unfortunately, division also made the task of constructing a parliamentary majority more difficult in an Assembly constricted by Communist Left and a Gaullist or Poujadist Right.

Economic structure

An explanation of decolonization based entirely on changes in the colonial economic structure was rejected in Chapter IV, but the choice between models in the metropolis was hedged: the political elite had some flexibility in interpreting the external orientation of the economy, and, whether consciously or not, used that margin of flexibility to erode the economic weight and political influence of those sectors in the economy that were most attached to a colonial orientation. Was there a closer connection between changes in political organization and strategy and those economic coalitions within France? Certainly party position was not divorced from evolving perceptions of economic self-interest: it is at least plausible that the *modérés'* willingness to support Moroccan decolonization was influenced by a shift toward acquiescence among French business interests in the protectorate; a possible link between Vosges textile interests and the campaign of Pierre Poujade may have found expression in the campaign rhetoric of the Poujadist movement.

Given its role in the final decolonization of Algeria and its dominance in the Fifth Republic, a more significant case is Gaullism. One explanation for the final episodes of decolonization could be the support that the UNR found in those

[7] Duncan Macrae, Jr., *Parliament, Parties and Society in France, 1946-1958* (New York: St. Martin's Press, 1967), p. 225.

sectors of a rapidly industrializing French economy that were not linked tightly to the colonial empire. The relationship between French business and Gaullism in the RPF years was a tenuous one. Like other groups, the *patronat* sought access to power, which the intransigent Gaullists could not offer until 1953; business also found the Gaullist notion of an activist state and its program of capital-labor association unpalatable.

By the mid-1950s, Chevrillon notes that business support for the Gaullist Social Republicans was severely reduced. The core of interests that remained as financial supporters of the movement does point toward support for decolonization rather than resistance to it.[8] Those firms most attached to Gaullism seem to be in technologically advanced sectors of the economy or in banking, two areas that were also characterized by substantial state involvement. For example, the dominant figure in the French aircraft industry, Marcel Dassault, was a long-time Gaullist supporter and eventually a UNR deputy; he would be sympathetic to Gaullist views on national autonomy and a modernized defense force. His banker, Albin Chalandon, was an Algerian "dove" who represented a principal target for the supporters of Jacques Soustelle as secretary general of the UNR. Other business support came from the director of Simca and a number of the largest chemical firms. The pattern suggests that business support for Gaullism resembled its geographic support; its strength lay in the dynamic sectors of French economy and society. These sectors were often intertwined with the state, but, apart from petroleum, they were seldom those most attached to the colonial empire.

Does this suggest that the decolonization of Algeria was simply the result of a redefinition of the interests of French capitalism, which found its expression in a revived Gaullist movement? Such an economic determinism, like that rejected in Chapter IV, omits the organizational struggles within Gaullism, which cannot be easily associated with any underlying

---

[8] Marie-France Chevrillon, "Les Républicains sociaux ou la traversée du désert, 1953-1958" (*Mémoire de maîtrise*, Institut d'Etudes Politiques, Paris), pp. 203-205; Henri Claude, *Gaullisme et grand capital* (Paris: Editions sociales, 1960).

pattern of interests. Political parties also played an independent role in defining the national economic interest, a process of aggregation that was not simply the addition of interests expressed by their supporters. Finally, the notion that a new economic coalition could dictate a change on the scale of the decolonization of Algeria underestimates the powerful resistance offered by the state and those economic interests threatened by change on the periphery. Still, in a sense, decolonization *was* the victory of "new France" over "old France," of European over colonial France. First *Mendèsisme*, and then Gaullism (the UNR) picked up the banner of a new nationalism based on French economic development and disengagement from empire. Unfortunately, like French economic development itself, that victory was halting and belated.

In addition to lending support to certain explanations for the contrasting courses of British and French decolonization and challenging other alternatives, this reexamination from the outside, which throws into relief the domestic effects of international change, has revealed a proportion of myth in the conventional wisdom about these events and cast doubt on some hoary precepts of political conduct. A number of Gaullist myths have been undermined: both Gaullist claims of consistent liberalism on colonial questions and Gaullist accusations of consistent failure in decolonization on part of the Fourth Republic and its parliamentary regime. The "system," despite its flaws, *was* capable of responding constructively to difficult international pressures. Had it not been so penetrated by those who sought its downfall, its performance might have been even more creditable.

Decolonization also punctures the adage that conservatives and nationalists are uniquely endowed to deal with international change; their capabilities may be highly dependent on internal organizational demands and the structure of domestic political competition. The comparative history of the Left suggests that attachment to ideology, often singled out by pragmatic Americans as the bane of European politics, in fact assisted in decolonizing the British Empire. Finally, the axiom that consensus is essential for a successful external policy must also be modified: the French political system demonstrated both too much consensus (from Center-Left to Center-Right during the Third Force and Algerian War years) and too little (leading to perverse competitive behavior, particularly on the Right).

THE DOMESTIC CONSEQUENCES OF INTERNATIONAL RELATIONS: TOWARD GENERALIZATION

A second task set in the Introduction was to begin the construction of a theory that would cover international-domestic linkages in the case of decolonization, and perhaps other cases as well. Existing accounts of the domestic consequences of international relations were criticized for remaining at the level of the society or the political regime. Here, the consequences of changes in international relations for political and economic actors below the level of the regime have been elaborated through four dynamics: that of organizational incentives and party competition, which can tie certain political organizations to their political environment; sensitivity to political change (political exposure) produced by the characteristics of firms; transmission of external shocks to the domestic polity by the state itself; and finally, the transformation of the politics of settler societies under external threat. Although several tentative generalizations can be advanced, the case of decolonization is more useful in pointing to avenues for additional research to help resolve the unanswered questions.

a) *Externally-induced political changes will not persist, unless they coincide with other preexisting social divisions (ethnic, class). International shocks may provide the opportunity for calling into question existing political alignments, however.*

Looking back on the experience of decolonization, the shape of British and French politics seems to have changed little, despite the divisions introduced at the time by external change. Although pessimists predicted the "Algerianization" of French politics, as terrified *pieds noirs* fled across the Mediterranean to France, the impact of the returning European settlers was slight. Their integration into French society, particularly in circumstances of economic prosperity in the 1960s, proceeded smoothly. Although they formed one electoral base for an anti-Gaullist extreme Right in the 1960s, the importance of that strand in French politics declined with the end of the Algerian War.[9] In both Britain and France, the post-colonial issue of race, already surfacing as colonial ties were challenged, remained to embitter metropolitan politics. Although post-colonial structures have survived at the international level—particularly in French relations with sub-Saharan Africa—in domestic politics, the empires seem to have disappeared with little trace.

Other external shocks or changes in international relations have also produced domestic alterations with short half-lives. The apparently deep fault between those who collaborated and those who resisted in France provides a supporting example. While many *Résistants* had hoped for a permanent realignment of French political life, the old boundaries soon reasserted themselves. Divisions within the Conservatives (between the Laniel and the Pinay factions) and between the Gaullists and the rest of the Right were based in part on Resistance records, but the split in Gaullist ranks and the investiture of Pinay signaled the fading of that division. Another international cleavage, the Cold War, had more persistent effects on French politics, largely because it overlapped the more powerful domestic division of class (reinforced by party).

Decolonization, however, was only weakly related to preexisting political divisions, although a certain Right-Left relationship could be detected. Disengagement from empire tended to split existing political formations, rather than reinforce the preexisting fissures as it did in Britain. Its last effects were

[9] Jane Kramer describes the state of the Europeans who returned to France from Algeria in *Unsettling Europe* (New York: Random House, 1980), pp. 171-217.

erased by the resurgence of traditional Left-Right conflict in 1968: de Gaulle's pardon of his old *Algérie française* opponents marked the end of a political epoch, just as the split in the RPF in 1952 had marked the close of another.

While the domestic political consequences of international politics rarely include permanent realignments, such external shocks may force into view dissatisfaction with the choices offered by the existing political structure. In at least two instances decolonization had such an effect. The Socialist opponents of Mollet during the Algerian War were in certain respects the ideological precursors of the new Socialist Party of the 1970s. The discontent that had erupted against the strategy and program of Mollet in the 1950s finally found organizational expression in the Parti socialiste unifié, which provided the New Left of the 1960s with many of its ideas, some of its leaders, (Michel Rocard, for example), though few of its electors. Decolonization was not the *basis* for the new Socialism, but it pushed the dissidents to give organizational expression to a deeper discontent with the old line. In Britain, the Monday Club posed a similar challenge to the leadership of the Conservative Party. Until the expansion of its membership during the fight against Labour's Rhodesian policy, the Monday Club had little influence on the course of African decolonization. Although it used the issue of support for the settlers to marshal financial and political support, the aims of the club's founders were far wider: it served as a center of fundamentalist opposition to the "Macmillan consensus" within the party, voicing the belief that the party was straying from the principles of Conservative ideology. Its combination of laissez-faire economic policies and a reassertion of the nationalism of "kith and kin" in external affairs soon became a force in the Conservative Party, and, with the election of Margaret Thatcher as leader, one of the dominant strands in Conservative ideology.

b) *Sensitivity to international politics can be produced by the organizational strategies of actors in the domestic political system; the "raw material" for their activities is often provided by previous external shocks or by the existing international environment.*

The political sensitivity of societies to changes in their international environments results in part from the traces left by previous intrusions of the external, but the persistence of those traces and amplification of the effects of any future international changes often results from strategies pursued by domestic political organizations. The link developed in Chapters II and III is one between the ideological incentives demanded for organizational maintenance and a particular set of international relations or foreign policies; other models, such as those based on ethnic ties, could produce similar results.

Creation and maintenance of sensitivity to the international environment can have important effects on political regimes through the route of subregime political actors. For the political parties examined above, the effects were two. First, the sensitivity of political parties to the changes implied in decolonization made their ability to mobilize the necessary power for carrying out the process doubtful; the sources of government support withered as change threatened externally. A more direct effect on the regime in France was a part of the Gaullist strategy (reminiscent of nationalist parties in the Weimar Republic): linking the internal legitimacy of the regime to its external performance, particularly the preservation of the French empire. Thus, the regime was not only saddled with ineffectual parties, but was itself attacked as it attempted to respond to international change.

The question of organizational strategy can be related to the persistence of externally induced cleavages within domestic politics, and further investigation could probably confirm that traces of external shocks will persist in those cases where organizations seek to keep them vital. That, in turn, leads to a more important question: why some organizations choose an external linkage as part of their domestic political strategy, particularly when control over the international environment is so much less certain than control over the domestic. In this regard, it is significant that, with a relative decline in the international weight of European societies, the degree of external political linkage (whether internationalism or pacifism on the Left or nationalist self-assertion on the Right) has also declined precipitously. Perceptions of international position, then, may influence the choice of external linkage.

c) *Boundaries defining participation in a political system are both permeable and variable over time. The penetration of domestic politics by external actors and their success in shaping policy is determined not only by access but by skill in constructing domestic political alliances. In times of rapid change in the rules of the political game, outside actors may be at a disadvantage in interpreting the requirements for success.*

These two liberal states exercised less control over their societies' transactions with the international environment than other, more closed societies, but access remained uneven and had to be won. In determining whether avenues of access were open, *nationalism*, so important in setting the boundaries of political membership, could be used to include or to exclude certain actors. The definition and redefinition of membership was made even more confused by the shifting criteria that nationalism set during these years. For colonial actors who directly participated in metropolitan politics, nationalism was a crucial weapon in keeping their rights of entry; nationalist appeals, in contrast to examples given in Chapter I, were *incorporating* rather than *exclusionary*.

Nationalism proved to be a fragile basis for secure participation in metropolitan politics, however. As empire and metropolis drew apart and the national self-image was defined anew, once-privileged insiders became suspect. Some, such as Sir Roy Welensky, were viewed as irritating intruders; others, if their opposition became more extreme, were condemned as traitors. To those who accepted the transition to a new, less extended France, the members of the OAS were simply terrorists; in their own eyes, the die-hard supporters of French Algeria were representatives of a tradition of resistance in the face of national betrayal.

Nationalism could serve to open the boundaries of participation in metropolitan politics, but success in influencing policy required domestic political allies (or compradors)—in political parties, interest groups, or the state itself—and an astute reading of the domestic political context. Some actors, such as subsidiaries of metropolitan firms, had automatic access and an ally in the form of the parent organization; others, such as the settlers, had to rely on constant and agile political performance to retain spokesmen in the metropolis. Even so, domestic political changes (such as the Mendèsist challenge in the Radical Party) could overturn longstanding ties, and colonial outsiders were often less able to detect changes that would affect the power that they could wield. As decolonization became an issue of national import and the arena of debate widened, the old pattern of quiet, behind-the-scenes influence that colonial actors relied upon crumbled. Here again, additional cases could illuminate why access to political systems changes over time. (The recent acceptance of lobbying by foreign governments within the American political process is an example of such a change.) Also, research should be directed to determining the reasons for choice of particular domestic allies on the part of external actors and the variation in political capabilities of such actors.

d) *The state serves not only as a gatekeeper between domestic politics and the international environment; it can also serve to transmit international shocks into the domestic arena.*
Certain parts of the state apparatus, such as the military, are particularly sensitive to external change, indeed, most societies *demand* such heightened sensitivity. Compared to civilian political actors, however, the military often define legitimacy to a greater degree in terms of external success. Unlike other externally sensitive parts of the state apparatus, such as the foreign or colonial ministries, the military has also had the means to change domestic political parameters. Two consequences follow. In certain circumstances of external change, the military may turn on the existing regime: colonial wars led two contemporary armies—the French and the Portuguese—to threaten the metropolitan regime during decolonization. But military regimes themselves are fragile in the face

of external failure: the de facto military regime in Germany in 1918, the Greek junta following the Turkish invasion of Cyprus in 1974, the Argentine military after the Falklands War—all are examples of surprising weakness after external shock. Although military regimes have been the subject of considerable attention from social scientists, the external dimension to military behavior—in inducing political activism and undermining military regimes—has not received the attention that it deserves.

CONSEQUENCES FOR THE STUDY OF INTERNATIONAL POLITICS

At the outset of this study, two implications for the study of international relations were noted. The first was the addition of another dimension to the analysis of foreign policy: rather than treating foreign policy as state-centered and its sources as wholly endogenous, the impact of external events and actors on those determinants would have to be assessed. Such an expansion would have more than theoretical interest. Alexander George and Richard Smoke, for example, have argued in favor of a general theory of influence to replace the prescriptions of an overly simplified deterrence theory that has dominated postwar American foreign policy.[10] Any such theory of influence would necessarily include some notion of the consequences of efforts on the part of states to affect other states *through* their societies.

Certain contemporary foreign policy debates center precisely on questions of assessing the domestic effects of external actors. Arguments about American policy toward South Africa tend to revolve fruitlessly around the question of whether "hard" line of pressure or a "soft" line of "constructive engagement" will be more successful. The argument cannot be resolved without a clearer estimate of whether this particular fragment society will respond to proposed external pressure

[10] Alexander L. George and Richard Smoke, *Deterrence in American Foreign Policy* (New York: Columbia University Press, 1974), chap. 21.

with a response of increased solidarity and resistance, or fragmentation and potential change. A subsidiary argument within the debate concerns direct external influence through foreign corporations acting as instruments of change. Here the question is one of what limits could they reach (assuming a willingness to serve as such instruments) before access to the South African economy would be denied.

A second case, peacemaking in the Middle East, increasingly revolves around similar questions, close to those of decolonization. Israel faces a situation of small-scale, but potentially traumatic decolonization in dealing with the future of the West Bank. Even the actors are roughly the same—a fragmented party system, militant settlers, an army with political tasks, and an external ally with its own strategic aims for the region.[11]

Other debates, riddled with clichés, could be investigated more precisely by looking more closely at the international-domestic linkage that is specified. The threat of "finlandization" in Western Europe seems to be defined by crude perceptions of European societies as supine rather than resistant. A credible argument about finlandization would rest on an examination of the ways in which Soviet pressure or military presence could be exerted to influence *internal* politics and produce acquiescence to Soviet wishes.

A final contemporary example concerns, not a conscious policy of influence, but the manner in which bureaucratized and organizationally determined decisions, such as those on weapons development, can effect the domestic politics and ultimately the foreign policies of other states. The present controversy over theater nuclear forces in Europe has been repeatedly shaped by American decisions (such as that to produce the neutron bomb) and declarations (such as those regarding limited nuclear war) which have been taken without attention to the intricacies of European political reactions. In

[11] Ian Lustick has drawn specific parallels with decolonization in "Considering the West Bank from Ireland and Algeria," *Moment* 7 (June, 1982), 19-24.

each of these cases, certain aspects of the history of decolonization could provide useful analogies: the impact of external events on political parties in the case of American weapons decisions; the manner in which indirect external changes enter the domestic political system (in this case the growth of Soviet military power), and the dynamics of threatened settler societies—South Africa could, in fact, be considered a case of delayed decolonization.

The domestic consequences of international relations also points to a second implication that goes beyond expanding conventional foreign policy analysis. It presents a paradigm or agenda for research that stands in contrast to the foreign policy model, as well as adding to it, one that has been labeled, for want of a better term, *structural.*

A structural perspective necessarily implies attention to the domestic consequences of international relations. In contrast to variants of the decision-making paradigm, foreign policy is not regarded as simply decision or even output, but, when viewed from the outside, as an *orientation*—a bundle of policies or a strategy—or, when viewed from the inside, as an *investment*—with a decided impact on domestic society. A second contrast to conventional foreign policy analysis, as these terms suggest, is examination of a longer slice of time; the dependent variable is less likely to be a discrete outcome than a *pattern* of outcomes. In contrast to a transactions model of international relations, a structural point of view analyzes not only the flows of trade, influence, and other elements of international relations across national boundaries, but also the ways in which those flows are embedded in societies, the attachments, often difficult to change, that are built up over time. Finally, as described above, there is greater attention to the feedback dimension of foreign policy and the manner in which the international affects the domestic determinants of foreign policy, as well as to the *costs* of foreign policy.

Certainly the account of relations between Britain and France and their empires qualifies as structural in the first sense of the "weak" definition given in Chapter I: emphasizing the relatively unchanging features of this particular set of relations, often embedded over a long period of time in the respective societies. The contrasting paths of economic and political development in the two European societies shaped the creation of these ties and their final demise. In France, industrialization before 1945 had occurred in fits and starts, failing to produce the highly organized and politically unified working class characteristic of Britain in the twentieth century.[12] The resulting fragmentation, on Right and Left in France, in contrast to the bipolar, class-based party system produced by Britain's rapid and complete industrialization, contributed to the relative ease of British decolonization. The clear divide in the British political system not only aided the decolonization of the Right and confirmed the anti-colonialism of the Left; it speeded the process of decolonization by providing an alternative route of access for colonial nationalists and a clear alternative government that could serve as a bargaining counter or tacit participant in negotiations between government and nationalists. France in the Fourth Republic, with its multiple political divides, offered a setting for competition on the Left and the Right, pushing parties toward an acceptance and even affirmation of the colonial status quo.

In producing contrasting party structures *internally*, the differences in British and French economic development affected the structural hold that the empires could exercise indirectly on the two European societies. The external dimension of their respective patterns of economic development shaped the *direct* impact of the empires even more. Not only did the French economy industrialize in fits and starts, it also lacked that outward dynamism, in the export of goods, capital, and population, that characterized its European rivals. The relative weakness of French international economic expansion, combined with France's beleaguered strategic position in Europe (and the perception of the empire as a strategic asset) resulted in a state-led strategy of colonial expansion and consolidation.

[12] On the pattern of French economic development and its external concomitants, François Caron, *An Economic History of Modern France* (London: Methuen & Co., Ltd., 1979), chap. 5.

In this respect, the two empires, and their manner of penetrating the metropolis, had differed from the start:

Comparatively, France lacked the colonists, overseas merchants, and investors to emulate the British kind of empire; but it was comparatively strong in the military and cultural resources for expansion. If the French were to build an empire at all, it had to be the kind of empire they could build. Throughout the century, France's typical imperial agents had been soldiers, technicians, and teachers rather than merchants and colonists: the exportable surplus of its standing army and efficient education, not those of its economy.[13]

Because of the strength of British overseas expansion, self-sustaining colonies could develop and the role of the metropolitan state was reduced. French overseas economic and demographic expansion was far weaker; despite an increased role for the state administration and the military, the empire that was constructed embedded itself more deeply in the metropolitan society; centralization implied that change would find its way to the center. Fearful for its possessions in a world of more economically advanced powers, facing strong movements of resistance in North and West Africa, the French *reinforced* the ties that bound empire to metropolis. Dependent development was the only form possible, but such an empire, despite its dependency, would prove more difficult to decolonize.

A second structural contrast also influenced the course of decolonization: the coincidence or separation of empires of prestige and empires of interest. For France, the loss of North Africa meant not only economic adjustment and hardship for the European populations, independence for those territories was perceived by some as the end of France as a great power. The empire of interests and the empire of prestige overlapped for the British Conservative elite only in the Middle East; decolonization in Africa, while touching ties to kith and kin, was not opposed on grounds of national status.

[13] Ronald E. Robinson, "Introduction," in Henri Brunschwig, *French Colonialism, 1871-1914: Myths and Realities* (New York: Frederick A. Praeger, 1964), p. ix.

Structural portraits of the two empires and the two European nations are in a sense mirror images: opposition to change in the British case was reduced by the diversity of the British Empire—the differing ideological holds of the Empire upon the Conservative party; the different estimates of political exposure perceived by economic interests; the representation, at least indirectly, of both settler and African populations in the metropolis through a political party resistant to fragmentation. In the French case, however, the *metropolis* was fragmented, Right and Left; the hold of the empire was not polarized but distributed more evenly across the political spectrum. The empire itself, on the other hand, appeared solidary: a high threat perceived by the European populations, the exclusion of the Arab populations from French political life, the alliance between settlers and the colonial state. Metropolitan divisions permitted the direct penetration of French politics by the representatives of empire and encouraged competition among political actors to strengthen the colonial attachment.

Although the study has employed a structural approach in the first sense of that term—emphasizing the persistent or relatively fixed features of a set of relations—it has departed from other structural models, such as dependency theory, in emphasizing that the structures tying together center and periphery, so deeply rooted in the histories of those respective societies, crumbled very quickly. What has been added is a dynamic quality to the structural perspective, pointing to the manner in which both resistance from the dominated populations, who often could not gain access to metropolitan politics, and changes in the European societies rendered the colonial system superfluous or even onerous. Too often structural accounts are static—concerned only with the "nouns" of a particular set of relations. Examining the case of decolonization and the linkings and detachments of societies that it includes, the cross-penetration and expulsion of external actors, adds the "verbs" that had been missing.

A structural perspective also produces standards of collective and individual judgment in international relations that differ from those in competing models. At least one measure of "success" in decolonization employed here derives from the structural point of view: minimizing the domestic effects of decolonization. Such a standard should be used with care, however. Although the immediate effects of decolonization may have been more severe for the French polity, divestment was more complete when it occurred. There were few analogues to the lingering imperial dreams of Britain, which proved to be so costly—the defense of sterling or a military presence east of Suez. "Success" in the British case also meant *externalizing* the costs of failure to decolonize: many of the most troublesome contemporary instances of conflict in the Third World—Palestine, southern Africa, even Ireland—are legacies of British decolonization. Britain was spared, but the world still lives with the consequences, which are not borne by British society.

The question of the judgment of individual action is complicated by the second aspect of a structural account—the avoidance of voluntaristic or subjective modes of explanation. Decolonization gave rise to "outcomes neither fully foreseen nor intended by—nor perfectly serving the interests of—any of the particular groups involved."[14] This structural portrait may seem unsatisfying or troubling to many, for it suggests a less certain control by actors over the course of events and a less certain responsibility for outcomes. Those who take a structural perspective, looking at the choices of individuals, often regard the choices of those who lost in such great historical changes as immoral or blind.[15] Bernard Bailyn, biog-

---

[14] Theda Skocpol, *States and Social Revolutions* (Cambridge: Cambridge University Press, 1979), p. 18.

[15] The first is the perspective of Albert Memmi, in *The Colonizer and the Colonized* (Boston: Beacon Press, 1965). Braudel verges on the second in some instances, as in the "paradox . . . that the true man of action is he who can measure most nearly the constraints upon him, who chooses to remain within them and even to take advantage of the weight of the inevitable, exerting his own pressure in the same direction. All efforts against the prevailing tide of history—which is not always obvious—are doomed to failure." *The Mediterranean and the Mediterranean World in the Age of Philip II*, Volume II, (London: Collins, 1973), pp. 1243-1244. How modest to admit

rapher of Thomas Hutchinson, an early casualty of decolonization, urges a tragic interpretation of history instead of such
heroic or Whig versions.[16] We are too close to the end of the
colonial empires, and too attuned to the moral concerns involved, to be capable of such a genuinely tragic view. We are
all Whigs in that our gods (in Max Weber's terms) include
national self-determination and freedom from alien domination. Still, we must be prepared to admit that men making
choices in such times, when once stable structures are being
shaken and overthrown, push Weber's ethics of responsibility to its limits. As Merleau-Ponty, writing of another
historical cataclysm, noted: "To govern, it has been said, is
to foresee, and the politician cannot excuse himself for what
he has not foreseen. Yet, there is always the unforeseeable.
There is the tragedy."[17] The individual choices made during
decolonization were of the most difficult sort—reading the
course of history and deciding whether to resist it or to ac-
commodate oneself to it. So much was unclear, and so many
were unwilling—after resisting another set of "inevitable" events
in the 1930s—to let go a place in the world and the particular
structures that guaranteed that place, even at the cost of great
violence. Some—Churchill, Eden, de Gaulle, Mollet—who had
led the resistance in the 1930s and 1940s, later misread the
national course on decolonization. Others, such as Daniel
Mayer and the Socialist dissenters, had also resisted yet read
the colonial future more clearly; punished politically, they
were eventually vindicated. The gamble was most difficult, as
Alfred Grosser notes, for nations such as these, declining in
influence, but the question of accommodation or resistance
remains open for all nations.

And so structure returns us to *drame*. Almost exactly twenty
years after France had conceded Algeria its independence, a

---

that the "tide of history" is not always evident to those attempting to swim
in it!

[16] Bernard Bailyn, *The Ordeal of Thomas Hutchinson* (Cambridge: Harvard University Press, 1974), p. ix.

[17] Maurice Merleau-Ponty, *Humanism and Terror* (Boston: Beacon Press,
1969), p. xxxiii.

mass grave containing the remains of more than one thousand individuals was discovered at Khenchela in the Aures where the Algerian revolt had begun. Despite the concern of Algerian authorities not to mar their anniversary celebrations, the cry was raised, "Who was responsible?" Like a bad dream, the old accounts of French atrocities surfaced, as well as those committed by the FLN against its domestic opponents and French collaborators. The question of individual culpability must always concern the scholar and the citizen. Many innocents died as new states were born. As our distance from the events grows, however, and our perspective lengthens, perhaps we will come to ask, not who was responsible, but how did this violence come to be?

BIBLIOGRAPHY

Party documents and publications

GAULLISM: LE RASSEMBLEMENT DU PEUPLE FRANÇAIS
Premières assises nationales. Marseilles, 16-17 April 1948. Speeches, reports, motions adopted.
Deuxième assises nationales. Lille, February, 1949. Speeches, reports, motions adopted.
Troisième assises nationales. Paris, 23-25 June 1950. Speeches, reports, motions adopted.
Quatrième assises nationales. Nancy, 1951. Speeches, reports, motions adopted.
Assises nationales. Paris, 9-11 November 1952. Speeches, reports, motions adopted.
Conseils nationaux. Reports, speeches, motions adopted. 1948-1953.
Dossier du candidat. Legislative elections of 1951.
L'Etincelle. 1947-1948.
La France sera la France: Ce que veut Charles de Gaulle. 1951.
ID: Service hebdomadaire d'information et de documentation. 1951-1953.
"Lettre à l'Union française." 1949-1958.
Notes hebdomadaires d'orientation politique.
"Pour un véritable regroupement national." Senatorial elections, May, 1952.
"Le Problème de l'Algérie." 1947.
Le Rassemblement. 1948-1954.

GAULLISM: CENTRE NATIONAL DES RÉPUBLICAINS SOCIAUX
Premier congrès national. Asnières, 18-20 November 1955. Typewritten transcript, microfilm.
Conseil national. Levallois-Perret, 1-2 June 1957. Reports and motions adopted.
Conseil national. St. Mandé, 22-23 March 1958. Reports and motions adopted.
Correspondence with departmental federations. Microfilm.
"Dossier du candidat." Cantonal elections, 1958.
"Dossier du candidat." Legislative elections of January, 1956.

Le Fait de la Quinzaine. 1955-1956. (Becomes Note d'Information: Le Fait de la Quinzaine.)

Les Idées . . . Les Faits. . . . 1954.

Journées d'études des cadres. Paris, 5 June 1955. Typewritten transcript, microfilm.

Lettre aux militants.

La Nation Républicaine et Sociale. 1955-1958.

Union Pour le salut et le renouveau de l'Algérie française. "Appel pour le salut et le renouveau de l'Algérie française." April, 1956.

―――. "La Vérité sur l'Algérie." February, 1958.

THE *modérés*

Action républicaine et sociale. "Eléments d'un programme de l'ARS." October-November, 1952.

Guesdin, René. L'Action républicaine et sociale: Mouvement politique. 1953.

Centre national des indépendants et des paysans. First Congress. December, 1954.

―――. Second National Congress. Versailles, November, 1956.

―――. Third National Congress. March, 1958.

―――. Fourth National Congress. Paris, 30 November-2 December, 1960.

―――. Fiches de documentation. 1956, 1958.

―――. Project de manifeste électoral. September, 1957.

―――. Statuts de l'Association. 1953.

Le Parti républicain de la Liberté. Le P.R.L.—Chemin de la Liberté. Third edition, 1948.

―――. Le P.R.L. a eu raison. 1949.

THE POUJADISTS

Fraternité Française. 1955-1957.

THE CONSERVATIVE PARTY

Conservative Commonwealth Council. Annual Conference Papers.

Conservative Political Centre. Commonwealth and Empire. (Address by Marquess of Salisbury on 24 April 1953.)

―――. The Commonwealth: Expanding Opportunity. September, 1958.

―――. The Expanding Commonwealth. October, 1956.

―――. The Expanding Obligation. March, 1961.

―――. Imperium et Libertas. (Address by Alan Lennox-Boyd.)

―――. Principles in Practics: A Series of Bow Group Essays for the 1960s. February, 1961.

———. Tradition and Change: Nine Oxford Lectures. December, 1954.

———. Wind of Change: The Challenge of the Commonwealth.

———. World Perspectives: Seven Oxford Lectures. December, 1955.

Conservative Research Department. Three Years Work: Achievements of the Conservative Government. December, 1954.

———. A Bi-monthly Survey of Commonwealth and Colonial Affairs (later Monthly Survey of Commonwealth and Colonial Affairs). 1952-1962.

———. Notes on Current Politics. 1956-1962.

Conservative and Unionist Central Office. Manifestoes and Campaign Guides.

———. The Baghdad Pact—Firm Base of Freedom. 1958.

———. Imperial Policy: A Statement of Conservative Policy for the British Empire and Commonwealth. June, 1949.

The Monday Club. Bury the Hatchet.

———. A Clear and Solemn Duty.

———. Rhodesia: A Minority View?

National Union of Conservative and Unionist Associations. Annual Conferences. 1948-1962.

———. Annual Conferences: Programme of Proceedings. 1955-1965.

———. Blueprint for Burma. 1944.

———. Colonial Policy and Administration. September, 1943.

THE FRENCH SOCIALIST PARTY (SFIO)

Archives du groupe parlementaire socialiste, 1949-1959 (Fondation nationale des sciences politiques, Service des archives d'histoire contemporaine.)

Le Populaire.

THE BRITISH LABOUR PARTY

Labour Party. Minutes of the National Executive Committee. 1950-1959.

———. Records of the Commonwealth Subcommittee. 1947-1963.

Fabian Colonial Bureau. Papers. (Oxford University Colonial Records Project, MSS. Brit. Emp. s 365).

Business organizations

Anglo-American Corporation of South Africa, Ltd. Annual Report. 1956, 1960, 1962.

The British South Africa Company. Director's Report and Accounts. 1959-1960.

The British South Africa Company. President's Statement. 1962.

Comité central de la France d'Outre-Mer. Archives deposited in the Archives nationales, Section Outre-Mer.

Commonwealth Industries Association. Annual Reports. 1946-1962.

————. Minutes of the Executive Committee and the Parliamentary Committee.

————. The Monthly Bulletin.

Compagnie Saint-Gobain Pont-à-Mousson. Archives of Verreries de l'Afrique du Nord and Société Commerciale et Minière pour l'Afrique du Nord.

Conferences of the Chambers of Commerce of the Mediterranean and of French Africa. 1949-1956.

Joint East and Central Africa Board. Annual Reports.

————. Annual Meetings.

————. "Chairman's Letter." 1953-1964.

————. "History of the Joint Africa Board." Mimeographed, n.d.

————. Minutes of the Standing Committee, the Executive Committee, the Executive Council, the Council. (The records of the Joint Board have been deposited in the Library of the Royal Commonwealth Society, London.)

Rhodesian Anglo-American Ltd. Annual Reports. 1961, 1962.

————. Statements by the Chairman, Mr. H. F. Oppenheimer.

Rhodesian Selection Trust Group of Companies. Statements by the Chairman, Sir Ronald L. Prain, O.B.E. 1959-1962.

Tanganyika Concessions, Ltd. Report and Accounts. 1959-1963.

United Central Africa Association. Birth of a Nation: The British Purpose in Central Africa, n.d.

————. Central African Federation: A Test of African Opinion. August 1952.

Interviews

Lord Brockway. London, 22 January 1980

Neville Brown. London, 31 July 1978

Sir Nigel Fisher. London, 18 October 1976

Adrian Fitzgerald. London, 26 August 1975

Lord Fraser of Kilmorack. London, 27 August 1975

Raoul Girardet. Paris, 29 June 1978

Cedric Gunnery. London, 20 August 1975

Miles Hudson. London, 24 August 1976

Patrick Keatley. London, 15 August 1975

Colin Legum. London, 9 January 1980
Margaret Legum. London, 3 August 1978
Sir John Peel. London, 15 January 1980
Lord Redmayne. London, 5 January 1980
Patrick Wall. London, 21 November 1979

Newspapers and Journals

The Daily Telegraph, London
L'Express, Paris
Le Figaro, Paris
France-Observateur, Paris
France-Soir, Paris
The Guardian, Manchester
Institut Français d'opinion publique. *Sondages*. 1950-1960
Le Monde, Paris
The Times, London

Unpublished works

Buchaillard, Pierre, and Contat, Bernard. "L'Union pour la Nouvelle
    République dans la Seine." *Mémoire*, Institut d'Etudes Poli-
    tiques, Paris, 1960.
Campbell, I. R. "Political Attitudes in France to the Algerian Ques-
    tion, 1954-1962." D.Phil. thesis, Oxford University, 1972.
Chevrillon, Marie-France. "Les Républicains sociaux ou la traversée
    du désert, 1953-1958." *Mémoire de maîtrise*, Institut d'Etudes
    Politiques, Paris.
Lange, Peter. "Change in the Italian Communist Party: Strategy and
    Organization in the Postwar Period." Ph.D. dissertation, Massa-
    chusetts Institute of Technology, 1974.
Lee, William S. "French Policy and the Tunisian Nationalist Move-
    ment, 1950-54." D.Phil. thesis, Oxford University.
Parodi, Jean-Luc. "Le 13 Mai 1958: Les Algériens d'origine euro-
    péenne et la politique." *Mémoire*, Institut d'Etudes Politiques, Paris,
    1960.
Saxe, J. W. "The Evolution of the Economic Structure of the French
    Union." D.Phil. thesis, Oxford University, 1958.
Schneider, William, "The Origins of Participation: Nation, Class,
    Issues, and Party." Ph.D. dissertation, Harvard University, 1971.

Tricot, Bernard. "La Décolonisation en Afrique du Nord." Paper presented at the Institut Charles de Gaulle, Paris, 24 November 1972.

Books

Almond, Gabriel A.; Flanagan, Scott C.; and Mundt, Robert J., eds. *Crisis, Choice, and Change: Historical Studies of Political Development.* Boston: Little, Brown and Co., 1973.
Alport, C.J.M. *Hope in Africa.* London: Herbert Jenkins Ltd., 1952.
————. *The Sudden Assignment.* London: Hodder & Stoughton, 1965.
Ambler, John Stewart. *The French Army in Politics, 1945-1962.* Columbus: Ohio State University Press, 1962.
Amsden, A. H. *International Firms and Labour in Kenya: 1945-1970.* London: Frank Cass & Co., Ltd., 1971.
Anderson, Malcolm. *Conservative Politics in France.* London: George Allen and Unwin, 1974.
Anderson, Olive. *A Liberal State at War: English Politics and Economics during the Crimean War.* New York: St. Martin's Press, 1967.
Anderson, Perry. *Lineages of the Absolutist State.* London: New Left Books, 1974.
Apter, David, ed. *Ideology and Discontent.* New York: Free Press, 1964.
Aron, Raymond. *La Tragédie algérienne.* Paris: Plon, 1957.
Aron, Robert. *Une Grande Banque d'affaires: La Banque de Paris et des Pays-Bas.* Paris: Les Editions de l'épargne, 1959.
Association Française de Science Politique. *L'Etablissement de la Cinquième République: Le Référendum de septembre et les élections de novembre 1958.* Paris: Armand Colin, 1960.
Astoux, André. *L'Oubli.* Paris: J. C. Lattès, 1974.
Auriol, Vincent. *Journal du septennat, 1947-1954.* Paris: Armand Colin, 1970.
Ayache, Albert. *Le Maroc: Bilan d'une colonisation.* Paris: Editions Sociales, 1956.
Barber, William J. *The Economy of British Central Africa.* Stanford: Stanford University Press, 1961.
Beer, Samuel H. *British Politics in the Collectivist Age.* New York: Knopf, 1967.

Bergquist, Charles W. *Coffee and Conflicts in Colombia, 1886-1910.* Durham, N.C.: Duke University Press, 1978.

Bernard, Stéphane. *Le Conflit franco-marocain, 1943-1956. Vol. III.* Brussels: Editions de l'Institut de Sociologie de l'Université libre de Bruxelles, 1963.

————. *The Franco-Moroccan Conflict, 1943-1956.* New Haven: Yale University Press, 1968.

Betts, Raymond F. *Assimilation and Association in French Colonial Theory, 1890-1914.* New York: Columbia University Press, 1961.

Birkenhead, Frederick Winston Furneaux Smith, 2nd Earl of. *Walter Monckton.* London: Weidenfeld and Nicolson, 1969.

Blake, Robert. *The Conservative Party from Peel to Churchill.* London: Collins, 1972.

Blank, Stephen. *Industry and Government in Britain: The Federation of British Industries in Politics, 1945-65.* Lexington: Lexington Books, 1973.

Bleuchot, Hervé. *Les Libéraux français au Maroc (1947-1955).* Aix: Editions de l'Université de Provence, 1973.

Blundell, Sir Michael. *So Rough a Wind.* London: Weidenfeld and Nicolson, 1964.

Borne, Dominique. *Petits bourgeois en revolte? Le Mouvement Poujade.* Paris: Flammarion, 1977.

Bouvier, Jean. *Un siècle de banque française.* Paris: Librarie Hachette, 1973.

Bowman, Larry W. *Politics in Rhodesia: White Power in an African State.* Cambridge: Harvard University Press, 1973.

Brett, E. A. *Colonialism and Underdevelopment in East Africa: The Politics of Economic Change, 1919-1939.* New York: NOK Publishers, Ltd., 1973.

Brockway, Fenner. *Outside the Right.* London: George Allen and Unwin, 1963.

————. *Towards Tomorrow.* London: Hart-Davis, MacGibbon, 1977.

Buffelan, Jean-Paul. *Le Complot du 13 mai dans le Sud-Ouest.* Paris: R. Pichon and R. Durand-Auzias, 1966.

Butler, D. E., and Rose, Richard. *The British General Election of 1959.* London: Macmillan, 1960.

Butler, David, and Stokes, Donald. *Political Change in Britain.* College ed. New York: St. Martin's Press, 1971.

Butler of Saffron Walden, Richard Austin Butler, Baron. *The Art of the Possible.* Boston: Gambit, 1972.

Caron, François. *An Economic History of Modern France*. London: Methuen & Co., Ltd., 1979.

Cerych, Ladislav. *Européens et marocains, 1930-1956: Sociologie d'une décolonisation*. Bruges: De Tempel, 1964.

Chandos, Oliver Lyttelton, Viscount. *The Memoirs of Lord Chandos*. London: The Bodley Head, 1962.

Charlot, Jean. *Le Gaullisme*. Paris: Armand Colin, 1970.

————. *L'Union pour la Nouvelle République: Etude de pouvoir au sein d'un parti politique*. Paris: Armand Colin, 1967.

Chiroux, René. *L'Extrême-droite sous la Vᵉ République*. Paris: Librairie de droit et de jurisprudence, 1974.

Churchill, Winston S. *India: Speeches and an Introduction*. London: Thornton Butterworth, Ltd., 1931.

Colliard, Jean-Claude. *Les Républicains indépendants*. Paris: Presses Universitaires de France, 1971.

Collier, David, ed. *The New Authoritarianism in Latin America*. Princeton: Princeton University Press, 1979.

Coser, Lewis. *The Functions of Social Conflict*. New York: Free Press of Glencoe, 1956.

Croft of Bournemouth, Henry Page Croft, Baron. *My Life of Strife*. London: Hutchinson & Co., n.d.

Cronje, Suzanne; Ling, Margaret; and Cronje, Gillian. *The Lonrho Connection*. Encino, Ca.: Bellwether Books, 1976.

Crossman, Richard. *Inside View: Three Lectures on Prime Ministerial Government*. London: Jonathan Cape, 1972.

Darby, Philip. *British Defense Policy East of Suez, 1947-1968*. London: Oxford University Press, 1973.

Debré, Michel. *Ces princes qui nous gouvernent*. Paris: Plon, 1957.

————. *Une certaine idée de la France*. Paris: Fayard, 1972.

Depreux, Edouard. *Souvenirs d'un militant*. Paris: Fayard, 1970.

Deutsch, Karl. *Nationalism and Social Communication*. Cambridge: MIT Press, 1953.

Dewey, Clive, and Hopkins, A. G., eds. *The Imperial Impact: Studies in the Economic History of Africa and India*. London: University of London, Athlone Press, 1978.

Douglas-Home, Charles. *Evelyn Baring: The Last Proconsul*. London: Collins, 1978.

Drucker, H. M. *Doctrine and Ethos in the Labour Party*. London: George Allen and Unwin, 1979.

Duchet, Roger. *La République épinglée*. Paris: Editions Alain Moreau, 1975.

Duverger, Maurice, ed. *Les Elections du 2 janvier 1956.* Paris: Armand Colin, 1957.

———. *Partis politiques et classes sociales en France.* Paris: Armand Colin, 1955.

———. *Political Parties.* London: Methuen & Co., Ltd., 1959.

Eden, Anthony. *Full Circle.* Boston: Houghton Mifflin Co., 1960.

Ehrmann, Henry W. *Organized Business in France.* Princeton: Princeton University Press, 1957.

Elgey, Georgette. *Histoire de la IVᵉ République: La République des contradictions, 1951-1954.* Paris: Fayard, 1968.

———. *La République des illusions, 1945-1951.* Paris: Fayard, 1965.

Epstein, Leon D. *British Politics in the Suez Crisis.* Urbana: University of Illinois Press, 1964.

———. *Political Parties in Western Democracies.* New York: Frederick A. Praeger, 1967.

Evans, Peter. *Dependent Development: The Alliance of Multinational, State, and Local Capital in Brazil.* Princeton: Princeton University Press, 1979.

Evans-Pritchard, E. E. *The Sanusi of Cyrenaica.* Oxford: Clarendon Press, 1949.

Faber, M.L.O., and Potter, J. G. *Towards Economic Independence: Papers on the Nationalisation of the Copper Industry in Zambia.* Cambridge: Cambridge University Press, 1971.

Farrell, R. Barry, ed. *Approaches to Comparative and International Politics.* Evanston, Ill.: Northwestern University Press, 1966.

Finer, S. E.; Berrington, H. B.; and Bartholomew, D. J. *Backbench Opinion in the House of Commons, 1955-1959.* Oxford: Pergamon Press, 1961.

Fisher, Nigel. *Iain Macleod.* London: André Deutsch Ltd., 1973.

Foot, Michael. *Aneurin Bevan, Volume II: 1945-1960.* New York: Atheneum, 1974.

Foot, Paul. *Immigration and Race in British Politics.* London: Penguin, 1965.

Fouchet, Christian. *Au service du Général de Gaulle.* Paris: Plon, 1971.

Furse, Sir Ralph. *Aucuparius: Recollections of a Recruiting Officer.* Oxford: Oxford University Press, 1962.

Gamble, Andrew. *The Conservative Nation.* London: Routledge & Kegan Paul, 1974.

Gann, L. H., and Duignan, P. *White Settlers in Tropical Africa.* Harmondsworth: Penguin, 1962.

Gann, L. H., and Gelfand, M. *Huggins of Rhodesia*. London: George Allen and Unwin, 1964.

Gardner, Richard N. *Sterling-Dollar Diplomacy*. Oxford: Clarendon Press, 1956.

Gaulle, Charles de. *The Complete War Memoirs*. New York: Simon and Schuster, 1964.

———. *Discours et messages: Pendant la guerre, juin 1940-janvier 1946*. Paris: Plon, 1970.

———. *Discours et messages: Dans l'attente, février 1946-avril 1958*. Paris: Plon, 1970.

———. *Memoirs of Hope: Renewal and Endeavor*. New York: Simon and Schuster, 1971.

Gendarme, René. *L'Economie de l'Algérie*. Paris: Armand Colin, 1959.

Gerschenkron, Alexander. *Economic Backwardness in Historical Perspective*. Cambridge: Harvard University Press, 1962.

Gilpin, Robert. *France in the Age of the Scientific State*. Princeton: Princeton University Press, 1968

Girardet, Raoul. *L'Idée coloniale en France, 1871-1962*. Paris: La Table Ronde, 1972.

———. *Le Nationalisme français 1871-1914*. Paris: Armand Colin, 1966.

Goguel, François, ed. *Le Référendum du 8 avril 1962*. Paris: Armand Colin, 1963.

———. *Le Référendum du 8 janvier 1961*. Paris: Armand Colin, 1962.

———. *Le Référendum de septembre et les élections de novembre 1958*. Paris: Armand Colin, 1960.

Goldsworthy, David. *Colonial Issues in British Politics, 1945-1961: From 'Colonial Development' to 'Wind of Change.'* Oxford: Clarendon Press, 1971.

Goodhart, Philip, with Ursula Branston. *The 1922*. London: Macmillan, 1973.

Goodsell, Charles T. *American Corporations and Peruvian Politics*. Cambridge: Harvard University Press, 1974.

Gordon, Michael R. *Conflict and Consensus in Labour's Foreign Policy, 1914-1965*. Stanford: Stanford University Press, 1969.

Grandval, Gilbert. *Ma mission au Maroc*. Paris: Plon, 1956.

Greene, Nathanael L. *Crisis and Decline: The French Socialist Party in the Popular Front Era*. Ithaca, N.Y.: Cornell University Press, 1969.

Grosser, Alfred. *French Foreign Policy under de Gaulle.* Boston: Little, Brown and Co., 1965.

———. *La IVᵉ République et sa politique extérieure.* Paris: Armand Colin, 1961.

Gupta, Partha Sarathi. *Imperialism and the British Labour Movement, 1914-1964.* London: Macmillan, 1975.

Guttsman, W. L. *The British Political Elite.* New York: Basic Books, Inc., 1963.

Hao, Yen-P'ing. *The Comprador in Nineteenth-Century China: Bridge between East and West.* Cambridge: Harvard University Press, 1970.

Hartz, Louis. *The Founding of New Societies.* New York: Harcourt, Brace & World, Inc., 1964.

Hauss, Charles. *The New Left in France: The Unified Socialist Party.* Westport, Conn.: Greenwood Press, 1978.

Heussler, Robert. *Yesterday's Rulers: The Making of the British Colonial Service.* Syracuse: Syracuse University Press, 1963.

Hirschman, Albert. *Exit, Voice, and Loyalty: Responses to Decline in Firms, Organizations, and States.* Cambridge: Harvard University Press, 1970.

Hoffman, J. D. *The Conservative Party in Opposition, 1945-51.* London: MacGibbon & Kee, 1964.

Hoffmann, Stanley. *Decline or Renewal?: France Since the 1930s.* New York: Viking Press, 1974.

———. *Le Mouvement Poujade.* Paris: Armand Colin, 1956.

Hopkins, A. G. *An Economic History of West Africa.* London: Longmans, 1975.

Horne, Alistair. *A Savage War of Peace.* New York: Viking, 1978.

Huxley, Elspeth, and Perham, Margery. *Race and Politics in Kenya.* 2nd ed. London: Faber, 1956.

Irving, R.E.M. *Christian Democracy in France.* London: George Allen and Unwin, 1973.

———. *The First Indochina War: French and American Policy 1945-54.* London: Croom Helm, 1975.

Jackson, Robert J. *Rebels and Whips: An Analysis of Dissension, Discipline and Cohesion in British Political Parties.* London: Macmillan, 1968.

James, Robert Rhodes. *Churchill: A Study in Failure.* London: Weidenfeld and Nicolson, 1970.

Jervis, Robert. *Perception and Misperception in International Relations*. Princeton: Princeton University Press, 1976.

Johnson, Chalmers. *Peasant Nationalism and Communist Power*. Stanford: Stanford University Press, 1962.

Joubert, Jean-Paul. *Révolutionnaires de la S.F.I.O.: Marceau Pivert et le Pivertisme*. Paris: Presses de la Fondation Nationale des Sciences Politiques, 1977.

Judt, Tony. *La Réconstruction du parti socialiste, 1921-1926*. Paris: Presse de la Fondation Nationale des Sciences Politiques, 1976.

Julliard, Jacques. *La IVᵉ République (1947-1958)*. Paris: Calmann-Lévy, 1968.

July, Pierre. *Une république pour un roi*. Paris: Fayard, 1974.

Kanya-Forstner, A. S. *The Conquest of the Western Sudan: A Study in French Military Imperialism*. Cambridge: Cambridge University Press, 1969.

Keatley, Patrick. *The Politics of Partnership*. Baltimore: Penguin, 1963.

Kelly, George Armstrong. *Lost Soldiers: The French Army and the Empire in Crisis, 1947-1962*. Cambridge: MIT Press, 1965.

Kennedy, David M. *Over Here: The First World War and American Society*. New York: Oxford University Press, 1980.

Kilmuir, Earl. *Political Adventure*. London: Weidenfeld and Nicolson, 1964.

Kim, Kyung-Won. *Revolution and International System*. New York: New York University Press, 1970.

Kirkman, W. P. *Unscrambling an Empire: A Critique of British Colonial Policy, 1956-1966*. London: Chatto and Windus, 1966.

Lacouture, Jean. *De Gaulle*. New York: Avon Books, 1966.

La Gorce, Paul-Marie de. *De Gaulle entre deux mondes*. Paris: Fayard, 1964.

Lammers, Donald N. *Explaining Munich*. Stanford: Hoover Institution, 1966.

Laniel, Joseph. *Jours de gloire et jours cruels, 1908-1958*. Paris: Presses de la Cité, 1971.

La Palombara, Joseph, and Weiner, Myron. *Political Parties and Political Development*. Princeton: Princeton University Press, 1966.

Lee, J. M. *Colonial Development and Good Government*. Oxford: Clarendon Press, 1967.

Leleu, Claude. *Géographie des élections françaises depuis 1936*. Paris: Presses Universitaires de France, 1971.

Lerner, Daniel, and Aron, Raymond. *France Defeats the EDC*. New York: Frederick A. Praeger, 1957.

Leys, Colin. *European Politics in Southern Rhodesia*. Oxford: Clarendon Press, 1959.

———. *Underdevelopment in Kenya: The Political Economy of Neo-Colonialism, 1964-1971*. Berkeley: University of California Press, 1974.

Lieber, Robert J. *British Politics and European Unity: Parties, Elites and Pressure Groups*. Berkeley: University of California Press, 1970.

Lijphart, Arend. *The Trauma of Decolonization: The Dutch and West New Guinea*. New Haven: Yale University Press, 1966.

McKenzie, R. T. *British Political Parties*. 2nd edition. New York: Frederick A. Praeger, 1963.

McKenzie, Robert, and Silver, Allan. *Angels in Marble: Working Class Conservatives in Urban England*. Chicago: University of Chicago Press, 1968.

Macmillan, Harold. *At the End of the Day, 1961-1963*. New York: Harper & Row, 1973.

———. *The Blast of War, 1939-1945*. London: Macmillan, 1970.

———. *Pointing the Way, 1959-1961*. New York: Harper & Row, 1972.

———. *Riding the Storm, 1956-1959*. New York: Harper & Row, 1971.

———. *Tides of Fortune, 1945-1955*. New York: Harper & Row, 1969.

———. *Winds of Change, 1914-1939*. London: Macmillan, 1966.

Macrae, Duncan, Jr. *Parliament, Parties and Society in France 1946-1958*. New York: St. Martin's Press, 1967.

Manin, Philippe. *Le Rassemblement du peuple français (R.P.F.) et les problèmes européens*. Paris: Presses Universitaires de France, 1966.

Marshall, D. Bruce. *The French Colonial Myth and Constitution-making in the Fourth Republic*. New Haven: Yale University Press, 1973.

Marwick, Arthur. *Britain in the Century of Total War*. London: Penguin, 1970.

———. *The Deluge*. Harmondsworth: Penguin, 1967.

Mauriac, Claude. *The Other De Gaulle*. New York: The John Day Co., 1973.

Micaud, Charles A. *The French Right and Nazi Germany, 1933-1939: A Study of Public Opinion*. Durham, N.C.: Duke University Press, 1943.

Miège, Jean-Louis. *Expansion européenne et décolonisation de 1870 à nos jours.* Paris: Presses Universitaires de France, 1973.

Miller, J.D.B. *Survey of Commonwealth Affairs: Problems of Expansion and Attrition, 1953-1969.* Oxford: Oxford University Press, 1974.

Milward, Alan S. *The Economic Effects of the Two World Wars on Britain.* London: Macmillan, 1970.

————. *War, Economy, and Society, 1939-1945.* London: Allen Lane, 1977.

Le Monde des affaires en France de 1830 à nos jours. Paris: Société Edition de dictionnaires et encyclopédies, 1952.

Monypenny, William Flavelle, and Buckle, George Earle. *The Life of Benjamin Disraeli.* London: John Murray, 1929.

Moran, Theodore H. *Multinational Corporations and the Politics of Dependence.* Princeton: Princeton University Press, 1974.

Moussa, Pierre. *Les Chances économiques de la communauté franco-africaine.* Paris: Armand Colin, 1957.

Murray, D. J. *The Governmental System in Southern Rhodesia.* Oxford: Clarendon Press, 1970.

Nehrt, Lee Charles. *The Political Climate for Private Foreign Investment.* New York: Frederick A. Praeger, 1970.

Nicolson, Harold. *Diaries and Letters.* New York: Atheneum, 1968.

Noël, Léon. *La Traversée du désert.* Paris: Plon, 1973.

Nora, Pierre. *Les Français d'Algérie.* Paris: René Julliard, 1961.

Nordmann, Jean-Thomas. *Histoire des radicaux, 1820-1973.* Paris: Editions de la Table Ronde, 1974.

Norton, Philip, ed. *Dissension in the House of Commons.* London: Macmillan, 1975.

Nutting, Anthony. *No End of a Lesson: The Story of Suez.* London: Constable and Co., 1967.

Oppermann, Thomas. *Le Problème algérien.* Paris: Maspero, 1961.

Owen, Roger, and Sutcliffe, Bob, eds. *Studies in the Theory of Imperialism.* London: Longmans, 1972.

Paxton, Robert O. *Vichy France: Old Guard and New Order.* New York: Knopf, 1972.

Peele, Gillian, and Cook, Chris. *The Politics of Reappraisal, 1918-1939.* London: Macmillan, 1975.

Philip, André. *André Philip par lui-même.* Paris: Editions Aubier Montaigne, 1971.

Pickles, Dorothy. *Algeria and France: From Colonialism to Cooperation.* New York: Frederick A. Praeger, 1963.

Pierre, Andrew J. *Nuclear Politics: The British Experience with an Independent Strategic Force 1939-1970*. Oxford: Oxford University Press, 1972.

Poncet, Jean. *La Colonisation et l'agriculture européennes en Tunisie depuis 1881*. Paris: Mouton & Co., 1962.

Price, Richard. *An Imperial War and the British Working Class*. London: Routledge & Kegan Paul, 1972.

Purtschet, Christian. *Le Rassemblement du peuple français, 1947-1953*. Paris: Editions Cujas, 1965.

La Quatrième république: Bilan trente ans après la promulgation de la Constitution du 17 Octobre 1946. Paris: Librairie générale du droit et de jurisprudence, 1978.

Quilliot, Roger. *La S.F.I.O. et l'exercice du pouvoir, 1944-1958*. Paris: Fayard, 1972.

Ramsden, John. *The Age of Balfour and Baldwin, 1902-1940*. London: Longmans, 1978.

Ranger, T. O. *Revolt in Southern Rhodesia, 1896-97*. Evanston, Ill.: Northwestern University Press, 1967.

Rasmussen, Jorgen S. *The Relations of the Profumo Rebels with their Local Parties*. Tucson: University of Arizona Press, 1966.

Rémond, René. *The Right Wing in France: From 1815 to de Gaulle*. 2nd American ed. Philadelphia: University of Pennsylvania Press, 1969.

Rosberg, Carl G., Jr., and Nottingham, John. *The Myth of 'Mau Mau': Nationalism in Kenya*. Stanford: Hoover Institution, 1966.

Rose, Richard. *The Problem of Party Government*. London: Macmillan, 1974.

———. *Studies in British Politics*. New York: St. Martin's Press, 1966.

Rose, Richard, ed. *Policy-making in Britain*. New York: Free Press, 1969.

Rosenau, James N. *The Scientific Study of Foreign Policy*. New York: Free Press, 1971.

Rosenau, James N., ed. *Linkage Politics*. New York: Free Press, 1969.

Roth, Andrew. *Enoch Powell: Tory Tribune*. London: MacDonald, 1970.

———. *Heath and the Heathmen*. London: Routledge & Kegan Paul, 1972.

Sampson, Anthony. *Macmillan: A Study in Ambiguity*. London: Penguin, 1967.

Schama, Simon. *Patriots and Liberators: Revolution in the Netherlands, 1780-1813.* New York: Knopf, 1977.

Seliger, Martin. *Ideology and Politics.* New York: Free Press, 1976.

Shannon, Richard. *The Crisis of Imperialism, 1865-1915.* St. Alban's: Paladin, 1976.

Shapiro, David, ed. *The Right in France 1890-1919: Three Studies.* London: Chatto and Windus, 1962.

Simmons, Harvey G. *French Socialists in Search of a Role, 1956-1967.* Ithaca, N.Y.: Cornell University Press, 1970.

Sklar, Richard L. *Corporate Power in an African State: The Political Impact of Multinational Mining Companies in Zambia.* Berkeley: University of California Press, 1975.

Skocpol, Theda. *States and Social Revolutions.* Cambridge: Cambridge University Press, 1979.

Smith, Tony. *The French Stake in Algeria, 1945-1962.* Ithaca, N.Y.: Cornell University Press, 1978.

————. *The Pattern of Imperialism.* Cambridge: Cambridge University Press, 1981.

Sorum, Paul Clay. *Intellectuals and Decolonization in France.* Chapel Hill: University of North Carolina Press, 1977.

Soustelle, Jacques. *Aimée et souffrante Algérie.* Paris: Plon, 1956.

————. *Le Drame algérien et la décadence française: Réponse à Raymond Aron.* Paris: Plon, 1957.

————. *Vingt-huit ans de Gaullisme.* Paris: La Table Ronde, 1968.

Stahl, Kathleen M. *The Metropolitan Organization of British Colonial Trade.* London: Faber, 1951.

Stein, Arthur. *The Nation at War.* Baltimore: The Johns Hopkins University Press, 1978.

Stepan, Alfred. *The State and Society.* Princeton: Princeton University Press, 1978.

Stewart, Charles F. *The Economy of Morocco, 1912-1962.* Cambridge: Harvard University Press, 1964.

Stohl, Michael. *War and Domestic Political Violence.* Beverly Hills: Sage, 1976.

Strange, Susan. *Sterling and British Policy.* London: Oxford University Press, 1971.

Talbott, John. *The War without a Name: France in Algeria, 1954-1962.* New York: Knopf, 1980.

Terrenoire, Louis. *De Gaulle et l'Algérie.* Paris: Fayard, 1964.

Thayer, George. *The British Political Fringe*. London: Anthony Blond, Ltd., 1965.

Thomas, Hugh. *The Suez Affair*. London: Weidenfeld and Nicolson, 1967.

Thompson, Neville. *The Anti-Appeasers: Opposition to Appeasement in the 1930s*. Oxford: Oxford University Press, 1971.

Tilly, Charles. *The Vendée*. Cambridge: Harvard University Press, 1964.

Tomlinson, B. R. *The Political Economy of the Raj, 1914-1947*. London: Macmillan, 1979.

Tricot, Bernard. *Les Sentiers de la paix: Algérie 1958-1962*. Paris: Plon, 1972.

Utley, T. E. *Enoch Powell: The Man and His Thinking*. London: William Kimber, 1968.

Wallerstein, Immanuel. *The Modern World-system*. New York: Academic Press, 1974.

Wasserman, Gary. *Politics of Decolonization: Kenya Europeans and the Land Issue, 1960-65*. Cambridge: Cambridge University Press, 1976.

Weinstein, Brian. *Eboué*. Oxford: Oxford University Press, 1972.

Welensky, Sir Roy. *Welensky's 4,000 Days*. London: Collins, 1964.

Wilkenfeld, Jonathan, ed. *Conflict Behavior and Linkage Politics*. New York: David McKay Co., Inc., 1973.

Williams, Phillip M. *Crisis and Compromise: Politics in the Fourth Republic*. New York: Doubleday-Anchor, 1966.

——. *The French Parliament (1958-1967)*. London: George Allen and Unwin, 1968.

——. *French Politicians and Elections, 1951-1969*. Cambridge: Cambridge University Press, 1970.

——. *Hugh Gaitskell: A Political Biography*. London: Jonathan Cape, 1979.

——. *Wars, Plots, and Scandals in Post-war France*. Cambridge: Cambridge University Press, 1970.

Williams, Philip, with David Goldey and Martin Harrison. *French Politicians and Elections, 1951-1969*. Cambridge: Cambridge University Press, 1970.

Williams, Philip, and Harrison, Martin. *Politics and Society in De Gaulle's Republic*. New York: Doubleday and Co., 1971.

Wilson, James Q. *Political Organizations*. New York: Basic Books, Inc., 1973.

Wolf, Eric R. *Peasant Wars of the Twentieth Century*. New York: Harper & Row, 1969.

Woolf, Leonard. *Downhill All the Way*. New York: Harcourt Brace Jovanovich, 1967.

Wright, Gordon. *The Reshaping of French Democracy*. Boston: Beacon Press, 1970.

Wylie, Laurence, ed. *Chanzeaux*. Cambridge: Harvard University Press, 1966.

Articles

Andrew, C. M. and Kanya-Forstner, A. S. "The French 'Colonial Party': Its Composition, Aims and Influence." *The Historical Journal* 14 (March, 1971), 99-128.

————. "The *Groupe colonial* in the French Chamber of Deputies, 1892-1932." *The Historical Journal* 17 (December, 1974), 837-866.

Ayache, M. A. "Les Mouvements de capitaux dans les sociétés au Maroc (1912-1955)." *Bulletin de l'Association de géographes français*, no. 275 (May, 1958), 17-27.

Barnes, Samuel H. "Ideology and the Origin of Conflict: On the Relationship between Political Thought and Behavior." *The Journal of Politics* 27 (August, 1966), 513-530.

Barry, Brian. "Review Article: 'Exit, Voice, and Loyalty.' " *British Journal of Political Science* 4 (January, 1974), 79-107.

Bodin, Louis, and Touchard, Jean. "L'Election partielle de la première circonscription de la Seine." *Revue française de science politique* 7 (April-June, 1957), 271-312.

Bourdin, Janine. "La Crise des Indépendants." *Revue française de science politique* 13 (June, 1963), 443-450.

"The Brass Behind the Copper," *Economist*, 7 October 1961, p. 55.

Calan, Pierre de. "Comment faire l'Europe cotonnière?" *Société belge d'études et d'expansion: Bulletin bimestrial*, no. 165 (March-April, 1955), 367-372.

Cameron, David R. "Stability and Change in Patterns of French Partisanship." *Public Opinion Quarterly* 36 (Spring 1972), 19-30.

Cornforth, James. "The Transformation of Conservatism in the Late Nineteenth Century," *Victorian Studies* 7 (September, 1963), 35-36.

"Defense des marchés cotonniers d'outre-mer." *Perspectives*, 23 July 1960, pp. 1-3.

Dresch, J. "Recherches sur les investissements dans l'Union française Outre-Mer; leur répartition; leurs conséquences." *Bulletin de l'Association de géographes français*, nos. 231-232 (January-February, 1953).

"Le Fonctionnement du 'lobby' marocain." *France-Observateur*, 2 September 1954, p. 14.

"La Française des pétroles joue l'avenir du Sahara." *Entreprise*, 15 September 1957, pp. 20-26.

"La France à la recherche d'un grand parti tory." *Entreprise*, 15 July 1957, pp. 36-41.

Gann, L. H. "The Northern Rhodesian Copper Industry and the World of Copper: 1923-52." *The Rhodes-Livingstone Journal*, no. 18 (1955), 1-18.

Girardet, Raoul. "Pour une introduction à l'histoire du nationalisme français." *Revue française de science politique* 8 (1958), 505-528.

Goldsworthy, David. "Conservatives and Decolonization." *African Affairs* 69 (July, 1970), 278-281.

Gourevitch, Peter A. "International Trade, Domestic Coalitions, and Liberty: Comparative Responses to the Crisis of 1873-1896." *Journal of Interdisciplinary History* 8 (August, 1977), 281-313.

———. "The Second Image Reversed: The International Sources of Domestic Politics." *International Organization* 32 (Autumn 1978), 881-912.

Guillemin, Philippe. "Les Elus d'Afrique Noire à l'Assemblée Nationale sous la Quatrième République," *Revue française de science politique* 8 (December, 1958), 861-877.

Hammond, Paul Y. "The Political Order and the Burden of External Relations." *World Politics* 19 (April, 1967), 433-464.

Harrison, Martin. "The French General Election, 1958: Paris 5: Safe Seat." *Political Studies* 7 (June, 1959), 147-156.

Hirschman, Albert O. " 'Exit, Voice, and Loyalty': Further Reflections and a Survey of Recent Contributions." *Social Science Information* 13 (1974), 7-26.

Hopkins, A. G. "Imperial Business in Africa, Part I: Sources." *Journal of African History* 17 (1976), 29-48.

———. "Imperial Business in Africa, Part II: Interpretations." *Journal of African History* 17 (1976), 267-290.

Horowitz, Dan. "Attitudes of British Conservatives Towards Decolonization in Africa." *African Affairs* 69 (January, 1970), 9-26.

Huntington, Samuel P. "Conservatism as an Ideology." *American Political Science Review* 51 (June, 1957), 454-473.

Irvine, William D. "French Conservatives and the 'New Right' during the 1930s." *French Historical Studies* 8 (Fall 1974), 534-562.

Kessler, Marie-Christine. "M. Valéry Giscard d'Estaing et les Républicains Indépendants." *Revue française de science politique* 16 (October, 1966), 940-957.

Kornberg, Allan, and Frasure, Robert C. "Policy Differences in British Parliamentary Parties." *American Political Science Review* 65 (September, 1971), 694-703.

La Gorce, Paul-Marie de. "De Gaulle et la décolonisation du continent noir." *Revue française d'études politiques africaines* 60 (December, 1970), 44-60.

Leonard, H. Jeffrey. "Multinational Corporations and Politics in the Developing Countries." *World Politics* 32 (April, 1980), 454-483.

Mack, Andrew. "Why Big Nations Lose Small Wars: The Politics of Asymmetric Conflict." *World Politics* 27 (January, 1975), 175-200.

Macleod, Iain. "Trouble in Africa." *The Spectator*, 31 January 1964, p. 127.

McWilliam, Michael. "Economic Policy and the Kenya Settlers, 1945-48." In *Essays in Imperial Government*, edited by K. Robinson and F. Madden, pp. 171-192. Oxford: Blackwell, 1963.

Masson, André. "L'Opinion française et les problèmes coloniaux à la fin de Second Empire." *Revue Française d'Histoire d'Outre-mer* 49, no. 324 (1962), 366-435.

Pinto-Duschinsky, Michael. "Central Office and 'Power' in the Conservative Party." *Political Studies* 20 (March, 1972), 1-16.

"Le Poujadisme: Un mouvement, un parti . . . et maintenant?" *Entreprise*, 1 July 1957, pp. 48-53.

Ranger, T. O. "Connections between 'Primary Resistance' Movements and Modern Mass Nationalism in East and Central Africa: Part I." *Journal of African History* 9, no. 3 (1968), 437-453.

Rosenau, James N. "Compatibility, Consensus, and an Emerging Political Science of Adaption." *American Political Science Review* 61 (December, 1967), 983-988.

Rutkoff, Peter M. "The Ligue des Patriotes: The Nature of the Radical Right and the Dreyfus Affair." *French Historical Studies* 8 (Fall 1974), 585-603.

Sartori, Giovanni. "Politics, Ideology, and Belief Systems." *American Political Science Review* 63 (June, 1969), 398-411.

Schuman, Robert. "Nécessité d'une politique." *La Nef* 10 (March, 1953), 7-9.

Seliger, Martin. "Fundamental and Operative Ideology." *Policy Sciences* 5 (1970), 325-338.

Semidei, Manuela. "De l'empire à la décolonisation à travers les manuels scolaires français." *Revue française de science politique* 16 (February, 1966), 56-86.

————. "Les Socialistes française et le problème colonial entre les deux guerres (1919-1939)." *Revue française de science politique* 18 (December, 1968), 1118-1124.

Seyd, Patrick. "Factionalism within the Conservative Party: The Monday Club." *Government and Opposition* 7 (Autumn 1972), 464-487.

Slinn, Peter. "Commercial Concessions and Politics during the Colonial Period: The Role of the British South Africa Company in Northern Rhodesia, 1890-1964." *African Affairs* 70 (1971), 365-384.

Smith, T. Alexander. "Algeria and the French Modérés: The Politics of Immoderation?" *Western Political Quarterly* 18 (March, 1965), 116-134.

Smith, Tony. "The French Colonial Consensus and People's War, 1946-58." *Journal of Contemporary History* 9, no. 4, (1974), 217-247.

Sternhell, Zeev. "Paul Déroulède and the Origins of Modern French Nationalism." *Journal of Contemporary History* 6, no. 4 (1971), 46-70.

Stohl, Michael. "Linkages between War and Domestic Political Violence in the United States, 1890-1923." In *Quasi-Experimental Approaches*, edited by James A. Caporaso and Leslie L. Roos Jr., pp. 156-179. Evanston, Ill.: Northwestern University Press, 1973.

Stultz, Newell M. "The Politics of Security: South Africa under Verwoerd, 1961-66." *Journal of Modern African Studies* 7 (April, 1969), 3-20.

Touchard, Jean. "Bibliographie et chronologie du poujadisme." *Revue française de science politique* 6 (January-March, 1956), 18-43.

Trimberger, Ellen Kay. "A Theory of Elite Revolutions." *Studies in Comparative International Development* 7 (Fall 1972), 191-207.

Library of Congress Cataloging in Publication Data

Kahler, Miles, 1949-
  Decolonization in Britain and France.
  Bibliography: p.
  Includes index.
  1. Great Britain—Politics and government—1945- . 2.
France—Politics and government—1945- . 3. Decolonization—History.
4. International relations. I. Title.
DA588.K34 1984   941.085   83-43078
ISBN 0-691-07672-3 (alk. paper)
ISBN 0-691-02224-0 (pbk.)

Miles Kahler is Associate Professor of Political Science
at Yale University.